THE ABINGDON PREACHING ANNUAL 2008

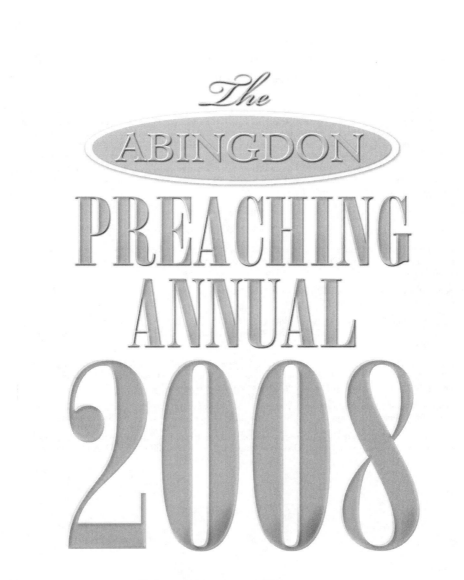

The ABINGDON PREACHING ANNUAL 2008

COMPILED AND EDITED BY
THE REVEREND DAVID NEIL MOSSER, PH.D.

ASSISTANT EDITOR RONDA WELLMAN

Abingdon Press
Nashville

*To Bishops John W. Russell and Ben R. Chamness
and to my treasured Central Texas Annual Conference
colleagues, lay and clergy,
with fond admiration and deep gratitude*

CONTENTS

❧❧❧

Introduction xvii

I. GENERAL HELPS

Four-year Church Calendar xx
Liturgical Colors xxi
Lectionary Listings xxiii

II. SERMONS AND WORSHIP AIDS

JANUARY

JANUARY 6 Epiphany 3
   The Winter of the Heart (Matthew 2:1-12)
   Lectionary Commentary (Isaiah 60:1-6; Ephesians 3:1-12)
   New Birth: Why Baptism Matters, *First in a Series of
      Three on the Sacraments* (Galatians 3:23-29)
JANUARY 13 Baptism of the Lord 11
   The Inelegance of It All (Matthew 3:13-17)
   Lectionary Commentary (Isaiah 42:1-9; Acts 10:34-43)
   Bread of Life, *Second in a Series of Three on the Sacraments*
      (John 6:51-58)
JANUARY 20 Second Sunday after the Epiphany 19
   Hope in the Lava Fields (Isaiah 49:1-7)
   Lectionary Commentary (John 1:29-42; 1 Corinthians
      1:1-9)
   A Sacramental Life, *Third in a Series of Three on the
      Sacraments* (Mark 12:28-34)
JANUARY 27 Third Sunday after the Epiphany 26
   Look Up to the Earth (1 Corinthians 1:10-18)
   Lectionary Commentary (Isaiah 9:1-4; Matthew 4:12-23)
   Sinners in the Hands of a Loving God: That's Not What
      I Intended, *First in a Series of Three on the Nature of Sin
      for Modern People* (Romans 7:14-25)

FEBRUARY

FEBRUARY 3 Fourth Sunday after the Epiphany 32
  Doing Justice, Loving Kindness, Walking Humbly (Micah 6:1-8)
  Lectionary Commentary (Matthew 5:1-12; 1 Corinthians 1:18-31)
  Sinners in the Hands of a Loving God: Following the Crowd,
      Second in a Series of Three on the Nature of Sin for Modern People
      (Matthew 27:24-26)
FEBRUARY 6 Ash Wednesday 39
  Prayers We Don't Pray (Psalm 51:1-17)
  Lectionary Commentary (Isaiah 58:1-12; Matthew 6:1-6, 16-21;
      2 Corinthians 5:20b–6:10)
  The Goat of God? *Third in a Series of Three on the Nature of Sin
      for Modern People* (John 1:29-36)
FEBRUARY 10 First Sunday in Lent 46
  Disabling Temptations (Matthew 4:1-11)
  Lectionary Commentary (Genesis 2:15-17, 3:1-7; Romans 5:12-19)
  God in Our Wilderness Wanderings, *First in a Series of Three on
      Wilderness and Pilgrimage* (Numbers 9:1-14)
FEBRUARY 17 Second Sunday in Lent 53
  Characters of Lent: One of Us (John 3:1-17)
  Lectionary Commentary (Genesis 12:1-4a; Romans 4:1-5, 13-17)
  Wilderness Community, *Second in a Series of Three on Wilderness
      and Pilgrimage* (Numbers 11:10-23)
FEBRUARY 24 Third Sunday in Lent 60
  Characters of Lent: Slow to Believe (John 4:5-42)
  Lectionary Commentary (Exodus 17:1-7; Romans 5:1-11)
  Looking Forward in Faith, *Third in a Series of Three on Wilderness
      and Pilgrimage* (Numbers 14:1-10)

MARCH

MARCH 2 Fourth Sunday in Lent 67
  Characters of Lent: Blind, but Now I See (John 9:1-41)
  Lectionary Commentary (1 Samuel 16:1-13; Ephesians 5:8-14)
  A Path, Not a Punishment, *First in a Series of Three on
      Spiritual Disciplines* (Luke 4:1-15)
MARCH 9 Fifth Sunday in Lent 74
  The Need for Prophets in the Valley (Ezekiel 37:1-14)
  Lectionary Commentary (John 11:1-45; Romans 8:6-11)
  Fasting—It's About Time! *Second in a Series of Three on
      Spiritual Disciplines* (Matthew 6:16-18)

Contents

MARCH 16 Palm/Passion Sunday 81
A Life Celebrated in Its Entirety (Philippians 2:5-11)
Lectionary Commentary (Matthew 21:1-11; Isaiah 50:4-9a;
   Matthew 26:14–27:66)
Listening for the Holy Spirit, *Third in a Series of Three on
   Spiritual Disciplines* (John 16:4b-11)
MARCH 20 Holy Thursday 89
Which Basin Do You Choose? (John 13:1-17, 31b-35)
Lectionary Commentary (Exodus 12:1-14; 1 Corinthians 11:23-26)
A Secret to Share, *First in a Series of Two on Holy Week*
   (Matthew 26:20-30)
MARCH 21 Good Friday 97
Remorse and Resurrection (John 18:1–19:42)
Lectionary Commentary (Isaiah 52:13–53:12; Hebrews 4:14-16;
   10:16-25)
Walking in the Light, *Second in a Series of Two on Holy Week*
   (Matthew 27:24-26, 45-54)
MARCH 23 Easter Sunday 105
Named and Claimed (John 20:1-18)
Lectionary Commentary (Acts 10:34-43; Colossians 3:1-4)
Glimpses of Easter, *First in a Series of Two on Easter*
   (Colossians 1:18-20)
MARCH 30 Second Sunday of Easter 112
Resurrection Reality (John 20:19-31)
Lectionary Commentary (Acts 2:14a, 22-32; 1 Peter 1:3-9)
Why Are You Surprised? *Second in a Series of Two on Easter*
   (Acts 3:1-16)

APRIL

APRIL 6 Third Sunday of Easter 118
Seeing the Risen Christ (Luke 24:13-35)
Lectionary Commentary (Acts 2:14a, 36-41; 1 Peter 1:17-23)
Are We Tending to Our Fruit? *First in a Series of Two on the Fruit
   of the Spirit* (Galatians 5:22-26)
APRIL 13 Fourth Sunday of Easter 125
Life in Abundance (John 10:1-10)
Lectionary Commentary (Acts 2:42-47; 1 Peter 2:19-25)
Are We Tending to Our Fruit? *Second in a Series of Two on the Fruit
   of the Spirit* (Galatians 5:19-25)

APRIL 20 Fifth Sunday of Easter 132
    Living Stones (1 Peter 2:2-10)
    Lectionary Commentary (Acts 7:55-60; John 14:1-14)
    The Seasons of Life, *First in a Series of Three on Easter*
       (1 Corinthians 15:50-58)
APRIL 27 Sixth Sunday of Easter 141
    Common Ground (Acts 17:22-31)
    Lectionary Commentary (John 14:15-21; 1 Peter 3:13-22)
    The Unexpected Jesus, *Second in a Series of Three on Easter*
       (Luke 24:13-35)

MAY

MAY 4 Seventh Sunday of Easter 148
    What Goes Up (Acts 1:6-14)
    Lectionary Commentary (John 17:1-11; 1 Peter 4:12-14, 5:6-11)
    Easter for All Seasons, *Third in a Series of Three on Easter*
       (Mark 16:1-8)
MAY 11 Pentecost 156
    Where's the Fire? (Acts 2:1-21)
    Lectionary Commentary (1 Corinthians 12:3b-13; John 20:19-23)
    The Church's Biblical Foundation, *First in a Series of Three on*
       "Is the Church Christian?" (Micah 6:8; Luke 10:25-28)
MAY 18 Trinity Sunday 164
    The Trinity: Relevant or Not? (Psalm 8; Genesis 1:1–2:4a;
       Matthew 28:16-20; 2 Corinthians 13:11-13)
    How Faithful a Church? *Second in a Series of Three on "Is the*
       Church Christian?" (Luke 16:10-13)
MAY 25 Second Sunday after Pentecost 172
    A Prayer of Humble Trust (Psalm 131)
    Lectionary Commentary (Isaiah 49:8-16a; Matthew 6:24-34;
       1 Corinthians 4:1-5)
    A Revitalized Church, *Third in a Series of Three on "Is the*
       Church Christian?" (Acts 2:43-47)

JUNE

JUNE 1 Third Sunday after Pentecost 179
    Beyond the Blessing and the Curse (Deuteronomy 11:18-21, 26-28)
    Lectionary Commentary (Psalm 31:1-5, 19-24; Matthew 7:21-29;
       Romans 1:16-17, 3:22b-31)
    The Perfect Pattern, *First in a Series of Two on Discipleship*
       (1 Peter 2:18-25)

Contents

JUNE 8 Fourth Sunday after Pentecost 187
 A Desire for Love (Hosea 5:15–6:6)
 Lectionary Commentary (Matthew 9:9-13, 18-26; Romans 4:13-25)
 Striving to Follow the Perfect Pattern, *Second in a Series of Two*
  on Discipleship (1 Thessalonians 5:16-22)
JUNE 15 Fifth Sunday after Pentecost 194
 Becoming a Part of God's Covenant (Genesis 18:1-15, 21:1-7)
 Lectionary Commentary (Matthew 9:35–10:8; Romans 5:1-8)
 Our Quest for Love and Belonging, *First in a Series of Two on*
  Family Life (Ruth 1:1-19a)
JUNE 22 Sixth Sunday after Pentecost 201
 Alive to God (Roman 6:1b-11)
 Lectionary Commentary (Genesis 21:8-21; Jeremiah 20:7-13;
  Matthew 10:24-39)
 God's Yes-I-Can Children, *Second in a Series of Two on Family Life*
  (Joshua 14:1, 6-14)
JUNE 29 Seventh Sunday after Pentecost 209
 God Will Provide (Genesis 22:1-14)
 Lectionary Commentary (Jeremiah 28:5-9;
  Matthew 10:40-42; Romans 6:12-23)
 Following Jesus: Grounded Upon Authority, *First in a Series of*
  Three on Evangelism (Matthew 10:1-4; 28:16-20)

JULY

JULY 6 Eighth Sunday after Pentecost 217
 Rest for the Weary (Matthew 11:16-19, 25-30)
 Lectionary Commentary (Genesis 24:24-28, 42-29, 58-67;
  Zechariah 9:9-12; Romans 7:15-25a)
 Following Jesus: Making Disciples, *Second in a Series of Three on*
  Evangelism (Matthew 28:16-20; John 1:35-42)
JULY 13 Ninth Sunday after Pentecost 225
 God's Gracious Rain (Isaiah 55:10-13)
 Lectionary Commentary (Matthew 13:1-9, 18-23; Romans 8:1-11)
 Following Jesus: An Abiding Presence, *Third in a Series of Three*
  on Evangelism (Matthew 28:16-20; John 14:25-27)
JULY 20 Tenth Sunday after Pentecost 232
 Adopted by God (Romans 8:12-25)
 Lectionary Commentary (Genesis 28:10-19a; Matthew 13:24-30,
  36-43)
 War . . . The Judgment of the Earth, *First in a Series of Two on*
  War and Peace (Isaiah 24:1-24)

JULY 27 Eleventh Sunday after Pentecost 239
    The Kingdom of Heaven Is for the Birds (Matthew 13:31-33)
    Lectionary Commentary (1 Kings 3:5-12; Romans 8:26-39)
    Peace . . . The Fulfillment of God's People, *Second in a Series of Two*
    on War and Peace (Isaiah 25:1-12)

AUGUST

AUGUST 3 Twelfth Sunday after Pentecost 246
    Wrestling God (Genesis 32:22-31)
    Lectionary Commentary (Matthew 14:13-21; Romans 9:1-5)
    An Odd Couple, *First in a Series of Two on Ruth* (Ruth 1:15-22)
AUGUST 10 Thirteenth Sunday after Pentecost 253
    Getting Wet (Matthew 14:22-33)
    Lectionary Commentary (Genesis 37:1-4, 12-28; Romans 10:5-15)
    Another Odd Couple, *Second in a Series of Two on Ruth* (Ruth 2–3)
AUGUST 17 Fourteenth Sunday after Pentecost 260
    A Brief Moment but a Long Look (Genesis 45:1-15)
    Lectionary Commentary (Matthew 15:[10-20], 21-28; Romans
       11:1-2a, 29-32)
    Singing Faith, *First in a Series of Two on Music and Worship*
       (Zephaniah 3:14-18)
AUGUST 24 Fifteenth Sunday after Pentecost 268
    Looking to the Rocks (Isaiah 51:1-6)
    Lectionary Commentary (Matthew 16:13-20; Romans 12:1-8)
    Dancing with God, *Second in a Series of Two on Music and Worship*
       (2 Samuel 6:12-15)
AUGUST 31 Sixteenth Sunday after Pentecost 275
    That's What I Like About That (Matthew 16:21-28)
    Lectionary Commentary (Exodus 3:1-15; Romans 12:9-21)
    The Mysterious Power of Prayer, *First in a Series of Two on Prayer*
       (James 5:13-16)

SEPTEMBER

SEPTEMBER 7 Seventeenth Sunday after Pentecost 282
    The Way to a Nation's Heart (Exodus 12:1-14)
    Lectionary Commentary (Matthew 18:15-20; Romans 13:8-14)
    The Mysterious Power of Prayer, *Second in a Series of Two on*
    Prayer (Matthew 7:7-8, 17:20)
SEPTEMBER 14 Eighteenth Sunday after Pentecost 290
    How Can I Make It Up to You? (Matthew 18:21-35)
    Lectionary Commentary (Exodus 14:19-31; Romans 14:1-12)

Healing Forgiveness, *First in a Series of Two on Health and Wholeness* (Mark 2:1-12)

SEPTEMBER 21 Nineteenth Sunday after Pentecost 296
Forgetting and Remembering (Exodus 16:2-15)
Lectionary Commentary (Philippians 1:21-30; Matthew 20:1-16)
The Nourishing Secret of the Meek, *Second in a Series of Two on Health and Wholeness* (Matthew 5:5)

SEPTEMBER 28 Twentieth Sunday after Pentecost 302
God with Us (Exodus 17:1-7)
Lectionary Commentary (Matthew 21:23-32; Philippians 2:1-13)
Little Children, Big Lessons, *First in a Series of Three on Children, Youth, and Ministry* (Luke 18:15-17)

OCTOBER

OCTOBER 5 Twenty-first Sunday after Pentecost 309
The Long Race (Philippians 3:4b-14)
Lectionary Commentary (Exodus 20:1-4, 7-9, 12-20; Matthew 21:33-46)
Be Transformed: Renew Your Mind, *Second in a Series of Three on Children, Youth, and Ministry* (Luke 2:41-52)

OCTOBER 12 Twenty-second Sunday after Pentecost 316
Prepare to Be Chosen (Matthew 22:1-14)
Lectionary Commentary (Exodus 32:1-14; Philippians 4:1-9)
Holding the Towel: The Value of Sharing, *Third in a Series of Three on Children, Youth, and Ministry* (John 13:1-20)

OCTOBER 19 Twenty-third Sunday after Pentecost 323
The Things That Are God's (Matthew 22:15-22)
Lectionary Commentary (Exodus 33:12-23; 1 Thessalonians 1:1-10)
What Is a Traditional Church? *First in a Series of Two on the Tradition of the Church* (Matthew 16:13-20)

OCTOBER 26 Twenty-fourth Sunday after Pentecost/
Reformation 331
The Great Commandment Times Two (Matthew 22:34-46)
Lectionary Commentary (Deuteronomy 34:1-12; 1 Thessalonians 2:1-8)
Is Religion a Private Matter? *Second in a Series of Two on the Tradition of the Church* (Acts 2:42-47)

NOVEMBER

NOVEMBER 2 Twenty-fifth Sunday after Pentecost 338
The Minister and Ministry (1 Thessalonians 2:9-13)
Lectionary Commentary (Micah 3:5-12; Matthew 23:1-12)

Contents

Commodities, Stocks, Bonds, and Inheritance, *First in a Series of Three on Stewardship* (Luke 12:13-21)

NOVEMBER 9 Twenty-sixth Sunday after Pentecost 345
What Does God Want? (Amos 5:18-24)
Lectionary Commentary (Matthew 25:1-13; 1 Thessalonians 4:13-18)
The Power of Compounding, *Second in a Series of Three on Stewardship* (2 Corinthians 9:6-15)

NOVEMBER 16 Twenty-seventh Sunday after Pentecost 353
Use It or Lose It! (Matthew 25:14-30)
Lectionary Commentary (Zephaniah 1:7, 12-18; 1 Thessalonians 5:1-11)
Thanksgiving and Generous Living, *Third in a Series of Three on Stewardship* (Proverbs 3:9-10; Psalm 116:12-14, 17-19)

NOVEMBER 23 Reign of Christ/Christ the King Sunday 361
The Shepherd King (Ezekiel 34:11-16, 20-24; Matthew 25:31-46)
Lectionary Commentary (Ephesians 1:15-23)
A "This End Up" Thanksgiving, *First in a Series of Three on Christian Thanksgiving* (Psalm 95:1-10)

NOVEMBER 27 Thanksgiving Day 368
The Way to a Thankful Heart (Luke 17:11-19; 2 Corinthians 9:6-15)
Lectionary Commentary (Deuteronomy 8:7-18)
Thank God! We Are All Keepers, *Second in a Series of Three on Christian Thanksgiving* (Psalm 121)

NOVEMBER 30 First Sunday of Advent 375
Waiting with God (1 Corinthians 1:3-9)
Lectionary Commentary (Isaiah 64:1-9; Mark 13:24-37)
Thanksgiving Leftovers, *Third in a Series of Three on Christian Thanksgiving* (Psalm 8:1, 3-9)

DECEMBER

DECEMBER 7 Second Sunday of Advent 383
Hope-filled Waiting! (Isaiah 40:1-11)
Lectionary Commentary (Mark 1:1-8; 2 Peter 3:8-15a)
Where Do Gifts Come From? *First in a Series of Two on Gifts* (Deuteronomy 26:1-19)

DECEMBER 14 Third Sunday of Advent 390
Will Anybody Know? (Isaiah 61:1-4, 8-11)
Lectionary Commentary (John 1:6-8, 19-28; 1 Thessonians 5:16-24)

Gift Cycle, *Second in a Series of Two on Gifts* (Deuteronomy 26:1-19)

DECEMBER 21 Fourth Sunday of Advent 397
  Let It Be! (Luke 1:26-38)
  Lectionary Commentary (2 Samuel 7:1-11, 16; Romans 16:25-27)
  Giving to Honor, *First in a Series of Three on Holidays and Emotional Health* (Luke 2:8-18)

DECEMBER 25 Christmas Day (or Christmas Eve) 405
  Life Interrupted . . . Or? (Luke 2:1-20)
  Lectionary Commentary (Isaiah 9:2-7; Titus 2:11-14)
  Time to Ponder, *Second in a Series of Three on Holidays and Emotional Health* (Luke 2:8-20)

DECEMBER 28 First Sunday after Christmas 412
  Redeeming Rituals (Luke 2:22-40)
  Lectionary Commentary (Isaiah 61:10–62:3; Galatians 4:4-7)
  Just Say No, *Third in a Series of Three on Holidays and Emotional Health* (Matthew 5:37a)

III. APPENDIX

Contributors 421
Scripture Index 425

IV. CD-ROM (THESE RESOURCES ARE FOUND ONLY ON THE ENCLOSED CD-ROM)

Entire Print Text plus the following (see the ReadMe.txt file on the CD for instructions);
Classical Prayers
  Morning Prayer
  Eucharistic Prayer
  An Orthodox Prayer
  A Covenant Prayer in the Wesleyan Tradition
  A General Thanksgiving
  Prayer of Saint Francis of Assisi
  A Prayer of Saint Chrysostom
  Serenity Prayer
  An Orthodox Evening Prayer
  Prayer from Saint Augustine
  A Collect for Peace
Classical Affirmations of Faith
  The Apostles' Creed (ca. 700 C.E.)
  The Nicene Creed (325 C.E.)

The Athanasian Creed (ca. 500 C.E.)
The Creed of Chalcedon (451 C.E.)
Contemporary Affirmations of Faith
A New Creed (United Church of Canada)
The Korean Creed
A Modern Affirmation
World Methodist Council Social Affirmation
Classic Sermons
Spiritual Worship (John Wesley)
Pray for Forgiveness (Clovis Chappell)
Pre-Sermon Prayers (David N. Mosser)
Pastoral Prayers (David N. Mosser)
New Year's
Epiphany
Baptism of the Lord
Transfiguration
Ash Wednesday
Lent
Holy Thursday
Good Friday
Easter
Ascension
Pentecost
Trinity
All Saints Day
Reign of Christ/Christ the King
Thanksgiving
Advent
Christmas Eve
Sermon Illustrations (hyperlinked to the text)
Annotated Bibliography (hyperlinked to the text)
Lectionary Verses (hyperlinked to the text)

INTRODUCTION

To slightly misquote a trusted friend: "As for me and my household, we will use the *Revised Common Lectionary*" (Joshua 24:15). As originally conceived, the *Abingdon Preaching Annual* was a homiletic resource that included three "sermon briefs" for each Sunday of the liturgical year. Each brief consisted of 600 words and was based on the day's lectionary readings. For some time the *Abingdon Preaching Annual* served preachers well. But in the intervening years circumstances came to our attention that encouraged Abingdon Press to provide an even more useful preaching resource to announce God's holy word. Thus, we present the 2008 incarnation of the *Abingdon Preaching Annual*, developed and improved through ongoing dialogue with our readers.

Several years ago, responding to a remarkably loyal readership, we decided to extend the length of the sermon entries and focus on only one of the day's lectionary texts. We supposed that a 1,000-word sermonic essay on a single passage might better serve our readers' needs. In addition we recognized that many preachers do not exclusively use the weekly preaching lectionary—or at all. Because we heard from many devoted readers, we decided to add a 1,000-word, topical sermon for each preaching day. We asked our writers to develop these supplementary sermons around specific themes. It was our hope that this new "series" feature would serve pastors who preach sermon series along with the lectionary. We consider, at least from our readers' responses, that this decision was born in happy judgment. In the 2008 APA all of our writers (for lectionary and series sermons) have also contributed worship aids that are directly related to the sermonic themes.

This year, again in response to reader comments and requests, we have expanded our coverage of the lectionary readings with additional commentary on those readings not employed in the main lectionary sermon for the week.

We have continued the General Helps section that, in this 2008 edition, includes: a four-year calendar of significant liturgical events, an overview of liturgical colors and their meanings, and lectionary listings for the calendar year.

In 2006, a CD-ROM with many supplementary features was added. The CD-ROM includes the full text of the print edition with the helpful feature of search capability. Hyperlinks also help readers quickly navigate to additional sermon illustrations, an annotated bibliography, and the full lectionary text for each week's readings. We also have incorporated pre-sermon prayers and pastoral prayers. And this year, the classical and contemporary prayers and affirmations that have been part of the print text can be found on the CD-ROM, along with two classic sermons from great preachers of the past. Electronic links help readers not only navigate easily among the CD-ROM features but also copy and paste prayers and scripture texts for use in worship bulletins and materials.

Yet, despite all these helpful elements, the real value of this resource is to put preachers in the arena of homiletical discourse with other preachers who know and perform their craft well. Few preachers have the opportunity to hear colleagues on a regular basis. The *Abingdon Preaching Annual* makes it possible for readers to see the homiletical work of some outstanding preachers, representing several Christian denominations. Sermon reading helps put all preachers in conversation about texts and homiletic strategies that will enhance the gospel's hearing. As Fred Craddock once commented with great insight: "The point of a sermon is not to get something said, but rather to get something heard." If we can study and muse over what our sister and brother preachers do with a text and how they present it homiletically, then perhaps we will be better able to assess and realize our own pulpit effectiveness. Preaching, after all, is a team effort as we listen carefully to both ancient preachers and contemporary ones.

My prayer for all readers who happen to be preachers is that as we walk through these texts and experience them with our preaching colleagues, we will all be better preachers for the experience. No doubt we have much to learn from one another. This is the ultimate purpose for the *Abingdon Preaching Annual 2008*. May each of you flourish in the ministry that God has entrusted to us and to Christ's holy church.

The Reverend David N. Mosser
The Nativity of Saint John the Baptist
June 24, 2006

I. GENERAL HELPS

FOUR-YEAR CHURCH CALENDAR

	2008	2009	2010	2011
Ash Wednesday	February 6	February 25	February 17	March 9
Palm Sunday	March 16	April 5	March 28	April 17
Holy Thursday	March 20	April 9	April 1	April 21
Good Friday	March 21	April 10	April 4	April 24
Easter	March 23	April 12	April 4	April 24
Ascension Day	May 1	May 21	May 16	June 2
Pentecost	May 11	May 31	May 23	June 12
Trinity Sunday	May 18	June 7	May 30	June 19
World Communion	October 5	October 4	October 3	October 2
Thanksgiving	November 27	November 26	November 25	November 24
First Sunday of Advent	November 30	November 29	November 28	November 27

LITURGICAL COLORS

If the gospel can be proclaimed visually, why should it not be? Color helps form general expectations for any occasion. Traditionally, purples, grays, and blues have been used for seasons of a penitential character such as Advent and Lent, although any dark colors could be used. White has been used for events or seasons with strong christological meaning such as the Baptism of the Lord or the Easter Season. Yellows and golds are also possibilities at such times. Red has been reserved for occasions relating to the Holy Spirit (such as the Day of Pentecost or ordinations) or to commemorations of the martyrs. Green has been used for seasons such as the Season after Epiphany or the Season after Pentecost. The absence of any colored textiles from Maundy Thursday to the Easter Vigil is a striking use of contrast. Colors and textures can be used most effectively in textiles for hangings on pulpits, on lecterns (if any), for the stoles worn by ordained ministers, or for ministerial vestments.*

Advent: Violet (purple) or blue

Christmas: Gold or white for December 24-25. White thereafter, through the Baptism of the Lord. (Or, in the days between January 6 and the Sunday of the Baptism, green may be used.)

Ordinary Time (both after Epiphany-Baptism and after Pentecost): Green

Transfiguration: White

Lent Prior to Holy Week: Violet. Black is sometimes used for Ash Wednesday.

Early Holy Week: On Palm-Passion Sunday, violet (purple) or [blood] red may be specified. For the Monday, Tuesday, and Wednesday of Holy Week, the same options exist, although with variations as to which color to use on each day.

Triduum: For Holy Thursday, violet (purple) or [blood] red may be used during the day and changed to white for the evening Eucharist. Then the church may be stripped.

Good Friday and Holy Saturday: Stripped or black; or [blood] red in some churches on Good Friday.

Great Fifty Days: White or gold. Or gold for Easter Day and perhaps its octave, then white for the remainder of the season until the Vigil of Pentecost.

Day of Pentecost: [Fire] red

Annunciation, Visitation, and Presentation of Jesus: White

Commemoration of Martyrs: [Blood] red

Commemoration of Saints not Martyred: White

All Saints: White

Christ the King: White**

---

* from *Introduction to Christian Worship Revised Edition* by James White © 1990 Abingdon Press. Used by permission.

** from *Calendar: Christ's Time for the Church* by Laurence Hull Stookey © 1996 Abingdon Press. Used by permission.

LECTIONARY LISTINGS 2008*
THE REVISED COMMON LECTIONARY

Date	First Lesson	Psalm	Second Lesson	Gospel Lesson
1/6/08	Isaiah 60:1-6	Psalm 72:1-7, 10-14	Ephesians 3:1-12	Matthew 2:1-12
1/13/08	Isaiah 42:1-9	Psalm 29	Acts 10:34-43	Matthew 3:13-17
1/20/08	Isaiah 49:1-7	Psalm 40:1-11	1 Corinthians 1:1-9	John 1:29-42
1/27/08	Isaiah 9:1-4	Psalm 27:1, 4-9	1 Corinthians 1:10-18	Matthew 4:12-23
2/3/08	Micah 6:1-8	Psalm 15	1 Corinthians 1:18-31	Matthew 5:1-12
2/6/08	Isaiah 58:1-12	Psalm 51:1-17	2 Corinthians 5:20b-6:10	Matthew 6:1-6, 16-21
2/10/08	Genesis 2:15-17; 3:1-7	Psalm 32	Romans 5:12-19	Matthew 4:1-11
2/17/08	Genesis 12:1-4a	Psalm 121	Romans 4:1-5, 13-16	John 3:1-17
2/24/08	Exodus 17:1-7	Psalm 95	Romans 5:1-11	John 4:5-42
3/2/08	1 Samuel 16:1-13	Psalm 23	Ephesians 5:8-14	John 9:1-41
3/9/08	Ezekiel 37:1-14	Psalm 130	Romans 8:6-11	John 11:1-45
3/16/08	Palm: Psalm 118:1-2, 19-29 Passion: Isaiah 50:4-9a	Psalm 31:9-16	Philippians 2:5-11	Matthew 21:1-11 Matthew 26:14-27:66
3/20/08	Exodus 12:1-14	Psalm 116:1-2, 12-19	1 Corinthians 11:23-26	John 13:1-17, 31b-35
3/21/08	Isaiah 52:13-53:12	Psalm 23	Hebrews 4:14-16, 10:16-25	John 18:1-19:42
3/23/08	Acts 10:34-43	Psalm 118:1-2, 14-24	Colossians 3:1-4	John 20:1-18
3/30/08	Acts 2:14a, 22-32	Psalm 16	1 Peter 1:3-9	John 20:19-31
4/6/08	Acts 2:14a, 36-41	Psalm 116:1-4, 12-19	1 Peter 1:17-23	Luke 24:13-35
4/13/08	Acts 2:42-47	Psalm 23	1 Peter 2:19-25	John 10:1-10
4/20/08	Acts 7:55-60	Psalm 31:1-5, 15-16	1 Peter 2:2-10	John 14:1-14
4/27/08	Acts 17:22-31	Psalm 66:8-20	1 Peter 3:13-22	John 14:15-21
5/4/08	Acts 1:6-14	Psalm 68:1-10, 32-35	1 Peter 4:12-14; 5:6-11	John 17:1-11
5/11/08	Acts 2:1-21	Psalm 104:24-34, 35b	1 Corinthians 12:3b-13	John 20:19-23
5/18/08	Genesis 1:1-2:4a	Psalm 8	2 Corinthians 13:11-13	Matthew 28:16-20
5/25/08	Isaiah 49:8-16a	Psalm 131	1 Corinthians 4:1-5	Matthew 6:24-34

* This list represents one possible selection of lessons and psalms from the lectionary for Year A (January 1–November 25) and Year B (December 2-30). For a complete listing see *The Revised Common Lectionary*.

Sunday	First Lesson	Psalm	Second Lesson	Gospel Lesson
6/1/08	Deuteronomy 11:18-21, 26-28	Psalm 31:1-5, 19-24; 46	Romans 1:16-17; 3:22b-31	Matthew 7:21-29
6/8/08	Hosea 5:15–6:6	Psalm 33:1-12	Romans 4:13-25	Matthew 9:9-13, 18-26
6/15/08	Genesis 18:1-15	Psalm 116:1-2, 12-19	Romans 5:1-8	Matthew 9:35–10:8 (9-23)
6/22/08	Genesis 21:8-21; Jeremiah 20:7-13	Psalm 69:7-18	Romans 6:1b-11	Matthew 10:24-39
6/29/08	Genesis 22:1-14; Jeremiah 28:5-9	Psalm 13	Romans 6:12-23	Matthew 10:40-42
7/6/08	Genesis 24:34-38, 42-49, 58-67; Zechariah 9:9-12	Psalm 145:8-14	Romans 7:15-25a	Matthew 11:16-19, 25-30
7/13/08	Isaiah 55:10-13	Psalm 119:105-12	Romans 8:1-11	Matthew 13:1-9, 18-23
7/20/08	Genesis 28:10-19a	Psalm 139:1-12, 23-24	Romans 8:12-25	Matthew 13:24-30, 36-43
7/27/08	1 Kings 3:5-12	Psalm 105:1-11, 45b	Romans 8:26-39	Matthew 13:31-33, 44-52
8/3/08	Genesis 32:22-31	Psalm 17:1-7, 15	Romans 9:1-5	Matthew 14:13-21
8/10/08	Genesis 37:1-4, 12-18	Psalm 105:1-6, 16-22, 45b	Romans 10:5-15	Matthes 14:22-33
8/17/08	Genesis 45:1-15	Psalm 133	Romans 11:1-2a, 29-32	Matthew 15:10-20, 21-28
8/24/08	Isaiah 51:1-6	Psalm 124	Romans 12:1-8	Matthew 16:13-20
8/31/08	Exodus 3:1-15	Psalm 105:1-6, 23-26, 45c	Romans 12:9-21	Matthew 16:21-28
9/7/08	Exodus 12:1-14	Psalm 149	Romans 13:8-14	Matthew 18:15-20
9/14/08	Exodus 14:19-31	Psalm 114	Romans 14:1-12	Matthew 18:21-35
9/21/08	Exodus 16:2-15	Psalm 105:1-6, 37-45	Philippians 1:21-30	Matthew 20:1-16
9/28/08	Exodus 17:1-7	Psalm 78:1-4, 12-16	Philippians 2:1-13	Matthew 21:23-32
10/5/08	Exodus 20:1-4, 7-9, 12-20	Psalm 19	Philippians 3:4b-14	Matthew 21:33-46
10/12/08	Exodus 32:1-14	Psalm 106:1-6, 19-23	Philippians 4:1-9	Matthew 22:1-14
10/19/08	Exodus 33:12-23	Psalm 99	1 Thessalonians 1:1-10	Matthew 22:15-22

*This list represents one possible selection of lessons and psalms from the lectionary for Year A (January 1–November 25) and Year B (December 2–30). For a complete listing see *The Revised Common Lectionary*.

Sunday	First Lesson	Psalm	Second Lesson	Gospel Lesson
10/26/08	Deuteronomy 34:1	Psalm 90:1-6, 13-17	1 Thessalonians 2:1-8	Matthew 22:34-46
11/2/08	Micah 3:5	Psalm 107:1-7, 33-37	1 Thessalonians 2:9-13	Matthew 23:1-12
11/9/08	A 18-24	Psalm 78:1-7	1 Thessalonians 4:13-18	Matthew 25:1-13
11/16/08	Zephaniah 1:7, 12-18	Psalm 123	1 Thessalonians 5:1-11	Matthew 25:14-30
11/ 08	Ezekiel 34:11-16, 20-24	Psalm 100	Ephesians 1:15-23	Matthew 25:31-46
11/27/08	Deuteronomy 8:7-18	Psalm 65	2 Corinthians 9:6-15	Luke 17:11-19
11/30/08	Isaiah 64:1-9	Psalm 80:1-7, 17-19	1 Corinthians 1:3-9	Mark 13:24-37
12/7/08	Isaiah 40:1-11	Psalm 85:1-2, 8-13	2 Peter 3:8-15a	Mark 1:1-8
12/14/08	Isaiah 61:1-4, 8-11	Psalm 126	1 Thessalonians 5:16-24	John 1:6-8, 19-28
12/21/08	2 Samuel 7:1-11, 16	Psalm 89:1-4, 19-26	Romans 16:25-27	Luke 1:26-38
12/25/08	Isaiah 9:2-7	Psalm 96	Titus 2:11-14	Luke 2:1-20
12/28/08	Isaiah 61:10–62:3	Psalm 148	Galatians 4:4-7	Luke 2:22-40

* This list represents one possible selection of lessons and psalms from the lectionary for Year A (January 1–November 25) and Year B (December 2-30). For a complete listing see *The Revised Common Lectionary*.

II. SERMONS AND WORSHIP AIDS

JANUARY 6, 2008

✦✦✦✦

Epiphany

Readings: Isaiah 60:1-6; Psalm 72:1-7, 10-14; Ephesians 3:1-12; Matthew 2:1-12

The Winter of the Heart
Matthew 2:1-12

The story of the Magi traveling from the East to Bethlehem is rich in imagery and begs the question, "Why did the Magi follow that star?" Perhaps the primary reason was because they were searching for a deeper meaning of life. What else could it be? They had everything else. They had their own religious beliefs. They had their own science of astrology, and they certainly had wealth and power. So why the trek? Why would they journey through the desert at night navigating by a star? Perhaps the long journey was made out of an awareness of their own emptiness. Somehow with all of their religion, science, and wealth, they were coming up empty. They were struggling with the all too common malady known as "the winter of the heart."

Their willingness to follow a star was an indication of their emptiness and their receptivity to God. These Magi were seekers who were willing to anchor their gaze on the star, trusting its guidance and meaning, while at the same time acknowledging their own limitations in spite of their reputations of being persons of royalty and scientific intellect of the stars. Out of their emptiness they were willing to search for meaning, identity, and purpose that perhaps they felt they were missing. This explains why these astrologers from the East would give themselves over to a lengthy and uncharted journey and would also explain why when they found the Christ, they worshiped and bowed down and paid the baby homage. In that manger they saw something and someone greater than themselves.

The heart of winter knows the bitter cold winds of emptiness. It knows the pain of uncertainty of meaning and purpose. It knows the need to

3

believe in something beyond itself. The heart of winter looks for reflections of itself everywhere: in the dreams of a quiet January night, in the sound of a name, in the touch of a familiar hand.

The heart of winter longs to be born again. It wants to test new ideas. It wants to make plans for the future. Throughout the month of biting winds, the human heart continues to ask, "Who am I and why? What is life's meaning and purpose?" Amid all the Christmas decorations we put up, amid all the Christmas carols we sing, amid all our Christmas activities, the heart of winter searches for an answer. Somehow the Magi knew that the presence of God had come into the world through human birth. That God could now be seen in human form, could be touched, embraced, offered gifts, and even worshiped.

When they arrived in the presence of the baby Jesus, they knew they had arrived. They had arrived at a new understanding of what life is all about. They had arrived at a new understanding of the meaning and purpose of life. They had arrived at a new understanding of their own identity, and there they fell to their knees and worshiped. There, in that humble setting, these three stalwarts from the East found their salvation. The story of the Magi is the story of our salvation as well. It is about us— our winter of the heart. It is about our emptiness, our journey, and our search for God. The story of the Magi is the story of our own quest for identity, which we, like the Magi, will find in the Christ.

Life doesn't make much sense until we can discover who we are and begin to grow into that person. Despite all of their wealth and power, the Magi wanted to find out who they really were and the star led them to a point of discovery. That star can lead us as well to the Christ child, where we can discover our reason for being. It is there, after the long journey, that we find inner meaning for our lives. The only proper response is to fall on our knees and offer our gifts.

Like the Magi, let us set forth on a journey seeking the Christ, realizing that as we each make our way closer to God, we are also drawing closer to one another. Is this not our only hope for world peace and reconciliation? If we follow the signs God gives us, we will find the presence of the living Christ.

Who knows how or where people find Jesus? Some spend their whole lives looking without success. We need to keep in mind that anything could be a sign if we could learn to relax our gaze, be open to any possibility, and be willing to be led to new, unusual, even dangerous places. Those who discover the presence of God in the Christ might be hard-pressed to explain what they saw because the meaning of epiphany might seem unlikely, outlandish, perhaps even shocking.

The fact is, not all who surveyed the starry sky that night saw what those astrologers from the East saw. But they followed that star until it led them to the place where they felt they now knew who they were and what the purpose was for their life. There, in the presence of God, they knelt and offered their gifts. Today, you are invited to come into the presence of Christ. Bring with you the gift of your life and you will know the experience of the Magi who, after encountering the Christ child, returned to their home a different way.

An elderly African American woman from the Bronx revealed herself to be a modern day Magi. Shortly after 9/11, she heard that a rescue worker at ground zero had injured a leg. She made her way down through intense security to Lower Manhattan and St. Paul's Episcopal Church— the center of rescue operations. There she left the cane that had supported her on her trek from home, through the mayhem and the rubble. And she hobbled off (*Celebration*, January 2003).

I don't know what motivated that simple but profound act other than her being willing to search for something or someone greater than herself. There she was, one of the Magi from the Bronx … in the intensity of searchlights and smoldering debris she came, offering her simple gift of homage, and went home. We don't know exactly how or why it happened that way. But it did. Epiphany is like that. (Rodney E. Wilmoth)

Lectionary Commentary
Isaiah 60:1-6

Five hundred years before the birth of Christ, a poetic prophet foresaw the impact of God's Christmas event. He issued the challenge of our text to the Hebrew people. A fascinating account of how the early church set the date for the observance of Christmas might be helpful. The early church fathers wanted to clearly represent the importance of Jesus as the "Light." No one knew exactly when Jesus was born, so they decided to set his birth to correspond with the winter solstice; that time in December when in an infinitesimal moment light and darkness change places. The birth of Jesus represents that infinitesimal moment. Although the early fathers made a four-day miscalculation, we nevertheless celebrated the fact that the light of Christ has come into our dark world and the darkness has never been able to put it out. So, "Arise, shine; for your light has come"!

Ephesians 3:1-12

Perhaps the greatest freedom we can experience is to be a prisoner for Christ. Such a concept is an oxymoron, but it speaks to the mystery of our faith. Such freedom allows us at the beginning of a new year to think about letting go of the past so that we can look forward to the possibilities of the future. Such freedom allows us "to see" what God may have in store for us. A more accurate translation is "to bring to light," "to enlighten," or "to illuminate." It is by being a prisoner of Christ that we are able to see "the plan of the mystery hidden for ages in God who created all things." This is a time of new beginning in Christ who sets us free. (Rodney E. Wilmoth)

Worship Aids

Silent Meditation

Neither you nor I nor anyone else ever saw a man like Jesus until he was born into the world. But what can we do about a man like that? If you are not willing to put an exclamation mark after his name and stand at attention, then you must put a question mark after his name and sit in silence. If you do not follow him, the least you must do is wonder about him. The one thing you cannot do is to ignore him. However unwitting our awareness of the impact of his life upon ours, the historical fact stands established that we are where we are today, doing what we are doing, in the way we are doing it, because a long time ago there lived a man named Jesus. Whatever our lives might have been without him, they are decisively different because of him. Even for those who are not committed to him, he is inextricably a part of the past that impinges upon the present of all who have lived ever since he lined. (Melvin E. Wheatley Jr.)

Affirmation of Faith (Responsive)

The star of divine promise shines before us still.
**Over a world of mute hopes, dim visions, dark fears, still
the light shines.**
In a world shrouded by darkness both tragic and willful,
Still we proclaim: our light has come.
The glory of God shines upon us.

For one born of God is born of our own flesh,
and that One is light for our lives.
**As we receive the light and let it shine through us, it raises
as a beacon for a darkened world.**
The peoples shall stream toward its promise; meek and mighty
alike share in its dawning brightness.
All: Then all shall say: Arise! The glory of God is upon us!

Dismissal with Blessing (Responsive)

May the God who established a covenant with those who seek to
enter the kingdom be always present with you.
Amen.
May Jesus Christ who sealed the new covenant with this meal
bring you peace.
Amen.
May God's Holy Spirit guide your life.
Amen.
Go in peace to serve God and your neighbor in all you do.
All: Amen. Thanks be to God.
(Rodney E. Wilmoth)

New Birth: Why Baptism Matters

First in a Series of Three on the Sacraments

Galatians 3:23-29

Scanning television, a prominent theme has emerged of late: our desire
for transformation, change, a makeover. In these programs a family
leaves, and then returns, and its home has been decorated in a new way.
Or people travel to a big city and then become a new person: new hair, a
new wardrobe. Or five guys come in and they teach you a new way to
cook, and they decorate, and they get rid of all the old stuff. Or, more
drastically, a team of surgeons, along with a very attractive model/
spokesperson, consult with someone and convinces them that they need
a new body and a new face.

It is all about makeover, transformation, change. Of course, the networks continue tapping into something powerful: the impulse to shed our
skin, to experience a metamorphosis, from an ugly duckling to a swan,
from a caterpillar to a butterfly.

For Christians, this impulse is deep within us as well, and the way we talk about makeover, transformation, change, and new life is baptism. In today's text, Paul speaks of an old way of life under the custodian, the disciplinarian, the pedagogy of the law, a law that we could not keep or live up to or fulfill. The law held sway over us until Christ came, Paul tells the Galatians. In Christ we become children of God. We are not speaking of natural childbirth, of the mark of circumcision, or any kind of ethnic heritage. We are children of God through faith.

This faith is expressed in baptism; we are baptized into Christ—into the body—and we "put on" Christ. The image is unmistakable—as if we are receiving a new wardrobe. And because we have put on Christ, we are made over, we are transformed, we are changed. The old camp song I learned in the mountains of western North Carolina said it well: "the best thing in my life I ever did do, was take off the old robe and put on the new."

Baptism is a visual symbol of the power of transformation. It is God's gift, God's work, God's act. Baptism also gives us a different way of perceiving ourselves. In these programs on television, the person leaves, and they return, and maybe they see a room or two in their homes, and everything is different, and the camera records their amazement. Or perhaps someone leaves and returns to see friends and family who cannot believe she is the same person. Or the surgically improved individual simply looks into a mirror and is overwhelmed. It is all about getting used to the change.

In the New Testament church, the converts needed some reassurance that they were worthy of God's gift, worthy of love. And so, Paul writes to them, and to us, "you are all children of God." Peter, in his letter, writes, "you are royalty" (1 Peter 2:9, paraphrased). You have a new identity. You belong to God.

A good friend of ours had her first child this spring, a boy. We saw him last week for the first time. As I picked him up, I was amazed first at how light he seemed, our children having grown almost to adulthood. I smiled at him, made some goofy noises and he looked at me as if he were going through some kind of internal biochemical reaction. Maybe he was doing that.

Then his mother took him back and said his name, and a huge smile came across his face. He knew the one to whom he belonged. This is a transforming truth. The primary identifying feature about you is not where you live or how you vote or how much money you have or where you came from or who your father is or even your gender or your race. You are a child of God through faith, in baptism.

In baptism we are marked, claimed, and given access to the grace that God wants to give us. This is our fundamental identity. Paul writes, "There is no longer Jew or Greek, there is no longer slave or free, there is no longer male or female; for all of you are one in Christ Jesus."

What we share in common—our identity in Jesus Christ—is more significant than all of our differences. Which is another way of saying we all belong. Baptism is about identity: we belong. Baptism is also about transformation: we can be changed. And baptism is a lifelong process. When we are watching television, transformation happens so quickly, and yet real change, authentic transformation, is different. We are becoming new creatures. We are being changed.

On television, transformation happens in an instant. But in reality, the transformation may take us a lifetime. So stay tuned. A sacrament is an outward and visible sign of an inward and spiritual grace. The change, the makeover, the transformation that matters is one that begins on the inside, what John Wesley called the "circumcision of the heart," what Jesus pointed to in so many of the teachings of the Sermon on the Mount.

The outward and visible sign is the water washing over us. The inward and spiritual grace is the acceptance, the unconditional love, the fount of every blessing, always a gift, a moment that extends into a lifetime. God is never finished with us . . . God will not give up on us. Our lives, our priorities, are being rearranged. Welcome to the family, God says . . . let's get you cleaned up!

And so we place ourselves in God's hands and we allow the waters to cleanse us, and our hearts are tuned to sing God's grace, and we see ourselves, and each other, for who we really are. We remember that we are baptized. We hear a voice calling our name, and if we are listening, a huge smile comes across our faces. We are children of God! (Kenneth H. Carter Jr.)

Worship Aids

Call to Worship

Come to the waters!
We have been called by God.
Come to the waters!
We have been claimed by God.

Come to the waters!
All: We are being cleansed by God. Come to the waters.

Prayer of Confession

We gather as unclean people, Lord. Our motives are not always pure. Our desires are not always appropriate. Our lives are not always ordered. Our actions are not always constructive. Remind us that we have been baptized, that you have created us, called us by name, taken us by the hand, and blessed us as your beloved children. Through the presence of your Holy Spirit, free us from all that is past, and empower us for all that awaits us in the future, through Jesus Christ, our Lord.

Words of Assurance

In the name of Jesus Christ, you are forgiven.
In the name of Jesus Christ, you are forgiven. Amen.

Benediction

Go forth into the world as new creatures, transformed by the word, cleansed by the spirit, washed in the waters of the one who saves and redeems you. In the name of the Father, the Son, and the Holy Spirit. Amen. (Kenneth H. Carter Jr.)

JANUARY 13, 2008

❧❧❧❧

Baptism of the Lord

Readings: Isaiah 42:1-9; Psalm 29; Acts 10:34-43; Matthew 3:13-17

The Inelegance of It All
Matthew 3:13-17

A Baptist minister tells of how he can still see the shock on the face of a woman when he explained to her that his tradition required immersion for baptism. She had been baptized as an infant in another church. But now she wanted to join the Baptist church. "Isn't there some other way?" she asked. "Dunking is so ... so ... inelegant!" (R. Wayne Stacy, "A Whole New Life," *The Minister's Annual Manual, 1998-1999* [Grove Heights, Minn: Logos, 1998]).

I have never thought of baptism as being inelegant, but it is a notion worthy of consideration. Baptism means, among other things, repentance, and repentance is not always the most elegant of experiences. Baptism by immersion can be pretty humbling. I have a retired Baptist minister friend who often referred to the baptistery as "the humility tank" and argued that was a good preparation for life in the kingdom of God, because God's kingdom is a countercultural movement that often sets persons apart by making demands that we live and work in a world that is at crosscurrents with what most everyone else believes, thinks, and holds dear.

While forms of baptism vary, immersion does help us see the symbolism of death and resurrection. John Westerhoff III describes a baptism in a small church in Latin America that certainly celebrates this theological view. He writes that the community of faith gathers and begins to recall God's gracious acts, which, by the way, is one of the reasons some traditions celebrate infant baptism:

The congregation began the mournful sounds of a funeral hymn as the solemn procession moved down the aisle. The father carried a child's coffin he made from wood; the mother carried a bucket of water from the family well; the priest carried the sleeping child wrapped only in a native blanket. As they reach the chancel, the father placed the coffin on the altar, and the mother poured the water in the coffin, and the priest covered the wakening baby's skin with embalming oil. . . . The priest slowly lowered the infant into the coffin amd immersed the child's head in the water. . . He exclaimed, "I kill you in the name of the Father and of the Son and of the Holy Spirit."

"Amen!" shouted the parents and congregation.

Then quickly lifting the child into the air for all to see, the priest declared: "And I resurrect you that you might love and serve the Lord."

Immediately, the congregation broke into a joyous Easter hymn (*Bringing Up Children of the Christian Faith* [Minneapolis: Winston Press, 1980], 3).

This gets at the heart of the reason for baptism, inelegant as it may be. There is nothing elegant about discipleship, because discipleship always begins with repentance, and repentance is a kind of death. As C. S. Lewis reminds us, "It is something much harder than merely eating humble pie. It means unlearning all the self-conceit and self-will that we have been training ourselves into for thousands of years. It means killing a part of yourself, and undergoing a kind of death."

Today we celebrate the baptism of our Lord. Some folks have often been puzzled as to why Jesus was baptized in the first place. After all, they argue, he was without sin. Why did he need to participate in a ritual that focused on repentance if he was sinless? The answer is that Jesus chose to immerse himself in the inelegance of life.

There is indeed something inelegant about baptism, but for that matter there is something inelegant about life! There is something inelegant about war, racism, and sexism. There is something inelegant about child abuse and spouse abuse. There is something inelegant about hunger and injustice.

The baptism of Jesus is linked to his being completely obedient to God's will. What gives us hope and encouragement when we observe the baptism of Jesus is that he was willing to enter the murky waters of the Jordan River as God's servant and one who serves with love and grace. Christ became the servant, and the primary work of the servant is to establish God's rule in the world, thus helping our world be more elegant. When Jesus emerged from the river, a voice from heaven was heard to affirm:

"This is my Son, the Beloved, with whom I am well pleased." The baptism of Jesus signals the fact that God is in the midst of all of life's inelegance.

The servant Christ comes into the inelegance of our life by humbling himself to be baptized. Baptism is the assurance that God is with us. Baptism is the assurance that we are welcomed into God's family long before we even ask to be invited. Baptism means that we experience the loving presence of God.

There are times when the inelegance of life cannot be denied. But thank God for the inelegance of baptism, for when our Christ was willing to get into the murky waters of life to give us the gift of dying to the old and being resurrected to the new so that each and every one of us can feel and experience the flowing love of God. (Rodney E. Wilmoth)

Lectionary Commentary
Isaiah 42:1-9

The first of the four suffering servant songs, this hymn focuses on a person, either an individual or the nation as a whole, specially chosen by God and entrusted with a mission not only on behalf of Israel but all the nations as well. This passage enables us to feel the weight of what God might be expecting of us. Too often we offer a gospel that has little depth and is rather light in terms of what might be expected of us if we are indeed chosen by God. There are some demands that go with being a servant of God, and one of those demands is doing what we can do to bring about God's justice. Being faithful to this calling may indeed lead us to experience what it means to be a suffering servant.

Acts 10:34-43

What happens when your mind is made up about some important matter and then something or someone comes along to suggest that we need to change our way of thinking? That is certainly what happened to Peter. He was not comfortable with the notion that God's love and salvation were for everyone. He probably believed that God shows favoritism, but now, in the presence of Cornelius and his household, Peter has to revise his thinking and in so doing is able to share his gospel with the household of Cornelius, which produces amazing results. This is a timely text for Christians living in a multicultural and multireligious world. Let us do what we can do to share the good news with a hurting world that is so in need of the healing balm that Christ can provide. (Rodney E. Wilmoth)

Worship Aids

Meditation

The most delicious piece of knowledge for me is that I am a child of God. That is so mind-boggling that [God] created everything, and I am a child of [God]. It means that I am connected to everything and everybody. That's all so wonderful. (Maya Angelou)

Call to Worship (Responsive)

The one who granted us the breath of life is present here to
> greet us.
**Praise God for the gift of life and the linking of our lives
with one another.**
God's own Spirit rests upon us, drawing us into the family of faith.
**We have been baptized into Christ and share in the mission
entrusted to Jesus.**
The good new of peace is for all people, for God shows no
partiality.
**We gather this morning to remember Jesus' baptism and
ponder its implications for us.**

Morning Prayer (Unison)

Great God, above all gods, we who fail so often and are so easily discouraged return for spiritual refreshment and practical directions. Take us by the hand and renew in us once more your holy covenant. Open the eyes that have been unable to see your truth. Release those of us who live in prisons of our own making and those bound by the sins of others. Grant us the help that we need to live freely in response to your Spirit. Amen.

Prayer of Confession (Unison)

Forgiving God, you embrace all through your Son Jesus, and we still show partiality. In him you proclaim the joyful news of peace, and we still talk war. In him, you wish to reconcile the whole human race in love, and we still put up walls of mistrust and fear one another. Jesus healed the oppressed and freed the captives, and we still reject his invi-

tation to new life. Have mercy on us, gracious God. Grant us the courage to pursue your way of love. Amen. (Rodney E. Wilmoth)

Words of Assurance

In the name of Jesus Christ, you are forgiven.
In the name of Jesus Christ, you are forgiven. Amen.

Bread of Life

Second in a Series of Three on the Sacraments

John 6:51-58

When asked for instruction in prayer, Jesus responded, when you pray, say "Our Father in heaven ... give us this day our daily bread" (Matthew 6:9, 11). In the Sermon on the Mount, Jesus likens God's nature to a parent: "What father," he asks, "would give his daughter a stone if she asks for bread? ... In the same way your heavenly Father never withholds good gifts from his children" (Matthew 7:9-11, paraphrased). When Jesus wanted to make visible the great gift of salvation offered to all people, near and far, he multiplied bread from a boy's basket and fed a multitude of people. When Jesus decided to leave behind a living reminder of the depths of God's love for a sinful world, he broke bread with disciples, even with the betrayer, and said, "take, eat: this is my body, which is broken for you" (1 Corinthians 11:24 KJV).

Bread is the gift of God made visible. That it is a gift may strike us as out of the ordinary, because we don't often think of bread given, but bread earned, bread worked for, bread gained by daily labor, the result of toil and sweat and stress. The bread of God is different. It is like manna, falling from heaven, new every morning. We do not earn the daily bread of God; it comes to us, like a miracle. In the same way Jesus comes to us. "For us and for our salvation he came down from heaven," the Nicene Creed reminds us. "I am the living bread that comes down from heaven," Jesus says.

When Israel was making a way through the wilderness, Israel's concern was about survival. Their basic human need was food. The immediate question was "what are we going to eat today?" In the wilderness Israel discovered that God would supply manna each day, and they were sustained. Jesus comes to a hungry people and feeds them; they wonder, they worry about the next meal; their basic human need is food; their question is "what are we going to eat today?" and in Jesus' gift they are sustained. End of story, right? No, there is more. The sixth chapter of John begins with the feeding of the five thousand, and continues with an extended teaching about the meaning of bread. Now that you have eaten, Jesus says, let me tell you what just happened.

"I am the living bread that comes down from heaven," he tells them. The people gathered don't understand, they disagree about what it all means, but Jesus continues: "eat this bread and you will live forever." Their concern is about what is going to happen today. Jesus speaks about eternity. We are often preoccupied with the immediate. Jesus always wants us to see a greater horizon: not just the immediate, but the ultimate.

Of course a lot of life is the immediate, what is needed right now. We'll just take some of the bread, thanks. We'll listen to the explanation later. Maybe at the end of the day, or maybe when the kids have grown up, or maybe when a crisis comes. Then we do want to know what it means. Then we may want to see the big picture.

We eat the bread; we receive the gift. But at some point we do need to know why we are eating the bread. Is it just to have the strength to wake up into the light of another day, so that we might eat the bread again? What is immediate is always there—we're hungry, give us bread—and Jesus does give us daily bread. God does provide. God's grace is sufficient. But there is more to life than daily bread. There is bread from heaven, bread that gives life to the world. That is the big picture, and Jesus is calling us in John 6 to move from our own immediate need to the greater horizon: not just another day of life, but eternal life.

It is true: there is always more going on here than we realize. In John there are layers of meaning—water and living water, birth and new birth, bread and bread of life; there are signs—water into wine, loaves and fishes, a towel and a basin; there are questions. After Jesus washes the disciples' feet he asks, "Do you know what I have done to you?" After Jesus' resurrection he asks, "Peter, do you love me?" Layers of meaning, signs, questions: there is always more going on here than we realize.

Of course, the same is true for us. Daily bread is a miracle. We all, to some extent, take the bread and eat it. I don't think too much about the farmer who planted the seeds, or those who prayed for rain in the midst of drought, their livelihoods at stake, or those who harvested, maybe migrants going from place to place, or those who drive the trucks to bring the bread to the store. I take a loaf off of the shelf and I throw it in the basket and I move on to the next thing. I miss the reality that there is more going on here than I realize.

Daily bread is a miracle. There are layers of meaning here. Those who eat my flesh and drink my blood abide in me, and I in them. Now something else is going on. It is communion with Jesus, a meal on a hillside in Galilee is likened to one in the upper room. Jesus becomes a part of us, and we become a part of Jesus.

What brings us together? Food. Bread. Bread of Life. A growing sense within us is that there is more to life than this life. The remembrance that we do not live "by bread alone, but by every word that comes from the mouth of God" (Matthew 4:4). A hunger for something that the world cannot satisfy.

Jesus says when you eat this bread and drink from this cup, I will live in you, and you will live in me. He gets inside of us, and we begin to see the world through his eyes. Suddenly we discover that there is more going on than we realize, and so we begin to live with an expectation of the miraculous. And life, the great theme of John's Gospel—whoever believes in him should not perish but have eternal life—life is not only what is happening all around us—in the immediate—but life extends into a horizon that is greater than we can see, and this is a foretaste of the living bread that comes down from heaven, that gives life to the world. (Kenneth H. Carter Jr.)

Worship Aids

Call to Worship

Come to the feast!
The table is prepared.
Come, you who hunger and thirst.
God will provide.
This is the day that the Lord has made.
All: Let us rejoice and be glad in it!

A Litany of Thanksgiving

For the gift of creation, for all that lives and grows:
We give you thanks, O God.
For those who till the earth and keep it:
We give you thanks, O God.
For those who harvest our food, especially migrant farm workers:

We give you thanks, O God.
For an abundance of food and drink, and for the sustenance of life:
We give you thanks, O God.
For those who share out of their bounty with others, especially in
soup kitchens:
We give you thanks, O God.
For the table of the Lord, a sign of your grace, a reminder of your
provision:
We give you thanks, O God.
For the Bread of Life, that comes down from heaven, giving life to
the world:
All: We give you thanks, O God.

Benediction

You have been fed at the table, nourished with bread and cup. Go forth
to be the body of Christ in the world. Go forth to share the Bread of Life
with those who hunger. In the name of the Father, the Son, and the Holy
Spirit. Amen. (Kenneth H. Carter Jr.)

JANUARY 20, 2008

❧❧❧❧

Second Sunday after the Epiphany

Readings: Isaiah 49:1-7; Psalm 40:1-11; 1 Corinthians 1:1-9; John 1:29-42

Hope in the Lava Fields
Isaiah 49:1-7

Leonora Tubbs Tisdale tells of visiting the Volcano National Park on the big island of Hawaii with her husband. She said that the mammoth craters on the top of the mountain intrigued her with their steam ominously rising out of their interior cracks and crevices. She indicated that up close and personal, these craters were a lot larger and more threatening-looking than the television pictures that she had seen.

So, too, were the lava fields that covered the mountainside where the craters had once spewed their steam and molten rock. She said that as she and her husband drove down toward the sea they would stop periodically to get out of the car and walk across the vast expanse of hard, gray-black rock, sometimes as much as ten to fifteen feet deep, that virtually covered over everything in its path. She said, "The sight of so much barren desolation was so grim; it was depressing. It was as if all hope of life and vitality had been snuffed out when the great mountain erupted." (Leonora Tubbs Tisdale, *Pulpit Resource*, February 23, 2003).

In our Scripture lesson from Isaiah, we hear a hopeful word from God to those who have been in the lava fields of exile. The mighty military powers of Babylon had overtaken them in years previous. Their homes and temple had been destroyed, their nation laid in ruin, and they were a captive people. Where was hope? How could anyone think of hoping when it appeared their God had deserted them altogether? With a future as bleak as an ash-gray lava field, why hope at all?

Indeed! Why hope at all? It is not an uncommon question today, especially for persons who feel that God has abandoned them. If you have felt that way from time to time, you need to know that you are not alone. Feelings of being abandoned in the lava fields of life are common even among the most devout. It is difficult to be hopeful when we find ourselves in the lava fields of troubles and unrest. And yet it is in the lava fields of life that we are told to "Sing for joy, O heavens, and exult, O earth.... For the LORD has comforted his people, / and will have compassion on his suffering ones" (Isaiah 49:13).

Imagine that! There is God speaking a word of hope, promise, and new life where one would never expect to hear the voice of God and where no one would probably expect to find any hope. But our God has a capacity to turn even deserts (or lava fields) into green acres where rivers flow freely. Is there anyone for whom this is not good news? God promises that we shall be brought home and that is a promise we are called on to share with others who are in the midst of despair. Our task is to look for this affirming presence of God and to proclaim Easter in the middle of any lava field.

One of the most significant theologians and pastors from Germany during the years of World War II was Dietrich Bonhoeffer. He remains today one of the most quoted persons of our time. Sent to a Nazi concentration camp by Hitler because of his refusal to recant his beliefs, Bonhoeffer was executed on April 9, 1945, just days before Allied troops freed the prisoners.

Bonhoeffer was in prison for two years. He was a great inspiration to his fellow prisoners as well as to the guards. A part of that inspiration was due to his courage and his deep spirit of gratitude. Even in the wilderness of that concentration camp, Dietrich Bonhoeffer was able to trust the presence of God. He saw every day in the prison as a day for serving God, and thanking God for what God shared with others. Shortly before his execution, he wrote a prayer of praise and thanksgiving for peace in the night and the new day. This powerful prayer also included pleas for love to blot out hatred and bitterness, faith for protection from despair, and hope for deliverance from fear. It ends with a poignant surrender to God's will in all things, regardless of what the day might bring.

Something quite wonderful can happen in the lava fields, a place where we might think is devoid of any hope. But look closer ... there in the cracks of the once molten lava are tiny shoots of new plant life. So we can sing for joy, "for the LORD has comforted his people, / and will have compassion on his suffering ones" (Isaiah 49:13).

For several years I had the privilege of living in Minneapolis. During those years I often drove Interstate 35. Somewhere between Minneapolis and Des Moines there is a small solitary sign that reads, "1 Mile to Hope." In all those years I have never turned off the Interstate to go to Hope, Minnesota. I knew I didn't need to. Just so long as I knew it was there that was enough to keep me on my journey. (Rodney E. Wilmoth)

Lectionary Commentary
John 1:29-42

The Gospel of John is seen as a devotional classic as well as a profound theological masterpiece. It is helpful to see this text as a part of a larger body of material that seeks to restate the faith. The reason for the restating has to do with the fact that Christianity, which had grown out of Judaism, was now predominantly a Hellenistic or Greek church. Christianity was confronted with multitudes of people, ideologies, and religions. The purpose of John's Gospel is to show that Jesus Christ is God's divine son and therefore life in the here and now can have meaning. In a day when seven out of ten people claim to be spiritual but not religious, this text forces us to think about our faith and what it means to be a Christian in today's world.

1 Corinthians 1:1-9

Paul's letter to the Corinthians is nothing short of amazing. One would think that the task of writing to a highly contentious church would involve some rather terse words of condemnation. But such is not the case, for Paul offers words of grace and understanding. Few other congregations could be more in need of the "grace and peace" of which Paul speaks. He writes, "To the church of God that is in Corinth, to those who are sanctified in Christ Jesus, called to be saints." The folks at Corinth are not acting very saintlike, but despite that Paul challenges that congregation to take a higher road by remembering their calling to be saints. Many churches today are in conflict over many issues. Such an inward focus can cause some churches to be contentious in nature. Let such congregations hear once again Paul's words of God's grace and love. (Rodney E. Wilmoth)

Worship Aids

Meditation

This is the true joy of life—being used for a purpose recognized by yourself as a mighty one; being thoroughly worn out before you are thrown out on the scrap heap; being a force of nature instead of a feverish, selfish little clod of ailments and grievances, complaining that the world will not devote itself to make you happy. (George Bernard Shaw)

Invocation

It is awesome, Holy God, to sense that you have chosen us for great responsibilities. You give us a light to the nations, so your salvation may reach the ends of the earth. Grant that we may reflect, and not block, the illuminating grace you intend for all whose lives we touch and the multitudes we will never know. We need this hour of worship to strengthen our resolve and equip us to represent you well. Amen. (Rodney E. Wilmoth)

A Sacramental Life

Third in a Series of Three on the Sacraments

Mark 12:28-34

When someone becomes a Christian, it's like a new birth. To shift the metaphor, someone has noted that acceptance of Christ is like a kickoff at a football game. You can't have a game without it, but there are still four quarters left. And so we ask, "What happens after the baby is born?" or "What happens in those four quarters?" John Wesley likened salvation to the process of entering into a house.

We have crossed the porch. We have opened the door. What happens next? I had a wonderful friendship with a farmer, and whenever I would go out to see him, he would remark with a deep laugh, "Come in the house!" That's what God is saying to us: "Come in the house!"

When we experience new birth, a wonderful adventure begins. But it is a tragedy if we never move beyond the experience of new birth. Births are always occasions for celebration. But a part of our celebration is the hope and expectation that the child will grow up and mature. Learn to walk. Leave home? Right?

Years ago I heard the great preacher Ernest Campbell reflect on the parable of the Prodigal Son, found in the fifteenth chapter of Luke.

The son goes away, hits bottom, wastes his inheritance. Then he comes to himself, returns home. The son says, "I'm back." The father rejoices: "My son was dead and is alive, was lost and is found!" They have a feast, that lasts long into the night. Everyone is happy!

The next morning, the son sleeps in. Everyone else rises early. The work begins. The son goes around to everyone who is at work, and says to them "I'm back." And they all respond, "Bless God, you're back." The next morning, the son sleeps in again, makes his rounds with everyone, "I'm back, I'm back." This goes on for awhile, until the day comes when someone finally says, "Bless God, you're back; here is a shovel, get to work!"

New birth is not enough. Paul, writing to the early Christians, let them know that by now he would have expected them to have moved beyond milk to solid food (1 Corinthians 3:2). Accepting Christ is like a new birth, but there is life after birth.

This life, according to Wesley, was called holiness, or growth in grace, or sanctification. This life was becoming a new creature—the image of God, disfigured by our sin, being restored in us. It is progress, maturity, discipleship.

The great key to what it means, for Wesley, that is to progress in the Christian life is to love. Wesley defined holiness as love of God and love of neighbor. We don't love God because God is perfect, although he is. "We love [God] because [God] first loved us" (1 John 4:19). It is also not enough to have faith. The only thing that counts, Paul wrote to the Galatians, is faith working through love (Galatians 5:6). If I have faith powerful enough to move mountains, but have not love, Paul wrote, "I am nothing" (1 Corinthians 13:2). This is the ultimate test of our belief, of our faith, of our maturity. Does it produce the fruit of love?

When God says, "Come in the house," it's all about love. When the scribe asks Jesus which is the greatest commandment, the Lord responds, "Love . . . God with all your heart, and with all of your soul, and with all of your mind, and with all of your strength . . . [and] love your neighbor as yourself" (Mark 12:30-31). The scribe repeats these words back to Jesus, and the Lord responds again, you are not far from the kingdom. In other words, "you've got it."

John Wesley had some specific and concrete convictions about love. Love didn't happen by accident. God uses ordinary channels to help us grow in grace. Prayer—private and public. Reading the Scripture, listening to others teach it and preach it. Receiving Holy Communion as often as we can. Wesley also believed in accountability—they were called class meetings—where we were reminded of the promises we had made before God.

Love is both internal and external. We need to pay attention to the inside of the house and the outside of the house. We are called to love God and to love our neighbor. In fact, they are connected and inseparable. The inside of the house, fundamentally, is gratitude. The outside of the house is benevolence. We are put on the earth to love God and our neighbor. That is the core of Wesley's belief about sanctification, becoming sacramental people. Wesley's mission called together a church that would help people to do this in practical ways.

Love is a work in progress. Something in us wants to accept the invitation, to live in the house. But some part of us wants to hang out on the porch for awhile, because we are resistant to change. Do you ever find yourself resisting change?

Once God begins the work of salvation in our lives, God is not content until we are remade into his image, which is love. God is love. Any understandings of salvation that settle for less than this deny the ultimate power of God's grace. We never find a resting place as Christians—we are always in the process of being saved, of becoming more like Jesus. God is never finished with us. There is a new birth, but we will also learn to walk, and run and not be weary; we will even mount up with wings like eagles. The ordinary channels of grace—including the sacraments of baptism and Holy Communion—will help us grow in grace. The good news is that our human efforts do not achieve this goal. The God who began a good work in us would be faithful to complete it (Philippians 1:6). (Kenneth H. Carter Jr.)

Worship Aids

Call to Worship

What does the Lord require of you?
Do justice, love kindness, walk humbly with God.
What is the great commandment?
All: Love God with all our heart and soul and mind and strength.

Prayer of Confession

O God, you bless us with gifts that are sometimes hidden and at other times evident. We are the signs of your life in this world. We are the visible body of Christ, his hands, his feet. And yet at times we have buried your treasures, squandered our inheritances, neglected your grace. Draw near to us as we hear your word, as we remember our baptisms, as we eat at your table. Forgive us, restore us, and use us to be the outward and visible sign of an inward and spiritual grace.

Words of Assurance

In the name of Jesus Christ, you are forgiven.
In the name of Jesus Christ, you are forgiven. Amen.

Benediction

Go forth to live in the grace of God, who created you for good works; in the love of Jesus Christ, whose blood cleanses you; in the power of the Holy Spirit, who makes all things new. Go forth in peace! Amen. (Kenneth H. Carter Jr.)

JANUARY 27, 2008

❧❧❧❧

Third Sunday after the Epiphany

Readings: Isaiah 9:1-4; Psalm 27:1, 4-9; 1 Corinthians 1:10-18; Matthew 4:12-23

Look Up to the Earth
1 Corinthians 1:10-18

Colonel Charles Duke was a member of the Apollo 16 crew who drove the lunar buggy on the moon. He described his feelings as he emerged from the space module and took his first tentative steps through the dust of the lunar surface, experiencing the sensation of weightlessness. Duke said he looked up and drank in the wonder of his situation as he was flooded by new feelings. It was a bit disorienting to look "down" at the earth. When he lifted his open hand toward the earth, he realized that he could completely block the view (as we do when we shield our eyes from the sun's glare). It was a powerful experience and altered Colonel Duke's perception of the world. He could see, for the first time, that all God's children could live together in community. (Harold W. Roberts, "Communion in a Divided World," *Pulpit Digest,* September/October 1985).

So what is the problem? Why don't we have a world where folks reach out and touch one another and communicate with one another? Why is it that we seem to have a lot of folks who are pretty good at lifting their hand and blocking out those with whom they disagree? The quick answer, of course, is that we are part of the human family and not everyone gets along with everyone else. Charlie Brown was heard to say, "I've given up the idea of being a physician and helping others." Linus says, "Why? I thought you loved humanity." Charlie Brown says, "I do love humanity. It's people I can't stand."

Most of us can understand Charlie Brown's dilemma. I always enjoy listening to Barbara Streisand sing, "People who love people are the luckiest people in the world." And then it dawns on me that most of my problems are caused by people! How many times do you suppose a teacher has said, "I would enjoy teaching if I didn't have to deal with the students"? Or a pastor say, "I would really enjoy being a pastor if I just didn't have to put up with some members of the congregation." One can almost hear the Apostle Paul say, "That congregation at Corinth would really be a great one if it just were not for the members."

Paul has heard disturbing reports about the extent to which bickering and backbiting have begun to threaten the stability of the Corinthian community. The congregation was dividing itself along certain lines within the community. Members were putting up their hands and blocking out those with whom they differed. Of primary concern for Paul was how folks were dividing Christ himself. In vintage style, Paul makes it very clear that Christ is not and cannot be divided if the church is to stand. "Now I appeal to you, brothers and sisters, by the name of our Lord Jesus Christ, that all of you be in agreement and that there be no divisions among you, but that you be united in the same mind and the same purpose."

While Paul was hopeful for the kind of world Colonel Duke visualized, he knew that there were Christian communities, like the one at Corinth, where folks plainly did not get along with one another. It was very easy for them to lift their hand and block out those with whom they did not get along.

Sadly we see forms of the Corinthian behavior in the Christian community. We are a divided people and we are part of a global family that is fractured. Even in our own Christian communities we are not always of the same mind and spirit of Christ. We have divided the Christ along the lines of laws and grace, along the lines of biblical interpretations and understandings, along the lines of exclusion and acceptance.

What is the solution? A starting place would be for the Christian community to realize that we are all one in Christ. We may not all look alike nor think alike, but what we share in common is Christ. I am an only child and I attended my first family reunion a few years ago. We gathered on the family farm in Alabama. I didn't know I had so many kinfolk. While standing in line to get some lemonade, a young girl turned to her grandmother and said, "Grandma, who are all these people?" Her grandmother, standing in front of me said, "Why, Honey, these are all your kinfolks. You're related to everyone here." The young girl looked past her grandmother to me and said, "Am I related to you?" I told her I probably was and sensed right away that did not make her day.

In some circles the word "kingdom" as been replaced with "kindom," suggesting that we are all part of the kingdom of God where we are all related to one another. I rather like that. (Rodney E. Wilmoth)

Lectionary Commentary
Isaiah 9:1-4

The setting for this passage is about 750 B.C.E. Israel found itself then, as now, sandwiched between two major powers, Egypt to the southwest and Assyria to the northeast. It was a time of violent conflict and unending destruction. Out of that darkness, the prophet Isaiah speaks of hope. The people of God will move out of the darkness of their existence into the light. The light will indicate divine presence and strength precisely to those who have felt godforsaken by the events of history. What a change the people will experience as a result of the light. Shouts of joy will be heard where before there was only weeping and wailing. The reason for the rejoicing is clear: God will break all the symbols of oppression. Our hope is in the faithful and powerful action of God who enables us to live in peace and with a sense of hope.

Matthew 4:12-23

"Location, location, location"—so goes the marketing slogan. For most successful people, this is the key. For all practical purposes, Jesus should have begun his ministry in Jerusalem, the capital city of the Roman province. In that location he could have contacted a great number of people in a short time. But according to the gospel writers Jesus chose not Judean soil but Galilee of the Gentiles. Why? Because the writers understood the universality of the gospel. Clearly, the church today is called to continue this universal mission of bringing the light, and being the light, in the darkness of the world. Let Christ teach us how to tell our faith story so that we can "fish for people." (Rodney E. Wilmoth)

Worship Aids

Call to Worship (Responsive)
> Come together, people of God, out of the gloom and shadow of a
> troubled world.
> **We come with joy to the great light that God has given us in
> Jesus Christ.**

Come away, people of God, from all that would mar your days.
**We come in the spirit of repentance to confront and
overcome all that divides us.**
Come to worship, people of God, leaving behind all else that
compels your attention.
**All: We come to refocus our priorities and to become alert
to God's actions among us. Amen!**

Benediction

Go now to the splendor of the universe; to enjoy the music of the
spheres. Go into the uncertainties of tomorrow; trusting that God
the Creator, Christ the Redeemer, and the Holy Spirit will guide and care
for you until we meet again. (Rodney E. Wilmoth)

Sinners in the Hands of a Loving God: That's Not What I Intended

First in a Series of Three on the Nature of Sin for Modern People

Romans 7:14-25

On July 8, 1741, Jonathan Edwards thundered a sermon entitled
"Sinners in the Hands of an Angry God" that established an era in
American Christianity. His spellbinding images of the sinner as a spider
over the pit of hell or of the floods of God's vengeance are indelibly
marked on the American psyche. After more than 265 years, we are still
living down that picture of preaching that some call with affection and
some in derision the era of "hellfire and brimstone" preaching.

The Bible is clear that there is sin, a fact confirmed by our own life
experiences. The problem is that the fear approach to sin causes people
to do what is already a natural tendency, to hide in self-denial and self-
deception. Thus we end up stuck in our sins and their consequences.
Furthermore, the Bible treats sin not just as personal attitudes and
actions, but even more often as attitudes and actions of groups
and nations. Because of sin personally and socially, we find ourselves
caught up in cycles of personal, family, community, and even global brokenness. Yet God invites us to take a look at what we think about, say,
and do, and face our sinfulness, not because God is angry as because God
is loving. We are sinners in the hands of a loving God.

But a startling realization awaits us when we take that look. James asks the question, "Does a spring bring forth good water and foul water at the same time?" (3:11). Well, James, when it comes to human beings, the answer is yes. In Paul's words, that which we would not, that do we do. We have within us an inner war between the part of us that is highly responsive to God and the part of us that is resistant and self-absorbed.

Today, I want to introduce you to the intentional Will Cotton. You have never met him and most likely never will. Will intends to keep his life well organized. He intends to always be joyous and even-tempered, especially with those closest to him, even when he is tired. Will intends to spend his time, his money, and his energy in ways that are consistent with what God asks of him. He intends to treat everyone fairly at all times and he also intends to make courageous decisions that are best rather than choose those things that are politically safe or expedient. Will intends to think right, eat right, speak right, and do right. Don't you admire him? Why, he's nearly angelic. How I envy the intentional Will, but I cannot be like him. Behold the spiritual split personality in me and in you.

One of the ways Paul deals with this "spiritual split personality" is to write that the old carnal nature no longer really exists. It's not really Paul that did it. What if you caught me doing something I shouldn't and I said, "That's not me that did that. That was the other me?" You would tell me that I was lying and irresponsible. Paul is not doing that. He readily admits that he talks one way and ends up living another. Rather Paul is trying to teach us a skill for life that is very important. We have to decide what we are going to allow Christ to claim us. We need to be able to say to ourselves and to others that some of our thoughts, words, and actions are not worthy of us, that they belong to that selfish individual who existed before we followed Christ. There is a "B.C." you that still hangs around: selfish, reactive, impatient, unloving—exceedingly sinful. But properly, because of amazing grace, you and I live in *ano domine,* in the year of our Lord, in which holiness and love reign. That's the "A.D." you. In this transitional time between who we once were and who we are yet to become, we have to decide in which era we will live.

But the truth is our track record in choosing which era we live is at best mixed. We can only admit that the "road to hell is paved with good intentions." For some of us that road is not only paved but striped, lined, and beautifully landscaped! We are hopelessly self-disappointing and stuck. So we understand Paul when he says in our scripture lesson, "What a wretched person I am! Who will rescue me?" Who indeed? For the war within is not one that can be wished way or corrected by New Year's resolutions or overcome with the latest self-help technique. We have a heart problem, one that leads to death. Every year, we learn of outstanding athletes who die on the court or on the field in the midst of a practice or game. The doctors report later that the athlete had an arrhythmia. You and I are much like those super athletes with such great giftedness and potential, and at the same time, a tragic flaw. We have spiritual and moral arrhythmia. The result kills us and those around us. For this arrhythmia, there is no cure ... in ourselves. But the good news is there is an outside cure. Paul says quickly, "Thanks be to God through Jesus Christ our Lord."

There is a spiritual cardiologist who has the treatment and a spiritual surgeon who can give us a needed bypass. Jesus is "the great physician" who leads us from what will kill us to what will make us eternally and wonderfully alive. Life is not about being all you can be. That will never be enough. Life is about becoming all that the grace of God can create in you and through you. Like all heart disease, early detection and treatment is better. And it's never too late to get a new heart. (Will Cotton)

Worship Aids

Prayer of Confession (Unison)

O God, we are not who we wish to be. We wish for closeness with you, yet we often stray. We wish to be holy, yet we are often inconsistent and rebellious. Forgive us and free us to be true to you, to ourselves, and to those around us. Amen.

Words of Assurance

In the name of Jesus Christ, you are forgiven.
In the name of Jesus Christ, you are forgiven. Amen.

Suggested Hymns

"Come, Ye Sinners, Poor and Needy"
"Just as I Am"

Enhancement for Preaching

Read an excerpt from "Sinners in the Hands of an Angry God" by Jonathan Edwards at the beginning of the sermon. (Will Cotton)

FEBRUARY 3, 2008

❧❧❧

Fourth Sunday after the Epiphany

Readings: Micah 6:1-8; Psalm 15; 1 Corinthians 1:18-31; Matthew 5:1-12

Doing Justice, Loving Kindness, Walking Humbly
Micah 6:1-8

One morning my eighth grade social studies teacher said, "The world is about one-third Christian, twenty percent Muslim, and thirteen percent Hindu." We thought it was the goofiest thing we had ever heard. I grew up with four religions—Baptist, Methodist, Presbyterian, and heathen—in that order. Almost everyone we knew was Christian. The small number of people who weren't at least had the decency to keep it to themselves.

The statistics aren't hard to imagine now. Our country is changing. America is increasingly home to Muslim mosques and Hindu temples. There are Sikh communities in New York and Buddhist retreat centers in West Virginia. My hometown has a Bahá'í congregation. By one count, the United States has 1,650 different religious movements with at least 2,000 members.

What should it mean that there are more Sunni Muslims than Protestant Christians? We hear a variety of religious viewpoints and it isn't easy to know how to respond as Christian believers.

It can be comforting to believe that we're in and everyone else is out, but it doesn't make sense. Believing that God's grace is only for a relative few of us insults God. We recognize that if we had been born in Indonesia, then we would probably be Muslims.

Because God is at work everywhere, we shouldn't dismiss the rest of the world as having nothing to say. We make a mistake when we try to divide most of the world into those who attend Christian churches and those who will never have a chance at God's grace.

There is, of course, the opposite mistake of believing that we shouldn't worry about anyone else, because deep down everyone believes the same thing. It's popular to say that all religions are about the same—as if we could combine all great traditions into one big melting pot. Those who think that all religions teach the same truths haven't listened. Christianity, Islam, Hinduism, Buddhism, Judaism, Confucianism, transcendental meditation, materialism, numerology, astrology, and jogging say very different things. Religious tolerance that discourages the honest evaluation of beliefs and practices also discourages commitment. To say that all religions are equal is to say that no religion makes any real difference.

So how should we feel about being a minority in a world filled with different religions? We should begin by recognizing that we're not the first to ask the question. While religious pluralism may be a new experience for us, it was the everyday experience of the Hebrew people. The Israelites were surrounded by thousands of gods and goddesses that belonged to their neighbors. Sometimes they responded by destroying their neighbors and sometimes they bought some of their idols just to be safe.

Seven hundred years before Christ, Israel is in the middle of a revival. The temple is crowded. People are sitting in the balconies. Giving is over budget for the first time in years, but the prophet Micah knows that something is wrong.

Israel is arrogant and uncaring. Micah pictures God charging Israel with a crime and taking them to court. God calls the mountains, hills, and foundations of the earth as witnesses for the prosecution. God's accusation is that Israel has forgotten God's generosity. God loved Israel, brought them out of slavery, and gave them a home. God speaks in pleading tones as a parent to a child who ignores the parent's love.

After they hear the accusation, the people, as usual, miss the point: "God, what more could you possibly want from us? Do you want more sacrifices, more expensive livestock? A thousand sheep? Just how religious can we be?"

They are religious, but their idea of what religion means is far from God's hopes for them. They think that religion consists of believing the right things and staying away from people who believe the wrong things. It's easier to appear religious than to be kind.

"What does God want?" the prophet asks. God wants us to do justice—to be a voice for the oppressed and unprotected; to fight for the rights of every person treated as less than God's child.

God wants us to love kindness. The Hebrew word is *hesed*—God's kindness. We respond to God's love by sharing it with others.

We are to walk humbly with God: listening for God's voice wherever God may be heard; listening to Jews, Muslims and Buddhists; learning how other people make sense of their lives; thoughtfully examining what it means to live with faith.

We will be better Christians not by refuting every idea that is Muslim, Buddhist, or Hindu, but by affirming the truth and continuing to search. We should find ways to say, "I have something I want to share with you and you have something that I hope you'll share with me."

We become more mature Christians by seeing that the great religions struggle with what matters, that each expresses a real human experience, and each deserves attention for the wisdom they offer the rest of humanity.

Could it be that having the right or wrong answers on theological questions is less important to God than whether we show compassion? Isn't that what the prophet Micah says?

When we see that other religions grapple with the truth, we understand that the great enemy is the partial practice of faith. The religious tradition of which I want to be a part includes Elie Wiesel, Mahatma Gandhi, Anwar Sadat, and Nelson Mandela. Do we have more in common with a person who says she's a Christian but has no real commitment or with the faithful member of another tradition who lives with God's kindness?

I want to be part of the religious tradition that includes the poor in spirit, those who mourn, those who hunger and thirst for righteousness, the meek, the merciful, the pure in heart, and the peacemakers. Christians should live out the best of our faith. We should cling to what we believe comes closest to truth, hold to the story we've been given, test it, doubt it, try it again, believe it passionately, share it, and celebrate it.

In a world of countless religions, what should we do? We should do justice, love kindness, and walk humbly with God. (Brett Younger)

Lectionary Commentary
Matthew 5:1-12

We spend our lives looking for fulfillment in the wrong places. The kingdom of joy is already here. "Blessed are the ..." The word for "blessed," *makarios*, doesn't describe a feeling, but a state of blessedness independent of the circumstances of life. True blessedness is not a question of whether or not we have problems.

In the original Aramaic, there was no verb at the beginning of these verses. An accurate translation would be: "Oh the happiness of the ..." God is congratulating those who have found the best way. This is not a blessedness of the future, but a kingdom of joy that is here right now.

1 Corinthians 1:18-31

No death has inspired more peculiar questions and strange theories than Jesus' death. Paul writes to the Corinthians, "the message about the cross is foolishness to those who are perishing." J. B. Philips translates it "nonsense." Much of what's been said about the cross is foolish nonsense.

Paul admits that the cross doesn't lend itself to easy analysis: "the discernment of the discerning I will thwart." If we have to have a formula, then the cross will be a stumbling block. Strength in weakness, gaining by losing, and hope through dying are hard to understand.

The cross pictures not only human nature at its worst but also the human spirit at its best. When Paul wrote about Jesus' death, he preached that the cross is, more than anything else, the forgiveness of God. (Brett Younger)

Worship Aids

Call to Worship

Welcome to worship. We are not, of course, the only people who will gather to worship today. Some will worship in ways much different from ours. But the yearnings of other hearts are much like our own. In worship, we recognize that God knows and loves us all.

Invocation

God and maker of us all, we come to worship remembering that your image lies in the hearts of all people. In the words of truth, the things of beauty, and the hope of faith, help us recognize the grace that makes us all your children. Amen.

Benediction

God has shown you what is good and has told you what God requires of you. Go from this place to do justice, love kindness, and walk humbly with God. (Brett Younger)

Sinners in the Hands of a Loving God: Following the Crowd

Second in a Series of Three on the Nature of Sin for Modern People

Matthew 27:24-26

In the last sermon I shared what would surprise most American Christians, that the Bible talks more about social sin, the sin of groups, than it does about personal individual sin. For example, on the last day of ninth grade we gathered in homeroom to receive our report cards. One guy, we'll call him Johnnie, was very shy and withdrawn, spending most of his time reading science fiction. Our teacher had mistakenly left the report cards in the office, so he left the room. One of our pranksters began to taunt Johnnie and then gathered a group that formed a circle around him. They all began to tease and taunt him: "Come on, Johnnie. The space creatures are coming to get you. Do we make you mad Johnnie? You wanna fight?" They howled in laughter. Finally, Johnnie threw down his science fiction book on the floor and ran out of the classroom with tears in his eyes. He never came back to our school after that. I get chills thinking what could have happened if it was today. Would he have done something to himself or would it have even been another Columbine? It's amazing what happens when a negative personal agenda becomes the agenda of a crowd.

Reinhold Niebuhr defined sin as "egoism," in which our own wants and desires become the center point of our lives. He wrote that crowds and nations develop a collective egoism, in which "the group is more arrogant, hypocritical, self-centered and more ruthless in the pursuit of its ends than the individual" (*The Nature and Destiny of Man*, Vol. 1 [New York: Scribner, 1964], 208). From a mosh pit to Abu Ghraib prison, from political conventions to church movements, groups take emotion and damage to a whole new level.

Consider world leaders who have taken our world to the edge of extinction—Hitler, Stalin, as well as some of the rogue dictators of today. I cannot explain their power except through the management of information in crowds. Similarly, I cannot understand the crucifixion of Christ without some of the same dynamics. Palm Sunday cheerers become Black Friday jeerers. Just manage information. Tell them that this healer and rabbi is really a blasphemer. Limit the crowd to only those who are likely to be cooperative. Dehumanize and demonize him until he eventually becomes crucifiable.

Further, no generation is more prone to be had by this kind of strategy than ours. On television and through the Internet, propaganda is thrown at us by international leaders, companies, competing politicians, and even preachers telling us who our evil enemies are. Because American Christians in particular have privatized sin and ignored how sinful group dynamics can become, we are often manipulated and co-opted into things we would never be if we were simply on our own.

Sin has a social face and we participate in it. One of the Bible's answers to sin's social dimension is found in 2 Chronicles 7:14, "If my people who are called by my name humble themselves, pray. . . . Then I will hear from heaven, and will forgive their sin." Notice that humility, not self-justification, is what is required.

When we lived in El Paso, my wife and I would go to Juarez, Mexico and see the huge *maquiladoras*, with recognizable corporate names. The workers there make 10 percent of the minimum wage in the U. S. Fuel costs are higher and resources are scarce. With pride, corporate leaders proclaim that they have tripled the income of those workers and provided you and me more affordable electronics. Open sewers run in the streets, partly because the Juarez citizens sided with the United States and our democratic policies. For a period of many years, no infrastructure money was sent from Mexico City for streets, sewer, or electricity. We enjoy the sale prices, not knowing that we have helped solidify a system that will keep people poor.

The Bible speaks strongly to economic sin from both Testaments. Why don't we? The same question can be asked about environmental sin or of racial sin. Our silence, our dulled consciences, and our complicit behavior indict us.

The Bible offers the church a two-part strategy for dealing with sin in groups, crowds, and nations. First, we are to clean up our own act. Peter writes in his letter, "For it is time for judgment to begin with the family of God" (1 Peter 4:17 NIV). How do we as a local church participate in power games and sinful behaviors? How do we as denominations and interdenominations justify ourselves while demonizing others, especially with non-Christian religions? Yes, the Bible calls for us to clean up our own act first, but the truth is we cannot. We can only confess we are not clean and ask for saving grace to become different.

Second, we are to become an alternative society in the world, what Jesus offered in his vision of "the kingdom of God." The church can give a constant picture of group redemption and salvation from sin. Negatively, that means playing the role of prophet and calling our world to Christ's standard. Positively, it means that we demonstrate that standard in the ways we treat people both in the church and outside the church. Just as we underrate the power of group sin, we underestimate the power of group redemption. In the face of natural disasters, we watch groups gather together in clubs, churches, and communities and do more than any could do separately. Jesus began the Christian movement by investing himself in a group. The church found its strength as a living organism known to one another as "the body of Christ." Jesus saw the potential of the church to transform the world when it became a collaborative force of the Holy Spirit. Do we still see that potential? Will our world around us find itself in the hands of a loving church? (Will Cotton)

Worship Aids

Prayer of Confession (Unison)

Forgive us, O Lord, when our faith becomes too personal. We seek wholeness with you and ignore our world's brokenness. We yearn for heaven and separate ourselves from those who experience individual and social hell. By your grace, turn us from isolation to involvement and from coldness to holy compassion. Amen.

Words of Assurance

In the name of Jesus Christ, you are forgiven.
In the name of Jesus Christ, you are forgiven. Amen.

Suggested Hymns

"Where Cross the Crowded Ways of Life"
"For the Healing of the Nations"

Sermon Enhancement

Read another excerpt from "Sinners in the Hands of an Angry God." It continues the intrigue and builds unity to this series of sermons. (Will Cotton)

FEBRUARY 6, 2008

❧❧❧❧

Ash Wednesday

Readings: Isaiah 58:1-12; Psalm 51:1-17; 2 Corinthians 5:20b–6:10; Matthew 6:1-6, 16-21

Prayers We Don't Pray
Psalm 51:1-17

The smells of spaghetti, French bread, and corn on the cob filled the kitchen. It was Carol's turn to say grace, "God, help us know when we have eaten enough and stop." She stunned everyone at the table. How cruel does a person have to be to pray something like that? Some things shouldn't be prayed. We know to avoid praying about things we have no intention of changing.

Hunger, for instance, is one of the subjects about which we've learned to be careful. If you pray too seriously for hungry people you'll end up skipping meals and giving your money away. One church member I know makes a point of not having cash in his wallet on World Hunger Day. He understands that if you're honest with yourself and God about hunger, then you have to give.

That's why most of us are careful not to pray too seriously for the homeless. It's awkward to pray for people who have no home when we have empty guestrooms. A pastor confessed, "If I don't stop just talking about helping the poor and start doing something to help the poor I'm going to be embarrassed to meet God." If you pray for poor people, then you have to help.

When our country is at war, we're careful about how we pray. If you're against a war, it's hard to pray honestly about the sense of moral superiority that may take up residence in your heart. If you're for a war, it's hard to pray honestly about Jesus' compassion for innocent children who are dying. If we pray too seriously, then God reminds us that there are people whose homes have been destroyed who need help. If we pray about it, we realize that there are things we could do that we haven't done.

We avoid praying about things that we don't want to change. It's frightening to pray about our careers. Does the senior pre-law major want to pray about whether God would like for her to be a social worker? Does the successful businessperson want to ask God if a lower paying job might make more of a contribution to the world?

We're careful about praying about the big questions. We know it would be dangerous to pray for orphans who need to be adopted. We're careful about praying about small stuff. What if you're going to a movie with some friends when a lonely person calls? If you pray about what you should do you might miss the movie.

We're especially careful about praying for people we don't like. Think of the person whose presence bothers you the most, who gets on your nerves and probably always will. When Jesus said "Pray for your enemies," he was inviting us to the kind of prayer that will lead us to say something kind that we don't want to say.

Most of the time we're afraid to pray about what we could be and do. In so many ways, we choose a life given to comfort over a life given in prayer. It's easier to live by the rules everyone follows and strive for the same version of the good life that everyone wants. We like what we have—including the vices we've gotten used to and the enemies we've carefully chosen. We don't avoid praying because our prayers go unanswered. We're afraid our prayers will be answered. We try not to see our potential, because we know far more of what we should be doing than we do.

We've learned to pray, "God, make me a better person, but not so much better that I have to change the way I live." Prayer is hard because we don't want to start doing what God invites us to do or stop doing what we've gotten used to doing.

King David went a long time without really praying. One afternoon a look turned into lust and David didn't pray about it. The lust turned into manipulation and David acted in ways that he never would have considered if he had the courage to pray. David was able to keep from admitting what he had done or what he needed to do for a long time. He didn't pray, because he didn't want to face the harsh realities.

Psalm 51 is the cry of a person who struggled to find the courage to pray. The amazing thing about this psalm is that for all of its agony, there's also a sense of relief. What David has ignored for so long is finally brought out into the open. It couldn't have been any easier for David to tell the truth about himself than it is for any of us. There is no painless way to stop protecting our easy lives and be honest to God. Yet, David's painfully honest prayer leads to joy.

When you think about the most courageous Christians you know, the ones who make sacrifices for their faith, do you feel sorry for them or is it clear that they have something we should want? People who pray passionately don't have easy lives, but they have abundant lives. God has dreams for us that we've been afraid to imagine.

What would be the result if we prayed for hurting people, the victims of tragedies, and our enemies? What would happen if we made a searching, fearless inventory of how much more we could be if we asked God for the courage to take chances?

Who's to say exactly what would happen, but we might know when we've eaten enough and stop; take a bag of food to someone who needs it; open our home to someone who needs help; write a check to help refugees; see our enemy with compassion; hear God inviting us to a different job or a different life; confess who we are and discover who we are meant to be; end up less comfortable and more saintly.

Ash Wednesday challenges us to pray courageously. When was the last time you prayed about anything that makes you uncomfortable? What will happen if we ask God, "What should we do?" (Brett Younger)

Lectionary Commentary
Isaiah 58:1-12

The temple in Jerusalem was standing room only. No one missed a service. They sang psalms, prayed, and gave offerings, but they didn't let worship trouble their consciences. If they kept their distance from God they could also keep their distance from God's hurting children. God told Isaiah, "Go tell them what's what. Blow the trumpet. Shout it loud. Tell them what hypocrites they are."

So the prophet let them have it, "If you're only going through the motions in worship, singing the songs but never engaging your hearts, hearing the scripture but not listening for God, giving an offering but not giving yourselves, then you should stay at home, because you're not doing God any favors. If you really worship God, you will share with the poor, listen to the lonely, and help those in need."

Matthew 6:1-6, 16-21

When Jesus tells the disciples to pray in secret, he is concerned with their motivation, "Don't pray for the sake of praise. Don't give to hear people say how generous you are. Don't fast for the satisfaction of others knowing that you are the kind of person who fasts. Instead, when you pray, go into your room and close the door. God who sees in secret will hear your prayers. When you give to the poor, don't let your left hand know what your right hand is doing. God will see the gift and reward you. When you fast, don't moan and grumble, and God will see the secret you keep and reward you. Lay up for yourselves treasure in heaven and not on earth—rewards that only you and God know about" (paraphrased). Jesus calls us to believe in God who sees in secret.

2 Corinthians 5:20b–6:10

While to the casual observer Ash Wednesday is about death, to the person who looks carefully, everything is turned upside down. What we thought was a focus on death becomes a call to life. What we think of as bringing life actually brings death.

Listen to Paul: "We are treated as impostors and yet are true; as unknown, and yet are well known; as dying, and see—we are alive; as punished, and yet not killed; as sorrowful, yet always rejoicing; as poor, yet making many rich; as having nothing, and yet possessing everything."

The season of Lent invites us to be honest about that in which we put our trust. The things that we hope will bring life—achievement, accomplishment, recognition—don't bring all that they promise. God offers a better way on this "day of salvation." (Brett Younger)

Worship Aids

Call to Worship

If you take the hymns seriously, you may realize that God is present. If you take the prayers seriously, you may see that you're doing something you shouldn't. If you take the scripture seriously, you may decide that your life has been invested in the wrong things. Be careful.

Invocation

God who knows our hearts, you are the source of our best thoughts, deepest wisdom, and greatest love. Help us be honest with you about our sins, shortcomings, and wondrous possibilities. May our worship be a gift of sacrifice and joy. Amen.

Benediction

May God save us from second-rate, routine, ordinary, comfortable lives. May God grant us the grace to pray and live with courage. (Brett Younger)

The Goat of God?

Third in a Series of Three on the Nature of Sin for Modern People

John 1:29-36

On this Ash Wednesday, I invite you to take a closer look at this Savior we all need to save us from our personal and group sin. John, in our scripture lesson, calls Jesus "the Lamb of God that takes away the sin of the world." There are many images of Jesus I treasure, but this isn't one of them! I like the Jesus who outsmarts all those who try to trap him, who does miracle after miracle, who forgives the worst of sinners, and confronts evil in the temple and those moneychangers. Jesus' disciples and the crowds who followed him liked that view of Jesus, too. Lambs are cute and pure, but they're also weak, passive, vulnerable, and, at least to all appearances, stupid. When we listen to some of the voices around Jesus' passion, he is often described similarly—weak, passive, vulnerable, and crazy. No wonder the disciples and the loyal crowds betrayed him, denied him, and ran for their lives. Jesus wasn't the hero they wanted or thought they needed. Who are you looking for this morning, "Jesus the Hero" (the one you want to get you out of this mess now) or "Jesus the Savior" (the one who will make you and your world new one moment at a time)?

This image of "the Lamb of God" makes no sense at all apart from the Old Testament. Numbers 28–29 gives a list of sacrificial offerings with instructions about how to carry them out. Some of the offerings were symbols of devotion to God, while others were for the sins of the people. The sacrificed lambs had to be one-year-old males. Two lambs were slain each day with two additional ones sacrificed on the Sabbath. On the first day of the month seven were slain. Seven were sacrificed on the first day of feasts like Passover. The bloodiest of the Old Testament feasts was the feast of Tabernacles in which fourteen lambs a day were slain for seven days and a final seven more on the eighth day (a total of 105). I guess you couldn't be squeamish if you were a priest! The sacrifice of lambs was then the key expression of the relationship between God and his people.

The thing that strikes me is that the animal sacrificed for the forgiveness of sins wasn't a lamb at all. Scholars debate what John could have meant. According to Leviticus 16, the actual animal was a goat. On the Day of Atonement, Yom Kippur, the ancient Jews would set apart two goats, both of which have much to say about salvation from personal and group sins. The first goat would be slaughtered and the blood would be placed on the altar by the priest in recognition that the blood of that goat was covering the people's sin before God. It's interesting that in the Old Testament sin is not so much forgotten as covered up by the grace of God. We talk about forgiving and forgetting, but for your spiritual health and mine, we are forgiven but we are not to forget what we have done or the grace that has covered it.

The second goat gives another powerful picture. According to Leviticus 16:20-23 (NIV), "He [Aaron] shall bring forward the live goat . . . and confess over it all the wickedness and rebellion of the Israelites— all their sins—and put them on the goat's head. He shall send the goat away into the desert in the care of a man appointed for the task. The goat will carry on itself all their sins to a solitary place; and the man shall release it in the desert."

How often we ask the question, "How can I get from under the burden of the things I have done?" Wouldn't it be great if we could just send our guilt and the brokenness out of town? Wouldn't it be great if we had our own personal scapegoat, a family scapegoat or even a national scapegoat, so we could start over in our relationships? How I wish Christians, Jews, and Muslims could get together and do that. We choose not to forget and energize our relationships with the wrongs that have been done to us. Hurt simply accumulates and deepens through the years, the generations, and even the centuries. We need a scapegoat.

Must we be reminded that there was a scapegoat according to Hebrews 13 that was taken outside the camp, outside the city, on whom the sins of the world were placed? With different groups and individuals, I have had people write letters they have burned, have had them write lists of their anger, sins, and regrets and placed them in trash cans that have been taken out and put in the dumpster. Why? If we don't have a place to send those things, they keep sabotaging our ability to move forward in healing and renewed relationships. We need a personal and group scapegoat, and according to God's word we have one.

Perhaps John should have called Jesus "the goat of God." But the Bible doesn't like goats. John's Lamb of God seems to be a combination of Passover and the Day of Atonement, a combination of salvation from death and salvation from sin. Isn't it true that Jesus did come to save us in both ways? So why would we live, continuing in the brokenness of our individual and group sin? Why not make a new beginning? I think that's what Jesus, the goat, the Lamb of God, is asking all of us. What a great way to celebrate Ash Wednesday, the people of God as sinners in the hands of a loving God. (Will Cotton)

Worship Aids

Prayer of Confession (Unison)

Deliver us, O Christ, from a Lent of empty self-denial, empty worship, and empty witness. Stir us to new awareness of our need for forgiveness and a new beginning with you. Move us from being admirers of the cross to being cross-bearers, reflecting your compassion, your servanthood, and your self-sacrifice. Amen.

Words of Assurance

In the name of Jesus Christ, you are forgiven.
In the name of Jesus Christ, you are forgiven. Amen.

Hymn Suggestions

"O the Lamb"
"Alas! and Did My Savior Bleed"

Sermon Enhancements

Read another excerpt from "Sinners in the Hands of an Angry God." Sing "O the Lamb" three or four times at different points of the sermon. (Will Cotton)

FEBRUARY 10, 2008

❧❧❧

First Sunday in Lent

Readings: Genesis 2:15-17, 3:1-7; Psalm 32; Romans 5:12-19; Matthew 4:1-11

Disabling Temptations
Matthew 4:1-11

Most of the time, without any real thought, we do what we want to do and make inferior choices. We trivialize sin when we think of it as an error in judgment. Sin is a flawed approach to decision making that leads us to the worst decision with which we can be comfortable. In a thousand ways we get used to making lesser choices. We're so used to choosing what's easiest that deciding to become more than we are doesn't occur to us.

Yet it's always possible to be true to the higher calling. Jesus is baptized in the muddy water of the Jordan River. The voice from heaven proclaims, "You are my child, my beloved, in you I am well pleased." Then Jesus goes to the middle of nowhere to decide what kind of child he's going to be.

The wilderness is hot and barren. The hills are dust heaps. The rocks are jagged. The wind howls at night. Jesus is so weighed down with the burden of choosing the direction for his life that he doesn't even think of food. It's been days, weeks since he has eaten. It's a great understatement when Matthew writes, "and afterwards, he hungered."

The silence is broken when from somewhere there comes a voice—a whisper, a screaming whisper: "If you are God's child, command this stone, so that it becomes bread." Jesus remembers John, the River Jordan, the sky opening and the voice saying, "You are my child, the beloved." Now it's a different voice, "If you are God's child."

Jesus was the first person tempted by fast food. A rounded stone becomes a loaf of pumpernickel; a flat rock becomes a tortilla. Who will it hurt? If he is God's child, then why shouldn't he have what he wants?

We struggle with the attraction of doing what's easiest. This first temptation is to make our decisions on the basis of what requires the least effort. We often pass on what's eternally best for what's momentarily satisfying.

We're tempted to choose the easy way when we realize how hard it is to forgive the guilty, listen to the lonely, and share what we have with the poor. It's much easier to settle for a tepid faith. We get so used to choosing what's easiest that we seldom consider the hard way of sacrifice. We'd like to believe that an easy life is a sign of God's approval, but if we're comfortable, then we've missed what's best.

Jesus understands the temptation of the easy way; "One cannot live by bread alone. Obedience to God is more important than my own comfort."

Satan tries again like a con man with an arm covered with Rolexes. This time it's from the steeple of the old First Church, "If you are God's child, throw yourself down. You know that the Bible says, 'God will protect you.'"

The first-century Jews believed that when the Messiah came, he would reveal himself from the temple roof. The tempter is reminding Jesus that he can be the Messiah the people want. He can be a great religious teacher and skip the hard parts. Jesus could have modified his ministry ever so slightly and been what they wanted him to be.

When Monty Hall offers us what's behind door number two, it's the temptation to look spiritual. We can keep up appearances even as we lower our expectations. In T. S. Eliot's play, *Murder in the Cathedral*, the tempter comes to Thomas Becket and offers the temptation of being a martyr, a religious hero. Becket understands, "The last temptation is the greatest treason: To do the right deed for the wrong reason."

We've figured out that we can look religious without truly seeking God. It's easy to meet people's religious expectations. We know how to pretend that we are living as God's children.

The screaming whisper returns with an offer of palaces and kingdoms, "Compromise and it's all yours." This is Frodo Baggins offering the one ring that rules them all. To worship Satan is to choose success. This third temptation is to want what everyone wants.

The evil one doesn't appear for us in a readily identifiable red suit with a pitchfork. The tempter appears as reasonableness. Evil's nagging voice is the desire for a little bigger house, a little more in savings, and a little better job.

Have you ever learned that someone who does the same job you do makes more money than you make? We know it doesn't do us any good to think about it, but we keep thinking about the injustice of it all and what we would do with the extra money. We choose to hang on to greed until it starts to crowd out things that matter more.

O. A. Battista wrote, "You have reached the pinnacle of success as soon as you become uninterested in money, compliments, or publicity." By that standard, most of us are still some distance from the summit.

Through cracked and bleeding lips, Jesus answers the master counterfeiter, "Bow down to God alone; worship only God."

The adversary retreats temporarily, but Jesus never stopped being tempted to make it easier for himself. Jesus faced the same temptations to compromise that we face. We choose every day between what seems okay and what's true to the gospel.

We need to remember this story of Jesus in the wilderness. There were no witnesses. Jesus must have told the disciples because he hoped that they would remember. Maybe you've had the experience of meeting someone so kind and caring that they made you want to be kind and caring, too. Remember that there was one who lived beyond comfort, praise, and affluence.

Remember whose we are. The voice at Jesus' baptism was the voice of assurance, "This is my beloved child." God has assured us that we too are God's children. We come to this Lenten season of repentance confessing our longing for the paths of least resistance and asking for new and honest hearts. (Brett Younger)

Lectionary Commentary
Genesis 2:15-17, 3:1-7

The Book of Common Prayer leads us to pray: "Almighty God to you all hearts are opened, all desires known, and from you no secrets are hid: Cleanse the thoughts of our hearts by the inspiration of your Holy Spirit, that we may perfectly love you and worthily magnify your holy Name."

Do we want to believe in a God who knows us that well? The writer of Genesis understands the desire to keep secrets from God. When Adam and Eve eat the fruit of the tree of the knowledge of good and evil, their eyes are opened and they know they are naked. Their story raises the question that leads to Lent, "Do we want our hearts cleansed?"

February 10, 2008

Romans 5:12-19

None of us like to admit that we are not who we ought to be. We don't want to be that honest. If a friend said, "I go to confession every morning, would you like to come with me?" most of us would pass. We think it would be depressing to start every day making a list for God of all of the ways we fall short.

Paul wants his readers to understand that if we have that idea, we have misunderstood. Sin leads to death. Forgiveness brings life. Christ provides a way of pardon: "One man's act of righteousness leads to justification and life for all." God invites us to live with a spirit free from deceit, a heart that's clean, and a soul that's true. (Brett Younger)

Worship Aids

Prayer of Confession

God, forgive us because the world needs our concern, and we think of our own comfort. Forgive us because the world needs genuine Christians, and we worry about appearances. Forgive us because the world needs love, and we daydream about riches. Hear our prayer and grant us your grace. Amen.

Words of Assurance

Hear the gospel. Christ Jesus came into the world for sinners like you and me. Believe the good news that we are forgiven. The life we'll have on our own is nothing compared to what's possible in God's grace.

Benediction

You have received grace, so share grace.
You have received forgiveness, so forgive.
You have received gifts beyond your need, so give.
(Brett Younger)

God in Our Wilderness Wanderings

First in a Series of Three on Wilderness and Pilgrimage

Numbers 9:1-14

Egypt is behind them, two years behind them. Can you imagine? Wandering in the wilderness for two years? Certainly there is relief from

the bondage of slavery in Egypt, and God has promised them a land flowing with milk and honey at the end of their pilgrimage, but will it really
be good enough to match up to their wandering for two years? In this
time, elderly loved ones have died, new babies have been born, new relationships have been forged, and all the while they walk and wander.

It is difficult for us to imagine a two-year span in the wilderness. For when
we enter our times of pilgrimage or wilderness wandering, it is often at our
own initiation. Life gets hectic and chaotic. Like the Israelites, we may feel
we have become slaves to our daily routines, our wants and needs, our jobs,
or any number of things that fill our lives with busyness. So to refocus and
rejuvenate ourselves, we choose to spend time alone; we need our time with
only us and God. Sometimes we are intentional about our wilderness time—
we go to a retreat center or get away for a while so that there are fewer distractions. Other times, the need for time with God creeps up on us and there
is no time for a getaway. We need to close a door, close our eyes, breathe
deeply, and focus on the fact that we are a beloved child of God.

As I revisit the story of the Israelites wandering in the wilderness, I
see a great deal of myself in them. They have been wandering for two
years, living in a chaotic, transient state, hoping and praying that the
God of Moses is one who keeps promises. And I don't know about you,
but I need some routine in my life. I like to know when, how, and why
things are going to happen. I work better in predictability and a controlled environment. But the wilderness is anything but controlled. It is
desolate, lonely, and at times out of control. It is time for some routine
and ritual.

Moses' announcement of God's command is met with immediate obedience. In fact, even those who are ritualistically denied the Passover rites
come forward requesting the ability to celebrate the sacred ritual. They
need to feel close to God. They are yearning for the familiar and the routine. They need to participate in a reminder of home.

While Passover is typically restricted to those who are ritualistically
clean, God has compassion on those who are unable to join the others at
the Passover table. Room is made for all at the table, for those who are
unclean from the touching of a corpse, and those who are considered
aliens or outsiders to the Israelite clan. Everyone is invited to participate
in the Passover celebration. Everyone is given a place in the ritual, drawing them all closer to God.

The reinstatement of the Passover ritual is not a random event in the
wandering of the Israelites. After surviving the wilderness for two years,

the Israelites are bound to be tired and frustrated. The scriptures record them remembering Egypt in an unrealistic hindsight, wishing for what they left behind rather than facing the unknown lying before them. They do not remember how terrible their lives of bondage really were because they easily become paralyzed in their fear of what may come. They need to reconnect with the God who granted them their freedom and has promised them the land of plenty at the end of their journey.

Bringing the Passover ritual back to the routine of the Israelites serves to remind them that God continues to be with them, even when they feel they are lost in the wilderness. The ritual serves as a reminder that they are not forgotten, that God remains with them in the midst of their chaos and distress.

The text serves as a reminder to us that when our lives are chaotic and in distress and we choose to take some time alone—some time in the wilderness to get away—that God remains faithful to us as God did with the Israelites. So often we think of time away as time alone with our thoughts, or "me time." But just as God supplies the routine of the Passover ritual to the Israelites as a means of drawing them closer in relationship, God seeks to draw close to us in our times of need.

Have you ever heard yourself use the phrase, "I just need to get away from it all"? This type of thinking may be what sends us into the need for our wilderness retreats. But we must be careful to not let the phrase mean that we need or want to get away from God. God seeks to be there with us when we need to get away from everything else. God wants to help us break the bonds of slavery when we have chained ourselves to our routines, our jobs, or our busyness. God wants to be with us without all the distractions so that we can be in communion with one another when we need God the most.

So next time the retreat center is calling or you suddenly feel the need to shut your office door to break the routine and be alone for a while, remember that running away from everything and everyone is not the answer. This is the time when God seeks intentional ways to be in relationship with us. It is a time when we can be most open to God's love and faithfulness to us because we are tired and weary from everything else. Like the Israelites, when we clear away the clutter of two years of chaos, our hearts are ripe for the gentle and meaningful reminders that God remains by our side in all that we do, but most especially in our wilderness wanderings. (Victoria Atkinson White)

Worship Aids

Invocation

God, we know you are present in this place because you are ever present with us. Draw us closer to you in this hour as our hearts come from many scattered places. Remind us that you walk with us in our wilderness journeys. Amen.

Litany

We walk in the wilderness.
God, walk with us.
We leave what is familiar.
God, walk with us.
We hope for promises foretold.
God, walk with us.
We look back and wonder.
God, walk with us.
We look forward and hope.
God, walk with us.
We put one foot in front of the other and dream dreams with you
     for what is to come.
We step with anticipation because you have delivered us.
We press onward because you are our God.
God, walk with us.
All: Amen.

Benediction

May the God who walks beside us in our wilderness wanderings walk beside us this day as we leave this place to be the children of God in a world crying out for meaningful rituals and reminders of hope in the midst of chaos and distress. May you be a reminder of hope. Amen. (Victoria Atkinson White)

FEBRUARY 17, 2008

❧❧❧❧

Second Sunday in Lent

Readings: Genesis 12:1-4a; Psalm 121; Romans 4:1-5, 13-17;
John 3:1-17

Characters of Lent: One of Us
John 3:1-17

This is the story of Nicodemus—and us. Nicodemus is a lot like us.
Nicodemus was part of the establishment and a respected member of the
community. He was educated, had some resources, and people looked up
to him. We are like him.

We're like him in that we are also mysteriously drawn to Jesus.
Nicodemus was curious about Jesus. He was drawn to Jesus. So are we.
Every one is here at worship because we are drawn to Jesus of Nazareth.
This mysterious figure of Jesus has an attraction, a draw on our hearts.
Nicodemus was also confused by Jesus. Nicodemus came to visit Jesus at
night. Nicodemus was in the dark. He didn't understand Jesus. They
never quite connected. Nicodemus applied his intellect, his education,
the values of his time and culture, and he missed Jesus' point. Jesus represented the ways of God that were, by definition, unconventional ways
in that time and in our time.

Jesus' ways are always unconventional. It's hard for establishment people like us, or like Nicodemus, to connect with Jesus. Jesus taught very
straightforwardly. He said, "If someone strikes you on the right cheek,
turn and offer the left to be hit also" (Matthew 5:39, paraphrased). Not
conventional thinking. Jesus had unconventional reactions to violence.
Jesus' way of responding to violence is inconsistent with ours. It's hard to
connect with this Jesus because what he teaches is so different than our
logic, our intellect, and our conventional thinking.

Jesus also said, "You have heard it said to love your neighbor and hate
your enemy, but I say to you love your enemy" (Matthew 5:43-44,

paraphrased). That's not human cultural logic, is it? Treat your enemy as if your enemy were your friend. That's hard. That's a difficult teaching and we have a difficult time with it.

In the conversation between Jesus and Nicodemus, we have another hard saying. Jesus said to Nicodemus, "You must be born again." Other English translations say "You must be born anew" or "born from above." The original Greek text contains a flexible phrase that has multiple connotations. Whether it is, "You must be born again," or "born anew," or "born from above," Nicodemus didn't get it. We in evangelical Protestant Christianity haven't gotten it either. We have all had the experience of being grabbed by the lapels, shaken, and asked, "Are you born again?" The implication is that being born again is something chosen, something you decide, something that happens by the force of your own will.

My birth had absolutely nothing to do with my decision making. If we are to be reborn, to be born again, then the analogy is birth. The metaphor is about how we came to life. Life is not a decision; it's a gift. It wasn't my decision to be born, nor did I decide to accept birth. Life was a gift, a wonderful gift of grace and love that is inexplicable and beyond comprehension. I was given this gift of life. It wasn't about decision or will or choice or effort. It's an experience that happens to us, not a thing we choose.

Jesus said, "It's like the way the wind blows. The wind blows this way, and it blows that way, and we don't know where it comes from, or where it goes." This new birth is an experience that just happens. One day we somehow, inexplicably, just know that we are loved by God eternally. It's an event, not a choice.

Twenty-five years ago when I was a young pastor the wind blew. It was a communion Sunday. In this particular little church the length of the little communion rail was fewer than fifteen feet. People would come forward and take a place as it was open.

We had a full house. A fellow I'll call Jim was in worship that day. These events took place right after the Vietnam War. During that time many congregations were sponsoring the resettlement of Indo-Chinese refugees. Our congregation had done just that. Twenty-two Laotians had come to live in our community and our little rural congregation had sponsored them all. Jim had been against it in almost ugly ways. Jim didn't think they belonged in our community. He didn't think the church ought to have brought those people to our community.

Jim was sitting on one side of the congregation and the Laotians were sitting on the other side. Both Jim and the Laotians started toward the communion rail at the same time. I could see what was going to happen and I was on tiptoe. You see, we administered the sacrament with each worshiper serving the person next to them.

I could see it coming. Jim came down one aisle and the Laotian family came down another. Jim and the head of the Laotian family found themselves kneeling beside each other. The bread began to make its way down the row. Someone on his right offered the body of Christ to Jim. Then Jim turned to his left to serve the one beside him. It was the person who Jim had tried to keep out of the community. You could hear a pin drop as Jim broke off a piece of the loaf and said, "This is my body, given for you."

The wind blew. Not everyone heard it. Some attendees were wondering where they were going to go to dinner; others were making grocery lists. Somebody else was thinking about the ball game. But for some, the wind blew that day. It wasn't a choice or an act of will. It wasn't a decision anyone made. It was just a moment when Christ came and we all experienced a rebirth.

Be alert. Pay attention. Keep your eyes and ears open because the wind is going to blow one day. If you notice, if you experience it, it's a new day. It's a new birth from above. Pay attention. Amen. (Carl L. Schenck)

Lectionary Commentary
Genesis 12:1-4a

These passages together form a powerful Lenten theme. God offered a covenant relationship to Abraham as a gift. God's promise was of land and posterity. In the ancient world nothing offered more security than land and posterity. Land was the assurance of sustenance. Children were security for one's old age. These promises to Abraham were God's gift. The mystery of God's providence was at work coming to Abraham as a surprise blessing. Abraham responded by putting his faith in the God of the promise.

Romans 4:1-5, 13-17

In Romans, Paul is writing to mostly Gentile Christians and connecting their faith in Christ with the faith of Abraham. Paul is writing here to address one of the major controversies of the early church. To what extent should a Gentile believer be required to obey the law of Moses? For Jews and some Jewish Christians to follow Christ required one to obey God's law as given to Moses. Paul explodes this logic in his analogy to Abraham who was given the promises and brought into covenant with God before the law was given. In the same sense, Paul says, the Gentile Christian is brought into covenant with God through faith. This powerful message sings throughout Lent. (Carl L. Schenck)

Worship Aids

Call to Worship

Nicodemus came to Jesus at night.
We are often in the dark concerning God's purposes.
We come to worship seeking light.
May we be born anew into Christ's light.

Invocation

Lord Jesus Christ make us mindful of your presence. When we grope in darkness, show us your light. With all the stain of the week past and all the hurt we carry to worship, we need to be made new again. We do not ask you to be present for we know you are. Instead we ask that we will be made aware of your presence and born anew by your grace. Amen.

Benediction

And now may Christ always lift the darkness of your life, may the Spirit blow afresh through your hearts, and may Christ's light dispel your darkness this day and evermore. Amen. (Carl L. Schenck)

Wilderness Community

Second in a Series of Three on Wilderness and Pilgrimage

Numbers 11:10-23

They are springing up in towns across the country. Carefully planned with zoning rules and in consultation with horticulture specialists, the buildings all look alike whether they are homes, movie theatres, or office buildings. They are selling out faster than they can be built. People are eager to move into these planned communities.

They are not all that different from the layout of a traditional small town. Everything is in walking distance. Your bank is down the street from your hair salon, your church, and your drug store. Ideally you get to know your neighbors just as you get to know the entrepreneurs in the business establishments because of your close proximity and your affinity for the luxury of the new neighborhood. I am sure they are quite convenient and nonetheless fashionable to live in, but because they are not exactly a new concept, I don't really understand the draw to them. But then I began to think about the name "planned community" and what that might mean to those who live in it. I wonder if the name "planned community" has anything to do with attractiveness of these new developments.

The name insinuates that the work of getting to know people and places is already done for you. Everything is planned out for you. You don't have to spend the first few weeks after moving in looking for the best route to the grocery store or the post office. There is no wondering what your neighbors might be like or fear of late night wild parties on the weekends, as many of these communities have rules about the kind of people who can live in them. There will always be someone around if you lock your keys in your car or need a cup of sugar for a last-minute recipe. Without the modern conveniences, Moses is living in a comparable situation. He has been traveling throughout the wilderness with the entire camp of Israelites fleeing from Egypt and heading for the promised land. He is likely surrounded by artisans of every kind, and men and women abounding with talents and gifts. Of course he is the God-appointed leader of the group, but it seems he has forgotten where he is, who it is that surrounds him, and who is providing him his true strength.

The Israelites have been wandering in the wilderness for years at this point in the text. They are tired and frustrated. God has promised, through their leader Moses, that they are bound for a land beyond their wildest dreams. Yet they are surviving day by day on bread and meager rations, carrying only the possessions they can fit in their caravans. They are being tested and pushed beyond their limits. They, like any of us, grumble and complain because at least it is something to do to pass the time. And as small children prove to us almost daily, sometimes grumbling to whomever is in charge will get us what we want.

Moses is bound to experience feelings similar to that of the Israelites. He too is wandering in the wilderness. He too, gets tired, hungry, and frustrated. Granted, Moses has the added entertainment, honor, and responsibility of being in conversation with God on a regular basis, but he is still wandering, sometimes aimlessly it seems, in the wilderness.

At this point in the text, the Israelites are extremely frustrated. They are crying among themselves in frustration, hunger, and exasperation. Moses takes their cries personally. He internalizes their pain and anger, and Moses, in turn, cries out to God.

Moses has lost his focus. In his own experience of the wilderness, he has forgotten that behind him walk thousands of people loyal to him, most of the time, and to God, when they are thinking straight. Instead of sharing the burden of his leadership with those around him, Moses tries to bear the entire burden of the Israelites' unhappiness himself. It is a weight far too heavy for any one person to bear, but nonetheless he tries. The result is disastrous. Moses cries out to God for release from the burdens through death.

God listens to the cries of the Israelites and of Moses. God asks Moses to gather seventy men who are leaders among the people to help bear the travelers' burdens. It is a seemingly simple solution to their cries. In battle language, it is divide and conquer; it is as easy as delegating authority or assigning responsibilities. Sharing burdens should have been part of the leadership structure of the Israelite camp from the beginning. It is part of what it means to be in community.

God's command points out what Moses should have seen all along. Moses is in the midst of a planned community, albeit different from the ones with which we are familiar. Everything the Israelites need to survive and thrive is right there among them. What things they may lack, God has been faithful in providing.

In this case, their irrationality and "why me?" syndrome got the best of them, something with which those of us who have experienced our own wilderness wanderings can sympathize. We forget that we are the only ones experiencing hurt, loneliness, frustration, and hunger for any number of things. We forget, like Moses, to turn around and see that we are not alone; we are never alone.

As the children of God, there is a planned community all around us. God does not expect us to bear our burdens alone. We don't have to look for the seventy leaders among us to find help. Among the children of God, there are helping hands in every direction. We simply have to use our voices and cry out for help as Moses did.

It is to be hoped that we can learn from Moses' experience and not wait until our burdens are so great we are crying out for death if we don't get help soon enough. The family of God is a planned community waiting to help one another and bear one another's burdens. Thanks be to God. Amen. (Victoria Atkinson White)

Worship Aids

We come today to worship, bringing our burdens to this gathering of the family of God. Let our loads be lightened as we share among one another.

Litany

God we cry out.
And we hear your voice.
We look for comfort.
And we see your face.
We seek answers.
And we see your handiwork.
We need help along the way.
All: And we meet you in the love of our neighbor.

Benediction

As we leave this place, may we not bear our burdens alone. God has given us brothers and sisters, mothers and fathers, friends and relatives to walk beside us, in front of us, behind us, but most importantly, with us. Take joy in knowing you are not alone in the journey. Amen. (Victoria Atkinson White)

FEBRUARY 24, 2008

❧❧❧

Third Sunday in Lent

Readings: Exodus 17:1-7; Psalm 95; Romans 5:1-11; John 4:5-42

Characters of Lent: Slow to Believe
John 4:5-42

The story of the woman at the well is Jesus' longest conversation with one person in the Gospels. In this story, the woman erects barriers. She finds countless things that get between her and Jesus. Let's look at the barriers that she erected and see if they are not ones that we also erect.

First, this woman erected a barrier of prejudice. Jews and Samaritans held deep animosity against one another. They had long standing hatreds. The woman said, "Why are you, a Jew, asking me to get you a drink?" The animosity she expressed was characteristic of the relationships between Jews and Samaritans. Expressing this animosity she created a barrier to Jesus. She couldn't understand him. The poet Maya Angelou wrote, "Prejudice is a burden which confuses the past, threatens the future, and renders the present inaccessible" (*All God's Children Need Traveling Shoes* [Boston: G.K. Hall, 1987], 155). That's exactly what she was doing. She was distorting the past and making the present inaccessible. She couldn't meet Jesus because she brought prejudice into the relationship.

What about the individuals or the groups toward which we harbor prejudice? It may be an individual or a group of people you reject because of the color of their skin or their religion or their way of life. God came to the Samaritan woman in the form of someone against whom she was deeply prejudiced. God may come to us in the same way. If we are to experience Jesus, we will have to look into the eyes and into the face of an individual or group against whom we harbor prejudice.

Another barrier the woman erected was social custom. In that time, Jewish men and any type of woman didn't interact in public. A good, upstanding, righteous, Jewish male would only talk to his mother, wife, or daughters—never to any other women. The Samaritan woman embraced the same cultural biases. It was a scandal for a Jewish man to talk to a strange woman. Today, we could use an ability to be so scandalized!

Social customs can separate us from people, also. How many of us know a person who is poor? Do you know a poor person as a real human being, knowing what their life has been like, knowing the names of their children? In our society, we segregate by economic status. Middle-class people only know middle-class people. Rich people only know rich people, and poor people only poor people. Social custom keeps us apart. Do you know someone who is desperately poor? Jesus came to the woman as someone social customs made a stranger. Jesus may come to us as a stranger.

A third barrier was that Jesus was an outsider for the Samaritan woman. Generally, Jews did not travel through Samaria. Most traveling Jews went out of their way to avoid Samaritans. To the woman, Jesus was an outsider to her community, an outsider to her way of life, and an outsider to her personal experience. That made it hard for her to take Jesus seriously.

Jesus is often an outsider to our lives. We'd like to make over Jesus into a middle-class American, but he's not. He's different from us. Jesus is deeply and profoundly different. His values and ambitions, the way he conducted his life, the things Jesus cared about, and the people for whom he cared, are all very different from us. He is an outsider to our way of life. If we choose to follow Jesus we will discover ourselves being different from our neighbors. Dare we associate with, become close to, or follow this outsider?

Finally, the woman was reluctant to be honest with Jesus. Jesus said, "Go fetch your husband" and she replied, "I have no husband." Jesus knew the truth. She had been married five times and was not married to the man she was with. She didn't want Jesus to know the truth. She would interact with him on the surface, but the real depth of her life experience—all the pain, all the trouble, all the mistakes, and all the heartaches of her life—she was trying to keep to herself. She was holding Jesus at arm's length.

We do it too. We dress up and get all pretty for worship. But how do we relate to Jesus when we get home from work and we're mad and frustrated and tired and beat up? Do we connect with Jesus then? Are we open with God and Christ about the messy parts of our lives; about the parts of our lives that aren't pretty, that aren't pious? We can pray when we're feeling pious, but can we relate to Christ when life's a mess and when we're a mess? Can we open these parts of our lives to Jesus? The Samaritan woman found it difficult and so do we.

Despite all the barriers this is a story with a happy ending. This woman eventually connected. She went back to her village and said, "I have met this wonderful, amazing man. Come meet him!" She becomes the first evangelist. She is the first to run and tell someone about Jesus. The story says the whole community came and many believed because of her.

It can work that way for us also. We are kept from Jesus by prejudices, social customs, fear of outsiders, and reluctance to expose the messy realities of our lives. We can get past those things and allow Jesus to be here, right in front of us. We can share what we have experienced with others and it can change everything. My hope and my prayer is that we can get past the barriers that get between us and Jesus. Then there's hope that even now we will meet Jesus too. (Carl L. Schenck)

Lectionary Commentary
Exodus 17:1-7; Romans 5:1-11

The Hebrew Bible lesson for the third Sunday in Lent is the Exodus story of God giving water to the thirsty Israelites from the rock in the desert. While this story could easily be linked to the gospel lesson, it also has rich Lenten possibilities standing alone. The story is one of dissatisfaction on the part of those who have been redeemed from slavery. The people cry out against Moses, accusing him of leading them into the wilderness to die of thirst. They did not believe that the God who had led them safely through the waters of the Red Sea would provide water in the desert. Lenten self-examination can call up many examples of the church and its people crying out to God as if God had not already redeemed God's people through the cross. Our current complaints shame us as we consider the work God has already done on our behalf. Additionally, how often do we fail to expect God's mercies when we have experienced them so richly in the past? (Carl L. Schenck)

Worship Aids

Call to Worship

Come to the well of living water.
We have come seeking Jesus Christ.

Draw deep from the well of life.
We have come to Christ to quench our thirst.
Drink deeply and be refreshed.
All: Quenched, we will then go to tell other about him.

Invocation

Living Christ, we often go to the well. We too often find ourselves parched by the pressures of life and in need of refreshment for body and soul. May we, like the Samaritan woman, discover you during the dry moments of our lives. Come to us and draw for us the living water of your presence. We pray in your holy name. Amen.

Benediction

Having drunk deeply of the living water of Jesus Christ our Lord, go now into his world to give water to the thirsty there. (Carl L. Schenck)

Looking Forward in Faith

Third in a Series of Three on Wilderness and Pilgrimage

Numbers 14:1-10

Are they sounding like a broken record to you yet? We have heard this story before at several different places along the Israelites' journey in the wilderness. You will recall that each time we hear this story, God remains faithful despite their whining and complaining. God is faithful, even when the Israelites are not.

This time it is not about wanting something different to eat or wondering how much longer their journey will be. This time the Israelites are scared. They are on the outskirts of all that God has promised them. They are almost there. Soon, it will all be worth it. They had to have wondered, as I am sure we would have, if it would be worth it. They have been through so much. They have wandered in the wilderness for years and years under the leadership of Moses, who didn't even consider himself fit for the job. They have lost loved ones. They have spent a generation feeling tired, exasperated, and lost. But here they are on the verge of entering God's promised land.

They are so close; they could feel the anticipation building. They sent spies ahead to see and report back what was in store for them. We imagine what they were hoping for, what they dreamt, for this new land.

Coming from a land of slavery and oppression, they may have hoped for a place where they would be kings and queens of the land and that others would work for them. Having been hungry and exhausted for years in the wilderness, they may have hoped for food growing plentifully and homes already built for them. They probably hoped for easily accessible water sources and high hills on which they could sleep. They may have dreamt of herds of animals wandering from plains to valleys, looking for a new shepherd. Their promised land was within reach.

But news of a land of plenty did not come from the spies without the crushing report of giants in the land. Yes, the land is the land of their hopes and dreams, it flows with milk and honey, the spies say, but it is also inhabited by giants.

At this point, we have the luxury of knowing the entire story. We know how God has delivered them in the past, and we know what the future holds for the Israelites. We know that God has been faithful to them all along and will continue to do so. We can see that if the Israelites will put their faith in God rather than focusing on their fear of giants, that their dreams will be their reality. God's faithfulness does not and will not leave them. God wants what is best for them and thus keeps the divine promises to them.

But they are scared. They are weak from wandering in the wilderness and the news of giants in their path is their breaking point. They lose sight of how close they are to the promised land and lapse into irrationally. Instead of trusting in God's faithfulness, they want to turn around and return to the slavery and bondage of Egypt. They are willing to accept the treachery and oppression of a life that is familiar rather than risk what is unknown in the light of God's love and faithfulness to them. They are that scared.

Thankfully, two leaders among them have a moment of clarity. Joshua and Caleb, two of the spies who have seen the giants, but have also seen the land of milk and honey, speak in the chaos. They remind their people of where they have been. They remind them of their power and abilities when God is on their side. They urge them not to turn their backs on God but to press forward in God's promises. Joshua and Caleb have seen the prize, they have seen the land that lies before them. They too are tired and weary from their years in the wilderness, but they are renewed by their hope of what is so close to their grasp.

We have all been where the Israelites are in this story. We can come so far in our journeys being grateful for the ways God delivers us and then we so easily and quickly forget. We think irrationally. We believe our lives would be so much easier if we had never filled in the blank with any number of things. We forget that God has been with us throughout our journeys in ways we could and could not see. We forget that God is faithful to deliver us until our journeys are complete. We forget and want to turn our backs on all that we have accomplished and learned because there are giants in our future.

What or who are the giants in your future? Who or what do you fear? Who or what do you know you cannot conquer or master or pass by alone? Is it debt? Is it something that may reappear from your past? Is it someone you think is smarter, quicker, funnier, or more successful than you? These may be scary thoughts or visions as you picture the giants in your path.

But now think of who in your life are the Calebs and Joshuas. Who are your champions? Who reminds you of where you have been and what they know is in your future because of the potential they know you have and the hope God holds for you? These people are the ones to keep in mind as you face your giants. They know you can conquer whatever giants lay ahead because they have seen you do it before. They want and desire a bright future for you.

We know, as Caleb and Joshua know, that God is with us in the wilderness. God provides rituals and opportunities for us to draw closer in our relationship with God. And we know that God does not expect us to bear our wilderness burdens alone. God provides community for us to journey alongside. And in that community, God provides leaders like Joshua and Caleb along the way to remind us that all our wilderness wanderings will be worth it when we maintain our faith in God.

Where are you in your wilderness journey? Where do you see God at work in your pilgrimage of faith? How are you being a Caleb or a Joshua to someone else? May we learn from the Israelites' story. May our eyes be fixed ahead and not behind. May our minds be fixed on God's faithfulness to us along the way. And may our hearts be open to new ways God is working in our lives. So may it be. Amen. (Victoria Atkinson White)

Worship Aids

Invocation

God, we know you are present in this place long before we begin to prepare our hearts for worship, because you are present in our lives long before we are born. Remain with us as we seek to give back to you a small portion of your generosity to us. Prepare our hearts to worship you, a good and faithful God.

Pastoral Prayer

God, there are those among us who need encouragement along the journey. They need reminders of your presence in the past and glimpses of the promises that are to come. Enable us to be your emissaries of peace, love, hope, and encouragement to those who need you. And when it is we who need to feel your presence, help us be mindful of your spirit ministering to us in ways we have not yet known. Amen.

Benediction

Leave this place with the knowledge of Caleb and the strength of Joshua. Stand up in chaos and speak for what is right and true. Embrace the power of God as only God's children can. Amen. (Victoria Atkinson White)

MARCH 2, 2008

Fourth Sunday in Lent

Readings: 1 Samuel 16:1-13; Psalm 23; Ephesians 5:8-14; John 9:1-41

Characters of Lent: Blind, but Now I See
John 9:1-41

ACT 1

"As Jesus walked along, he saw a man blind from birth."

Thus begins the first act of the story. Jesus sees a blind man who survives by begging. Jesus does a very strange thing. He puts mud in the man's eyes and sends him to a pool of Siloam to wash. The word *Siloam* meant "sent." The blind man was sent to "Sent" and told to wash. He came back seeing, but by this time Jesus has disappeared. Jesus in fact, disappears from the story for a long time.

Now the formerly blind man's neighbors begin to argue. Was the man before them the same man who was born blind? The man says, "Yes, it's me."

"Well, who did it?"

"Jesus."

"Where is he now?"

"I don't know."

We have the man who is able to see with his eyes, but not with his heart. He does not know the one who had sent him.

It's not so different with us. Jesus has sent us all. We know that Jesus sends us into the world to address the needs of the people like the blind man. Although we may be uncertain just how to do the task, we know what the task is. Jesus sends us to the hungry, the sick, the lame, the lost, and the lonely.

Like the blind man, we are sent, but we may not understand who sends us. We too, are people with mud in our eyes. Life is messy. Our family lives, our work lives, the whole world is a mess. Jesus invites us to wash the mud out of our eyes. Jesus challenges us to clean up the world. We know we have been sent, but we are not always convinced of the wisdom of the sender. We are hesitant to go where Jesus sends us. We find excuses to avoid Jesus' instructions.

ACT 2

"They brought to the Pharisees the man who had formerly been blind.... The Pharisees also began to ask him how he received his sight."

In this part of the dialogue the man sees a little better. Our subject is confronted by a hostile interrogation. Healing of his physical sight had occurred on the Sabbath, and the religious leaders were the Sabbath police. The religious authorities have a dilemma. Healing of blindness is good. Healing on the Sabbath is not.

With a delicious irony, the authorities turn to the beggar and ask him to explain what had happened. Pressed in this way, the man who earlier had said Jesus was the one who sent him now reaches for a fuller understanding. The blind man says, "He's a prophet." A prophet is a person with a message.

For many that's who Jesus is. He's a man with a moral and ethical message. Jesus' message is about caring for those in need. But the message grows larger. Jesus teaches love of neighbor and enemy—an idealistic, perhaps unrealistic, message, but a high moral teaching. He's a prophet. For many that is the most light to be shed on the question, "Who is Jesus?" He is one with a great idealistic and perhaps unrealistic message.

ACT 3

"The religious leaders, a second time, called the man who had been blind, and they said 'Give glory to God. We know that this man is a sinner.' He answered, 'I do not know whether he is a sinner. One thing I do know, that though I was blind, now I see ... if this man were not from God, he could do nothing."

The blind man has gradually elevated his view of Jesus. First, Jesus was the one who sent him to the pool. Next he said "He's a prophet." Now the man elevates his understanding of Jesus another notch higher. He says Jesus is from God. You see how that raises the stakes? It is one thing to say Jesus is a moral philosopher, a teacher. But now these teachings that seem idealistic, but unrealistic, have become not just the idealism of a great moral philosopher, but a message sent from God. We can dismiss the ranting of an idealist, but if his message comes from God, then the message cannot be easily discarded as naïve idealism. The message becomes not the message of a dreamer, but the command of the creator of the universe. How do we say that God is naïve and unrealistic? It is easy to dismiss Jesus as an idealistic teacher who doesn't understand the real world. But God's message can't be so easily dismissed. Have we joined the blind man in believing Jesus' message is a message from God?

ACT 4

Jesus reappears after having been absent from the story since he sent the blind man to the pool.

"Jesus heard that they had driven him out and when he found him, he said, 'Do you believe in the Son of Man?' He answered, 'And who is he, sir?' Jesus said to him, 'You have seen him, and the one speaking with you is he.' He said, 'Lord, I believe.'"

First, he's the one who sends us. Next he's a human teacher of morality. In Act 3, he becomes the one with God's message. Now the formerly blind man sees with spiritual insight. Jesus is not only the person with God's message, but he is God's message.

At Christmas, we talked about the birth of a baby with a title: Emmanuel, God with us. Not just a man, not just a prophet, not just a person who has insight into God's ways and purposes, but Jesus is God with us. The formerly blind man worshiped him. Messengers are not worshiped. The gospel writer has staged a story of enlightenment. The one who formerly couldn't see with his eyes or his heart now sees in crystal clarity—"the light of the world."

It is an amazing story. Who do you say he is? Sender, teacher, messenger, or God? May Jesus wash our eyes so we too may see. (Carl L. Schenck)

Lectionary Commentary
1 Samuel 16:1-13

Lent is a time for self-examination, but it is also a time for repentance—change. If we stay the same after our journey through Lent, we have missed its purpose. In this text we find Samuel tempted to be stuck in the past. The Lord asks Samuel, "How long will you grieve over Saul?" The message is clear. Move on. Then the Lord gives instruction on next steps toward a new beginning. Samuel remains reluctant. "If Saul hears of it, he will kill me." Change can be dangerous. It can also feel more dangerous than it really is. This text invites us to consider the change, the repentance, the new direction God has for us this Lent.

Ephesians 5:8-14

As the days lengthen during Lent, the writer of Ephesians invites us to reflect upon the image of light. The text makes it clear that Christ is the light source. Having moved from the reign of darkness to the reign of light, the Christian is called upon to let Christ be the light that illuminates life.

The light of Christ throws everything into perspective. The preacher or teacher can travel with text into the inner life of the disciple, in keeping with the traditional Lenten theme of self-examination. Where are the dark places, the self-serving motives, the twisted relationships, the unholy ambitions that the Christian can expose to the light of Christ in Lenten self-examination?

Or just as easily, the preacher can call upon the church to shine the strong light of Christ upon the ills of society. Any age and any society can offer countless examples of darkness, injustice, violence, poverty, and exploitation. The complacent Christian, church, or society stands in need of the bright light of Christ. (Carl L. Schenck)

Worship Aids

Call to Worship

Come to this house to be changed.
But we come to be comforted.
Be careful, the living Christ is here.
The living Christ comforts.
Yes, Christ will comfort, but for those who will see, he will
    challenge.
**May we be comforted by Christ, but may we also have the
eyes to see his challenge to change.**

Opening Prayer

O Lord, we journey these roads of Lent and more and more see ourselves in the people Jesus encountered on the roads of his life. We do not always like what we see. Jesus keeps calling for us to repent. He offers to clean the mud from our eyes that we might see him clearly. When we see Jesus clearly we are changed. When we see our world clearly, we are called to change it. O Lord, help us see and make us the people you desire us to be. In Jesus name, amen.

Benediction

Now that Jesus has opened our eyes, let us go into his world seeing clearly the tasks he has for us there. (Carl L. Schenck)

A Path, Not a Punishment

First in a Series of Three on Spiritual Disciplines

Luke 4:1-15

Jesus knows a great deal about paths. He was born in the small village of Bethlehem, only a narrow road—not much more than a path—from the nearby city of Jerusalem. Jesus followed the path that his parents led to work and family, synagogue and temple. He set his sights on the path to Jerusalem and the Palm Sunday highway, knowing that mere days later, it would lead up the path of Calvary.

When John baptized Jesus, Christ took a path that led to the wilderness. Although it was likely not an actual forty-day journey as the Hebrew euphemism suggested, Jesus spent an enduring time in solitude in the wilderness. It was not a punishment, but a path of his choosing. Jesus showed us the way to go.

Spiritual discipline is not about punishment, but about taking a journey along a path that leads to grace. Spiritual discipline, whatever the nature of that discipline, is a path of one's own choosing that reveals God's own design. It is an opportunity to open our hearts and minds to the presence and grace of Christ and to the power and guidance of the Holy Spirit.

Spiritual discipline is a path to nourishment and redemption of our soul. In whatever form, and there are many, such discipline can be a powerful means of God's grace for those who seek it. Prayer, fasting, giving, serving, worship, biblical study (*lectio divina*), spiritual reading, journaling, the Lord's Supper, confession, and spiritual writing are all disciplines of God's grace. They are paths that lead us onward in our journey with the opportunity of growing closer to the presence of the living Christ.

In his time in the wilderness and at other times of personal retreat, Jesus taught the value of looking inside so that we can better understand and face the world outside (see also Mark 1:35; Matthew 14:13; 26:36). When we follow the path of Christ, it is the path that leads to God's grace. It is to discover God at work in life—in all our lives—and to share that good news and the joy that such truth brings. We can discover God at work in the ordinary and routine activities of life, for God's grace is found in both the mundane and magnificent.

I am the servant—not the owner—of a dog and cat, Gracie and K. C. They have me disciplined quite well. I feed them when they go into the kitchen, I let them out when they go to the door, and I pick up after them, which is something that they never do for me. Animals need discipline to help manage their behavior, but I have found that it is sometimes less stressful for the human to do the adapting. I learned long ago that when my dog goes to the front door to walk with me, she will kneel, not sit, so that I may attach the leash to her collar. She never learned to sit, so she kneels. We can be creatures of both good and bad habits.

Sometimes we neglect to make the time to listen to the presence of God. We have gotten into patterns and routines that perpetuate bad habits. When we do not discipline ourselves to listen, it is easy to be distracted by the many competing voices that lead us away from the Holy. We may think that we are listening, but experience tells us otherwise.

I am puzzled when my child says that I am not listening to him. I think that I am listening to him. Did he say something that I did not hear, or did I not understand what I heard him say? What my son is trying to tell me is this: what he needs from me and what I give him are not the same things. We both become frustrated when we are unfulfilled by this disconnect. When you and I feel disconnected from God, it is a disconnect on a transcendent scale that influences every level of our ordinary life.

My home study is a sparsely furnished upstairs room. It has a small desk, some bookshelves, a standing lamp, and a chair sitting by the window. The window overlooks the front yard and the street below. I enjoy looking out in the morning and watching children pass by on their way to the bus stop. I see runners and walkers. I watch a couple have an intense debate as they fast-walk down the block, and see a stay-at-home-day-trader get very bad news while walking with his "Bluetooth" headset. What I also see from my chair is a clearer picture of my life and an understanding of some of the struggles that I face.

It is my place to be still and to know that God is. I do not need to know all about God, but I do sense the reality of God's presence and the love of God's grace. My problems take on new perspective and my challenges seem less powerful and ominous. This is my spiritual discipline. It is not punishment. Yes, I may set the morning alarm a bit earlier to make the time, but when I take the time I rarely regret it.

Such time is a place along a path that is the journey of the Christian life. I like to get off of culture's highway and stay on that path as much as I can. There is greater quiet and serenity there. There are birds that sing, flowers that bloom, people who love, and unexpected treasures that delight.

Luke's Gospel says it. Jesus had just come back from the wilderness— from his spiritual discipline that fed his soul. Luke says that Jesus "filled with the power of the Spirit, returned to Galilee, and a report about him spread through all the surrounding country. He began to teach in their synagogues and was praised by everyone." Jesus knew; it is a path, not a punishment. (Gary G. Kindley)

Worship Aids

Call to Worship

We gather together this morning on the journey of life.
Our separate journeys are one, in this hour, as we become
    God's community of faith in this place.
We are people invited to follow a disciplined path.
It is not a discipline of punishment, but a path of grace.
Come, people of God, let us share the journey together!

Invocation

Holy Lord, who was led by the Spirit into the wilderness, lead us to where you would have us to go. Teach us the value of the Way, and let us follow the path that you have laid before us. Amen.

Benediction

Follow the path of the spiritual life. Be a spiritual people. Seek grace and offer it to all whom you meet. Amen. (Gary G. Kindley)

MARCH 9, 2008

❧ ❧ ❧

Fifth Sunday in Lent

Readings: Ezekiel 37:1-14; Psalm 130; Romans 8:6-11; John 11:1-45

The Need for Prophets in the Valley
Ezekiel 37:1-14

A family is fighting a battle against one of life's most feared enemies, cancer, and they watch their loved one as she literally wastes away from the disease. A community is ravaged by a natural disaster, and the residents return to find their homes, schools, and businesses lying in ruins. A man is facing an unknown future as his company conducts layoffs, and he is unsure of how his bills will be paid. A country is in the midst of war, and it watches as its young women and men enter into the dangers of combat. A woman is struggling with an illness no one sees, and she struggles to make it through each day against the waves of depression. As we look at the world around us, it is easy to become discouraged and wonder about God's presence in the midst of all the despair.

The prophet Ezekiel faced a situation that caused great despair in the lives of his audience. It was one of the darkest times in the history of God's people. The Babylonians had conquered their land and carried many people off into captivity. The nation of Israel experienced tremendous physical and emotional losses. Their confidence in themselves and in Yahweh was at an all-time low. The people needed to be reminded about the God who loved them and sustained them. The people needed to have their hope restored and their vision enlarged. It was in this time of need that the Spirit provided Ezekiel with an experience that still speaks to us today.

The Spirit of God carried Ezekiel out to overlook what might be described as the ruins of a battlefield. There were many bones scattered upon the ground, and they had obviously been there for quite a while. There was no sign of life left in them, as they were old and dried out from the ravages of time. The Spirit then asked Ezekiel a pivotal question,

"Mortal, can these bones live?" Ezekiel, like many of us, hedged his bets. He didn't say no, yet he wasn't willing to say yes either. Ezekiel's answer was evasive at best, and in his uncertainty he turned the question back on God—"O Lord GOD, you know." As he was faced with the lifeless bones, Ezekiel was uncertain. He had been called to answer the question that haunted the house of Israel. He was called to consider whether God could work a miracle in the life of a nation that appeared as good as dead. Ezekiel was called to examine his faith in the God who delivered them from slavery and gave them the land.

Can these bones live? It is a difficult question to answer. It is difficult because it is a question that challenges the prophet to view the world around him not with the eyes of reality, but with the eyes of faith. Ezekiel is called to imagine the divine power working to bring life where there was death. He is called to trust in God who has acted on their behalf in the past. Ezekiel is called to imagine a future filled with hope, boldly proclaiming promise even while those around him are uttering words of despair. Can these bones live? God says yes.

Still, the most interesting part of the story is that God calls the prophet to play a part in the reanimation of the dry bones. It is only when Ezekiel has prophesied to the bones that they will live. The prophet must say to the dry bones, "O dry bones, hear the word of the LORD." It is only when the prophet proclaims the word of God to the bones that they begin to reassemble and be covered with flesh. Then, even after this initial stage of the miracle, there is no breath in the bones. God calls the prophet to prophesy yet again. "Then he said to me, 'Prophesy to the breath, prophesy, mortal . . . that they may live.'" At each step of the miracle, God uses Ezekiel to proclaim the divine words and to announce the new thing that God is about to do in the midst of the valley of dry bones. The proclamation for the word is central to the miracle!

God knows that the bones can live again. Could it be that by inviting Ezekiel to name the acts of God, God is helping Ezekiel discover the answer to the question "Can these bones live?" God engages Ezekiel's help in the miracle, and does so in order that the proclamation of God's word and actions may continue. God desires human witnesses to speak of God's miracles of life. Even at the conclusion of our lection, we find God articulating that very reason for this powerful act, for "then you shall know that I, the LORD, have spoken and will act."

As I look at the world around me, I find myself surrounded by piles of dry bones. There are individuals, communities, and nations that are at the end of their ropes. I look around and there is great reason for despair. We are wandering in "the valley of the shadow of death" (Psalm 23:4) and some around me seem to have no reason to hope. We are surrounded by a broken and hurting world. People all around us ask, "Can these bones live?" That is why God needs prophets in the valley today. God needs men and women who will stand knee-deep in bones and proclaim that death and destruction do not have the final word. God needs preachers and prophets who will prophesy to the bones, who will speak the word of truth. God needs us to remind those who are lost, alone, and afraid that God will "bring you up from your graves . . . put [God's] spirit within you, and you shall live." May God continue to use us to proclaim the good news and the promise of new life to those who need it the most! (Wendy Joyner)

Lectionary Commentary
John 11:1-45

This prolonged narrative about the death and resurrection of Lazarus provides many opportunities for preaching. First of all, we are invited to reflect upon the nature of death and its permanence. Lazarus's death was real and it affected those who loved him in powerful ways. In fact, we are provided with a rare glimpse into the emotional life of Jesus as he confronts the death of his friend. The good news in this passage is revealed at the conclusion of the narrative, however, as we are reminded that with God, death does not have the last word. Jesus resurrects Lazarus, bringing life where there had been death. The parallels with the Ezekiel passage are clear. However, one helpful train of thought to consider is the statement of Jesus to Martha, "Did I not tell you that if you believed, you would see the glory of God?" We sometimes focus so much on the miracles themselves that we fail to see their purpose. Both the dry-bones miracle and the resurrection of Lazarus find their purpose in the revelation of God. They draw our eyes to a powerful God who is always working for our good, bringing new life from the jaws of death.

Romans 8:6-11

In this beloved text, the Apostle Paul gives us one of the most complete reflections in Scripture upon the gift of God's Spirit. He begins this section by contrasting God's spirit with the spirit of those who dwell in the flesh. Paul states, "the Spirit is life and peace" while "the flesh is death." He then spells out, in detail, the new life we receive through God's Spirit.

Our newness of life is compared to the newness of life experienced by the resurrected Christ. This provides perhaps the strongest parallel with the Ezekiel passage. Both passages remind us of the new life that is possible through the movement of God's Spirit. It is most helpful to place these passages in conversation with one another because doing so enables us to understand that resurrection is not only about eternal life after death, but also the newness of life we experience through the power of Christ in our lives each day. Just as the dry bones received new life, so we can live anew with God's Spirit working in and through us. (Wendy Joyner)

Worship Aids

Call to Worship

We gather together today in faith. We boldly proclaim that death and despair do not have the last word in our lives, for with God all things are possible. May God's Spirit blow through our flesh and bones, bringing new life and renewed hope.

Prayer of Confession

Gracious God, we confess that we are a people with a short memory. We fail to remember your mighty acts and do not always trust you in times of adversity. Remind us of your powerful love and care—that we might be filled with a bold and courageous faith.

Words of Assurance

In the name of Jesus Christ, you are forgiven.
In the name of Jesus Christ, you are forgiven. Amen.

Benediction

May the Spirit of God bring new life to our old and tired bones. May God knit together and renew our lives this day, equipping us for service and strengthening us for the proclamation of God's amazing acts. May we be prophets of grace in the darkest valleys. Amen. (Wendy Joyner)

Fasting—It's About Time!

Second in a Series of Three on Spiritual Disciplines

Matthew 6:16-18

Food takes time. We spend time growing food, harvesting food, selling food, shopping for food, preparing food, and consuming food. We store leftover food, clean up after we've eaten food, and take medication when we've had too much food. We read books, peruse magazines, and eagerly watch television cooking shows to learn new ways of preparing food. Children (and sometimes church youth groups) play with food, while millions in this world do not have enough food. Fasting is a vital spiritual discipline that is vastly overlooked and misunderstood. As Christ's disciples, we have much to learn and to teach to restore the need for fasting. When I was newly married, my wife decided that she would fast for Lent. It was not a diet or a fad, but an opportunity that she described as a spiritual and physical cleansing. For several weeks into the forty days of Lent, she consumed only liquids and vitamins. At her doctor's insistence, she added soup and then some fish. Friends did not understand. They asked her where she got the diet. They wanted to know how much weight she had lost. They asked if she was working out with her fast and if she was monitoring her measurements.

Some church members asked if she had come from a Roman Catholic family. Others wondered if she was Lutheran. I suspected that these folks listened to Public Radio's "Prairie Home Companion" for their understanding of what it meant to be Lutheran. Still others, unable to comprehend or relate to her spiritual perspective, merely considered her strange or perhaps a bit fanatical about her religion.

The experience led me to devote a sermon addressing the spiritual nature of fasting. I explained that fasting is distinctly not dieting but a spiritual discipline to allow someone to draw closer to God. I reported that there is medical research that has determined how fasting brings about physiological changes to one's body. Fasting can increase blood flow to the brain, the organ that is the center of cognition, emotion, and our sense of well-being.

The spiritual discipline of fasting is a means of stepping off the path of consumption and chaos. Fasting is a means of making time for God by focusing our life on something besides activity, entertainment, and self-satisfaction. Fasting is not only about what we don't consume but also about what we do not do. Fasting is essentially about time—intentionally setting aside time for listening and growing in the spirit of Christ by giving up time for physical pleasure.

Because fasting is a choice, a path that we choose, the Gospel tells us that fasting is not meant to be a public display of punishment and agony. Once again, spiritual discipline is not punishment but a path that leads to grace. Matthew's account of Jesus' teaching on fasting is a declaration. Jesus declares: "Whenever you fast, do not look dismal, like the hypocrites, for they disfigure their faces so as to show others that they are fasting."

Jesus then goes further in that same verse, pointing to the true value of fasting versus the self-serving attitude of those who see it as a means of appearing pious. "Truly I tell you, they have received their reward." For those who treat fasting as an opportunity for self-importance, they have gotten out of it what they expected to get out of it. Spiritual opportunists want others to look at them and see what they believe to be piety and spiritual greatness. Jesus is saying that what they really desire is to feed their own ego, so that is all that they shall gain.

The true value of fasting comes from what we are willing to put into such a discipline. It is a path that can lead us closer to God, to better knowing God's presence, and God's call upon our life. True fasting is a path of spiritual discipline that leads us nearer to the blessing of God's grace. Like prayer, fasting is a means of growing a deeper and clearer comprehension of the holy mystery of Christ's love.

Fasting and prayer go together, for they are complimentary spiritual disciplines that move us from the secular world without to the holy kingdom within. Prayer and fasting are a means of changing our focus, of clearing our bias, and setting aside our prejudice. Together, prayer and fasting help us reorder our thinking, reassess our concerns, embrace our challenges, establish our priorities, banish our fear, cease our worry, and liberate our soul. Life can tarnish our spirit, and our soul becomes toxic.

Culture teaches us to be consumers. Our most precious commodities are not our possessions and professions but our love and laughter. Christ made it clear that the purpose of the incarnation is to offer abundant life. We find true abundance in the richness of our relationships and the serenity of our soul.

Fasting is most commonly considered as refraining from feeding our body, but it can also be a matter of stewardship of life. Fasting can include refraining from consumption or reexamining our need for entertainment.

Fasting might mean decreasing time spent with objects (computer, television, electronic games, and audio gadgets), and increasing time spent with God, family, and friends. Love is something from which we need never fast.

Matthew's sixth chapter is a great beginning for anyone desiring to grow in spiritual discipline. The path of grace is a disciplined path, but such discipline is not a stranger to joy and peace. Fasting is a matter of time, both what we do with it and how we consume it. Fasting is a vital spiritual discipline that engages the mystery of faith and unlocks doors of grace that we have failed to explore for far too long. (Gary G. Kindley)

Worship Aids

Call to Worship (Unison)

Come, people of God! Enter into God's presence with prayer and fasting. Make this time of worship a fast from all that distracts or consumes you, and be consumed by the eternal love that never lets you go.

Prayer of Confession (Unison)

Holy God, we confess that we have wasted our life in consumption of what does not satisfy. In truth, we have not permitted ourselves to be consumed by your unconditional grace. Teach us the value of fasting—of refraining from what robs us of time for the truly important. Remind us of those whose lives and love we cherish, and teach us that love is something from which we need never fast. Amen.

Words of Assurance

In the name of Jesus Christ, you are forgiven.
In the name of Jesus Christ, you are forgiven. Amen.

Benediction

Go out as people consumed by God's love. Do not be consumed by this world. Live a disciplined life. Feed on the grace of our faith. Go out and be the church! (Gary G. Kindley)

MARCH 16, 2008

❧❧❧

Palm/Passion Sunday

Palm Readings: Psalm 118:1-2, 19-29; Matthew 21:1-11
Passion Readings: Isaiah 50:4-9a; Psalm 31:9-16; Philippians 2:5-11; Matthew 26:14–27:66

A Life Celebrated in Its Entirety
Philippians 2:5-11

I remember vividly the first time I saw a professional production of the life of Christ acted out upon the stage. There were beautiful sets, talented actors, and lots of activities to focus upon as many extras moved about the stage. I saw many familiar scenes from the life of Jesus recreated before my eyes. I saw a nativity scene where Mary and Joseph welcomed the Christ child in humble surroundings. I witnessed some of the healing miracles as Jesus laid his hands upon the sick and the outcast. I heard the words of Jesus delivered in the Sermon on the Mount. I gazed upon the scene of the final Passover meal that Jesus shared with his disciples. I even experienced anew the horrors of Jesus' crucifixion, and celebrated as I watched Jesus come forth from the tomb following his resurrection.

The thing that was most impressive to me however, was the final scene of the play. The play concluded with a reenactment of the ascension of Christ. The disciples were gathered around to hear Jesus' departing words of commission and as they watched Jesus ascended into the sky. I am not exactly sure how they did it so convincingly, but through the use of lighting, screens, and an elaborate scaffold, the actor playing Jesus ascended into heaven surrounded by angels. The angels held trumpets and offered arms outstretched in praise, as they celebrated Christ's majesty and his glory. I remember standing there with goose bumps on my arms. It was a transformative scene for me. I realized, for perhaps the very first time, the entire scope of Jesus' experience. I had caught glimpses of the story before, but I had never been able to reflect upon the entire sweep of the divine drama that was played out in the life of Christ. In this play I had not only beheld the human experience of Jesus' life, but also now beheld the divine celebration of Jesus' life.

The gift of this passage in Philippians is that it also invites us to take into account the entire sweep of the divine drama that took place in the life of Christ. In the space of these few verses, Paul reminds us of the very nature of Jesus as it was revealed in his actions. We are encouraged to celebrate both the divinity and the humanity in the experience of the Christ event. First, Paul reminds us that Jesus was the preexistent Lord, who indeed was "in the form of God." Jesus' existence did not begin in a manger in Bethlehem, but rather he was present from the beginning, at the right hand of God. The one who came and dwelt among us was the Son of God. As the Son of God, Jesus had every reason to enjoy the status and rights of the divine life.

Yet, Paul tells us, Jesus "did not regard equality with God / as something to be exploited, / but emptied himself, / taking the form of a slave." Here Paul reminds us of the mystery of what we call the incarnation. We are sometimes guilty of celebrating the mystery of Jesus' incarnation only at Christmas, but it is perhaps here, during this season of the journey to the cross that the incarnation most fully realizes its scandal. Jesus' birth in the humble surroundings of poverty lies at one end of the incarnation, but Jesus' suffering and death at the hands of humanity lies at the other end. Paul marvels at the wonder of Jesus' willingness to lay aside his divine privileges and power, "taking the form of a slave" and ultimately becoming "obedient to the point of death—even death on a cross." Jesus, the divine Son of God, literally pours out his life on our behalf. Jesus sets aside his own will for the will of God so that we might know that power of God in and through him.

Finally, once Jesus had lived this human life of radical obedience and humility through his death on the cross, Paul reminds us that God exalted Jesus to the highest level. We are shown the divine approval of Christ's actions on our behalf, "that at the name of Jesus, / every knee should bend ... and every tongue should confess that Jesus is Lord, / to the glory of God the Father." It's this final scene in the drama that gives us goose bumps. It is only when Jesus loses his life for our sake that he receives it back again. It is when Jesus humbles himself that he is most highly exalted. Jesus' act of self-emptying is the act that God works in most powerfully.

I believe that during this most holy season of the year the church sometimes fails to focus on the big picture of Jesus' journey. As we approach Holy Week we sometimes look only at the human suffering of Jesus on the cross. Yet when we focus only on the humanity of Jesus' experience we lose the very essence of its mystery and power. Palm/Passion Sunday calls us to celebrate the tension inherent in Jesus' self-emptying and radical obedience. We are called to lift up both the humanity and the divinity of Christ, for only in doing so can we realize the power of Jesus' surrender. We are called to struggle with our cries of "Hosanna" one moment and "Crucify him!" the next. We are called to ponder anew the mystery that God is most glorified in the moment of Jesus' most profound weakness and suffering. We are called to remember that the one crucified "King of the Jews" is also the "King of the Universe." We are called to remember that Jesus' radical obedience in death leads ultimately to his resurrection, glorification, and ascension through the power of God. The overwhelming love of Jesus is revealed to us most fully when we contemplate the fullness of all that he offered up and sacrificed on our account. If that doesn't give us goose bumps I don't know what will. (Wendy Joyner)

Lectionary Commentary
Matthew 21:1-11

This scripture passage, commonly called the triumphal entry, recounts Jesus' journey into Jerusalem. In this scene, we can see the beginning of the paradox that will carry us through Holy Week. Jesus enters Jerusalem hailed as a king, yet he is unlike any king that has come before. The crowds welcome him with jubilation and praise. They shout words celebrating God's saving power, and prepare a runway of cloaks and palm branches for Jesus to enter town upon. He is welcomed as a conquering hero might be welcomed. Yet, even in the joyous procession, there are reminders of Jesus' uniqueness. He comes not in power, but "humble, and mounted on a donkey." Like the passage in Philippians, we see the entire scope of Jesus' life and ministry alluded to—he is both king and humble servant as he enters the town where he will meet his death.

Isaiah 50:4-9a

The Suffering Servant narratives in the book of Isaiah include many parallels with the narratives of Jesus' passion. The servant undergoes deep humiliation through persecution, as he states "I gave my back to those who struck me, and my cheeks to those who pulled out the beard; I did not hide my face from insult and spitting." Yet, even in the midst of the worst that his enemies have to offer, the servant remains faithful and "set [his] face like flint." Ultimately, the faithfulness of the servant is recognized and rewarded by God. The servant states, "it is the Lord GOD who helps me.... All of them will wear out life a garment; / the moth will eat them up." The grand sweep of self-giving, humiliation, and ultimate vindication parallels that found in the Philippians hymn.

Matthew 26:14–27:66

Matthew's account of the passion of Jesus includes many of the pivotal moments in his final days. The faithlessness and denial of Jesus' closest followers are contrasted with the faithfulness and obedience of Jesus. Jesus is shown as one who ultimately does the will of God even when faced with times of doubt, fear, desertion, misunderstanding, and persecution. These texts provide an opportunity for us to reflect upon Jesus' human struggles, and what it looked like for Jesus to "empty himself" of divine power and privilege. The story also provides us with a chance to reflect upon our own discipleship while looking at the struggles of Jesus' disciples. Do we have the same mind in us that was in Christ Jesus or will we deny, abandon, or forsake the way of our Lord? (Wendy Joyner)

Worship Aids

Call to Worship
Let us gather now to worship him who comes to us as king. The herald of God's salvation is in our midst. May we graciously receive this one who is mighty in deed, but also not what we expected, who comes into our midst lowly and meek.

Prayer of Confession
Eternal God, we confess this day that we are all too often caught up in the excitement and jubilation of the crowd. Our cries have become the same as theirs. We have become fickle, as we celebrate your salvation one moment and call for the death of your son in the next. Forgive us, we pray, and help us voice your will alone.

Words of Assurance

In the name of Jesus Christ, you are forgiven.
In the name of Jesus Christ, you are forgiven. Amen.

Benediction

Now may the same mind be in you that was in Christ Jesus. Through the gift of the Holy Spirit, may God bless you this day with strength, courage, humility, and compassion. May you be faithful as you seek to follow Jesus. Amen. (Wendy Joyner)

Listening for the Holy Spirit

Third in a Series of Three on Spiritual Disciplines

John 16:4b-11

I began this three-part series on spiritual disciplines with the idea that discipline is a path and not a punishment. Spirituality is an essential part of who we are as people of God. Spiritual discipline is an opportunity to strengthen and grow our spiritual self as well as our relationship with God and others. Such discipline is not undertaken because we must, but because we desire. It is a path and means of our choosing, not an arduous task of someone else's demand.

In part two, I focused on the discipline of fasting, a means of stepping off the merry-go-round of consumption and chaos. Fasting means focusing our life on something besides activity, entertainment, consumption, and self-satisfaction.

This third part of the series may feel like a Pentecost sermon, but it is a message that is relevant every season of the church year. We are daily in need of the power, guidance, and wisdom of the Holy Spirit, yet most of us do not discipline ourselves to "be still and know."

We wander about, sometimes aimlessly, sometimes purposefully, but whose direction are we following? Is the purposeful life one that follows our own direction, the self-made woman or man who is known for their accomplishments, acumen, wealth, or power? If we say that power and wealth are so important for us, then why not tap into the greatest and richest source of power humankind has ever known?

Jesus told us that he was leaving to be with the Father but that he would send the Advocate or Comforter who would help and guide us along our path as Christian disciples. It is this Comforter whom we need to know more, and to whom we must listen if we are to discover who we are and where we are going.

It was a Sunday morning when we gathered in the carpeted gym of the church's Family Life building. There was a long piece of green yarn that snaked across the room, around several chairs, through the handle of a two-wheeled cart dolly, and up on the stage, tied off at the railing of the ramp. Two student volunteers from the sixth grade Sunday school class each wore a blindfold and were led by the hand to the yarn. They were told that this was their lifeline. They were to follow it to its end. There would be obstacles along the way, they were warned. People could help them, but it was their life and they could accept, ignore, or even seek help from the nameless classmates who were placed strategically to keep them from harm.

When the exercise was over, we sat in a circle on the floor and talked about what had happened. The string represented our journey; the chairs, steps, and dolly, the obstacles that we encounter along the way. The class-mates were the presence of the Holy Spirit—encouraging, guiding, guard-ing, and prompting, but never forcing us to take a path.

One student got confused and started going the wrong way. He was moving backward on his journey. We do that, too. We allow the voices of others to distract us from our true path and calling. We may revert back to old ways, bad habits, lousy choices, and even dangerous lifestyles. The Holy Spirit is still there to help us, but we can be so con-vinced of our own self-sufficiency that we ignore divine guidance. For this reason, we require time apart from our daily routine. We can be too close to the route we are taking to see the larger picture of where we are headed. We must pause and look from a distance at our life and see where we are along our journey.

I took one month as a time for sabbatical. It was more than a vacation; it was Sabbath time. It was recreation, but in the form of being recreated and renewed during a time of intentional introspection, reflection, study, prayer, worship, travel, dialogue, interviews, and writing. I learned some-thing about myself and my life. I realized that change was required if I was to become the whole person of God whom I was intended to be.

I worshiped in many different towns, in many different churches, of various denominations. Through such an experience I discovered that faith is not limited to a certain type of church organization or even the-ology, but that spiritual nourishment can be found in many places and many cultures when we seek and open our souls to find.

There was a time when I heard the oft-repeated phrase, "Stop trying and start trusting," with little inspiration. It seemed rather trite to me, as if one simply could turn on a "belief switch" and make doubt turn into unrelenting faith. Then one day I grasped what it meant for me.

I was journaling—or attempting to journal—in my upstairs study. It is a great space to be, and a quiet retreat from the day, but there was no inspiration coming to or through me. I decided to stop trying to be inspired and tried to offer encouragement and inspiration to others. I began writing pastoral notes to people on our church prayer list. They were simple, handwritten, and from-the-heart letters that offered a word of hope to people who were struggling. "God is with you in your grief," "I am praying for you today," "You are surrounded by friends who care for you," were some of the sentiments I penned. Thirty minutes later, I felt a sense of relief and fulfillment. Rather than working for inspiration, I was inspired to be a source of inspiration and hope for others.

A friend's 100-year-old grandfather died recently following a brief illness. He was a vibrant and vital man all of his life. He had no need for dentures or eyeglasses. On the wall of his hospital room, he could read from his bed the plaque someone had given him in honor of his hundredth birthday. I especially liked his obituary that read, "He was active in his business until a week ago." That's how we ought to go! That is the sort of disciplined living that says, "I choose to celebrate and embrace life, rather than allow the detours and disappointments of life to determine my attitude." There are events, illness, and circumstances in life that we cannot control, but we are responsible for how we respond and live with what life gives us.

The red bird—a cardinal—that sits on the fence I can see from my window goes about its life doing what birds are supposed to do. With jerking motions, he cocks his head in all directions from his perch, lest some predator sneak up on him. He enjoys the breeze of this mild Texas springtime afternoon and knows that at his choosing he can lift his wings and fly off to destinations unknown to me. Discipline is a path, it is a way of living, and it is a gift from the Divine, the God whose grace sustains and redeems us. We humans have the opportunity to take a path of spiritual discipline in order to nourish ourselves. It is within our ability to do it. Like the cardinal up on the fence, if we choose not to use the skills we have been given, we may turn around to find that evil has come upon us because we failed to be still, to look, to listen. (Gary G. Kindley)

Worship Aids

Litany

Listen!
Whom are we listening for?
Listen for the Spirit!
How do we listen?
With open hearts and open minds.
Come, Holy Spirit, we are waiting and listening!

Prayer

How is it, O God, we can have two ears and technology to amplify sound, and yet we do not listen? How is it, O God, we can hear the sound of money and culture but ignore the voice of your Spirit? Shout to us, Holy Spirit, for we are a deaf people who need to hear a word from you. Amen.

Benediction

Listening can be a sign of faith. Listening can take courage. Listening can lead to change. Go forth to be the church, listening with faith and courage, prepared to act! (Gary G. Kindley)

MARCH 20, 2008

Holy Thursday

Readings: Exodus 12:1-14; Psalm 116:1-2, 12-19;
1 Corinthians 11:23-26; John 13:1-17, 31b-35

Which Basin Do You Choose?
John 13:1-17, 31b-35

Approaching his trial and death, Jesus had supper with his disciples. There was likely an underlying tension in the room because the disciples' feet were still dirty after the meal began. Lacking a servant, the disciples may have taken turns performing this important hospitality duty. Because, according to the other Gospels, the disciples had been arguing about who was the greatest and jostling for position, perhaps no one wanted to do servant's work.

The room must have grown silent with disbelief as Jesus stood up, removed his robe, put a towel around his waist, took up a basin of water and began to wash the disciples' feet. What is Jesus doing? That's a job for a servant! Peter tried to object, but Jesus made it clear that Peter must accept his foot washing and that he would soon understand. When Jesus finished and sat down, every eye must have been on him, awaiting an explanation. Jesus said, "Do you know what I have done to you? You call me Teacher and Lord—and you are right, for that is what I am. So if I, your Lord and Teacher, have washed your feet, you also ought to wash one another's feet." With a basin of water, Jesus demonstrated servanthood and called his disciples to follow his example.

Jesus gave a gift to his disciples and to the world that night: the gift of service. Service is a gift because it gives us a way to respond to God's love and because loving God and our neighbor enables us to live an abundant and joy-filled life. We need the gift of service as a way of blessing our world.

I remember when, at the age of ten, I first bought Christmas presents for my parents. They had been giving me presents all my life and had expressed their love in many other ways. I needed a way to give back to them. My grandmother paid me for helping her gather and sell pecans and then took me shopping so I could buy my own gifts for my parents. That gift from my grandmother was the most memorable because she gave me a way of expressing my love and gratitude through giving.

Jesus said, "Truly I tell you, just as you did it to one of the least of these who are members of my family, you did it to me" (Matthew 25:40). When we give a drink of water to the thirsty, visit someone who is sick or in prison, give clothes to one who is naked, or food to someone who is hungry, we do it to Jesus—that is how closely Jesus relates to the poor, the hungry, the naked, and the ill. The gift of service is the opportunity to respond to God's love by loving and serving those with whom Jesus identifies completely.

In his early days, Saint Francis of Assisi was quite wealthy and spent his time partying and acquiring as much as he could get, yet he was not happy. One day, riding alone in the country, he saw a leper with a mass of sores on his body. Francis was deeply moved. Instead of backing away in fear he got down off his horse and embraced the leper. In that moment the face of the leper became the face of Christ. Francis' life was transformed—as was the life of the leper—by the gift of service.

Jesus made clear the responsibility that accompanies the gift: "You also ought to wash one another's feet. For I have set you an example, that you also should do as I have done to you." What Jesus expects from his disciples is that we serve—that we take up the basin of service.

Matthew's Gospel tells of another basin wielded by a corrupt and cruel leader named Pontius Pilate, the Roman Governor. When the religious authorities brought Jesus to Pilate and demanded Jesus' crucifixion, Pilate knew what was right because his wife had reminded him that Jesus was righteous. Pilate took a basin of water, literally washed his hands of the matter, and handed Jesus over to be crucified (Matthew 27:1-24). History reveals however, that Pilate could not wash Jesus' blood off his own hands. Only Pilate—and not the Jews—had the power either to kill Jesus or to set him free. That is why we say in the Apostles' Creed that Jesus "suffered under Pontius Pilate." Pilate didn't drive the nails, but with a basin of apathy he killed Jesus.

Apathy is, after all, deadly. No wonder the early church leaders included sloth on their list of seven deadly sins. Sloth doesn't just mean "laziness." It means not caring enough to do anything. That describes the basin of Pilate. When we see the plight of a brother or sister in need and turn away, or when we know what is right and absolve ourselves of the responsibility, then we are choosing Pilate's basin.

Two basins were used within a few hours of each other: Pilate's and Jesus.' Holy Thursday is an especially appropriate time to ask ourselves the question again: *Which basin do I choose most consistently in my life? Do I give of myself and my money for the sake of others? Do I serve Christ by serving others in Christ's name? Do I care and put that caring into action? Which basin do I choose—the basin of service or the basin of Pilate?* The answer to that question makes all the difference in the world because the difference between Pilate's basin and Christ's basin is the difference between night and day. Service is the way of Christ because it brings peace where there is turmoil, love where there is hate, fulfillment where there is emptiness, and meaning where there is meaninglessness. Service is the mark of the Christian disciple.

There is an old legend—told in many faith traditions—of a person being granted a vision of heaven and hell. That vision confronts us with the truth of the difference between the two basins. The vision of hell is a huge banquet table loaded with all kinds of wonderful foods—everything good to eat that you can imagine. The problem is that the people around the table are starving to death. In their faces the dreamer sees pain and misery, for on their arms are splints holding their arms straight so they are unable to bend their elbows to get the food to their mouths.

Immediately another vision takes the individual to heaven and to his surprise he finds a room that looks exactly the same: the same table, the same delicious food, people sitting around the table. Only these people are happy. They are laughing and talking and enjoying one another's company. They also have splints on their arms. There is only one difference, and it's a big difference—the difference between night and day, the difference between the basin of Pilate and the Basin of Christ. The difference? They are feeding each other.

Which basin will you choose? (Tim K. Bruster)

Lectionary Commentary
Exodus 12:1-14

Right in the middle of the dramatic events leading up to the exodus, there is a pause to talk about remembrance and worship practices related to the events that are unfolding. The month of these events will become the first month—a new beginning each year. The saving events of liberation from slavery to a new inheritance will be commemorated in concrete ways as biblical memory is acted out in worship each year. Some of the elements of the first night of this worship practice will be: (1) the sacrifice of a lamb, its blood put it on the two doorposts and the lintel of the houses; (2) the sharing of the roasted lamb together with unleavened bread and bitter herbs; (3) eating the meal in a hurry and poised to leave with loins girded, sandals on, and staff in hand and, later in verse 26; (4) the inclusion of children in the service.

On Holy Thursday, we remember and enact one of those subsequent meals that Jesus and the disciples shared. In the Synoptic Gospels, Jesus redefines the elements of bread and wine. They become a remembrance of Christ's body broken and Christ's blood shed for our sake and for the sake of the world. In John's Gospel, Jesus is the Passover lamb who gives his life that we may be set free from slavery to sin and death and given abundant life. In John the meal shared with the disciples precedes Passover and includes Jesus washing the disciples' feet and calling on them to go and do the same. On Holy Thursday, we look back to the exodus and the cross and remember all God's mighty acts. We remember and celebrate the presence of Christ in the meal we share together. We share it with young and old alike—teaching the children about the power, grace, and love of God through the sacred meal. We eat it rather hurriedly, poised to go out from the gathering as free people: free to live abundantly, free to love extravagantly, and free to wash one another's feet—to serve in the name and spirit of Christ our servant.

1 Corinthians 11:23-26

It is clear from the preceding verses that not everyone in the Corinthian church is appropriately observing the worship practice Paul calls the Lord's Supper. It is evident that the Lord's Supper—at least in Corinth—is part of a complete meal, likely held in a home. Some are hoarding the food and becoming drunk so that others are going hungry. Paul even writes in verse 20, "When you come together, it is not really to eat the Lord's Supper." The practice has become marked by something that has nothing to do with Christ: selfish hoarding, the desire to be served instead of to serve, and lack of caring for the poor and hungry.

These attitudes don't belong to the kingdom feast. These attitudes are foreign to the life and teachings of Jesus and to the last meal Jesus shared with his disciples.

Interestingly, if Paul hadn't had this problem with the Corinthian church, he wouldn't have written to straighten it out, and we wouldn't have these words on the subject. But we do have them and they are instructive for our faith and worship life in the church today. Paul makes it clear in the verses preceding our lectionary text that the Lord's Supper is communal, not individual, and should make no distinction between the wealthy and the poor—between those who have the luxury of arriving early and those who do not, for example (see vv. 21-22). Paul then reminds them that what he received from the Lord and what he had earlier handed on to them: "The Lord Jesus on the night when he was betrayed took a loaf of bread, and when he had given thanks, he broke it and said, 'This is my body that is for you. Do this in remembrance of me.' In the same way he took the cup also, after supper, saying, 'This cup is the new covenant in my blood. Do this, as often as you drink it, in remembrance of me.' " Paul then reminds them that the meal is actually a proclamation: "For as often as you eat this bread and drink the cup, you proclaim the Lord's death until he comes." The importance of appropriate observance of the Lord's Supper is that the heart of the proclamation—the self-giving love of Jesus—be clearly seen and heard and experienced in the community of faith. (Tim K. Bruster)

Worship Aids

Call to Worship

As our Lord gathered his disciples on the night in which Jesus gave himself up for us, so we gather in Jesus' name and at his table. As our Lord took a basin of water and washed the feet of the disciples, so may we experience the presence and call of our servant Lord.

Prayer of Confession

Our gracious God, Jesus taught us to love you with all our heart, soul, mind, and strength, and our neighbors as ourselves. Jesus taught us to serve as he served. We confess that we have often failed to learn, and what we have learned we have often failed to put into practice. Forgive us, we pray, in the name of Jesus. Amen.

Words of Assurance

In the name of Jesus Christ, you are forgiven.
In the name of Jesus Christ, you are forgiven. Amen.

Benediction

Go and take up the basin of Christ, serving God and your neighbor in all that you do. And may the peace of Christ the servant be with you now and forevermore. Amen.

A Secret to Share

First in a Series of Two on Holy Week

Matthew 26:20-30

Walking through Holy Week is a precious opportunity to journey with Jesus through the streets of Jerusalem, through jeering crowds, through dinners of disappointment, all the way to the cross of death and despair. With those "joyous" thoughts in mind, we can hardly be surprised to find a smaller crowd on Holy Thursday worship than what we saw on Palm Sunday or hope to see on Easter Sunday. And yet, this journey, like so many other difficult journeys, brings an opportunity for growth that no easy road could offer.

When I was a child, I never attended a worship service between Palm Sunday and Easter. I don't think the church I attended even offered any such worship service in those days. I do remember always wondering where my dear Catholic friend Sharon was on that Friday before Easter. But I was far too busy decorating Easter eggs and choosing an Easter dress with my mother to worry all that much about Sharon's absence.

Then in my young adult years, I experienced my first Holy Thursday worship service. I loved it because it reminded me a bit of Christmas Eve. Only the faithful few were occupying the dark and quiet sanctuary, the people I knew as my mothers and fathers and sisters and brothers in the faith. The pastor invited us forward to tear off a piece of bread and dip it in the grape juice, something I found far superior to the wafers and cups we passed on Sunday mornings. To this day, I love communion by intinction. I love the way the bread soaks up the grape juice. I love the way the two tastes combine in my mouth and smoothly make their way down my throat into my body. Even now, Holy Thursday is easily my favorite time of worship in this six-week Lenten season.

In thinking about this day and all the memories I have of Last Supper dramas, foot-washing services, and Holy Thursday communions gathered around the communion table in a circle, I'm a bit awestruck. And a bit worried that I like keeping this secret to myself! I still enjoy that this is a worship service attended by the faithful few who are my closest and dearest sisters, brothers, children, and parents in the faith. I love that I know almost every person's name here and can call each one by name as the bread and cup are offered. Perhaps this is a secret to share. But in order to share this secret, we need to figure out what's so special about this night. What is it about this secret service that touches our spirits so profoundly that we would hurry home from work at the end of the week and stay out late to worship with our church family before returning to work and the Friday rush awaiting us early tomorrow morning?

Certainly, the intimacy of this night is precious. Much like the intimacy Jesus experienced in that Last Supper with the disciples, this is a time of quiet reflection and mysterious ponderings. No matter how many times we repeat the story, we are still puzzled by the journey that Jesus embarked upon. We wonder, as those first disciples wondered, why Jesus walks the road toward his own death. We wonder how all of that pain and despair relates to the lives that we live as Christians. We wonder which of the disciples we imitate on a daily basis. Am I the one who betrays, the one who denies, the one who hides, or the one who follows? "Surely not I" is more of a prayer than a question on this night, for this is a night to take a deep breath and wonder.

This is a night when our prayer is answered as we take the bread, dip it in the cup, and taste the strange dusty sweetness of bread and juice filling not only our mouths but also our very souls. For on this night, we are reminded that it is a dusty road through Jerusalem to the cross. And yet, it is tainted with sweetness, for at the end of this road is not so much death as love. At the end of this road is a Christ who loved us so much that compassion and forgiveness were Jesus' guiding laws. At the end of this road is a God who loved his own Son so much that resurrection, not death, was the final word. Indeed, this bread is not just Christ's life, but our very lives. This cup is filled not just with juice, but with the compassion and forgiveness and love that only God could offer so completely that it soaks through every pore of our lives.

This is a night that is precious. To walk with Jesus on this part of the journey is a profound gift. To know that even though the road is dusty and hard, Jesus chose this road and walks it with us. To know that even though the journey includes death and despair, God offers new life and hope as the final destination. This is something magnificent on our Lenten journey. This is a secret not to be kept, but to be shared. This is a night to remember all year long and to carry in our hearts as strength for the journey we live each day. When next we gather for this precious night, may we gather with a few more friends who want to know the secret gift of bread soaked in juice, life infused with forgiveness, compassion, and love. (Mary J. Scifres)

Worship Aids

Call to Worship

Come to the table, for all things are ready.
Come to the feet of Jesus to worship and remember.
Come to this holy evening with hearts open to the holiness
of God.
Come to this holy worship with trust that Christ is with us.
Come to the table, for all things are ready.

Invocation

Loving God, as we come into your presence, surround us with your Holy Spirit. Fill us with your nourishing grace that always fulfills. Open our hearts and minds to hear your Word and to receive the nourishment you offer.

Pastoral Prayer

God of humility and grace, walk with us through this Holy Week journey. Gather us at your table, and fill us with your grace. Help us live as people who serve and love. Guide us to be disciples who stay awake, even through dark and troubling times. Strengthen us to be disciples who are steadfast and true. In Jesus' name, we pray. Amen. (Mary J. Scifres)

MARCH 21, 2008

❧❧❧

Good Friday

Readings: Isaiah 52:13–53:12; Psalm 22; Hebrews 4:14-16, 10:16-25;
John 18:1–19:42

Remorse and Resurrection
John 18:1–19:42

Guilt, regret, remorse: Jesus' first disciples experienced these emotions
powerfully. Following the arrest of their Lord and friend, the disciples
scattered—just as Jesus said they would. It was even worse for Peter, however, because when Jesus said that they all would scatter, Peter rather
arrogantly said, in effect, "Not me, Lord! They may all go running, but
not me! I would never desert you." Jesus quietly told Peter right there in
front of everybody that in fact he would deny him three times before the
rooster crowed. Sure enough, when the rooster crowed at daybreak on
Friday, Peter had done just that.

Can't you imagine that Peter was haunted by every little detail of that
awful night? He could remember the supper with Jesus, Jesus washing the
disciples' feet and insisting that they follow Jesus and do the same. Peter
remembered crossing the Kidron Valley to the Garden of Gethsemane,
the soldiers and police approaching with their lanterns and torches and
weapons, drawing his sword in panic and cutting off the right ear of the
high priest's slave and Jesus' strange words, "Put your sword back into its
sheath. Am I not to drink the cup that the Father has given me?" And,
of course the arrest of Jesus.

Peter especially remembered the courtyard of Caiaphas, the high priest.
When the woman guarding the gate said, "You are not also one of this
man's disciples, are you?" He heard himself say, "I am not." Peter could
remember the charcoal fire burning in the courtyard and trying to fit in
with the others warming themselves by the fire. In his memory he could
still smell that fire, hear its crackle, feel its warmth, and see its light

causing shadows to dance all around. Peter could hear the question being asked again; "You are not also one of his disciples, are you?" He could hear himself say a second time, "I am not." Peter could hear one of the slaves ask him, "Did I not see you in the garden with him?" A third time he could hear himself deny Jesus. He would never forget the sound of that rooster crowing after his third denial. He remembered seeing his friend and Lord being led by in shackles and their eyes meeting for a brief moment. What a horrible memory! Nothing, Peter must have thought, could erase the pain, guilt, and remorse he felt. It was forever burned into his memory.

Mark's Gospel gives us a clue about how bad it may have been for Peter. When the women discovered the empty tomb on Easter morning, a young man sitting in the tomb dressed in a white robe announced that Jesus had risen and then he said, "But go, tell his disciples and Peter that he is going ahead of you to Galilee" (Mark 16:7). Why "his disciples . . . and Peter?" Had Peter removed himself from the group? Had Peter's denial been too much for him to take? Maybe it was that Peter no longer considered himself worthy to be called a disciple and to be a part of the group. It was very difficult for Peter. His remorse burned like a charcoal fire as every detail of that awful night came to mind. How in the world could Peter ever receive forgiveness and be restored? For that matter, how can we?

In Luke's Gospel Jesus prayed for forgiveness for all those who crucified him and who participated in his crucifixion (23:34). Jesus gave himself completely that we might have forgiveness and new and abundant life. Good Friday is called good because of this amazing grace and love of God in Christ. But, how does forgiveness come? I believe it comes to us something like it did for Simon Peter—through the experience of the resurrected Christ. The end of the Gospel of John brings the wonderful continuation of Simon Peter's story as he experiences the resurrected Christ. Following the death and resurrection of Jesus, the disciples retreated to the familiar—they went fishing. They fished all night and caught nothing. Just as day was breaking, they saw a stranger on the beach who said to them, "Children, you have no fish, have you?" They answered him, "No." He said to them, "Cast the net to the right side of the boat, and you will find some" (John 21:5-6a). This time their net was teeming with fish and the disciple John turned to Peter and said, "It is the Lord!" Always impulsive, Simon Peter jumped into the water and headed toward shore, while the more reserved disciples steered the boat on in.

When they got to the shore they saw a charcoal fire Jesus had built. He was cooking breakfast for them. The Greek word translated "charcoal" is used only one other place in all of Scripture—for the fire in Caiaphas's courtyard. When Peter sees the fire, hears it crackling in the semi-light of dawn, smells it burning, feels its warmth and sees its light dancing on the face of Jesus, what do you suppose Peter thought of? As the roosters began to crow in the Galilean countryside what do you suppose was on Simon Peter's mind?

I believe Christ carefully set up the whole scene to bring to Simon Peter the healing of memories and forgiveness. Simon Peter had three times denied even knowing Jesus and Jesus gave him the opportunity to say three times, "Lord, you know that I love you." The whole event was tailored to meet Peter's need for forgiveness—as it called to mind Caiaphas's courtyard and his denial. The sight, sound, and smell of the charcoal fire in the semi-darkness of early dawn would call to mind the darkest moment in Simon Peter's life. But, it would call that dark moment to his mind for one purpose: to bring forgiveness and healing to Peter's troubled soul. Jesus loved Simon Peter and reached out to him in just the way he needed at that moment in his life.

The good news is that the Lord loves you and me that much today! Saint Augustine said, "God loves you as if you were the only one in the world to love." Christ loves us in just that way. Christ knows our needs, he knows our pain, he knows our sin, he knows our joys, he knows our sorrows, and he loves us each one as individuals. The risen Christ gave Simon Peter just what he needed for his estrangement and painful memories. Then, they broke bread together—always a sign of reconciliation and peace and friendship.

Jesus' forgiveness and reconciliation was transforming for Peter and his forgiveness still transforms today! (Tim K. Bruster)

Lectionary Commentary
Isaiah 52:13–53:12

This passage is the final of the four Servant Songs in Isaiah. It is really a song of triumph, beginning and ending with the exaltation of the servant of Yahweh. The interpretations of this song vary widely in both the Jewish and Christian traditions and most commentators discuss multiple meanings. The song is reminiscent of psalms of thanksgiving and focuses on God's work in the world. The identity of the servant changes among the Servant Songs and other references to the servant, depending on the passage. Sometimes the servant is Israel, sometimes a subgroup of Israel, and sometimes an individual called by God to serve the people of God.

While the song does begin and end with a word of triumph, the path to the exaltation of the servant is the path of suffering and death for "our sake." This can be—and has been—understood as either for the sake of Israel in exile or for the sake of the nations. It isn't clear who is speaking in the first person plural. Likewise, the identity of the servant can be—and has been—understood either collectively as Israel or individually as a person called by God to fulfill this role. The suffering of this servant is appalling to everyone who reads it. Yet, the servant carries the infirmities and diseases of the people, is wounded—even crushed—for the sins of the people and takes on the punishment for everyone. The suffering, however, brings healing to everyone. It is a prophetic message of hope to a people in exile whose central traditions and institutions were destroyed by a cruel foreign power. Understood collectively, the suffering the people are undergoing in exile is ultimately redemptive both for them and for the world. Understood as an individual, the Suffering Servant answers the need of Israel in the face of their persistent sin that led to the exile and the need for forgiveness and restoration. Because the people have not turned from their evil ways, God accomplishes atonement in a way that is shocking—by allowing the punishment to fall on a single innocent person. It is, as Isaiah puts it, "a perversion of justice," yet the people are restored through this sacrifice of this servant who is close to the heart of God.

Christians see Christ and his self-giving in this Suffering Servant who takes on the sins of the whole word for the redemption of the world.

Hebrews 4:14-16; 10:16-25

In both of these passages, the writer of Hebrews uses imagery from the sacrificial system of temple worship. The writer compares and contrasts both the sacrificial practices and the priesthood with the work of Christ. Rather than continual animal sacrifices, Jesus has made one sacrifice that accomplishes forgiveness of sin once and for all. The writer of Hebrews brings to mind Jeremiah 31:33-34, in which the Lord promises a covenant written on the heart and that the Lord will "remember their sins and their lawless deeds no more" (Hebrews 10:17). The communal nature of this understanding comes through clearly. The writer uses the first person plural to describe the meaning of Jesus' work in our lives. The writer calls the community of faith to mutual accountability and encouragement, as well: "Let us consider how to provoke one another to love and good deeds, not neglecting to meet together, as is the habit of some, but encouraging one another." Finally, there is an escatological urgency.

The understanding of Jesus as the great high priest is at the heart of Hebrews. Not only has this great high priest "passed through the heavens," but the high priest also is able "to sympathize with our weaknesses" and who "in every respect has been tested as we are, yet without sin." This comes close to expressing the classic theological formula: fully divine and fully human. Although fully divine, Jesus experienced what we experience and therefore understands fully the struggles, temptations, joys, and sorrows we share. While God is holy, that is, "different" or "other than," Hebrews says that God is intimately involved in humanity and fully understands what our lives are like. (Tim K. Bruster)

Worship Aids

Call to Worship

Go to dark Gethsemane, ye that feel the tempter's power;
Your Redeemer's conflict see, watch with him one bitter hour,
Turn not from his griefs away; learn of Jesus Christ to pray.
("Go to Dark Gethsemane" by James Montgomery)

Prayer

Our gracious God, with deep gratitude we acknowledge that you set before us a table loaded with the food of love, mercy, forgiveness, and new life. You ask only that we feast, that we are transformed, and that we go from this place to feed others the food that has given us life. In the name of Christ we pray. Amen.

Benediction

Go forth in silence, remembering God's grace poured out for you in Jesus Christ. Thanks be to God for this indescribable gift! In the name of the Father, the Son, and the Holy Spirit. Amen. (Tim K. Bruster)

Walking in the Light

Second in a Series of Two on Holy Week

Matthew 27:24-26, 45-54

As we journey through Holy Week, we are invited into some of the darkest and most troubling moments in Jesus' life. Surely today's story is the darkest and most troubling of all. A holy man of God, who spent three years of his life preaching and teaching, healing and caring, is put to death. Not a very fitting end to a life of compassion and kindness, is it?

Yet that ending is too often the story of so many who bring light to our world. It is almost as if the very light that they bring offends and must be snuffed out. We could compose long lists of the early church martyrs who followed in Jesus' footsteps as people offering compassion and healing only to face brutal deaths. In modern times, great leaders like Martin Luther King Jr. and Mahatma Gandhi have been assassinated cruelly. When we think of such deaths, we are tempted to think that the assassins and the politicians who would cause such deaths are evil or crazy, nothing like the rest of us. Likewise, when we read the stories of this last week of Jesus' life, we are tempted to think that disciples who betray and deny are weak willed or filled with evil sinfulness, nothing like the rest of us. The gift of this Holy Week journey is to remember not only Jesus' story but also the story of the disciples and the politicians. For in this story, we are invited to learn valuable lessons from each person's place on this journey.

On the disciples' journey, we see fear ruling the day. Judas betrays, Peter denies, others fall asleep or hide. Betrayal and denial and fear are not unfamiliar themes in today's world. If we each took a few minutes, I suspect all of us could come up with several stories in our own lives when we betrayed or were betrayed, when we denied someone's importance in our lives or were denied by someone important to us. Living up to our relationship commitments with unwavering loyalty is no easy task. Living up to our ethical and spiritual commitments with similar dedication is a mighty challenge. On this journey to the cross, I am reminded of many places where I need forgiveness for betraying and denying. On this journey of life, fear too often haunts my steps and guides my actions. These are the aspects of my life that need Christ's forgiveness, coupled with the Spirit's strength if I am to walk as a disciple of Jesus with steadfast faithfulness.

When I journey as a follower of Christ with that steadfast faithfulness, however, I run right into the all-too-familiar theme of being light in a dark world that too often wants to thrive on that darkness. I love thinking I might occasionally be a bit Christlike in my life. After all, that is a major goal of the Christian journey, is it not? But being extinguished doesn't sound inviting, and having our light extinguished is not something that only happens to great saints of God. Even everyday disciples like you and me run the risk of being an affront to people who are frightened of the light. We are called to be the light of Christ in this dark world. But shining light into dark closets or shadowy corners where people hide their fears and inadequacies, their darkest secrets and sins, is dangerous work. For light that reveals truth is never an easy light to face. Even light that reveals love and forgiveness where we are harboring anger and hate can seem offensive.

Knowing all of this, Jesus went on preaching and teaching, healing on the Sabbath, and including the excluded. We are challenged as followers of Christ to do the same. Knowing the painful death he would face, Jesus journeyed to Jerusalem even as that journey ended at the cross. We are challenged on this day to find the strength to walk this journey with Jesus. We are promised that we can walk this journey because of Christ's compassion and love for us. When we betray or deny, when we accuse or crucify, we are still invited into the brilliant light of God's forgiveness. When we are afraid or want to hide, God's Holy Spirit offers us strength and courage to endure whatever may transpire on this journey. When we live this journey as disciples who walk all the way to the cross, who truly strive to walk in the way of Christ Jesus, we make this Friday truly good. We make Jesus' teachings come alive. We make Christ's sacrifice a worthwhile gift rather than a tragic demise.

May we walk as disciples who are steadfast and true, who are filled with light and love, and who offer forgiveness and compassion as readily as we receive these gifts. May we trust in the Easter joy of new life and hope even as we embrace the reality of Friday's death and despair. (Mary J. Scifres)

Worship Aids

Prayer of Confession

Christ of compassion and kindness, we confess that often we avoid this Friday because we want to feel good. On this Good Friday, forgive us for seeking after feelings that flee and things that don't satisfy. Help us embrace the goodness of this day. Help us embrace the peace and joy that your compassion and love offer to us. In your gracious name, we pray. Amen.

Words of Assurance

Know that our good God has given every good thing to us, forgiveness and love being the greatest gifts of all. Know without a doubt that these good gifts, forgiveness and love, are ours to claim through Jesus Christ. Amen.

Benediction

Go forth with Easter hope in your heart. As we live in the darkness of death's shadow, may we still be a people who know the light and love of Christ Jesus. (Mary J. Scifres)

MARCH 23, 2008

❧❧❧

Easter Sunday

Readings: Acts 10:34-43; Psalm 118:1-2, 14-24; John 20:1-18; Colossians 3:1-4

Named and Claimed
John 20:1-18

We have all walked "tomb-ward" like Mary, on a morning of defeat or despair or deep grief. Pick up the daily paper. Evidence that evil is growing, death reigns, and sin is triumphant is splashed across the front page. It is not the newspaper's fault. That is just life. Defeat, despair, and deep grief are all around us and yes, within us. I recall walking into the hospital in Corpus Christi years ago and encountering a fellow pastor, now a retired bishop. We exchanged greetings. I asked why he was there. He shared a tale of a member of his church battling serious illness. In responding to his queries, I spoke of a beloved grandmother in my congregation slowly dying of cancer. He sighed and said, "Every family has some kind of heartache or tragedy they have to battle." I concurred.

In the joy of Easter morning, we must start where the biblical story does, with a journey to the tomb. We all know what it is like to walk that road with Mary. It is as ancient as the first Easter and as contemporary as today. The reality of defeat, despair, and grief are as near as the loss of loved ones in accidents, the heartache of a child gone astray, the sinking feeling of never quite measuring up, and the deep grief of death. The reality of such a tomb-ward journey is as global as the tragic loss of life in conflict or a hurricane hitting the shore. Mary's journey that morning is our journey on many a morning.

In life's all-too-common journeys, we encounter small signs of a great victory. Those signs were there on that first Easter. The Bible says, "Mary Magdalene came to the tomb and saw that the stone had been removed from the tomb." She does not understand its meaning. She runs to get others. She jumps immediately to the common supposition that "They have taken the Lord out of the tomb, and we do not know where they have laid him."

Whatever else is to be said, at this point it is clear that the grave is not the end. I remember a colleague telling of pausing in a cemetery after he had finished a funeral. He looked at a massive stone crypt set near where he had just concluded the service. Clear, specific instructions had been left. "Not to be opened upon any circumstance" was chiseled on the stone door facing of the crypt. And yet, there it was. The tiny shoot of a plant, possibly a tree in the making, had slowly but inexorably forced the door of the crypt open. A shaft of light was streaming in.

So it is for us this day. A shaft of light breaks through the darkness. Mary struggles to believe; so too do Peter and the other disciple as they peer in to examine what is left behind. They examine the grave like befuddled detectives, one starting to believe; the other, Peter, clearly not knowing what to make of the empty tomb.

We are so like them that at times it is painful. We believe, and yet we are overwhelmed in grief and loss. We believe, and yet we shake our heads at how awful the world is. We believe and yet ... we are not sure. We believe, and see small signs of a great victory.

Notice what the disciples and Mary did. They relegated the extraordinary—the stone rolled and the tomb empty—to the ordinary. They sought to explain it all with a sensible supposition—the body has been taken. All the while they confronted massive evidence of the truth. Christ has been raised from the dead. Death and sin are conquered. Belief dawns slowly with the light. The Bible says, "For as yet they did not understand the scripture, that he must rise from the dead."

This too is our struggle. Small signs of this colossal victory are all around us. Mary and the two disciples of that first Easter morning would teach us to look for signs of the extraordinary in the ordinary. In love shared, in care given, with hope amid despair, and laughter in the place of grief, comes the dawning of belief. One of the followers gets it. "Then the other disciple, who reached the tomb first, also went in, and he saw and believed." Let that be us. Begin to see the extraordinary—God in resurrection action—amid the ordinary.

In a scene that could be taken from any cemetery, Mary encounters the triumphant Jesus. It is so ordinary that she, at first, doesn't recognize him. She thinks Jesus is the gardener.

It is important for both proclaimer and listener to pause and catch the full impact of what is being said. Jesus is first encountered near the tomb! Angels are inside the tomb, at the very epicenter of defeat, proclaiming the triumph. We encounter Jesus first, often best, at the very place of our defeat, despair, and deep grief. Where we struggle to believe, God is most present. Where we have come to the end of our resources, there God breaks through in triumph.

Focused on her grief, Mary teeters on the edge of faith. "Sir, if you have carried him away, tell me where you have laid him, and I will take him away." Then the full impact of the gospel hits. "Jesus said to her, 'Mary!'" In the naming, she is claimed by the Lord. Christ's triumph becomes her destiny! Our morning begins in a graveyard. It ends in a shout. "I have seen the Lord."

Our path of faith is similar. Near the tombs of our life, be they physical or symbolic, we are named and claimed by the risen Lord. Lift your head when defeat, despair, and deep grief settle in. Look for the triumph of Christ. It is at hand. You are named and claimed.

Death is defeated. Oh, to be sure, death is real. Jesus wept by a grave and so should we. Our grief is a sign of our love, but it is not the end. The story is not finished. Through the triumph of Christ, "in life, in death, in life beyond death God is with us. We are not alone" (The New Creed). The Lord names you and claims you this day!

Sin is conquered. Oh, to be sure, sin is still with us. We know the pain of its wounds too well. But it does not have the final word over your life or mine. Sin remains, but it no longer reigns. However scarred and marred your past, the triumphant Lord of the resurrection offers new life for you this day. In triumph, you are named and claimed. (Mike Lowry)

Lectionary Commentary
Acts 10:34-43

This passage is Peter's great kerygmatic sermon. Its designation for Easter is appropriate, because it offers the core gospel message. Contextually, it comes in response to the inquiries of the Roman centurion Cornelius. Peter launches into the sermon with the stunning confession, "I truly understand that God shows no partiality." It is as radical a message today as it was then. The lesson of Peter's vision is now clear. Christ has been raised as the redemption of all. Easter is not just about resurrection but also forgiveness and new life in Christ now.

Scholars note that the passage follows the standard outline of many kerygmatic sermons in Acts—proclamation, scriptural evidence, and summons to repent and believe. Peter's bold assertion, "he is Lord of all," forms the basis of the conversion to inclusiveness. The affirmation of who Christ is propels Christians to reach out to all people. Failure to reach out is to deny the very lordship of Christ.

Colossians 3:1-4

The Epistle lesson for Easter morning rings with an opening affirmation. We have been raised with Christ! The whole passage reverberates on this towering proclamation. It was an early Christian practice to baptize new converts on Easter morning. Thus, many scholars see in this passage of dying and rising a baptismal reference. Exegetically the affirmation forms a bridge to how one ought to live as a child of the resurrection.

Twice we are admonished and encouraged to refocus our living based on the truth of the resurrection. This is not another worldly preoccupation but a theological conviction that with Christ's rising, baptized Christians are citizens of eternity. We are in the world but not of it. With the resurrection, the old has died and a new way of living is born. Verse 4 closes with an eschatological reference. Christ is the hope of glory for people of the resurrection. (Mike Lowry)

Worship Aids

Call to Worship

Whom do you seek at the tomb?
We seek Jesus of Nazareth.
He is not here; He is risen!
He is risen, indeed!

Prayer of Confession

Lord God who triumphed over sin and death, we confess to you our casual disbelief. Despite the celebration of this day, there have been times and places we doubted the truth of your resurrection. We have succumbed to sin. We have embraced defeat. We have submitted to despair. Forgive, we pray, the timidity of our faith. Free us from the chains of doubt and despair. Deliver us into the joy of eternal life through Christ our risen Lord. Amen.

Words of Assurance

Hear the good news! "Death has been swallowed up in victory.... The sting of death is sin, and the power of sin is the law. But thanks be to God, who gives us the victory through our Lord Jesus Christ" (1 Corinthians 15:54, 56-57) Christ is risen and goes before you. (Mike Lowry)

Glimpses of Easter

First in a Series of Two on Easter

Colossians 1:18-20

Martin Luther wrote, "Our God has written the truth of resurrection not in books alone, but on every leaf of springtime."

We can find the truth of resurrection in books, our Bibles as well as the volumes of spiritual and theological books in our homes, churches, offices, and libraries.

And at this time of the year as Luther pointed out, nature proclaims it too. Spring buds break forth from dry branches; shy pastel flowers emerge from winter-hard dirt and newborn grass; and leaves spring forth in that shiny, yellow-green newness that is only born in the spring.

I believe though, that God has written the truth of resurrection in a few other places as well. I see it on people's faces and in certain momentary glimpses that remind me over and over again of God's power to make all things new.

"Jeff, will you have Susan to be your wife?" I look into the groom's eyes. My mind flashes back to a pastoral counseling session eighteen months earlier. I remember looking into those same eyes, filled with tears and rocked with grief after Jeff's first wife's sudden death. Jeff did not know which way to turn. He did not know how he would go on. He was lost. And yet now, somehow, new life and a new relationship emerged.

I look at the bride. "Susan, will you have Jeff to be your husband?" Susan is a survivor too. For years she endured an abusive first marriage. In much pain and fear and with great struggle, she finally shed that destructive relationship and stepped into a life on her own, not knowing what the future would hold. Now, somehow, new life has been born where she least expected it.

I look down and into the baby blue eyes of little Anna as she stands between the bride and groom. She was once an abandoned infant living in a foreign nation's orphanage. Now she is a radiant flower girl with a new mommy and daddy. "Anna, do you take Jeff and Susan to be your parents?"

New life, resurrection, always seems to affect me the same way. It surprises me. It takes my breath away. It causes a lump in my throat. I'm left speechless and amazed. I find myself wanting to run and share the news with someone else, "You are not going to believe this! Guess what just happened?"

I've seen glimpses of new life in so many unexpected places, and you have too:

- in dwindling churches that discover a fresh mission
- in people deeply hurt by life who manage to turn that very hurt into a ministry
- in families where relationships have been cut off and yet, somehow, connection begins again
- in individuals who believe they are empty, used up, and find, surprisingly, a new bud of life emerging where they least expected it

In one particular week in our church, we experienced two tragic, sudden deaths within our church family. Our congregation was rocked with grief and certainly the particular families were devastated. In the course of that week, countless meals were delivered, tears shed, visits made. We had two very large funerals. I remember at the end of that week, being drained from the sorrow and the pastoral load, returning to my office and finding a freshly baked loaf of bread sitting on my desk. It was still warm and the fragrance of it filled the room. It was from a church member and had a thank-you note attached. It surprised me, this gift. It took my breath away, the fragrance of it. I sat at my desk alone, broke the bread and ate it, reflecting on the wonder of the body of Christ. Each bite of that warm, soft bread ushered a bit of new life into my soul.

Eugene Peterson paraphrases our text from Colossians:

> Christ was supreme in the beginning and—leading the resurrection parade—he is supreme in the end. From beginning to end he's there, towering far above everything, everyone. So spacious is he, so roomy, that everything of God finds its proper place in him without crowding. Not only that, but all the broken and dislocated pieces of the universe—people and things, animals and atoms—get properly fixed and fit together in vibrant harmonies. (*The Message*)

Christian songwriter and singer Bebo Norman says it in his own way, "The God of second chances will pick them up and let them dance / through a world that is not kind" ("A Page Is Turned").

Those are all amazing Easter images: a resurrection parade, the God of second chances picking us up, letting us dance, a Christ so spacious and roomy that all that is broken and dislocated in the universe has hope of new life, wholeness, being properly fixed.

The truth of resurrection is so real, so central to life and faith that we can only take it in, I think, in glimpses. We can only behold such an awesome truth in little doses.

This Easter I will take my resurrection snippets as they come: in the shiny eyes of a child adopted into a family, a church with a fresh mission, a new bud on the branch, a life going one direction now turned slightly in another direction, a bite of warm bread, and a stone rolled away. And each time I glimpse resurrection—breathless, speechless, and amazed—I will try to find a way to say an Easter thank-you to the God of second chances. (Cindy Guthrie Ryan)

Worship Aids

Invocation

God, here and there, in springtime signs all around us, we see the wonder of the resurrection. Show us again and again, the Easter hope. Open our eyes; open our hearts; we don't want to miss Easter. Amen

Litany

New life is all around us.

We see it in the leaves, the flowers, and the new green grass of springtime.

We see it in the eyes of a new believer.

We see it in a relationship healed, a grief comforted, a hope renewed.

All: We celebrate new life all around us. Alleluia. Amen.

Benediction

As we leave this place, turn our attention to each leaf, each flower of springtime. Wake us up so we might celebrate Easter over and over again. Amen. (Cindy Guthrie Ryan)

MARCH 30, 2008

✥✥✥

Second Sunday of Easter

Readings: Acts 2:14a, 22-32; Psalm 16; 1 Peter 1:3-9; John 20:19-31

Resurrection Reality
John 20:19-31

Do you remember how Walter Cronkite used to close his broadcast by saying, "And that's the way it is"? Such is a world vision that reflects the painfulness of reality. It is an echoing of the somber words of agnostic Bertrand Russell: "Brief and powerless is Man's life; on him and all his race the slow, sure doom falls pitiless and dark."

Life on Easter evening for the disciples opens in a somber, fearful mood. John reports, "When it was evening on that day, the first day of the week, and the doors of the house where the disciples had met were locked for fear of the Jews." Huddled behind locked doors, the followers of Jesus are struggling with the reality of the resurrection.

Today, we struggle with reality. In fact the biggest venue on television is the genre of so-called reality TV. I've got this great idea for reality TV. It would be the ultimate survivor show. Take a guy who is obviously a religious fanatic. So much so that he believes he's the messiah, the savior of the world. Then you could have authorities who are out to get him. Let's say they succeed and put him to death. But how's this? He rises from the dead after three days. Now that is a survivor! His reality changes our reality. He didn't just survive. He triumphed! Now that is real reality, resurrection reality. It is way beyond the survivor. Now comes the really great part; you can be a part of the show.

Resurrection reality takes us way beyond the survivor. "Peace be with you," the Savior said. Jesus offers reality that is so much better than just struggling to survive. In resurrection reality, our Lord and Savior offers a spiritual peace that triumphs in the midst of the raging storms of modern living. Reality TV says that the purpose of life is to claw your way ahead, to do everything you possibly can to make money, to win in the end, to survive by being number one regardless of what happens to others. Resurrection reality with Jesus offers a purpose that is far beyond just looking out for number one or just advancing your career or just earning money.

Jesus said, "As the Father has sent me, so I send you." Resurrection reality is about living your life to the mighty purposes of God. It is about advancing the kingdom of God through evangelistic witness and the deeds of love and mercy.

Reality television is about living life for insignificant goals. Resurrection reality is about the opposite—living life for the greatest goal of all, the advancement of God's kingdom here on earth, the sharing of the gospel of Jesus Christ by words and deeds. To what purpose are you living? Is it reality TV or resurrection reality?

One thing that strikes me is how powerless reality TV seems to be. People work hard to survive, but only one makes it. You can be voted off the island through no fault of your own. The only energy you have is your own energy; and when that is spent, when you've reached the end of your rope, you are out of luck.

Resurrection reality is just the opposite. It is not all up to you. Jesus "breathed on them and said to them, 'Receive the Holy Spirit. If you forgive the sins of any, they are forgiven them; if you retain the sins of any, they are retained.' "

Many of us live with the functional atheism of reality TV. Resurrection reality is completely contrary to that. It is living in the conviction that God is not asleep or in a coma but will act with you and through you, empowering you to accomplish the impossible for God's kingdom. We are not alone. God is with us, in history and in our lives, transforming them with a resurrection reality. "Receive the Holy Spirit."

Which do you choose? Will you live on your own power, exhausted and struggling, or will you open yourself to the mighty power of God?

Peace, purpose, power—three things we all desperately need. TV reality offers no peace, only the running of the rat race. It offers no purpose beyond the accumulation of money, place, or pleasure. It offers no power beyond your own limited resources. Resurrection reality offers peace for a purpose with power. It breaks through locked doors and banishes fear. This can be yours. You won't be voted off the island but rather have reality shaped day by day and moment by moment through the risen Lord and

Savior who, in the power of the Holy Spirit, stands in our midst this hour. (Mike Lowry)

Lectionary Commentary
Acts 2:14a, 22-32

This segment from Peter's Pentecost sermon shares the core kerygmatic confession of who Jesus is. It follows the pattern of such affirmations by detailing what Jesus has done, his crucifixion and death in fulfillment of the scriptures, and his resurrection. There is an uncompromising proclamation of Jesus as the Christ. The Gentiles may have been the instruments of Jesus' death, but the Israelites were responsible for it. There is a deliberate, almost crude, contrast between the Israelites killing in verse 23 and God's raising up in verse 24. Verses 25 through 28 quote Psalm 16:8-11. Peter follows by asserting that Jesus is the fulfillment of this messianic hope to whom David could only at best point.

1 Peter 1:3-9

The great resurrection theme of Easter morning continues in full force. This text is a blessing addressed to God in fulsome praise and gratitude. Within the blessing are the great themes that will be explored in the letter—salvation and new birth, joy and perseverance in trials, a living hope and inheritance. It is all put in the context of worship with a language directed upward to God.

The sermonic outline might begin in praise of the resurrection based on verses 3 and 4. It might then unpack key concepts: new birth, living hope, imperishable inheritance, the triumph of God through Christ. The context of 1 Peter is framed by trials and suffering. The great resurrection promise is much greater than a simple feel-good mentality. You are receiving the outcome of your faith in salvation. (Mike Lowry)

Worship Aids

Call to Worship
> Peace be with you.
> **And with you also.**
> The risen Christ is with us.
> **All: We are not alone! Thanks be to God!**

Prayer of Confession

Lord God, we confess to huddling behind locked doors. We know the truth of your resurrection and yet distrust its peace, spurn its purpose, and reject its power for our lives. Forgive our failure to fully embrace your presence. Transform our doubt into vibrant faith and compassionate sharing. We pray in the name of our risen Lord, Amen.

Words of Assurance

Receive the good news! The risen Christ stands among us and says, "Peace be with you ... receive the Holy Spirit." In the name of Jesus Christ your sins are forgiven! Thanks be to God! (Mike Lowry)

Why Are You Surprised?

Second in a Series of Two on Easter

Acts 3:1-16

A bit of amazing new life is described in the book of Acts. Peter and John are on their way to the temple. At the same time, scripture tells us, someone is carrying a man with a disability to the temple gate so he may beg from those going to the temple. This is a daily occurrence, we are told.

The beggar asks Peter and John for a handout. They look the man in the eye and heal him. The man jumps to his feet and walks. Then he goes into the temple. And, not only does he walk, he dances and praises God! Everyone, the scripture says, is astonished and can't believe it. Peter, never missing a great preaching opportunity, looks at the people and says, in so many words, "Why are you surprised? This is God we are talking about. Faith in Jesus Christ made this happen. Why are you surprised?" I'm pretty sure if I somehow became a part of this text, I would be in the crowd and not in the pulpit. I would be one of the amazed multitudes with my mouth open wide in disbelief. I would be murmuring to my friends, "That can't be the one with the disability over there dancing ... it just can't be!" I would be rubbing my eyes, trying to shake myself awake. New life surprises me every time. When my children were born, even though I'd been anticipating their births for months, when the actual time of birth arrived, I was shocked. When I held my firstborn daughter for the first time, I found myself astonished and breathless. I marveled over her soft newborn skin, her tiny little fingers and toes, and looked into her little face for hours. I still can't quite believe it. Looking at her still takes my breath away and I've had seventeen years to absorb that miracle.

When spring arrives and green grass emerges from the brown, dead grass, it amazes me. When tiny buds pop out on bare branches and daffodils poke out from under cold, hard winter dirt, I am always surprised.

My theological training and my study of Scripture have taught me well. I know God specializes in new life. Yet when it happens my heart is always caught off guard.

One of the classical spiritual disciplines is the act of attentiveness. It is an act of discipline to become awake and attentive to God's presence in all of life.

Sometimes I wonder what astonishing glimpses of new life you and I are missing simply because we haven't been looking for resurrection and healing in certain places. The man with a disability, we are told, sat at the temple gate every day, begging. He was a fixture there. No one expected anything different from him. I imagine most people didn't even notice him after the first few times they passed that way. I'm sure most people didn't even look him in the eye.

I wonder what you and I might be missing right now because our eyes have stopped seeing. I wonder who might dance before us if we could only focus. I wonder; are there places in our lives where new life will emerge if we will only pay attention?

Peter and John, perhaps because of their relationship with Jesus, saw something different in this man. They looked him right in the eye, the scripture says. They saw him. They paid attention.

Who or what in your life deserves a longer look from you today? Our relationship with the risen Christ infuses our lives with the sweet possibilities of new life. It is literally all around us for the seeing.

At the gates of the temple one who used to beg is now dancing. From a grief healed to a life transformed, God specializes in the dancing. From the promise of eternal life to the glimpses of newness in our everyday lives, God specializes in the dancing.

I am a hospice chaplain. Much of that ministry involves counseling with people at the end of their life. Sometimes I get used to the routine of some of my pastoral visits with people. Most visits follow a pattern, a time of visiting, light chatter, and then sometimes the conversation goes deeper and we talk of death or life after death. Sometimes the person shares hopes and dreams and regrets and worries. Usually at the end of the visit, I pray. Recently, I visited a ninety-four-year-old woman. Our visit followed the usual pattern. I read some scripture to her from her well-worn Bible. We talked about life and death. I said, "Shall we pray before I go?" She said, "Sure." I took her hand, closed my eyes and opened my mouth to pray. Before my first word emerged ... she grasped my hand tightly and she started to pray. She prayed for me and my children and my ministry. She prayed that I might be close to God and be faithful in helping people to see God. She prayed for my husband and my marriage. Then, she said "Amen." It surprised me, that prayer. It took my breath away. It touched me deeply. I looked in her eyes and saw a twinkle of new life and a spirit that was dancing. She said, "I just love to talk to God."

This is, after all, God we are talking about. Why are you surprised? (Cindy Guthrie Ryan)

Worship Aids

Invocation

God, by now we should know you will do it every time. You are the God of new life. You specialize in bringing new from old, life from death, hope from despair. You know how to change sinners into saints and beggars into dancers. Be with us today as we, your surprised children, celebrate the wonder of new life. Amen.

Litany

He sat at the gate every day.
Disabled and begging, every day.
You and I have our ruts too . . . our paralyzed places.
Places we sit every day, disabled and begging.
But then, eyes locked.
Healing happened.
And he walked! He danced! He praised God!
All: And we walk! And we dance! And we praise God! Amen.

Benediction

God of new life, we leave this place today surprised and amazed at the wonder of new life. We leave, dancing and praising you. Go with us. Help us pay attention. Resurrection is all around us. Amen. (Cindy Guthrie Ryan)

APRIL 6, 2008

❧❧❧

Third Sunday of Easter

Readings: Acts 2:14a, 36-41; Psalm 116:1-4, 12-19; 1 Peter 1:17-23; Luke 24:13-35

Seeing the Risen Christ
Luke 24:13-35

More than anything else, the Bible is about relationships and attitudes, especially about God's relationship with the people of faith.

Our text today is about two disciples on the evening of the day of resurrection. These two disciples had spent quality time with Jesus. They had seen Jesus feed thousands of hungry people. They had seen Jesus cure the blind, the sick, and the lame. They had seen Jesus walk on water. They had seen Jesus give life to a young girl, a young man, a servant, and his good friend Lazarus. They had heard Jesus preach great sermons like the Sermon on the Mount. They had learned from the teachings of Jesus. They had walked with Jesus into Jerusalem on Palm Sunday and then gone to the temple with Jesus. They had a great expectation that Jesus would become the next king of Israel and throw out the Romans and the despised sons of King Herod.

However, things had turned out differently. Jewish and Roman authorities would arrest, try, and crucify Jesus in a matter of hours. Chapter 24 of Luke reports that the two disciples who were on their way to a small village near Jerusalem were sad. Sad can mean different things. First, surely these two disciples were in shock that after a glorious entry into Jerusalem the government authorities arrested Jesus a few days later. Perhaps besides being sad they were depressed. They were so sad and depressed that they did not recognize the Lord Jesus when he joined them in their walk to Emmaus.

Surely, these two disciples were frustrated and perhaps they were even angry with the Lord Jesus. They were so sure that Jesus was the

Messiah, the one who would become the king of Israel, throw out the Romans, and get rid of the immoral sons of Herod. Jesus had come so close to being king. The two disciples thought of the big crowd that welcomed Jesus to Jerusalem barely a week ago. Rather than fight for the throne, Jesus angered people at the temple when he overthrew the tables of the money changers. Instead of avoiding the Roman soldiers, Jesus surrendered meekly. Look at what happened to him: a horrific death on a cross!

As the two disciples wallowed in their grief, their disappointment, their frustration, their sadness, their depression, and their anger about how badly things had gone, they did not notice, they did not see that the Lord Jesus was walking with them! Luke's story of Emmaus is a superb commentary about how life attitudes keep us from seeing the Lord Jesus as Jesus walks with us. Bad attitudes in life keep us from rejoicing in the presence of the Lord Jesus.

This story of these two disciples on their way to Emmaus on the evening of Jesus' resurrection is a call to us that we might just be like those two disciples. Like the two disciples, we know about Jesus and the great miracles. Like the two disciples, we know about Jesus' teachings and preaching. Moreover, like the two disciples, we just might be disappointed, frustrated, or angry that things in life have not turned out the way we wanted them to be. Just when we think we have it made, we do not get what we want. We feel let down by the Lord Jesus. We are sad and perhaps even angry about our failed expectation. We end up having a bad attitude, which in turn ruins our relationship with the Lord Jesus Christ.

That is what happened to Judas Iscariot. Judas was close to the Lord Jesus, but ultimately Judas Iscariot was blind as to who Jesus really was and what Jesus was doing. The two disciples on their way to Emmaus let their bad attitude get in the way and thus they too were blind and could not see or recognize Jesus walking with them.

The good shepherd always walks with the lambs. The Lord Jesus Christ is always with his people, his followers. If you are a follower, a disciple, then the Lord Jesus Christ walks with you. What a great thing, what a beautiful thing, what an awesome and holy thing to be walking with the Lord Jesus Christ! But, to see Jesus walking with you, you have to have the right attitude, an attitude that includes love first of all, peace, and joy. That is why when the Lord Jesus appeared to the disciples in the Upper Room, Jesus spoke first of peace and then of forgiveness—that is, loving God and loving one another. The first words of

Jesus to his disciples after the resurrection are about attitude and relationship: peace and forgiveness.

What is going on in your life? Are you sad because things have not turned out in ways that favor you? Are you depressed because of losses in your life? Are you upset because you feel God did not give you what you wanted? Do you feel spiritually empty? If you do, it could be that your attitude in life is keeping you from seeing the Lord Jesus. It could be that your attitude may be getting in the way of your relationship with the Lord Jesus.

At the end of the day, the two disciples invited the friendly stranger to join them for supper. Jesus joined them and ate with them. As Jesus broke and blessed the bread, their eyes opened and they saw the resurrected Jesus. If you invite the Lord Jesus into your life and let him break bread with you, then you will see him and be blessed by him! Don't let bad attitudes keep you from seeing the Lord Jesus. Get right attitudes of peace and forgiveness, of love and joy, and you will see Jesus walking with you and blessing you. Amen. (Roberto L. Gómez)

Lectionary Commentary
Acts 2:14a, 36-41

In the Gospels, Peter is a strong, determined person who depends on himself. Yet when the Roman soldiers arrest Jesus, Peter runs away—a very frightened individual. Peter tries to stay close to Jesus, but when a young girl asks him about his relationship to Jesus, a frightened Peter denies the friendship. Still, God is not finished with this scared disciple who denies Jesus. In due time, Peter is blessed by the anointing of the Holy Spirit. Peter's blessing is receiving power and courage to preach openly and give witness to Jesus. Thus, in Acts 2 we see a new Peter, brave and enthusiastic, preaching with the power of the Holy Spirit. How wonderful it is to preach with the power of the Holy Spirit!

1 Peter 1:17-23

The language and imagery of 1 Peter 1:17-23 may seem strange to us. We just do not hear it in our secular culture and we do not hear it in our churches. "Ransomed from the futile ways ... with the precious blood of Christ" is foreign to our daily living. Yet in my experience, these words are alive and powerful.

Some friends invited me to attend a Gideon's dinner for clergy. The speaker was a middle-aged man. While in prison for illegal drugs and serving a lengthy sentence, he gladly received the Gideon New Testaments. He would tear up the New Testaments and use the fine paper for cigarettes. One day as he rolled a paper for a cigarette, he paused and read it. It was John 3:16. He had never read the Bible before, but it caught his attention. He read it over and over again. Later, he got another New Testament. He read it from cover to cover. Alone in his cell he had a conversion experience. The prison staff noticed a difference in him. They released him from prison ahead of schedule, due to his good behavior and rehabilitation, or we could say transformation. Now he is an evangelist working with prisoners. Purified by the blood of the Lord Jesus Christ, the former drug dealer shares the love of Christ with others as he helps them know a better life. (Roberto L. Gómez)

Worship Aids

Call to Worship

God, Easter has occurred but the shock of the crucifixion keeps us
> from seeing the resurrected Christ.
Have mercy on us.
Open our eyes and ears that we may see and hear the living Christ
> speak to us.
Have mercy on us.
Let the loving presence of the living Christ warm our hearts.
All: Glory be to God! Amen.

Invocation

Dear God, you walk with us from moment to moment. Yet our thoughts and feelings about things past or things to come keep us from acknowledging your presence. We miss the precious moment of your holy presence. As we worship this morning, touch us that we that we may rejoice in your loving presence. Amen.

Benediction

Lord, you have blessed us today with your love, joy, and peace. Send us as your children to share your blessings with grateful hearts for what we have seen and heard. Amen. (Roberto L. Gómez)

Are We Tending to Our Fruit?

First in a Series of Two on the Fruit of the Spirit

Galatians 5:22-26

Outside the parsonage of my first church there was a cherry tree. The tree produced cherries for a two-week period each year. Unfortunately for me, I was living in the parsonage for three years before I realized this fact. The berries grew on the tree and at the peak of ripeness, you had to harvest them or the squirrels, birds, and other little creatures that lived near the tree were sure to eat them all up. One year during a particularly wet winter, the tree produced an overabundance of fruit for me and the various woodland animals. The cherry tree for me serves as an analogy for some people's idea about the fruit of the Spirit that Paul talks about in Galatians 5:22-26. Paul writes, "The fruit of the Spirit is love, joy, peace, patience, kindness, generosity, faithfulness, gentleness, and self-control."

The Holy Spirit produces fruit inside each and every believer of Jesus Christ. Unfortunately, not all Christians seem to realize this fact. As we grow in our faith, we need to pay special attention to the fruit within us. We should tend to our harvest by developing these character traits in such a way that they can serve as an example others of what it means to be a Christian. The seed at the core of an apple is responsible for the reproduction of another tree, which in turns produces more apples. When one brother or sister in Christ shares the fruit of the Spirit with another it helps develop the fruit inside the Spirit of the receiving believer, thus producing more fruit.

The fruit of the Spirit can be broken down into two categories. First, those traits that exist out of the agape love of Jesus Christ: love, joy, peace, and kindness. Second are the traits that seem to show themselves best when we are able to control our own will and allow the Spirit and the will of God to guide our lives: patience, faithfulness, gentleness, generosity, and self-control. In this sermon, we look at the "love traits" of the fruit of the Spirit.

Can any of us remember the very first time that we felt love? For most people, love begins when their mother holds them in her arms for the first time. But to actually recall when we first felt love is a different matter all together. God demonstrates love to us in so many different ways in the Bible. The ultimate act of love is Jesus' willingness to submit to his crucifixion on a cross. A wise pastor and teacher once told me that if you had to sum up the Bible in two words, they would be, "God loves." In 1 John 4:19 we are told, "We love because he first loved us." Agape love is that expression of love that expects nothing in return. Although it may be difficult for us to remember the first experience of love in our life, there is no doubt that we recognize the love that comes from the Spirit.

There are many events, people, and possessions that may bring joy into our life. One time, as a young man, I hit two home runs in the same inning of a baseball game. The pictures of this event show a boy who is full of joy and happiness. By the next game or the next strikeout, that joy had quickly gone away. Individuals can bring joy into our lives and promptly turn around and disappoint us. Possessions bring about a temporary emotional uplift but as we grow bored with the object, we begin to look for the next source of excitement. The joy that comes from the Spirit is an everlasting joy that creates a special feeling inside of us that is sometimes difficult to explain. There is a special sense of joy that seems to permeate a room when Christians fellowship together. When a person can smile and wish you goodwill when they are bedridden with cancer or some other debilitating condition, that is the joy that comes from the Holy Spirit.

Paul writes "the peace of God, which surpasses all understanding, will guard your hearts and your minds in Christ Jesus" (Philippians 4:7). True peace exists when we live our lives in harmony with Jesus Christ. Throughout the Gospels, Jesus tells us not to worry—a peaceful life is a life with little worry. When the disciples were hiding after the crucifixion, Jesus appeared to them and offered them "Peace." We will have peace when we allow the Holy Spirit to guide our lives, and let the will of God be our will. Does that peace guarantee us a life with no stress and no chaos? No. However, the Spirit's guidance does provide a sense of tranquility to help us navigate the difficult storms of life we sometimes face.

Have you seen the bumper sticker that reads, "Practice Random Kindness & Senseless Acts of Beauty"? The world knows that kindness displays power and love. Perhaps more heads have turned because of a kind act or deed than by any other action. God calls us to practice kindness in all that we do, not just on a random basis. To be kind is to do what is right—no matter the cost. We have to look no further than the parable of the Good Samaritan in Luke's Gospel to learn what it means to be kind. The Holy Spirit empowers us to share the love of Christ with the world through routine acts of kindness.

These acts share the agape love of Jesus Christ with the world. May God's love, joy, peace, and kindness flow through us. (John Mathis)

Worship Aids

Call to Worship

The Lord gives love freely. Where there is love,
There is joy. The Lord gives joy daily.
Where there is joy, there is kindness.
The Lord calls us to be kind to one another.
Where there is kindness, there is peace.
Lord, grant us the love, joy, and kindness to bring about peace in your world.

Pastoral Prayer

Gracious Lord, teach us to love one another as you have loved us. Bring joy into our lives and allow us to share that joy with the world. Help us develop a spirit of kindness. Grant us peace as Christ offered the disciples. Allow the fruit of the Spirit to grow in our lives as we learn to walk in faith.

Benediction

As we leave this place of worship, let us love God and love one another. Bring joy to the world with kindness. Peace be with you forever and always. (John Mathis)

APRIL 13, 2008

❧❧❧

Fourth Sunday of Easter

Readings: Acts 2:42-47; Psalm 23; 1 Peter 2:19-25; John 10:1-10

Life in Abundance
John 10:1-10

Most of us will remember the name of Columbine High School for a long time. We will remember that two misguided young men went to their home school, Columbine High School, and killed twelve of their school colleagues and a teacher. We now know that hatred filled these two young men. They planned their murderous attack for over a year. They meant to kill many more students and teachers. They left notes indicating their growing anger, resentment, and racism. In one final tragic action, they sought to find meaning and power in a senseless violent event.

Littleton, Colorado, seemed to be a wonderful community full of peace and prosperity. Families moved to Littleton looking for a good place to live and raise their children. Now the memory of bloody bodies in classrooms and hallways in Columbine High School stir emotions of sadness, grief, and shock.

What went wrong? We might blame any number of people and things. We might blame the boys' parents, the school environment, their schoolmates, the Internet, cable TV, the movies, or their church, or whatever. We will never know exactly what went wrong.

Sometimes it seems as if we live in a mad, crazy, and cruel world. Sometimes it seems that pain, hurt, grief, horror, and terror dominate. Sometimes it seems there is no faith, hope, or love.

John 10:1-10 speaks to such circumstances. Jesus tells us that we are like sheep. He tells us that we get to the pasture of food and water by a gate. Jesus speaks of thieves and bandits who enter the sheepfold in ways other than the gate to steal and kill the sheep. In today's world, thieves and bandits steal our minds and hearts with false promises. Thieves and bandits lure us away from God's plan for our life. Thieves and bandits will confuse us and put us on a road to perdition and evil suffering.

A new friend in Christ told me about evil suffering. He was a drug addict. To support his drug habit he stole things from his parents, his brothers, his sisters, and his friends, from everybody! He felt guilty for hurting those persons he loved, yet he continued stealing. He took his drugs, felt okay for just a little while and then he felt terrible, and each time his terrible feelings lasted longer. The longer he used drugs, the more he abused his body and his soul. Talk about evil suffering!

A psychologist named Abraham Maslow once said that humans have several basic needs that Maslow described in five levels. We all have physiological needs: hunger, thirst, and fatigue. We all need safety: the need to avoid pain, feel secure, be free from chaos, and the need for structure. We all need belongingness and love. We need esteem and self-respect, adequacy, and competence. Finally, the highest level is the need for self-actualization, understanding, and aesthetic pleasure. (Rodney J. Hunter, ed., *Dictionary of Pastoral Care and Counseling* [Nashville: Abingdon Press, 1990], 691).

Most of us get our needs met at the first two levels. We run into problems at the third level. There are crucial moments in life when we lack the belongingness and love we so badly need and want. We suffer. We are stuck in the third level: wanting to belong and be loved, but getting neither. My guess is that those two young men in Littleton wanted badly to belong and be loved.

We can have everything in the world, but without love and a strong sense of belonging somewhere to someone life is empty. Recently there was a television show about one of the richest women on earth. She was intelligent. She was pretty. She was super wealthy. Sadly and tragically, she had no loved ones and felt she belonged nowhere. This wealthy and beautiful woman died alone and sad of a broken heart.

My hunch is that most of us are looking for a good life. It would be nice to have a wonderful home, a well-paying job, a happy family, a neighborhood without crime, good health, an inspiring church, and so on. Yet deep in our hearts, we realize that lots of money, great fame, influence, or a long life will not always bring us happiness. What we really want is someone to love us, someone to care for us, someone to be a true, loyal friend.

I have good news for you. Jesus Christ is that someone. Jesus Christ loves you. Jesus Christ cares for you. Jesus Christ is that true and loyal friend. Jesus invites you to join his group of friends. You can belong to Jesus Christ, the Son of God, and his friends. In this fellowship of Jesus, you will experience love, true love, honest love, and sacrificial love. Jesus is the gateway to the sheepfold. He is the one who takes care of us. Jesus does not come to steal and kill. Jesus comes to give you life, and give it in abundance!

I had the privilege of visiting an elderly church member. She had lived a long life, had a good family, and loved the Lord Jesus. One day when I went to see her, I noticed that she had many nice, fresh, homegrown vegetables in her living room. When I saw the vegetables I knew who had brought them to her. A certain church brother was romantically interested in her. I said, "Sister, I think brother likes you a lot." She smiled at me and said, "Yes, I know he likes me, but he is not the only one. There are others who like me too!"

Jesus said, "I came that they may have life, and have it abundantly."

You can have life and have it abundantly. Let Jesus Christ be your shepherd. Let Jesus Christ be your friend. Let Jesus Christ be your brother. Let Jesus Christ be your Savior. Let Jesus Christ be your Lord and bless you with the abundance of his grace. Open your heart and let Jesus Christ come in. (Roberto L. Gómez)

Lectionary Commentary
Acts 2:42-47

This passage shows what happens when the love of God that is in the Lord Jesus Christ transforms individuals, families, and an entire community. God's grace and the gift of unity of the Holy Spirit overcome greed, envy, hate, mistrust, and lack of cooperation among individuals and families. This narrative from Acts sets a high standard of living for families and churches. In turn, this standard helps people of faith and their faith communities witness to a broken, hurting world in need of God's grace, joy, and peace. Furthermore, the Holy Spirit gives individuals, families, and faith communities the power to witness, to overcome divisions, and to resist evil. It is true that such grace, joy, and peace do not last even in faith communities, but while they do, what a glorious glimpse of God's kingdom!

1 Peter 2:19-25

Verse 18 in 1 Peter 2 indicates that the writer of this letter directed this portion of the letter to slaves. In 1 Peter 2:19-25 are words of encouragement to slaves who suffer unjustly that the Lord Jesus Christ, the Son of God, himself suffered unjustly, but that his suffering is redemptive suffering for all who follow him. (Roberto L. Gómez)

Worship Aids

Call to Worship

When we take our eyes off the Lord Jesus Christ, we hunger and thirst.
We feel our cup of life is empty.
The Lord Jesus gives life and gives it abundantly.
Let our cup overflow with the presence of the Lord Jesus in our daily living.

Invocation

Heavenly Father, the world tries hard to convince us that it can feed our soul, mind, and body. We fall to temptation and binge on things that neither satisfy us nor bless us. Bless us with your Holy Spirit that we may open our hearts and minds to your Son, the living Christ who feeds us at his table with abundant food from heaven that truly nourishes our soul, mind, and body. Amen.

Benediction

Dear God, today we came to praise your holy name, to worship you, and to rejoice in your presence. In your love, you have blessed us with the spirit of your Son, Jesus, resurrected from the dead. Now, send us forth to share the good news of true and abundant life in the Lord Jesus Christ. Amen.

Are We Tending to Our Fruit?

Second in a Series of Two on the Fruit of the Spirit

Galatians 5:19-25

As we continue to explore at the fruit of the Spirit, we now concentrate on those traits that rely on the self-control given by God: patience, generosity, faithfulness, gentleness, and self-control. These qualities directly contrast with the "works of the flesh" listed in Galatians 5:19-21. If we maintain self-control over "the flesh," we can prevent ourselves from falling into the traps of sin. Many people feel that they can personally control every aspect of their life without the power of the Holy Spirit. Many well-meaning people have tried—only to fail. Peter tells us that we must "support ... [our] knowledge with self-control" (2 Peter 1:6). If we are to grow in our walk as followers of Jesus, we must learn to temper our impulses, our emotions, and our desires. Patience requires us to have self-control over our anxieties and stresses. Generosity requires us to have self-control over our personal finances and time. Faithfulness requires us to have self-control over our daily routines and rituals. Gentleness requires us to have self-control over our emotions and attitudes toward other people.

As a child growing up in Northern Virginia, I felt as though I always had to wait. I waited after football practice, after basketball practice, and after baseball practice. My parents were diligently trying to chauffeur three boys around to different sporting events and games. Sometimes I wondered, "Have they forgotten about me?" Perhaps God was using this time to help me develop patience. Patience, as one of the fruits of the Spirit, is more about the ability to bear pains or trials evenly without complaint. God blesses me whenever I meet someone who is suffering through some tragedy in his or her life calmly and patiently. I wonder if I too could possibly demonstrate such joy and faithfulness. The Holy Spirit empowers us to bear witness to the power of God through the difficulties of our life.

We must continue to seek God's guidance in our life to maintain a life of faithfulness. A lack of faithfulness may be a sign of spiritual immaturity. It is very important to participate in spiritual disciplines to grow in our relationship with God. Through prayer, we communicate with a loving God who desires to hear from us. We need to read the Scriptures looking for ways to do God's will in our lives. Weekly worship is a good habit for anyone to develop. As we enjoy fellowship with one another, we help one another grow together as the family of God. We all should take a little quiet time each day and concentrate on the living God. Furthermore, journaling is an excellent way of expressing our experiences with the living Christ in the world. All of these activities lead to a life of faithfulness. Children sometimes have difficulty controlling their emotions. We have walked through church or a store where some child is screaming and crying at the top of his lungs until he gets his way. The parents who seem to have the best response to their children are the ones who demonstrate patience and a good deal of gentleness. They are able to exhibit authority while maintaining peace and not losing their temper. We see gentleness in those who speak softly, touch lightly, wait patiently, and work together with others with patience and kindness. The fruit of the Spirit produces this kind of gentleness. Mary shows signs of gentleness as she sits at the feet of Jesus. Jesus Christ best embodies gentleness in the Bible. Jesus was able to rebuke sinners with tenderness instead of with harsh admonishment. Jesus Christ laid down his life freely for us in atonement for sin. This was the definitive act of gentleness. As John writes, "The law indeed was given through Moses; grace and truth came through Jesus Christ" (John 1:17b). We see gentleness in other believers who allow God's grace to guide every ounce of their being. It is through their gentleness that we see Jesus within their Spirit.

Sometimes a person will ask me, "How do you know that someone is truly a believer in Jesus Christ?" This is a difficult question at best and perhaps an impossible one to answer. The Pharisees, Sadducees, and the people in the crowds frequently questioned Jesus about who would inherit the kingdom of God. Unfortunately, outward appearances often mask the inner heart of a human being. Paul tells us that a believer in Jesus Christ will exhibit the fruit of the Spirit. Paul suggests that, "If we live by the Spirit, let us also be guided by the Spirit." Fruit of the Spirit seems impossible to develop in our lives. We do not want to love everybody.

Sometimes we enjoy being angry at a person. We do not want to be patient. We want things to happen and happen now. We do not want to be kind. We want to repay an adversary with the animosity shown to us. However, if we allow the Spirit of the living Christ to work in our lives we can grow in our life of discipleship. One of the greatest joys I have as a minister is when I see somebody grow in their walk with the Lord. The fruit of the Spirit shines bright and everyone can see the light of Christ within him or her. As we tend to our spiritual gardens, the fruit of the Spirit will become more evident in our lives and we will be able to spread the seed of Christ's love throughout the world. (John Mathis)

Worship Aids

Call to Worship

God, grant us your grace so that we may live by the spirit.
Lord, let your spirit guide us.
God, grant us your grace so that we may be generous and faithful.
Lord, let your spirit guide us.

God, grant us your grace so that we may be patient and gentle.
All: Lord, let your spirit guide us.

Pastoral Prayer

Eternal God, you give each of us the fruit of the Spirit to share your grace to the world. Let us rely upon the Spirit to guide our lives and teach us self-control. Give us the power to be your witness to the world, sharing all that the fruit of the spirit bears: love, joy, peace, patience, kindness, generosity, faithfulness, gentleness, and self-control. As we share the fruit of the spirit with the world, we share the character and grace of Jesus Christ. Amen.

Benediction

Go forth and plant a seed. Where the works of the flesh abound, sow the fruit of the spirit. Love generously. Be gentle and kind. Be faithful and patient. Let peace and joy flow constantly from your heart. Let other see Jesus Christ reflected within you as the fruit of the Spirit abounds in your life. (John Mathis)

APRIL 20, 2008

※ ※ ※

Fifth Sunday of Easter

Readings: Acts 7:55-60; Psalm 31:1-5, 15-16; 1 Peter 2:2-10; John 14:1-14

Living Stones
1 Peter 2:2-10

Peter, in his first letter, tells us that we are to be living stones: "Come to [Christ], a living stone, though rejected by mortals yet chosen and precious in God's sight, and like living stones, let yourselves be built into a spiritual house, to be a holy priesthood, to offer spiritual sacrifices acceptable to God through Jesus Christ." *Living stones*, what in the world does that mean?

I don't think we as a people who live in a fertile land with hills and trees and grass can truly understand this passage, until we understand the land from which Peter writes. When I was in Israel, I was constantly amazed at the landscape. It was beautiful, but very different than anything we usually see. Jerusalem is a city built on a hill, with valleys on every side. As you look out to the Mount of Olives from the Temple Mount, you can see patches of grass, but you mostly see rocks and stones. You walk in sandals and the dirt gets under your feet and between your toes and you are constantly watching your footing.

The city itself is stone. All of the houses, churches, and even the city walls are made out of limestone. There is really no color to the city architecture; it just looks like stones piled on top of each other to create the city. In fact, in the early 1950s and 1960s, construction was all done with cinderblock because it was cheaper than using stone. But unfortunately the cinderblock ruined the look of the city; now there is a law that every building being constructed must look like limestone on the outside. Today in modern Israel, they are creating "fake" stone structures so that everything will continue to look like stone.

Peter, in writing this letter, looks around and sees all these stones. Imagine Peter sitting at a desk, looking out of a small window, and writing to encourage new Christians and followers of Jesus. Peter looks out that window and all he sees are the stones. Peter then looks down at his parchment and begins to encourage the Christians. "Come to Christ, a living stone." Peter looks out, sees all these stones and knows that if they were alive in Christ, they would prove an amazing witness. They would rise up in power and strength and build wonderful things for the Lord, because they were the foundations of a building alive for Christ.

These stones that decorate the church remind us that we too are to be living stones. We are to take heed to Peter's words and become living stones. We are to be so filled with the love of Christ and the power of the Holy Spirit that we are alive and strong and hard and yearning to do Christ's work in the world. These stones will be with us for the next few weeks. As we travel towards Pentecost and the birth of the church, these stones are a reminder that we too are to be alive and living stones of faith.

God has a plan for us. First Peter goes on to tell us that we are "a chosen race, a royal priesthood, a holy nation, God's own people, in order that you may proclaim the mighty acts of him who called you out of darkness into his marvelous light. Once you were not a people, / but now you are God's people; / once you had not received mercy, / but now you have received mercy." Being living stones embraces the knowledge that we are all special.

But the passage isn't done. The scripture tells us that we are chosen "in order that you may proclaim the mighty acts of him who called you out of darkness into his marvelous light." Being a living stone is proclaiming the mighty acts of Christ. It means getting involved in your faith. It's not just sitting in a pew on a Sunday morning, but living out the faith because you are a living stone. Christians are to be hard and strong and alive through the power of Jesus Christ.

Peter says, "Let yourselves be built into a spiritual house." As we come together, each of us a living stone, we are built into something greater through the power of Jesus Christ. We are special and important and Christ is alive in us and waiting for us to actually be a living stone. To take risks and live and breath everything through the power of Jesus Christ.

The stone is such a remarkable image because it seems so dead. It lays on the ground and does nothing. But when you look closer at a stone, you can see how alive it can truly be. Living stones built God's city, Jerusalem. A living stone is hard and strong and stays in its place for hundreds and thousands of years, telling the story of where it came from. A living stone is waiting for the Creator to come along and build it into something beautiful.

Peter, the disciple known as the Rock says, "Come to [Christ], a living stone, though rejected by mortals yet chosen and precious in God's sight, and like living stones, let yourselves be built into a spiritual house." Be a living stone this week. Rise from your pew. Leave this plain stone structure and allow God to work in your life and become a living stone. Listen to God, let yourself be built into a spiritual house and serve God in some way.

Worship Suggestion

Pass baskets of stones along the pews. Invite the congregation to take a stone from the basket as it is passed. Tell those present, "Hold it in your hand. Feel its curves and strength and how hard it is to the touch. Let this be a reminder to you that you too are to be a living stone for Christ." (Jennifer H. Williams)

Lectionary Commentary
Acts 7:55-60

This passage marks the beginning of the transition from the disciples who knew Jesus directly to the early church and Saul/Paul. In the midst of Stephen's death, the witnesses and possibly participants "laid their coats at the feet of a young man named Saul." The phrase seems to be out of place during the murder scene, but it sets the stage for the church's next phase of life. Saul was an active participant in the death of the first Christian martyr, yet comes to be the founder of the church throughout the world. Stephen's final words are not only a prayer, but a statement of faith as well. "Lord, do not hold this sin against them." Saul becomes the proof that Christ forgives and uses every one of us despite our past sins.

John 14:1-14

It seems that the Christians who sit in our pews have been taught that it is inappropriate and even sinful to question God. The disciples in this passage show us that the act of questioning is not the problem; our questions can lead us to greater answers. Although Jesus is in their midst, the disciples still question and ask for signs. "Lord, we don't know where you are going, so how can we know the way?" (v. 5 NIV). "Lord, show us the Father and that will be enough for us" (v. 8 NIV). The disciples' lack of faith in the presence of the Messiah highlights the human quality to question and doubt. Although we may not always get the answer we desire, Jesus does provide answers. Trust in God—At the beginning of the passage, Jesus says, "trust in God" (v. 1 NIV). However, all of us at some point fail to trust in God and put our trust in others or ourselves. When Thomas asks for the way, he fails to trust. But instead of rebuking him, Jesus patiently responds. Jesus is our way; our task as Christians is to be patient and just "trust in God". (Jennifer H. Williams)

Worship Aids

Call to Worship

Come to Christ a living stone.
We come to be filled with Christ's power.
Let yourselves be built into a spiritual house.
We come to learn how to be the church.
You are a chosen race, God's own people.
Jesus has led us into the light. We will proclaim his mighty acts!

Prayer of Confession

O God, we have not been your people. Instead of being your living stones, we remain solid rocks of denial and complacency. We have stumbled on the stones of the world and not held onto you as our rock and our salvation. Forgive us, we pray. Amen.

Words of Assurance

In the name of Jesus Christ, you are forgiven.
In the name of Jesus Christ, you are forgiven. Amen.

Invocation

God, our solid rock, move us by your word. Help us be your living stones in this sanctuary and in your world. As we strive to be your people, may we proclaim your mighty acts and be alive through your Holy Spirit. In the name of Jesus we pray. Amen. (Jennifer H. Williams)

The Seasons of Life

First in a Series of Three on Easter

1 Corinthians 15:50-58

It was Job who asked: "If a man die, shall he live again?" (Job 14:14 RSV). Can we trust what we have been taught about the meaning of death and what lies beyond? What comfort can we find for the future, when the wrinkles in our faces, the illness in our bodies, and the accidents in an unsafe world remind us that life in this dimension is not permanent? For some, these questions may seem academic, but for most of us they are as real as life and as serious as death. Is there a season we do not see that this brief interim of earthly life is but a preparation for? This is a question that prowls the cellars of our souls like a restless ghost through every age and stage of life.

We live in a predictable world where we move logically from day to night and from one season to the next. In some similarity to the season of nature, there are seasons in our lives. Those seasons are described with such terms as: prenatal, infancy, childhood, adolescence, adulthood, middle age, and old age. We move almost imperceptibly from one season to the next, never being quite able during one season of life to anticipate what the next season will be like. In our prenatal state we have absolutely no intimation of the kind of world into which we will be born. If we could be consulted on the matter of being born, we would probably reject the idea as strongly as we reject the idea of death. In childhood and adolescence, we press eagerly toward adulthood in anticipation of its privileges and opportunities we see available to those who are living ahead of us. With most of us, the eagerness to press on to the next season begins to diminish in our middle years. We lose some of our adventurousness as we know less and less about what lies ahead, and more and more about what is behind us. We become cautious and afraid lest our years run out and time for us will be no more. John Keats spoke of this in one of his greatest poems: "When I have fears that I may cease to be / before my pen has gleaned my teeming brain . . ." We do not usually pass willingly into a season we cannot see and with which we have no familiarity.

In the thirteenth chapter of 1 Corinthians, Paul speaks of the normal progression of life from one season to the next. "When I was a child, I spoke like a child, I thought like a child, I reasoned like a child; when I became a man, I gave up childish ways" (v. 11 RSV). Here Paul refers to the plan in which persons move from one season to the next in order to suggest one's ultimate destiny—which consists of fullness far more complete than anything we can possibly imagine. Paul suggests another season that lies around the bend in the river of life that we call death—a season about which we now know only by intimation, and in which the need for former things will no longer be, and in which there will be no lack of knowledge and no lack of love. "Now we see through a glass darkly, but then we shall see face-to-face—understand as we are understood and know even as also we are known" (v. 12, paraphrased). Paul and the whole New Testament suggest that the full meaning of life is not attained in this world, but that beyond the dark veil of death there is another season. It is a season which, by its very nature and quality, will not only have meaning within itself but that will give meaning of the confusing parts of all past seasons of life that presently we do not fully understand.

I do not mean that we can offer technical proof of everlasting life, for the power of God lies beyond the puny rationality of the human mind. But, there are intimations of immortality that come with our growing understanding of this created universe and the life that we know in it. While we do not presume to understand the full meaning of death or what lies beyond, we do see that there are vast inequities in life and in death unless there is a season that lies beyond in which a just God will square things. There is almost a universal consensus that we live in a world in which good is ultimately rewarded and evil is ultimately punished. Yet, we see the wicked prosper and the good die young. This plain fact draws to mind numerous examples of inequities in this life. If we believe that God is just, then there must be a season in which accounts are settled. Logic and justice will not let us abandon Socrates drinking the hemlock or Joan of Arc at the stake, and will not allow us to leave Hitler forever in his bunker in Berlin. Neither will logic and justice allow death to end it all for the little child who died before life here could get underway. And while we do not believe that God took the child, we do believe that God received the child.

When we see some life cut short just as genius was beginning to bloom, or some life end with death in the middle of a great and creative project, all the reason and logic that is in us cries out that there must be more. Someone said that Robert Louis Stevenson died with a thousand stories in his heart. If death is the end of our being and doing, the Creator of this universe is a very poor manager of his world. It is not logical that when we are just beginning to get some grasp on the handles of life and just beginning to do our best work we end up forever on the junk pile of death. There must be more.

There is a strange and beautiful passage of scripture buried deep in Ecclesiastes. Listen to what it says. "[God] has made everything beautiful in its time; also [God] has put eternity into man's mind, yet so that he cannot find out what God has done from the beginning to the end" (3:11 RSV).

This passage of scripture takes a quantum leap beyond its own time and setting. In a time when human understanding of any sort of afterlife was still dim, in a time when there was no theological formulation of eternal life, the writer of Ecclesiastes felt something in his bones that was not in his books. He wrote down this powerful statement, the details of which were not to be spelled out for hundreds of years. From the very beginning there has been some vague feeling in human beings that once is not enough, that there must be something more. Here it is all the way back in the book of Ecclesiastes, as big as life: God has put eternity into the human mind.

I do not ultimately believe in life after death because of any mind-boggling philosophical arguments, as convincing as they may be. Any rational arguments, taken individually or collectively, leave enough unanswered questions about life after death to seriously impair a confident approach to the grave. I believe in life after death because Jesus said, "Because I live, you shall live also" (John 14:19 RSV). For the Christian person, belief in life after death hangs finally not upon any rational arguments that the mind can frame but upon faith in the veracity of one solitary person whom we believe to be the divine Son of God, Jesus of Nazareth, who lived and died and indeed rose from the dead, giving final substance to his most radical promise and claim.

Jesus, in his teachings, assumes the everlasting quality of life. Jesus admits no possibility that a person may escape from life by dying. When we die we leave behind all that we have, and take with us all that we are. It is a sobering thought to realize that with death we are not done with life. We do not really cash in our chips, but rather exchange them for another currency.

There is a season we do not see. (Thomas Lane Butts)

Worship Aids

Prayer of Confession

Dear God, we confess to the fragmentation we experience when we try to draw all the pieces of our lives into a unified whole. We confess how we have divided our lives into so many frustrating cul-de-sacs. We have looked to others for approval and self-worth, oblivious to the truth that self-worth comes from you and from within. As we reflect on the meaning of resurrection, we pray for resurrection in our own lives. Through Jesus Christ, our Lord; Amen.

Words of Assurance

In the name of Jesus Christ, you are forgiven.
In the name of Jesus Christ, you are forgiven. Amen.

Pastoral Prayer

Almighty God, Father and Mother of us all, we come before you today in the reflected light of the glorious resurrection of Jesus, the Christ, in whose life and death and resurrection we find all that is essential to our salvation. We are thankful that your unconditional love for us is not dependent upon our understanding of you, and that your acceptance of us is not dependent upon the purity of our lives or the perfection of our ways.

How grateful we are for unnumbered blessings that have come to us in such strange ways, at such strange times, and from such strange people—to save us from trial and tragedy of such magnitude as would have destroyed us. How thankful we are for the saving people in our lives, for rare, beautiful, and sensitive friends who heard the song in our hearts, and then when we forget our own song, they come and sing it back to us.

We pray for your people here and everywhere whose lives are filled with frustration and pain. We pray for those who are sick in any of the ways in which we may become ill. Be with those who wait anxiously for results of examinations and tests. Grant them courage and strength to face scary prospects concerning their health and the health of those they love. Keep us ever sensitive to the needs of those around us. Save us from choosing to do nothing because we cannot do everything.

May our songs, the Holy Scripture, and our recollection of the resurrection of Jesus give us a sense of security and hope in an uncertain world. In the name of Jesus, our Lord; Amen.

Benediction

Grant us an abiding awareness of your loving presence as we walk out into the world. Help us leave our burdens here in the church so that we may function with dignity and full effectiveness as human beings each day of this week. Touch us with love so that we may touch others with love. Amen. (Thomas Lane Butts)

APRIL 27, 2008

❧❧❧

Sixth Sunday of Easter

Readings: Acts 17:22-31; Psalm 66:8-20; 1 Peter 3:13-22;
John 14:15-21

Common Ground
Acts 17:22-31

When I was in seminary I was chosen as a student representative for the Curriculum Selection Committee. I remember getting all dressed up to go to my first meeting, sitting in the oversized chairs, and feeling so small in comparison to the professors and deans sitting around that table. At this point, my memory starts to get fuzzy and my stomach starts to rumble with butterflies of embarrassment. I remember talking a lot during that meeting, sharing all my excellent ideas and being virtually laughed out of the room by the professionals and academics. At one point, I remember a respected professor telling me, in a very polite way, to be quiet. I wanted too much in too little time; I thought I knew everything that would make the seminary better. I saw what could be and wanted it all done immediately. Honestly, some of my ideas were worthy of being heard, but my actions and overzealous presentation caused a rift between myself and those whom I wanted to influence. Overall, the meeting was a disaster; I felt so awful that I never attended another meeting and rode out the final months of my seminary career in silence. Looking back, I would say that I was overly enthusiastic, overzealous, and far too impatient.

After years of ministry, I like to think that my ability to work with others has improved. In the local church, I have learned that there are times to speak up, but also times where silence and patience are worthy qualities. In this world, it is necessary to have patience, love, and understanding to accomplish a goal.

I take heart in knowing that Saint Paul also struggled with sharing his message. Paul has had a difficult journey prior to this passage from Acts 17. Paul was on fire with the Holy Spirit and was sharing the message any way that he could. In Acts 16, Paul finds himself in prison, narrowly escapes and then finds himself at the hands of an angry mob in Thessalonica. Paul is young in the faith, knows he has a message to share, and enthusiastically (and some might say overzealously) presents the gospel to everyone he encounters. It is Paul's enthusiastic, if impatient, presentation that gets him into trouble.

In this passage from Acts 17, Paul finds himself in Athens. Paul is now an experienced and wise evangelist who decides to try another tactic to get his point across. In Thessalonica, the scripture says, "Paul went in, as was his custom, and on three sabbath days argued with them from the scriptures" (v. 2). Prior to Athens, Paul argued his points; he was certain about Jesus' lordship and he presented it in a manner that caused severe problems between Paul and the synagogues of several prominent towns. But entering Athens, Paul learned from his previous experience. Rather than argue with the citizens, Paul begins by praising them, saying, "Athenians, I see how extremely religious you are in every way." Paul takes the time to experience their city and observes their religious statues and idols. Paul tries to understand the Athenian people before he shows them the message of salvation. In his patience and understanding, Paul finds a way to share Jesus, saying, "For as I went through the city and looked carefully at the objects of your worship, I found among them an altar with the inscription, 'To an unknown god.' What therefore you worship as unknown, this I proclaim to you." Because Paul took the time and was patient, he was able to find a way to reach the Athenian people by touching upon what they already knew. Because Paul observed that the Athenians believed in an unknown god, he was able to spread the gospel by revealing God through the presence of the Messiah, Jesus Christ.

I have come to dislike the word *evangelism*. It makes me think of people standing on the street with signboards or college friends who tried to convert me by asking if I had accepted Jesus Christ as my personal Lord and Savior. While those evangelism techniques may reach a certain segment of the population, I do not believe they are the example that Paul sets forth for us in this passage. Paul's success in Athens comes because he is able to find common ground with the Athenians. Only after he finds the common ground is he able to share his own testimony of the Messiah who is grander than any stone or metal idols the Athenians have worshiped before.

Spreading the gospel is not about an overzealous presentation that hits the hearer over the head; it did not work for the young Paul and it will not work for us. Sharing Jesus means finding the common ground with your friend and neighbor. Sit down with that person and listen to them; discover their beliefs and then start to share your own. Evangelism is what Paul does in this passage, he understands his listeners and he starts with what they know and then opens their minds to the power of Christ. Evangelism for us is sharing our story of Jesus in a patient and understanding manner. When you are sitting beside your coworker and she's having a bad day, pray for her and share that prayer with her. When your friend is going into surgery, tell him how Jesus has been with you and given you the strength to persevere. Sharing the gospel takes patience, understanding, and love.

This scripture teaches us that no matter how important our message, even the message of salvation, it will not be heard unless it is presented in a manner that is appropriate to unbelievers. Paul shows us that we cannot hit others over the heads with the message of Christ. Our task as Christians is to find the common ground and then begin. Amen. (Jennifer H. Williams)

Lectionary Commentary
John 14:15-21

While the 1 Peter text from this Sunday addresses suffering, the gospel lesson promises an Advocate. The New International Version (NIV) translates the Greek word as "Counselor." In recent years, the cable networks have had a rush of law programs with lawyers, often called counselors, who advocate ferociously for the truth. At some time in our life, we all need an advocate or counselor to work on our behalf. In the postmodern, post-9/11 world, individuals often feel isolated and alone, craving true community. The John text shows us that we have an Advocate; God provides such comfort through the gift of the Holy Spirit and the presence of the church.

1 Peter 3:13-22

It is difficult for many of us in the United States to understand what it means to suffer for Jesus Christ. While we may know suffering, it usually does not come because of our beliefs. This sermon time could be used to highlight how people throughout history and in our current world actually suffer for being Christian. Persecution of Christians still occurs and people do lose their life for Christ's sake. In a world divided over religion, Christianity can be cause for suffering or can cause the suffering. And although our national context may not be cause for great suffering for a Christian, in what ways can we stand up to the world's values and risk our safety in service to Christ? (Jennifer H. Williams)

Worship Aids

Prayer of Confession

The One God, we may not have idols of gold or silver, but we still put other idols ahead of our love for you. Our money, cars, homes, and toys all overshadow your commandments to be your people. Forgive us for creating idols out of worldly items. As we grope for you, reach out to us. Amen.

Assurance of Forgiveness

Hear the good news. While we wallow in our human desires, Christ's love abounds. Our Lord is not an unknown God. Through his sacrifice, death, and resurrection, Christ reveals himself and forgives our sins. In the name of Jesus Christ, we are forgiven.

Invocation

O God, reveal yourself to us. We know that you are not an unknown God, but that you desire to be in relationship with us. May we hear your word in order to go into your world and reveal your presence to others. We pray in the name of the Father, the Son, and the Holy Spirit. Amen. (Jennifer H. Williams)

The Unexpected Jesus

Second in a Series of Three on Easter

Luke 24:13-35

There is no Eastertide story more meaningful for the human situation in any age than Luke's enchanting narrative of Jesus' appearance on the road to Emmaus. It is a starburst of spiritual insight that offers hope and help for the hopeless and helpless. In it we see how the unexpected Jesus is more likely to show up in the atmosphere of honest uncertainty, emptiness, and frustration than in the human *hubris* of those who are quite sure they already know everything they need to know.

Those of us who live two thousand years after the event have too much closed knowledge, standardized theological interpretation, and deadly and deadening certainty to be naturally open to the unexpected Jesus. The accumulated layers of refined theological interpretation often shield us from the startling joy of the unexpected Jesus who slipped up on the blind side of the two dispirited pilgrims who had given up and were on their way home to Emmaus.

Perhaps the most helpful thing earnest seekers can do to create an atmosphere for a life-changing encounter with Jesus is to empty ourselves of all that we know or think we know to make room for the unexpected Jesus. The persons on the road to Emmaus did not have answers. They had questions—frustrating questions. They were genuinely puzzled and discouraged. They had hoped and trusted that Jesus was "the one," but it appeared they were sadly mistaken. They were as empty as the empty tomb. The women came back saying they saw a vision of angels who said Jesus was alive. Some of those who were gathered went to the tomb and found it as the women had said, but they didn't see him. What were they to do? There was only one thing left to do—pack up and go home. They were going back where they started, empty and out of hope.

If they had known what we now know they would have stayed in Jerusalem and probably would have been sitting around a conference table writing an early draft of the Apostles' Creed. But they were ignorant, empty, and hopelessly discouraged, which provided the exact atmosphere for the most unexpected and saving experience of their lives.

Several years ago one of my counseling clients gave me a desk plaque that reads: "When the pupil is ready the teacher will come." Just as Jesus came into the world at the right time, there is a real sense that Jesus shows up in our lives at the right time—when we are ready. There is no universal formula we can circulate to designate when we are ready. Our readiness and openness to Christ coming into our lives is a condition that is far more specific to each individual than general and applicable to all. It is not that God in Christ is not always standing at the door of our lives ready to come. God is always ready. We are the ones who must be ready to receive God into our lives.

When we are bursting with self-assurance we are not ready. When we feel no need for divine assistance, we are not ready. Have you ever wondered why Jesus said: "Truly, I say to you, it will be hard for a rich man to enter the kingdom of heaven. Again I tell you, it is easier for a camel to go through the eye of a needle than for a rich man to enter the kingdom of heaven" (Matthew 19:23-24 RSV)! It was not that Jesus had something against rich people. Jesus knew, as we know, that riches tend to confer a false sense of independence and make people think they have no need for God or anyone. When we count on our wealth to save us, wealth becomes our god, and we are not ready.

We are more likely to be ready to recognize Jesus when we find ourselves in the zone of desperation. We are open to divine intervention in our world when we see no way out on our own. When I was a fuzzy-cheeked young preacher, I remember one of our old preachers being asked to offer the opening prayer one morning at Annual Conference. He opened his prayer by saying: "O Lord, if you saw the *Montgomery Advertizer* this morning you know we are in serious trouble." I chuckled to myself to hear this old man address God in such a way, but upon reflection I realized that this was a signal in prayer that we are ready. Come, Lord Jesus!

I am not suggesting that we should seek conditions of crisis in order to lure God into our lives. Not to worry, life will provide all the crises we need without our contriving a crisis. Neither wisdom, wealth, good planning—not even luck—will save us from those unbidden occasions when the bottom drops out—when life splits open at the seams and we find ourselves in over our heads. It happens to us all and then the God you thought you did not need will become the object of a fervent search. When the gods you made for yourself topple, when your life falls in shambles at your feet, when something happens that money cannot fix and all your virtues cannot prevent and life becomes dark at noonday—you will be ready, and God will show up in ways and places and persons you least expected.

Easter stretches into all of the rest of our lives. You may not be able to recreate the experience in which God showed up in your life, but you will never be the same again after you realized he was right there with you and you did not know it until he was gone. The afterglow of the unexpected Jesus lingers to flavor all the rest of life, and you will never feel alone again. (Thomas Lane Butts)

Worship Aids

Prayer of Confession

We confess how the disillusionment of disappointing outcomes overshadows our lives and weakens our will and witness. Save us from giving up too soon and going home too quickly when things have not worked out as we thought they should. May Jesus show up in our lives when we are walking the wrong way. Amen.

Words of Assurance

In the name of Jesus Christ, you are forgiven.
In the name of Jesus Christ, you are forgiven. Amen.

Pastoral Prayer

Dear God, whose way is mercy and whose name is love, stand among us today in one of the many ways you come to encourage your people. We do not ask for complete knowledge, but we pray to know enough to be saved from complete ignorance. We do not pray for a blinding light, but enough light to keep us from being blind. Help us open our lives to the gifts of wisdom and insight you know that we need.

We sense the hurts of people around us and pray for the wisdom and insight to reach out in your name to touch and heal. We pray for those among us and around us whose hearts are troubled over the death of a loved one. In your mercy, O Lord, help us reflect the light of the resurrected Jesus into their darkness and gloom.

We pray for peace in the world, peace in our nation, peace in the church, and peace in our hearts. Save us from our inclinations to solve problems with violence that can only be solved by love. In the good name of Jesus, amen.

Benediction

In our rush to get home today, let us not leave this holy place without enough of the reflected light of the resurrection to save us from despair about the death and dying we will see in ourselves and others this week. Help us, Jesus! Amen. (Thomas Lane Butts)

MAY 4, 2008

❧❧❧

Seventh Sunday of Easter

Readings: Acts 1:6-14; Psalm 68:1-10, 32-35; 1 Peter 4:12-14, 5:6-11;
John 17:1-11

What Goes Up
Acts 1:6-14

(Rather than using a dated television reference, a movie with an uncertain ending could be substituted; a good example might be Gone with the Wind.*)*
Some of you already know, but over the past few months I have been absolutely obsessed with JAG. That's right, that awesome family friendly law/military show on Friday nights. The newsletter crew has heard me bemoan for months now that the show was cancelled and my two favorite characters on television, Mac and Harm, had not gotten together. For nine years I have watched these two banter around a relationship and I vowed that the last episode they should get together. Well, they finally did, but neither could decide who would give up their Navy career. It looked like the show would end without that happy conclusion. Then the two characters decided that they would let fate decide by tossing a coin in the air. The show ended with all the characters gathered around, while Mac and Harm decided their careers and their lives on the toss of a coin. As I watched, it felt like all Americans had done the same thing, sitting on the end of their couches just waiting for that coin to land. And suddenly, the coin started to spin and hit its height and … the end. The show ended with that coin up in the air. "What?" I protested, probably quite loudly as I looked at my husband, looked back at the TV, and back at my husband again. But I wanted to know the answer; who would head to a new billet in San Diego or London? Would Harm remain in the Navy? Would Mac remain a Marine? Alas, I shall never know, because that coin was left flipping up in the air.

Welcome to Jesus' ascension. Today the proverbial coin is left hanging in the air. It has been forty days since Easter. During this time, Jesus has been with the disciples, teaching them, feeding them, and spending time with them. Now it is time for Jesus to go. Jesus leads those disciples out to the Mount of Olives near Bethany. He rises into the sky and ascends into heaven. Jesus must go up.

With Jesus' ascension we, like those disciples so long ago, are left wondering what is going on; we're left hanging in the air, so to speak. We know that something has been promised; Jesus said something about being clothed on high. But what does he mean?

We humans don't really like not knowing, do we? We want it made clear and outlined, otherwise we are left with questions. What really will happen with Harm and Mac? What is Jesus talking about? Who's coming? Now we know some of these answers, maybe not the JAG answer, but we know that next week we will celebrate Pentecost. The church will be born and we will receive the Holy Spirit. But we celebrate Ascension Sunday each year as a reminder that faith isn't about knowing all the answers. Those early disciples didn't know everything and certainly, neither do we. Faith is about the not knowing, the leaving it all up in the air, leaving it up to God, and trusting in God's promises.

But none of us likes the up-in-the-air choices. We want definitive answers, we make the safe choices, and we trust in ourselves rather than in God.

Jesus' ascension is about placing our faith and trust in our Lord Jesus Christ. Jesus led those disciples out to Bethany, he went up into heaven, and then Jesus left them with only his words as a promise. But it is the response of the disciples that reminds us of our own actions. Those disciples didn't despair, they didn't leave in tears and mourning thinking it was over, they watched him go up into heaven and then they trusted in his words and devoted themselves to prayer. "All these were continually devoting themselves to prayer, together with certain women, including Mary the mother of Jesus, as well as his brothers."

The disciples respond with praise and worship. Despite their fear of the unknown, their need for control and their questions, the disciples responded with faith. That is what makes us Christians different. Our response to the unknown is prayer and faith. Those early disciples teach us that we need to have faith that even in the questions, when everything around us is up in the air, faith will push us along and keep us strong.

Our faith is assurance, even when the going is tough and everything is in question. In the moments of our lives when things are left up in the air and we just don't know, that is when it is crucial to place our faith in Jesus Christ.

The ascension is our reminder to retain hope even when it all seems in question. Those disciples didn't stand on that mountain and mourn Jesus' departure; they trusted in his promises and knew that even then they weren't alone. The disciples continued through the fear of the unknown and trusted in their Lord and Savior. They gathered together, surrounded themselves with a community of faith and prayed for the answer and for God's time to be revealed.

The next time you are filled with questions and it seems like only a coin toss can decide, place your trust in your true Lord, pray, have faith, and wait for the presence of God. Amen. (Jennifer H. Williams)

Lectionary Commentary
John 17:1-11

The John passage precedes Jesus' arrest and passion narrative. Before going to the Mount of Olives, Jesus prepares himself through prayer. This week's Gospel shows Jesus praying for the disciples. In his prayer, Jesus teaches the church how we are to pray for the world and ourselves. In the final verse, Jesus prays, "Protect them by the power of your name—the name you gave me—so that they may be one as we are one" (v. 11 NIV). This statement of faith, highlighting the unity of the Holy Trinity, also teaches us about the unity of the church. As we prepare for our own tribulation and trials, we are to be a people protected by the Holy Spirit and united by our faith in Jesus Christ. Unfortunately, the church is all too often separated by our beliefs rather than united by them. Our message to the world is one of imperative importance and needs to be spread. However, our own schisms within the local church and the global church provide fodder for a world discounting us. We fail to remember and work towards unity with the goal of spreading the message of Jesus Christ.

1 Peter 4:12-14, 5:6-11

The 1 Peter text ties nicely to the gospel passage. Just as we are a people who needs to be unified, we also need to be aware that there is evil that desires to penetrate the boundaries of the church. "Be self-controlled and alert. Your enemy the devil prowls around like a roaring lion looking for someone to devour" (v. 5:8 NIV). The task of the church is to resist evil and stand firm in our faith. What are ways that the church is being attacked from outside? From the inside? And how can the people of God called the church stand firm? The church is a countercultural movement that may provide a different path from the world around it. As we prepare for Pentecost, this passage reminds us that to receive the gift of the Holy Spirit entails a calling to stand firm in faith despite the forces that would like to see us fail. (Jennifer H. Williams)

Worship Aids

Invocation

God, help us sing your praise throughout the world. As we gather together this morning, fill us with your Holy Spirit to be your people beyond these walls. You came to show us how to live and to give us eternal life; may we share that message of joy with the world around us. Amen.

Prayer of Confession

Forgive us, heavenly Lord. All too often we stand basking in your presence instead of serving you in our midst. Help us see you in our brothers and sisters and extend ourselves in ministry to you. Move us beyond ourselves to be your people in the world. Amen.

Words of Assurance

In the name of Jesus Christ, you are forgiven.
In the name of Jesus Christ, you are forgiven. Amen.

Benediction

Toss a coin in the air and say, "Our future is uncertain and it may feel like everything is up in the air, but wait, for Christ will provide." May Christ be with you in this community and as you go through your ministry in the week ahead. In the name of the one God, Father, Son, and Holy Spirit. Amen. (Jennifer H. Williams)

Easter for All Seasons

Third in a Series of Three on Easter

Mark 16:1-8

Religion has always developed around those areas and aspects of life we do not understand, not around those areas we do understand or think we understand. When our world is manageable we may tip our hats toward some sort of higher power in a conventional fashion. Some people do not feel they need anything religious to help negotiate life when they are doing all right on their own. But, when life breaks open at the seams and we are standing before some mystery that is larger than life and beyond comprehension, we begin to look at and think of life in a different way.

It is no accident that when we are looking for spiritual insight and power we walk up a hill outside Jerusalem and stand as close as we dare to the tragic scene of a crucifixion, where a gaunt figure hangs between heaven and earth and between life and death, and we hang on to every word we hear. "Father forgive them, for they know not what they do"— "To day shalt thou be with me in paradise"—"Father, into thy hands I commend my spirit" (Luke 23:34, 43, 46 KJV). What tragedy! What mystery! But, we are drawn to it like a magnet.

When our souls are empty and our hearts ache and we do not understand life, we walk on out to a graveyard, to a tomb that is open and empty. In the presence of that tremendous mystery, which nobody can begin to explain, where by some divine alchemy death and tragedy get transformed into light and life we find hope, encouragement, and the will to go on.

Every now and then, just when we think we cannot go on, something strange, sometimes simple, happens and we get a quick glimpse into the heart of God's eternal mysteries. A stranger says or does something and then disappears forever. A tragedy turns into a triumph; a miracle happens before our eyes; a child is born or dies or says or does something; and our eyes are opened, our hearts are melted with love and for a few seconds the mysteries of the universe are laid bare before our very eyes.

Sometimes Easter happens on a dark Tuesday afternoon in December, and for a moment we feel in touch with someone or something important with which we have been out of touch for a long time. Sometimes an angel touches your life in midsummer and suddenly you see and understand things gloriously differently. You stop being afraid of old ghosts that have haunted you ever since you can remember. You quit caring about all the wrong things and learn how to empty your life of junk. After all, Easter is a day of miracles for the dead, and all of us are or have been or will be dead. Whenever that happens we need an Easter happening.

Let me tell you an Easter story. Several years ago one of my unusually smart (and sometimes smart-aleck) preacher friends, who knows how I love a story, called me and said: "Dr. Butts, I am sending you a story. It is yours to tell only if you can be professional enough to tell it without a tear in your eye or quiver in your voice." I took the challenge but lost. You want to try? I do not know the origin of the story, but here it is.

Once upon a time there was a little boy named Philip who was born with Down's syndrome. He was a very pleasant and happy child it seemed, but increasingly aware of the difference between himself and other children.

Philip went to Sunday school each Sunday with nine other eight-year-old children. The Sunday school teacher was a very sensitive and creative man. Philip, with his increasingly noticeable difference, was not readily accepted as a member of this third-grade Sunday school class. But this teacher knew how to facilitate a class of eight-year-old children. They learned and they laughed and they played together. They really cared about each other, even though, as you know, eight-year-olds don't say they care about each other out loud very often. But the teacher could see it. He also knew that Philip was not really a part of the group. Of course, he did not choose or want to be different. He just was.

The Sunday school teacher had a marvelous design for his class on the Sunday after Easter. You know those things that pantyhose come in—the containers look like eggs. The teacher collected ten of them to use on that Sunday. The children loved it. Each child was given an egg. It was a beautiful spring day, and the assigned task was for each child to go outside on the church grounds and find a symbol of new life, put it in the egg, and bring it back to the classroom. They would then mix them all up and then all open and share their new life symbols and surprises together, one by one.

It was wild as they ran around outside and then came back in and put their eggs on a table. The teacher began to open them one by one. There was a flower in one. Another had a butterfly.

He opened another, and there was a rock. Some laughed and some said, "That is crazy! How's a rock supposed to be like new life?" But the smart little boy about whose egg they were speaking spoke up. He said, "That is mine. I knew all of you would get flowers, and buds, and leaves, and butterflies, and stuff like that. So, I got a rock because I wanted to be different. And for me, that's new life—the rock that was rolled from the tomb."

The teacher opened the next one, and there was nothing there. The children said, "That's not fair. That's stupid! Somebody didn't do right." About that time the teacher felt a tug on his shirt, and he looked down and Philip was standing beside him. "It's mine," Philip said. "It's mine."

And the children said, "You don't ever do things right, Philip. There's nothing in it!" "I did so do it right," Philip said. "I did do it. It's empty—the tomb is empty!"

The class was silent, very silent. And for you people who don't believe in miracles, one happened that day. From that time on, it was different. Philip suddenly became a part of that group of eight-year-old children. They took him in. He was set free from the tomb of his differentness.

Philip died in the summer of that year. His family had known since the time he was born that he would not live out a full life span. Many other things had been wrong with his tiny little body. In late July, with an infection that most normal children could have quickly shrugged off, Philip died.

He was buried from the church where he went to Sunday school. At the funeral nine eight-year-old children marched up to the altar—not with flowers to cover the stark reality of death. Nine eight-year-olds, with their Sunday school teacher, marched up to that altar and each laid on it an empty egg—an empty old discarded holder of panty hose.

Sometimes Easter happens in the strangest ways, at the strangest times, and in the strangest places. It never lasts long, except as we remember it. It is like a door that opens for a moment and then it closes. We keep on looking for it again and again to remind ourselves that things are not as they seem. There is a different world out there that is more real than the world we see.

Do you understand that? I don't but I do believe it. (Thomas Lane Butts)

Worship Aids

Prayer of Confession

We confess, O Lord, to the sin of frozen doubt that we have been unwilling to expose to the light of faith and insight, which you freely give to all who earnestly search. Save us from our little fears that seem so big from where we stand and how we are looking at reality. And when the circumstances of life bend us out of shape and we begin to doubt what we thought we really knew, let us hear again the words of Jesus who said: "Because I live you shall live also." Amen. (Thomas Lane Butts)

Words of Assurance

In the name of Jesus Christ, you are forgiven.
In the name of Jesus Christ, you are forgiven. Amen.

Pastoral Prayer

Most holy Lord God, whose ways are not our ways and whose thoughts are higher than our thoughts, shine the light of higher things on our lowly lives. We want to know, O Lord, and what we cannot know, we want to believe; and for what we cannot believe, help our unbelief. May something be sung or said or preached or prayed that will help us with the dark spots in our lives.

Help us act and live in such ways as to contribute to the church really being church. Forgive our impulsive and thoughtless words with which we have sideswiped people around us this past week. Help us be more sensitive to the needs of people who do not clamor for attention, but who need attention. Teach us the fine art of extracting ourselves from people who are emotionally greedy so that we will have time for the quiet and shy and even the unlovely people whose needs are obvious, but who are afraid to ask for anything.

Save us from all our sins, especially those sins that are so much a part of who we are that we do not notice them any more.

Bless our worship today that it may touch the lives of people who haven't experienced church at church lately.

In the name of Jesus. Amen. (Thomas Lane Butts)

Benediction

May the grace of the Lord Jesus save you from sin, and the love of God give you something to tie to in a world that buffets the insecure, and may the pervading presence of the Holy Spirit keep you properly stirred up. Amen. (Thomas Lane Butts)

MAY 11, 2008

❧❧❧❧

Pentecost

Readings: Acts 2:1-21; Psalm 104:24-34, 35b; John 20:19-23;
1 Corinthians 12:3b-13

Where's the Fire?
Acts 2:1-21

Today is Pentecost Sunday, a day we remember and celebrate when the Holy Spirit was first given to Jesus' disciples. For the past few years, every time Pentecost Sunday has rolled around, a particular memory has come to my mind.

It's something that happened years ago when I was a young, naïve associate pastor. It was Pentecost Sunday, and I was offering the pastoral prayer in worship. It went something like this: "We thank you today, O God, for the gift of the Holy Spirit. We thank you for sending it among us."

After the service the senior pastor I was working with at the time pulled me aside and said, "The Holy Spirit is not an 'it.' The Spirit is a person of the Trinity to whom we relate. We pray to the Spirit; we love the Spirit; we commune with the Spirit. You can say 'he' or 'she,' I don't care, but don't say 'it.'" I'd never thought about that before. His words caused me to reflect a long time on my relationship with the Holy Spirit.

To be honest, the fact that I called the Spirit "it" showed the distance I felt from the Spirit. I never prayed to the Spirit. I never thought about loving the Spirit. And I certainly didn't think of her or him as being as important as God the Father and God the Son. In fact, I rarely thought about the Spirit at all.

The truth is many of us in the church today are baffled by the Holy Spirit. We gather on Sunday mornings and recite the creed together, "I believe in the Holy Spirit." But how often do we really talk about the Spirit?

Sure, we have our vague notions about how the Spirit works. When we think of the Spirit, we think of the comforter. We think of divine nudges, soft whispers, gentle presence. And all of that is true. The Holy Spirit is our Comforter and our Advocate.

In fact, this morning I was going to preach a sermon about that very thing: how the Holy Spirit is not just loud and fiery, like she was on the day of Pentecost. The Spirit is often quiet, gentle and subtle, easy to miss. We don't all have to be fiery to be filled with the Holy Spirit. And that's all true.

But then I went back to the second chapter of Acts and realized there's no getting around it in this story. The Holy Spirit is loud, fiery, and earth-shattering. Listen to how Luke recounts the story of Pentecost: "Suddenly from heaven there came a sound like the rush of a violent wind, and it filled the entire house ... divided tongues, as of fire, appeared among them, and a tongue rested on each of them. All of them were filled with the Holy Spirit." Did you hear Luke's words? "Suddenly," "rush," "violent wind," "fire."

There's nothing subtle here. The Holy Spirit arrives loudly and dramatically. And she sets the disciples on fire. They were never the same after that. And neither was the world.

The Spirit brought about radical change. In that moment on the day of Pentecost, the Spirit transformed a ragtag gathering of Jesus' disciples into the body of Christ, the church. Peter the impulsive, James and John the competitive, Mary the meek, Thomas the doubtful—everyone in that room that day was changed. Some became prophets, some healers, some preachers, some caregivers—some would travel the world preaching, others would stay behind-the-scenes caring for the poor—but all of them were set on fire. With the power of the Holy Spirit, they changed the world.

Now, here we are today—the church of the twenty-first century. Up and down our street this morning there are churches celebrating Pentecost. Some will have birthday cake to celebrate the birth of the church. Some will have red and white balloons. Some will ask their members to wear red. Some will have liturgical dancers waving red banners. We know very well how to celebrate Pentecost.

But, the story of Pentecost raises to us the question: "Where's the fire?" When we invited the Holy Spirit into our worship this morning, did we really know what we were asking for? Yes, we want the Comforter. We want the Advocate. We want to come here and feel the gentle presence of the Spirit. We wouldn't even mind a little nudge or two.

But do we really want the fire? We like the Holy Spirit to be warm . . . but hot? Do we really want to be changed? Would we call upon the Spirit if we knew it meant that we'd have to live and love differently? Do we realize what we're doing when we call upon the Holy Spirit?

When those first disciples were anointed with the Holy Spirit, it was a pretty wild scene. People on the street thought the disciples were drunk. The disciples were so excited, so fired up, so full of the Spirit that people thought they were crazy.

Do people on the street ever look at us Christians and think we're crazy? Do we look different enough from the world that people notice us at all? Don't get me wrong. I don't think we're necessarily called to be "shoutin' Christians." We don't all have to be fiery and loud. I'm not talking about that kind of heat.

What I want to know is, are our hearts really on fire? Is God really at the center of our lives? Do we love in a way that is radical? Are we extravagantly generous? Do we forgive the unforgivable? Do we reach out to the least and the lost? Are we so loving, so compassionate, so giving, so humble, that the world thinks we're crazy?

This morning is Confirmation Sunday in our church. When someone is baptized among us, we all pray for the Holy Spirit to work within that person. Do we take that prayer seriously? Do we really want the Holy Spirit to fill these young people?

To those of you who are being baptized and confirmed, I could say nicely and warmly, "Welcome to the church. I hope you get involved in the youth group. I hope you have fun. I hope you grow up to be nice and well rounded. I hope your activities at church are as enriching to you as band camp, as a soccer season, or as your many other activities."

But I feel led to say something else this morning. What I really want to say to you is—Watch out! If you really want to take this step, if you really want to take this journey with Christ, if you really want the Holy Spirit to work within you, then put on your crash helmets. Get ready because the Spirit can set a fire in your hearts.

Your relationship with God in the Spirit is not just another good activity to keep you busy. It is the most important thing in this life. It is everything. And if you really want to say yes to God, then be ready. The Spirit will make you do crazy things like loving your enemies. The Spirit will make you reach out to people who are outcast. The Spirit will make you spend your money differently. The Spirit will make you cry for the suffer-ing of others. The Spirit will make you want to change the world.

Now ... for all of us who welcome these confirmands today, we as a church must let the Spirit do the Spirit's work. As these confirmands join us on the journey, we dare not try to quench their fire. We dare not cool down the message of the gospel.

Let us not teach them to be sensible and moderate. Let's not teach them how to fit in. Let's teach them instead to be drunk with love for God, crazy in their compassion for others, unreasonable in their faith, extravagant in their kindness, and radical in their commitment to God and God's people. And let's do more than that. Let's teach them how to stir up a little trouble in the world.

May we teach them not so much with our words as with our lives. (Carol Cavin-Dillon)

Lectionary Commentary
1 Corinthians 12:3b-13

When we read this familiar passage, we often focus on the variety of gifts named here. We use this passage as a foundation to talk about the diversity of spiritual gifts in the Christian community. On Pentecost Sunday, however, we might focus instead on the one source of all gifts: the Spirit.

When it comes to spiritual gifts, we often assume that some gifts are better than others. Not only that, but we assume that the people with those gifts are better. We think some people are more worthy or more honored than others because of the gifts that they have.

But Paul proclaims to the Corinthians that all gifts are from God. Our gifts are not deserved. They are not a reflection on us at all. They are for God's glory and for the building up of the community. Moreover, all gifts are of equal importance. So our gifts must not separate us and place some of us over others. Our gifts should unite us, reminding us that we all are dependent on the Holy Spirit.

John 20:19-23

Since this passage comes to us on Pentecost Sunday, we would do well to focus on the gift of the Holy Spirit. John's version is very different from Luke's version in Acts. Here, Jesus is still with the disciples and he breathes on them.

By saying that Jesus breathed on them, John calls to mind God's creation of humankind in Genesis 2:7. Adam was made out of the dust of the earth, but God's breath gave Adam a soul, a spirit. Likewise, Jesus' disciples were sinful human beings, wrapped up in their own status and their own security. (They were so afraid for their lives that they locked the doors!) But when Jesus breathed onto them, the Holy Spirit gave them the power, the gifts, and the boldness to change the world. (Carol Cavin-Dillon)

Worship Aids

Call to Worship

When the day of Pentecost had come, they were all together in one place.
Come, Holy Spirit! Break into our gathering!
And suddenly from heaven there came a sound like the rush of a violent wind.
Come, Holy Spirit! Stir us with your power!
Divided tongues, as of fire, appeared among them.
Come, Holy Spirit! Set our hearts on fire!
And all of them were filled with the Holy Spirit.
Come, Holy Spirit! Fill us again with your love!

Prayer of Confession

O Holy Spirit, we remember today how you came to the disciples with a rush of wind and tongues of fire. Yet we confess to you that our faith has become stagnant and lukewarm. No wind blows. No fire burns. We have become comfortable and complacent. Forgive us, we pray. Fill us again with your power. Set our hearts on fire again that we may give ourselves completely to you. In Christ's name we pray. Amen.

Words of Assurance

In the name of Jesus Christ, you are forgiven.
In the name of Jesus Christ, you are forgiven. Amen.

Benediction

Go from this place knowing that the Holy Spirit goes with you. But be warned, when you follow the Spirit, you never know where you might end up. But there are some things you will know. You will know that you are not alone. You will know power. And you will know peace. Amen. (Carol Cavin-Dillon)

The Church's Biblical Foundation

First in a Series of Three on "Is the Church Christian?"

Micah 6:8; Luke 10:25-28

Karl Barth writes, "There can be no thought of the being of Jesus Christ enclosed in that of His community, or exhausted by it, as though it were a kind of predicate of this being. The truth is the very opposite. The being of the community is exhausted and enclosed in His" (*Church Dogmatics*, IV/2 [Edinburgh: T & T Clark, 1958], 655).

References to the church are few in Scripture. The Greek word for "church," *ekklesia*, is found only five times in the Gospels, all in Matthew. Jesus anoints Simon as Peter and declares, "on this rock I will build my church" (Matthew 16:18). We find all other references in the eighteenth chapter of Matthew where Jesus outlines an agenda of caring and forgiving among members of the church. "If another member of the church sins against me," asks Peter, "how often should I forgive? As many as seven times?" "Not seven times," says Jesus, "but, I tell you, seventy-seven times" (Matthew 18:21-22).

While the institutional church is not a central focus in Scripture, making disciples is central. The word *disciple* appears two hundred forty one times in the NRSV New Testament. Jesus is constantly inviting people to follow him and encouraging others to be inviting. "Go therefore," says Jesus, "and make disciples of all nations" (Matthew 28:19). Disciple making is clearly the primary function of Jesus' followers, the church.

Luke records that a group of seventy were dispatched by Jesus on a disciple-making mission and returned overjoyed. "Lord, in your name even the demons submit to us!" (Luke 10:17). These disciples discovered the shocking authority in Jesus Christ.

Paul was the church builder. The authority of the church lies in Christ, but its foundational principles may be more Pauline. Paul was a Pharisee. However, Paul clearly attempted to create a new church based on faith and love rather than on law and judgment. "For the promise that he would inherit the world did not come to Abraham," writes Paul, "or to his descendants through the law but through the righteousness of faith" (Romans 4:13). For Paul, the law fulfills through the commandment to love your neighbor as yourself (Romans 13:9-10).

The definition of *neighbor* became a point of conflict in the early church, especially between Peter and Paul; Paul desired to extend fellowship to Gentiles, and Peter was reluctant. Paul refers to Peter as hypocritical in his stance against the inclusion of Gentiles (Galatians 2:13). Paul's inclusive vision of the church eventually won favor, but this conflict was the first demonstration of the church's fallibility. The scars of conflict are evident in Paul's letters. Paul refers to the conflict in the Corinthian church discovered through Chloe's people (1 Corinthians 1:11) and between Euodia and Syntyche in the Philippian church (Philippians 4:2). Paul hoped to raise the church above human conflict through faith in Christ where people no longer see each other from a human point of view, but as a new creation in Christ (2 Corinthians 5:18).

The earliest Christian believers were Jews who had no vision of a church separated from Judaism. While Jesus was constantly at odds with Jewish leadership, it is unclear whether he intended a separate faith community, or to reform Judaism.

Jesus taught obedience to the authority of Jewish leaders, while disapproving of their behavior. "They tie up heavy burdens, hard to bear, and lay them on the shoulders of others; but they themselves are unwilling to lift a finger to move them" (Matthew 23:4). They were purveyors of judgment without offering God's grace.

The early motivation of the Christian church was to share the good news of Jesus Christ. Jesus roamed the countryside teaching, healing people, and inviting them to follow, but he did not seem interested in institutionalizing his movement. The church found authority in Christ, but its organizational principles are Pauline.

The guiding principles of the early church were faith in God through Jesus Christ, and love of neighbor. When a scribe asked Jesus how he could gain eternal life, Jesus asked him, "What is written?" He answered, "You shall love the Lord your God with all your heart, and with all your soul, and with all your strength, and with all your mind; and your neighbor as yourself." These principles are central to Deuteronomic and Levitical law and to the prophet Micah's declaration that the Lord requires us "to do justice, and to love kindness, / and to walk humbly with your God." The foundation of the church is found in the principles of justice and faith.

Rather than offering a prescription for his church, Jesus modeled expected behavior. Jesus healed the sick and ate with sinners. Jesus sat at table with Pharisees and with tax collectors, leading the Jewish leadership to say, "Look, a glutton and a drunkard, a friend of tax collectors and sinners!" (Luke 7:34). Jesus' ministry had no boundaries. Jesus extended the love of God to all who would respond.

The early church lived out Micah's call for justice and loving kindness. They invited all neighbors to the table and cared for one another as they worshiped God together. They lived the model of Christ's inclusive and caring ministry.

Paul hoped the church would be the new creation in the image of Christ. The early church was modeled after Christ's ministry, claiming Jesus' authority. The foundation of the church was found in God's radical grace and its inclusive invitation.

Karl Barth recognized the church as a potentially fallible human institution. However, its power and its hope lie in the authority granted by Jesus Christ to extend God's grace to all. The underlying principles of the church of Jesus Christ are to love God, and to live justly with our neighbors. (Dan L. Flanagan)

Worship Aids

Call to Worship

We gather as the church of Jesus Christ.
We gather with the authority of Christ.
Jesus called Peter and calls us to be his church.
All: As his church, we are called to care for each other, and to care for our neighbors.

Prayer of Confession

Lord, we have failed to be your church. You call us to love you and our neighbor. Instead, we live self-centered lives. We have built the church around our needs rather than the needs of our neighbors. Forgive our lack of compassion. Lord, help us be a church faithful to your call. Amen.

Words of Assurance

In the name of Jesus Christ, you are forgiven.
In the name of Jesus Christ, you are forgiven. Amen.

Benediction

May we walk humbly with God and do justice. May we be the church of Jesus Christ! (Dan L. Flanagan)

MAY 18, 2008

❧❧❧

Trinity Sunday

Readings: Genesis 1:1–2:4a; Psalm 8; 2 Corinthians 13:11-13; Matthew 28:16-20

The Trinity: Relevant or Not?

Psalm 8; Genesis 1:1–2:4a; Matthew 28:16-20; 2 Corinthians 13:11-13

Several years ago in another church where I was serving, the children's minister asked me if I would speak to the first-grade Sunday school class. The topic was worship, and he wanted me to meet with the children in the sanctuary so that we could get a close look at the baptismal font, the altar, and the paraments. Of course, I agreed. I love children and I think it's so important to teach them about why we do what we do in the church.

So, at 9:45 on that Sunday morning, I met the youngsters at the front of the sanctuary. The children's minister had asked me to wear my robe so that the children could see it and we could talk about it. After we toured the sanctuary and talked about colors and symbols, I sat down with them and asked if they had any questions. One little girl looked down, pointed at my white stole and said, "What's that thing?"

I looked at my stole and said, "It's a symbol of the Trinity."

"What's the Trinity?" she asked.

"Uh...." For the next five minutes (which seemed like an eternity) I found myself trying to explain the Trinity to a group of first graders. I failed miserably. By the time I finished hemming and hawing, they looked so confused! How in the world do you teach a bunch of six-year-olds about the most complicated theological concept in the book? I guess the answer is just to wait until they're older. A six-year-old is too young for *Narnia*, much less the Trinity!

Wait until they're teenagers. Or even adults. We adults can handle such theological complexities, right? We've been to school. We've studied literature and algebra and biology and philosophy. Heck, some of us

164

even have a Masters and PhD! Surely it's easy for us to understand and explain the Trinity.

"Uh…"

One of my professors in seminary jokingly tried to explain it to us: "It makes perfect sense. God is three … is one … is three. Get it?"

"Uh…"

Let's be honest. It's hard to wrap our brains around the Trinity. Sure, we've all heard the shamrock idea: Just as the shamrock is one plant with three leaves, God is one God with three faces. Or maybe we've heard the water image: Just as H_2O can take three forms in ice, liquid, and steam, so God has three forms. Helpful? Yes. Especially when faced with thirty first-graders looking to you for answers. But these images don't answer many of our questions.

The truth is, the Trinity is a great mystery that is hard to understand and even harder to explain. And yet, it lies at the foundation of what we Christians believe about God. Almost every creed of the church affirms our belief in God the Father, Jesus Christ the Son, and the Holy Spirit. We even devote a high holy day of the church to this mystery. This morning we celebrate Trinity Sunday. But do we have any idea what we're doing?

Is the Trinity just an obscure doctrine that we give lip service to because the church calendar tells us to? Does it have anything to do with our daily living? Think about it—what does the Trinity mean to you? It's worth pondering and praying over.

In our Scripture readings this morning and throughout our worship, we have heard about the three persons of the Trinity. We have recalled how God revealed Godself to us in three distinct ways.

Genesis 1 recounts the power of God the Creator. In the beginning God created the heavens and the earth. A loving and powerful God made the universe in all its vastness and mystery. Psalm 8 sings of the wonders of the universe and how they reveal to us the power of our Creator. The stars, the planets, the oceans, and the mountains—all of it came from the hand of God. But this creator God is not just concerned with the grandness of the universe. God is also our loving parent who created each strand of our DNA with care. God our Father/Mother created each one of us to be unique, to have special gifts, and special purpose. Your life and my life matter to God. We have a place in this universe and a calling to fulfill. It is God who has created us in love and calls us to live in love. So, yes, that makes sense. That's relevant to our daily lives.

One way that God teaches us how to love creation and one another is in the person of Jesus Christ. As Matthew and the other gospel writers tell us, Jesus walked alongside us on this earth to show us the face of God. And in Jesus' death and resurrection, God becomes our Redeemer. Now, we spend a lot of time in the church talking about Jesus. We learn about Jesus' teaching, his example, his healing, and his love. The gospel stories give us something tangible to hold onto. Jesus gives us all sorts of guidance on how to live our lives. It's not hard to find ways that Jesus is relevant to our lives. Just count how many cars have the bumper sticker: "What Would Jesus Do?"

What about the Holy Spirit? For many of us, the Spirit is very relevant to our daily living. We recognize the Spirit's activity all around us: in those little nudges to call someone or pray for someone, in the peace that surrounds us when we undergo surgery, in the inspiration that comes when we're teaching Sunday school or praying, in the committee meeting where truth is spoken and consensus is reached. Many of us know the Spirit as our sustainer, our inspiration, our daily guide.

We see daily evidence of God our Creator. We strive to follow the concrete example of Jesus the Christ. We look for signs of the Holy Spirit around us. Individually, the three persons of the Trinity make sense to us. But what does it mean for the three to be one and the one to be three? God the Father, Son, and Holy Spirit. Creator, Redeemer, Sustainer. One in three in one. Ice and liquid and steam. Three leaves of a shamrock. What power can this mysterious doctrine have for us?

Whether you relate most to God the Creator, Jesus the Redeemer, or the Holy Spirit Sustainer, the mystery of the Trinity has something to teach us this morning. There is something beautiful and powerful about a God in three persons. There is something God can reveal to us when we ponder the mystery of the Trinity.

In the Hermitage Museum in St. Petersburg, Russia, there is an icon of the Holy Trinity painted by Andrei Rublev sometime around 1400 C.E. For those of you who are unfamiliar with icons, they are pictures that are used in prayer. Believers are to gaze at them prayerfully until they become like a window into the heart of God. God can reveal Godself to us as we are praying through the image of an icon.

This particular icon portrays the three persons of the Holy Trinity as three angels sitting together at a table. The head of each angel is inclined toward one of the others, so that there seems to be a circular movement around the table, connecting the three to one another. On the table is a chalice. What this image reveals to me is that in God there is a living, loving community. From the beginning of time until the end of the age, God the Father, God the Son, and God the Holy Spirit have existed as a holy community of love and grace. To put it another way, God is community.

And now we, as God's children, are invited into that holy community. We are invited into the holy dance of the Creator, Redeemer, and Sustainer. We join in the dance when we respond to the love of God by loving God in return.

So, as we reflect on the Trinity, don't let it be just a vague, dry doctrine for us. Don't write it off as something that's just too complicated for us to understand. Don't leave it to the seminary professors to debate about.

Let's think about the community of love that has been within God since the beginning of time. Let's accept God's invitation to join in that community. As we see real, concrete examples of how God has created us, redeemed us, and sustained us, let us respond with love and gratitude. Let us add our love to the Trinity's communion of love.

What's more, let God be revealed in our community. The Trinity teaches us that no one ever stands alone. As soon as we accept God's love and redemption, we are members of a community. We cannot be Christians without being connected to one another. Sorry. If we're going to embrace God the Creator, Redeemer, and Sustainer, then we're going to have to embrace each other. Not just the folks who are inside the church's four walls this morning, but everyone who calls upon the Triune God.

If that weren't hard enough, God calls us to do more. Not only do we have to love other believers, but we have to go out and share God's love with the world. Jesus commanded his followers: "Go therefore and make disciples of all nations, baptizing them in the name of the Father and of the Son and of the Holy Spirit, and teaching them to obey everything that I have commanded you" (Matthew 28:19-20). The love we find in the Trinity, the communion we find with one another, is not just for our own sakes. It's for the sake of the world. It's meant to be shared.

The world needs love. The world needs grace. The world needs community. May the Triune God—Father, Son, and Holy Spirit—Creator, Redeemer, and Sustainer—help us to share the message of the Trinity with all of creation. (Carol Cavin-Dillon)

Worship Aids

Scriptural Call to Worship (Genesis 1:1; Psalm 8:1; John 1:14, 20:22)

In the beginning God created the heavens and the earth.

O Lord, our Sovereign, how majestic is your name in all the earth!

And the Word became flesh and lived among us.
O Lord, our Sovereign, how majestic is your name in all the earth!
Jesus breathed on his disciples and said to them, "Receive the Holy Spirit."
O Lord, our Sovereign, how majestic is your name in all the earth!
O Lord, our Triune God, how majestic is your name in all the earth!
All: O Lord, our Triune God, how majestic is your name in all the earth!

Scripture Reading

Since this Sunday is Trinity Sunday, it would work well to read all of the lectionary passages in worship. Each reading points to a different person of the Trinity and could give shape to the liturgy.

Pastoral Prayer

Holy God, we thank you for the many ways that you have revealed yourself to us. This morning, we thank you especially for the mystery of the Trinity. You are one God, yet you are three: Father, Son, and Holy Spirit. Although we don't fully understand this mystery, we recognize its power for us. In you, there is community. In you, three faces smile upon us. In you, we find our Creator, our Redeemer, and our Sustainer. Help us now as your creatures to be grateful for all your creation. Help us believe in our bones that you have forgiven and redeemed us through Jesus Christ. Help us turn each day to your Holy Spirit so that you might sustain us with your love and peace. And lead us out into the world to make disciples of all nations, that they too might know you as Lord. We pray in the name of the Father and of the Son and of the Holy Spirit. Amen.

Benediction (2 Corinthians 13:13)

The grace of the Lord Jesus Christ, the love of God, and the communion of the Holy Spirit be with all of you. (Carol Cavin-Dillon)

How Faithful a Church?

Second in a Series of Three on "Is the Church Christian?"

Luke 16:10-13

The commandments to love God and neighbor are intended to transform the world. Often the church is transformed by the world.

The church of John Wesley's time had embraced culture. John Wesley tried to revive the church by holding it accountable for both spiritual and human needs. Wesley attempted to revitalize religious practices and initiated social reforms in the agricultural fields and in the prisons.

Wesley and the evangelical Anglicans fought against slave trade, the greatest social injustice of Wesley's day. Similar work against slave trade came from the Quakers and the Congregationalists in America, while the issue divided the Methodists, Presbyterians, and Baptists.

The relationship between church and state has had an impact on the church's faithfulness to its mission. There has long been a marriage between the Roman Catholic Church and the Spanish- and Portuguese-speaking nations of Latin America and Europe. There have also been state-controlled churches in Europe, such as in Germany.

Because he saw the church as a potential unifying force, Adolph Hitler drew the church into his empire-building plans in the 1930s. While many of the Roman Catholic and Protestant churches draped the Nazi flag over their altars and expressed allegiance to Hitler, the confessing church movement organized in 1934 stood in opposition to Hitler. It declared no human führer could stand above God. Confessing leaders such as Martin Niemoller and Dietrich Bonhoeffer were executed for their witness against the state.

The framers of our American constitution tried to prevent creation of a state religion. Our ancestors came to American seeking to practice their religion freely. Today's American religious landscape is increasingly pluralistic and there seems to be a desire among some Christians for a closer relationship between church and state. The American flag holds prominence alongside the cross in many church sanctuaries. The Christian right and left both clearly try to influence public policy in the political forum. The line between church and state in America is at best hazy.

For their first three hundred years, Christians were persecuted by the Roman Empire. Constantine changed that relationship by making Christianity the official state religion. He tried to control the church as well as his empire. Constantine's organization of the Council of Nicea in 325 C.E. was a failed attempt to unify the church.

Jesus himself warned against dancing with the state. When the scribes and chief priests asked if they should pay taxes, Jesus said "give to the emperor the things that are the emperor's, and to God the things that are God's" (Luke 20:25). And the Apostle Paul taught that Christians were separate from culture, in that "our citizenship is in heaven" (Philippians 3:20). The church and state have historically danced around the issues of control and power.

The church has also experienced an internal power struggle centered on clergy and laity. The clergy quickly limited authority around the sacrament of Holy Communion and interpretation of Scripture. Only the Latin Vulgate translation of Scripture was used in worship. The early church leadership resembled the self-centered Jewish leadership of Jesus' time. Clergy, including the pope, were enjoying their privileged position within the church.

The eleventh and twelfth centuries witnessed the construction of thousands of beautiful Gothic cathedrals. Church buildings became symbols of the church's power and the authority of the clergy surged. Within a few centuries, Christians had moved from meeting in homes and tenement houses into ornate churches.

The fourteenth and fifteenth centuries, however, saw the decline of the papacy and the church's authority. In 1378, John Wycliffe, claiming Scripture as authoritative, sponsored a translation of the Bible into English so more people could read it. Martin Luther was so concerned about corruption in the church that in 1517 he posted his 95 Theses on the door of the Wittenberg church. The Protestant Reformation was born, and the role of the laity increased.

Rather than being faithful to its call to social justice, the church was reveling in privilege. Instead of loving neighbor, churches allowed their walls to exclude their neighbors. The erosion of the church's authority has been exacerbated over the last century, especially in mainline churches.

The young adults in my Christian Ethics class at Morningside College hold traditional, even conservative values on almost every issue, except on the issue of homosexuality. They see gays as a part of the American fabric and the church as unjust when it excludes gays. Homosexuality is not a sin to most young people, and they are critical of the church's lack of hospitality toward gays. Young adults ask how excluding gays from our churches is consistent with the commandment to love our neighbors.

The church has struggled with its relationship with culture, especially with the state. The church has fallen in love with buildings and laws rather than with justice and grace. It has failed to maintain spiritual commitment among the faithful. The church has lost its original evangelistic fervor and passion for justice and has failed to walk humbly with God. (Dan L. Flanagan)

Worship Aids

Call to Worship

In the midst of an ever changing world, we come to worship.
We come to find peace within these walls.
We look for peace while Christ calls us to change the world.
All: Let us be the church and change the world!

Invocation

We gather routinely, Lord, expecting something to happen. Through the power of the Holy Spirit, energize our worship. Move us to be the church. Open our hearts to your love. Open our doors to our neighbors. Open our souls to the joy of commitment. Help us worship with desire, and then to serve with passion. Amen.

Benediction

Having renewed your faith through worship, go forth to live your faith in service. Be the church in the world. Amen. (Dan L. Flanagan)

MAY 25, 2008

Second Sunday after Pentecost

Readings: Isaiah 49:8-16a; Psalm 131; 1 Corinthians 4:1-5;
Matthew 6:24-34

A Prayer of Humble Trust
Psalm 131

Before my final year of seminary I took a much needed two-month
break from my studies. I headed for La Antigua, Guatemala, a place
famous for three things: its coffee, its colorful celebration of Easter, and
its language schools. Because I happened to make my sojourn at the right
time of year, I was able to experience all three, studying Spanish by
immersion, participating in the Easter festivals, and drinking a lot of
great coffee.

Although it was an amazing journey, it was far from carefree. There was
a storm cloud of theological questions rolling in my head, made more
acute by the culture shock provoked by my first experience of living
abroad. Everything seemed foreign to me—not only the sights, sounds,
and scents of this new country—but even those things that previously
seemed essential to who I was. My cultural assumptions, my self-
understanding, and my theological commitments all felt uprooted,
floating perilously out of my reach.

During my language lesson one morning, my internal unrest was obvious. One foot tapped nervously, my attention faded in and out of verb
paradigms, and I went through a few too many cups of fine Guatemalan
coffee. My tutor, a sweet woman who patiently endured the slings and
arrows of my rough Spanish, asked what was on my mind. Since I could-
n't figure out how to translate "dark night of the soul" into Spanish, I
tried to deflect the question, saying that I was just a little preoccupied. To
this she replied with the gently ironic equivalent of, "Really?" She could
see through the diversion. Taking a deep breath, I attempted to unload

the burden. I don't remember the content of the conversation, though I am certain that she did not pull my free-floating world out of the sky and reroot it for me. But she did manage to help me see it through new eyes. My Spanish tutor was no scholar. She was a woman of moderate education and meager social status. She was not a pastor or theologian; but she had the wisdom to not offer easy answers or cheap advice. Somehow this humble woman was an instrument of grace, redirecting my attention to God, to whom I could entrust my uncertainty and unrest. She did not dispense with my questions; she reframed them. And with that I found rest. Of course, this experience of spiritual unrest is hardly unique. Anyone who has spent much time traveling along the road of faith has bumped into questions that feel insurmountable, crises that are devastating, and situations where God seems painfully absent. It is in these times that our trust is worn thin and our attention is drawn away to the ever-present "cares of the world."

The Psalms, the prayers of the people of God, are familiar with this spiritual state of affairs and they address the situation with surprising honesty. This is true of the Psalms generally: thanksgiving psalms shout, "Hooray for God!" while the laments call out to God for assistance in terms we might find irreverent, daring to ask "Where on earth are you?" or "What is taking you so long?"

Psalm 131 is a special prayer of humble trust that addresses us and our care-filled lives. If we are preoccupied and distracted, rather than living in the trust and faith described in today's gospel passage, this prayer is meant to redirect us, guiding us back to the right path.

The psalmist begins by saying, "O LORD, my heart is not lifted up, / my eyes are not raised too high; / I do not occupy myself with things / too great and too marvelous for me."

Sometimes we forget that we are finite. We forget that there are things too great and marvelous for our comprehension. This happens easily enough. Tragedy strikes and we want to know why. We look around our world and see pain and suffering, wars and unfathomable cruelty, and we find ourselves asking how those things are possible in a world created by a good God. We look to our faith and find it full of mysteries about who God is: God is one, yet God is three; Jesus Christ is fully God and fully human. Before we realize it, we are consumed by questions that—although good and worthwhile—can paralyze us if allowed to become an end unto themselves. But, if we are to offer a humble prayer of trust along with the psalmist, we must make a humble assessment of our ability to understand and then loosen our grasp on these questions. Only then can we redirect our attention toward God who loves us with the concrete love of a caring mother or father.

The psalmist continues: "But I have calmed and quieted my soul, / like a weaned child with its mother; / my soul is like the weaned child that is with me."

Once we have undergone the difficult work of stilling our souls, redirecting our gaze toward the God who loves us simply, we are able to be with God in peace, as a weaned child and its mother. Unlike the newborn who weeps in response to every perceived need, the weaned child has learned to trust its mother's loving provision and is capable of extended, restful presence. These are the first glimmers of love that are not motivated by the immediate prospect of food.

This is why Christ commands, "do not worry about your life, what you will eat or what you will drink, or about your body, what you will wear" (Matthew 6:25). Because, when we are overrun by our cares and desires, shrilly crying like newborns, we cannot experience the peace and joy of being at rest with the one who loves us as only God can.

In the wise words of my Spanish teacher: "*No te preocupes.*" "Do not worry." Or in the words of the psalmist: "O Israel, hope in the LORD from this time on and forevermore." Amen. (Cameron Jorgenson)

Lectionary Commentary
Isaiah 49:8-16a

This passage mentions a string of promised blessings common to the prophets: that God will hear, answer, and save; that the people will be established in the land; that prisoners will be released and that God will provide, guide, and restore. But these promises are future-oriented and the prophet knows that this delay can lead the people to wonder whether they have been forsaken. Just as in the psalm, however, we are reminded that we are God's children. The image of the nursing mother is used to suggest the permanence and the depth of God's love. We have been nursed by God and we have been inscribed on God's hand—how, then, could we ever be forgotten?

Matthew 6:24-34

The Sermon on the Mount is known for its extension of the Mosaic law, penetrating to the spiritual roots of the ancient prohibitions. It is also known for its reversal of the "normal" order of things: the mourning are comforted, the meek inherit the earth, one's enemies are to be loved. Beyond this, the theme of divine parenthood is at work. We are called to address God as "Our Father" (Matthew 6:9). We are reminded that God will not give us snakes and stones when we ask for fish or bread; rather, God will give good gifts as a loving father would (Matthew 7:9-11). This theme of divine parenthood provides a fascinating perspective on Jesus' teaching about wealth. We see that Christ is primarily concerned with wealth's power to distract us and erode our faith in God's provision. As in Psalm 131, Jesus suggests that the cares of the world can reduce our relationship with God to need fulfillment—calling to mind a demanding child who is unaware of the parent's love.

1 Corinthians 4:1-5

The Apostle Paul, having scolded the Corinthians for their divisive attitudes, turns his attention to a defense of his ministry. The embattled apostle defends himself in a surprising way, appealing to the image of stewardship. As a steward, Paul and the other apostles are simply caretakers of what God has given. They are not innovators or "religious geniuses," they are caretakers of the Word who both protect and distribute what is God's. Ultimately, God can be the only judge who determines their fidelity as stewards. Paul implies that this image of stewardship has relevance for us all. In these opening chapters of 1 Corinthians, and in the other lectionary passages for today, what becomes clear is that all of life is a gift. And, as Paul reminds us in 1 Corinthians 4:1-5, God is the loving Judge who holds us accountable for what we do with what we have been given. (Cameron Jorgenson)

Worship Aids

Prayer of Confession

Lord, we confess that our hearts have been divided. We have been anxious and distracted and our attention has been scattered. We confess that these weeds are choking out life and causing us to wither. Come, uproot the weeds, prune the vines, and make us alive. Amen.

Prayer of Response

Lord, teach us to pray. Teach us to pray in humility and trust. Teach us to turn our attention from our cares to you who cares for us. Teach us to rest in you with a calmed and quieted soul. We hope in you, O Lord, now and forevermore. Amen.

Benediction

Friends, don't worry about tomorrow for tomorrow has enough worries of its own; rather, go from this place in the peace that surpasses all understanding, knowing that we serve a God who knows our needs and loves us unreservedly. (Cameron Jorgenson)

A Revitalized Church

Third in a Series of Three on "Is the Church Christian?"

Acts 2:43-47

The title of Eugene Kennedy's final chapter in *Tomorrow's Catholics, Yesterday's Church* is intriguing: "Where God Is Homeless and All Men Are at Home" (Harper & Row, 1988, 187). It is a great image of what the church ought to be.

The foundation of the church is in the scribe's response to his own inquiry about the path to eternal life (Luke 10:25). The vitality of the future church depends on our ability to love the Lord and our neighbor. The commitment called for in this Deuteronomic law is all encompassing. "You shall love the Lord your God with all your heart, and with all your soul, and with all your strength, and with all your mind" (Luke 10:27). What is left? Our whole life should be loving God, a precept of faith softened by the contemporary church.

Jesus invited people into sacrificial discipleship. The sons of Zebedee left their father to follow Jesus. When told his own mother and brothers were near, Jesus replied, "Who are my mother and my brothers?" (Mark 3:33). When a disciple said he would follow once he buried his father, Jesus said, "Follow me, and let the dead bury their own dead" (Matthew 8:22). Faith in Christ requires total commitment.

Those from mainline church traditions ask members to support the church by their prayers, presence, gifts, and service. However, the depth of commitment to those vows has waned in the modern church.

The task of Christians must be to determine what total commitment means for them. The task of the church is to encourage faith development, model the faithful life, and share God's grace.

God is not bound by the walls of the church. God is homeless or as Paul reminds us "[God] is not far from each one of us. For 'In him we live and move and have our being'" (Acts 17:28). Through its sacramental authority, the church offers a reminder of the spiritual meaning of life. Jesus encouraged us to share the bread and cup to remember him. Jesus also sends us out. The church must reaffirm its sacramental role and prepare people to become disciple makers.

The role of the church is to provide a worshiping and caring community that strengthens the faith of Christians and provides tools to transform the world. In the early church model, Christians lived with one foot in the sanctuary and one in the world. The modern church, too, must extend its meeting space beyond the sanctuary into homes and other secular places. "Day by day, as they spent much time together in the temple, they broke bread at home and ate their food with glad and generous hearts, praising God and having the goodwill of all the people."

The nurturing church could look something like John Wesley's system of classes. From seekers to the mature Christian, small groups offer support and accountability. In small groups, loving God and each other is encouraged.

Early church fellowship was primarily centered around a meal. While the celebration of Holy Communion helps us remember, it hardly qualifies as a fellowship meal. True fellowship and social justice began around the table for early Christians. They invited people from all social strata to form a new family. The love of God and the love of neighbor were modeled at table.

The church of the future cannot simply stand at the doors and welcome people. It must move outside the doors. A significant challenge is to understand the homeless God and to take seriously Jesus' commandment to make disciples of all nations.

Evangelism of the future must be first recruiting and then welcoming. The church must listen to the spiritual needs of those who feel disenfranchised, especially young people. The church will revive itself only as it nurtures internally and responds to the needs of those outside the door. The future vitality of the church depends on its ability to renew itself. Mature Christians should be comfortable in the sanctuary and in the world, sharing their story on campuses, on the streets, and in the prisons. The church must embrace diversity and break down walls that divide. Today's walls look eerily similar to those of Jesus' day: economic and social status, gender and sexual preference, skin color, and political power. The church must, with the example of Christ's ministry, find a way to offer God's grace to all people.

We can love only because God first loved us. The commitment required of our relationship with Jesus Christ pales in comparison to his sacrifice for us. All that we are stems from his authority. Paul's letter to the Romans warns of apostasy and offers direction, "Do not be conformed to this world, but be transformed by the renewing of your minds" (Romans 12:2).

Christ granted the church the power to transform the world. The church exists to remind us of God's sacrificial love (Holy Communion) as we commit our own lives to praising God and inviting our neighbors to the table of fellowship. Our task is to share the story of the boundless God and make disciples of all nations. The faithful church models justice and walks humbly with God. (Dan L. Flanagan)

Worship Aids

Call to Worship

Jesus calls us to be disciples and to make disciples.
Jesus invites us to live sacrificially.
Jesus invites us to change lives and to change the world.
We come to renew ourselves so we can help transform the world.

Prayer of Confession

We have failed as your church, O God. You call us to live faithfully and to act justly. Instead, our lives reflect more of our needs than the needs of others. Move us beyond ourselves to hear the cry of the needy. Your Messiah sacrificed himself for us. May your grace shine through a church that accepts its call to justice and faith. Amen.

Words of Assurance

In the name of Jesus Christ, you are forgiven.
In the name of Jesus Christ, you are forgiven. Amen.

Benediction

Christ gives us the authority to change the world. Share Christ's grace with all whom you meet. Be the church that was called to faithfulness by Jesus Christ. Amen. (Dan L. Flanagan)

JUNE 1, 2008

❦❦❦

Third Sunday after Pentecost

Readings: Deuteronomy 11:18-21, 26-28; Psalm 31:1-5, 19-24; Romans 1:16-17, 3:22b-31; Matthew 7:21-29

Beyond the Blessing and the Curse
Deuteronomy 11:18-21, 26-28

In Deuteronomy we see Moses telling the story again, reminding the people where they have been and what God has done among them. Soon he comes to a critical juncture in the story: descending the mountain with the Ten Commandments only to discover the people worshiping a golden calf. After destroying the tablets and disposing of the idol, Moses ascends the mountain again to receive new tablets of stone to replace those he symbolically destroyed. When he returned, Moses called the people to follow and obey. These were not empty words without teeth, rather, with the commands came promises of blessing for those who follow, and curses for those who turn away.

When you hear the words of Deuteronomy—words that pronounce divine blessing on obedience and a divine curse on disobedience—how do you find yourself responding? Several gut level responses seem natural. You might find yourself nodding in approval because of the justice this implies. What we see is a personalized, Judeo-Christian version of karma: good guys get rewarded; bad guys get punished. This is grade-school common sense on the cosmic scale. Not only is it the case that what goes around comes around but also with the "principal" watching the playground with an all-seeing eye, one had better be on her best behavior because no one wants to be on the receiving end of that punishment.

However, it is entirely possible that you hear the words of Deuteronomy in a very different light. Rather than being instinctively attracted to the idea of a God who blesses and curses, you might find yourself squirming. It is not hard to see why. The community of faith has a long, less than

179

gracious history of connecting tragic events to divine retribution. Just think of the public statements made by some religious leaders following 9/11, Ariel Sharon's stroke, and the tsunami in Asia. It seems that one can count on two things every year: the hurricane season and the harangue season—that time of year when self-proclaimed prophets connect the dots between catastrophes and the particular sinners God had in the crosshairs.

Beyond the unattractiveness of this approach to life, there seems to be an even more fundamental objection. We may find ourselves asking: *Could this picture of God be right? Is God one who showers blessings on a few and relishes striking down everyone else? Could it be that God is sitting at the divine laptop with his finger twitchily hovering over the "smite" button?* If we honestly assess our own shortcomings, we should hope this is not the case.

It may be tempting to chalk up this quandary to some inadequate, "Old Testament," wrath-filled picture of God, in contrast to the God of love and mercy described in the New Testament. But if this is the temptation, we must resist it. Not only does that mischaracterize the God portrayed by the Old Testament, it gets the picture of the New Testament wrong as well.

In the Gospel of Matthew, we see Jesus calling his followers to himself on a mountainside, delivering to them a new teaching. In this Sermon on the Mount Jesus proclaims the Beatitudes, God's blessings on certain ways of being and living in the world. Then, like Moses, he proclaims the demands of the law, taking them one step further to address the sins of the heart. After he gives these commands, Jesus does something we might not expect. He says, "Not everyone who says to me, 'Lord, Lord,' will enter the kingdom of heaven, but only the one who does the will of my Father in heaven" (7:21). Just like Moses, Jesus begins his message with blessing and ends with a stern warning that amounts to a curse.

So, does all of this serve to reinforce the picture of the karmic God of divine wrath? Are the holy pundits right? Does Jesus endorse their picture of God waiting anxiously to smite?

Perhaps part of our problem is the way we have framed the question. Perhaps our discomfort with the idea of God blessing and cursing has blurred our vision, causing us to miss what both Moses and Jesus are doing.

What if they did not come to announce a long list of ethical rules to be followed for their own sake? What if the intent was not to institute an ethical system of holy obligations or divine demands?

Instead, is it possible that both are painting a picture of the good life, crafting an image of what life could be if lived according to justice and holiness? What if their intent was to point a way forward, a path that leads to abundant, overflowing, joy-filled life? What if they intended to engage the moral and spiritual imaginations of the people of God, as if to say, "If you could just see what life could be when lived God's way, nothing could hold you back from pursuing it"?

If this is what they were attempting, then blessings and curses make more sense. Living life as God meant it is its own blessing. Refusing this way twists and disfigures life in unnatural and unhealthy ways that amount to a built-in curse. Therefore, when we see God punishing people in Scripture, the situation is often portrayed as a parent disciplining errant children, redirecting them away from self-destructive ways, and blessing those who embrace life as God intended it.

Why are we called to put God's words in our hearts and souls, on our heads, on our hands, and on our doorposts? Why are we to spend our lives talking about them and meditating on them? So that our lives might be long in the land. These words give life—not according to a spiritual quid pro quo—but because God's words and ways are good and true. Why are the poor in spirit, the meek, and the pure in heart called blessed? Because these are the ways of God, and that way is the way to life—abundant life. (Cameron Jorgenson)

Lectionary Commentary
Psalm 31:1-5, 19-24

In the second half of this psalm we see both blessing and curse. God shelters, protects, and stores up great goodness for the faithful; God also pays back "the proud" in full. An interesting dynamic here is the role of trust and faith. The proud enemy does not trust in God and, consequently, he wars against the faithful. The faithful hero of the psalms, on the other hand, is favored precisely because of his trust. This trust is made explicit in verse 5 when the psalmist commends his spirit into the hands of God, relying on God for redemption. This element of faith helps us reimagine who the "good guys" and "bad guys" might be, while helping us avoid the age-old mischaracterization of the Old Testament's view of salvation as consisting solely of "works of the law."

Matthew 7:21-29

One question raised by these passages is how "active" the blessing and cursing of God is. Although the picture in the Old Testament is mixed, writings associated with Deuteronomic theology suggest that God showers blessings on those who live according to God's commands, while rebels are punished. Other books are less actively retributive (note the difference between Proverbs and Ecclesiastes). The picture Jesus offers is similarly mixed. In this passage he claims that some will be judged as evildoers because they did not act according to the will of the Father. Yet, he concludes by appealing to the contrasting images of buildings with foundations of rock and sand, suggesting the passive judgment that comes to those who must face the natural consequences of living in a way other than God's intent.

Romans 1:16-17, 3:22b-31

In characteristic fashion, the Apostle Paul provides a helpful counterbalance to a discussion that necessarily emphasizes human action. While the other passages emphasize the significance of human deeds, calling the people of God to fidelity, Paul reminds us of the basis for those actions—faith. The apostle proclaims that all have sinned and are in need of salvation, a restoration that comes as a divine gift that is received in faith. So, while it is appropriate to speak of blessing and curse—even in response to human action—Paul reminds us that basis for human action is faith or unfaith. For this reason, boasting is not so much prohibited as nonsensical. (Cameron Jorgenson)

Worship Aids

Call to Worship

Today, like the children of Israel, we gather at the mountain to hear the words of the covenant. Like the disciples, we follow Jesus up the mountain to hear what the Lord has to say. Let us boldly approach the throne of grace together. Friends, lift up your hearts!

Prayer of Confession

Lord, we come to you humbly, knowing that we have fallen short. We have missed the mark. We have sinned. Though we know that we have earned judgment, we also know that you offer us grace. We receive your grace, and for this we give our thanks. Amen.

Words of Assurance

Friends, you are beloved of God. Know this truth. Allow it to transform your life. Know that God is not waiting to pounce; rather, God loves you enough to warn you of the lion who is. Let us lovingly follow Christ who is the life and light of all humankind. (Cameron Jorgenson)

The Perfect Pattern

First in a Series of Two on Discipleship

1 Peter 2:18-25

Christ is described as the perfect pattern and example for us to emulate as disciples. "For to this you have been called, because Christ also suffered for you, leaving you an example, so that you should follow in his steps."

Some Christians during the time of this Scripture writing were household slaves who found it easy to work diligently for kind and temperate masters. Like all human beings, it was difficult to submit when faced with unjust treatment. Peter encouraged Christians to be loyal servants so that they could win people to Christ through their example. They were asked to follow in the steps of Jesus—no easy task when we all know Jesus was willing to mingle with the sick and afflicted, dine with tax collectors, and even provide miracles to people of different race and beliefs.

In Matthew, Jesus emphasizes the point to illustrate what is required of his disciples. "For if you love those who love you, what reward do you have? Do not even the tax collectors do the same? And if you greet only your brothers and sisters, what more are you doing than others? Do not even the Gentiles do the same? Be perfect, therefore, as your heavenly Father is perfect" (Matthew 5:46-48). When we live as Christ lived, we may suffer, but we are called to face anguish in relationships as Jesus did, calmly, patiently, and with confidence that God is in control. To be faithful Christians, we can pattern our lives after Jesus' life.

Schoolchildren in the early 1800s were given a wax tablet to help them learn to write. The letters were grooved on the tablet so the students would have a perfect copy to follow. The form of the letter was as it should be written, and by tracing the letters, they enhanced their writing skills. The children simply copied the line to learn to write.

Like those tablets, Christ left the perfect example for all disciples. I can only imagine the discipline Christ must have experienced as a child, a youth, and as a young person. Through thirty years, Jesus subjected himself to three basic disciplines that are examples for Christians today.

First is the discipline of childhood. Jesus took responsibility for the chores of the family, learned to care for his belongings, and to have social graces, just as children do now. I enjoy picturing Jesus tending to the needs of a younger brother or helping Mary with common household chores. Moreover, I do not believe it is far-fetched to believe Jesus may have been disciplined during those formative years.

Secondly, Jesus was subjected to the discipline of labor. One tradition tells us that Jesus carved his father's coffin and drenched it with tears. Jesus may have even fashioned crosses as he worked in his father's carpenter shop. I believe Jesus was faithful to business and understood keeping the business alive. This is discipline Jesus learned in his early life, and perhaps disciples in our churches and even in our country have lost the discipline of labor.

Jesus also knew the discipline of worship. Jesus learned Scripture. It was difficult to study, but we know that he did and that Jesus went to the temple to study with the great rabbis of his time. Remember that his family lost him at the age of twelve. Jesus was discovered learning about the Jewish traditions, establishing his own beliefs and value system, and in a way, teaching others about his role in Jewish tradition and in light of what would become Christian teaching.

Worship and studying the texts of his day were not easy tasks. Scrolls were typically many feet long. There were no vowels, no capital letters, no division of words, or of sentences. When will we learn that the church is the most important institution in our midst? When will we learn that worship is critical to our growth in discipleship? When will we learn that studying God's word in not easy? When will we see the rewards of our study and know that it is good?

What can we learn from these lessons? I believe we may learn to salvage life's leftovers. After sorrow, disappointment, unjust treatment, loss of life of friend or family member; take the leftovers. It is a sad thing when the soul has no life, while the body perseveres. Some people give up on life at a young age and physically die many years later. Too often, the painful things in life keep Christians from focusing on the disciplines and the perfect example that Christ left for us.

To be Christlike, we must have the courage to endure whatever life offers. In each of us, there is a secret self that is totally invincible. There is an ancient story of Alexander the Great: A chieftain gave Alexander some hunting dogs. Alexander released deer and antelope in anticipation of seeing them attack. The dogs yawned and lay down. Alexander had them killed and accused the chieftain of giving him a gift with no courage. The chieftain said, "If only you had released lions and tigers."

To be Christlike, we must learn to face up to our fears and defy them. It is important to have faith in an almighty God. My dad raised Hereford cattle on a small lease in the Texas panhandle. He believed in the Hereford breed and was confident they could survive the devastating winters in the Great Plains. Dad often pointed out that they face into the wind when other cattle turn their backs to the wind and walk as far as they can, usually to their death at a fence as much as four miles away. He was sure that the fence and the backside of the cows acted as a snow catcher and they would potentially suffocate under snow. Jesus faced his fears and did not run away even as death became imminent.

To be Christlike, we must learn to rest in Jesus. I believe that Jesus had a secret life at rest while his public life was under pressure. Jesus went to the Garden of Gethsemane to pray and find peace. Jesus tried to escape the throngs of people by taking a boat to the other side of the lake. Jesus sought solace. To be good disciples of Christ, we may find ways to rest so we can give to others whose needs exceed our own.

All of these are examples that Jesus left us. Jesus is the perfect example. Amen. (Ted L. McIlvain)

Worship Aids

Call to Worship
When we feel faint in spirit,
we seek God's will so our bodies persevere.
When we face adversity,
we turn and face our fear.
When we are weary,
we find rest in Jesus.
When we worship,
All: we are servants to others and our God.

Pastoral Prayer
Gracious and loving God, we bring our worries and fears to you and seek your guidance and comfort. We are humble servants who search for refuge in the confines of our church and among the friends that you have provided in this place. Today we trust you to protect and give courage to all who believe in you. Help us, O God, to be true disciples with a will to reach out to those less comfortable.

Hear this prayer and bless us through your Son, Jesus Christ. Amen.

Benediction

May the Lord bless you as a true disciple.

May you find peace in the world you occupy.

May the Lord guide you on your journey to offer help to those in need.

And, may you rest in the peace and comfort of God.

Amen. (Ted L. McIlvain)

JUNE 8, 2008

❧❧❧❧

Fourth Sunday after Pentecost

Readings: Hosea 5:15–6:6; Psalm 33:1-12; Romans 4:13-25; Matthew 9:9-13, 18-26

A Desire for Love
Hosea 5:15–6:6

Can you imagine a world where love of God and love of others is the focus of everyone you meet, read about, or see? Can you imagine a world where everyone worships God and where everyone cares for their neighbor more than they care about themselves? On the evening news we would see highlights about the birth of a new baby and an interview of the family who will love that baby all their days together. Another story in the paper might be about a food and clothing distribution center that has plenty of supplies, but no one to give them to, or a town where the rumor is about how loving a family has been to another. In this world, nations would make peaceful arrangements between each other, poverty would not exist, and diversity among all people would be celebrated. I cannot help but think that God created us to live in such a world.

We all know what the real world is like. It is a world that lacks love and prides itself on selfish needs. Only a few voices around the world work towards this steadfast love that God desires. The steadfast love that Hosea speaks about is a deep love. It is the same love between God and Abraham, God and Jacob. It is a love that God gives and we receive; yet God desires us to respond with such a love.

Today we find ourselves in a place not so different from the people of Israel in Hosea. Israel and Judah show their love for God only when they are in need. God sits high above ready to intervene, but frustrated by the lack of sincerity in the hearts of these nations. God has tried tough love, keeping a distance and killing the disobedient. God is like a parent at the end of the rope who throws up her hands saying, "What shall I do with

187

you?" In God's sorrow, God simply states, "I only want you to acknowledge my existence and love me as I love you."

It is pretty simple really; God desires love and recognition. That is it. From the beginning of time, God has been making God's presence known in the garden of Eden, the stories of Abraham, Moses, the kings, the prophets, and Jesus Christ. Over and over again God has reached out in love to be worshiped and loved in return. Why is it so difficult for the people of Hosea's time, and the people of today, to simply love and acknowledge God with sincere hearts?

The first challenge is convenience. Currently I am in the process of practicing intensive journaling. I learned about this unique feedback-style of journaling more than four years ago and it is a wonderful life tool for me. It helps me to focus on the "now" moment in my life such as balancing work, family, and personal time, and it helps me to see where my life is going. It is a valuable tool for me, but it is just not convenient. In order to journal, I have to find some quiet time, a pencil, and my journal. I have to be willing to give up a significant part of my day or evening to do some productive work. It is hard and I find myself only going to my journal when I am in a stressful, emotional, or in a transition time in my life. But I know if I went to my journal more often I would gain much more insight to the "now" moment and have a better idea of where my life is going. It is a wonderful gift, but often I find excuses for not using this gift that I possess.

The same was true for the Israelites in Hosea's day, and I suspect the same is true for many of us today. They only turn to God when it is convenient. We only turn to God when times are difficult or uncertain. Yet, God desires a relationship with us in good and bad times, whether it is convenient or not. God desire a loving relationship with us at all times. We want our God to be like a drive-through window. We pull up to the menu, place our order, and in a few minutes we are happily satisfying our craving. We want our God to be an ATM God. Our energy or funds are running a little low; we slide in our card and out slides our money. Even if we want an "on demand" God, we still have to give to receive. In order to receive a hamburger at a local drive through window, we have to pay the price. In order to receive money from an ATM, we have to have money in our account. And in order to recognize the steadfast love of God, we have to throw convenience out the window and give God our love and time first.

Secondly, commitment is necessary to fully love God. I have a ninety-pound black labrador retriever named Sarah. Sarah is 100 percent committed to me. Sarah is there when I get home, ready to eat. Sarah is there in the morning to make sure I am awake by 7:00 a.m. No matter where I go or what I do I know that Sarah will be with me or waiting for me. It is a good feeling to receive a love like that. A love that doesn't ask questions and a love that quickly forgives.

It is the same kind of commitment God gives to us. Wherever we go and whatever we do, God is committed to us, but how committed are we to God? How often do we nourish our soul with Scripture and prayer, with praise and worship? How long has it been since we stepped up our commitment to God? If we are comfortable with where we are in our commitment to God, we need to take on one more spiritual discipline, sign up for one more Bible study, worship God in a different way, or serve God through the needs of others. There is always more we can do to connect to our God. It only takes commitment.

The words of the prophet Hosea speak to us through the ages. We too have made God fit into our world instead of submitting to God's call on our lives. If we will return the steadfast love of God that we freely receive through grace, and commit to God even when it is not convenient, God will not sit high above us. God will be in our midst. When we are filled with God's steadfast love completely, it begins to overflow into the lives of those around us. And maybe, just maybe, one day we will have a world where love of God and love of neighbor are priorities. And maybe, little by little, we will help usher in the kingdom of God! (Meredith Remington Bell)

Lectionary Commentary
Matthew 9:9-13, 18-26

Jesus reveals the focus of his mission in this passage from Matthew. Although Jesus entertains the challenges of the Pharisees, his true focus is on the people existing on the fringes of society. In this case, it was the tax collectors, whom no one liked or appreciated, the physically ill, and the spiritually deprived. Jesus taught the tax collectors to follow him and learn to find faith from his example. In the crowd, Jesus healed one with a strong faith. In a home, Jesus taught about faith by waking the "sleeping" girl. Jesus shared God's desire for the world to worship and love

God. Jesus also gave us the new commandment of loving our neighbors. It is through Jesus' example of teaching others about the steadfast love of God that we can help build the kingdom of God.

Romans 4:13-25

It is through faith, not the law, that Abraham became the father of many nations. Abraham's faith was unquestioning and unwavering, even when he fathered a child as a very old man. With every challenge and encounter with God, Abraham grew in faith. The challenges made Abraham stronger. Through our faith we believe in the triumph over death and the resurrection in Jesus Christ. We cannot fully understand the complete act of forgiveness and grace we are given through the love of God, but through loving God and others we are able to grow in our faith in hopes that we will someday share the strong, unwavering faith of Abraham. (Meredith Remington Bell)

Worship Aids

Opening Prayer

Loving God, as we gather together to hear your word for us today, help us pause our busy minds and open our hearts to hear your message for us. We praise you for the way you work in each of our lives and we pray that we will leave this time closer to you and willing to share your love with your children whom we encounter everyday. Amen.

Call to Worship

Through scripture, song and prayer, teach us, O God, who you are.
God is love.
Through our actions, thoughts, and lives help us show others who
    you are.
God is love.

Benediction

Go from this place filled with the love and grace of our God. May your faith grow and may you share the steadfast love that is poured into your heart. Amen. (Meredith Remington Bell)

Striving to Follow the Perfect Pattern

Second in a Series of Two on Discipleship

1 Thessalonians 5:16-22

All I know about my brother is what I read on a tombstone in a cemetery in White Deer, Texas. Von's name and two dates are chiseled into the stone. November 25, 1934–February 4, 1953 ... just nineteen years. I know everything there is to know about the month, day, and year of his birth and death, but there is a personal mystery about that chiseled dash between the two. I was three years old at the time of his death, and there are no memorable experiences to draw from. However, there are stories from the family that give me an inkling about his life and faith in God. More than five hundred people attended his funeral in 1953 and it is said that most of them had been touched by his spiritual life. He made the determination to stay away from radiation treatments for the cancer that had attacked his body and, according to our mother, he said, "I put my life in the hands of God, and I'm ready for a heavenly home." I believe he followed the example of Jesus, and in so doing, touched the lives of many. All Christians are called to be examples to others. In a letter to the family, Von wrote, "I tried to be a Bible for people who never read a word of it." To be the pattern that others will follow, we can learn to be good disciples by praying, worshiping, and studying God's word.

Paul's writing to the church in Thessalonica emphasizes that the road to strong discipleship begins with prayer and ends with us doing what is good and avoiding evil. As we prepare our lives to be good disciples for our Lord, we must be ever attentive to the perfect example that Jesus left for us, and it begins with a faithful prayer life. We are aware of the prayers of Jesus. He prayed in Gethsemane. He prayed to multiply morsels to feed 5,000. Jesus prayed from the cross. He taught the twelve original disciples to pray. The purpose of praying daily is to open ourselves up, to rejoice in the presence of God, to listen to God, to lift others to God in prayer, to praise God, and to give thanks to God.

I believe that prayer is adoration, praise, and the spontaneous yearning to worship, honor, and magnify God. It is like the moments of thanks when a child curls up in your lap, looks into your eyes and says, "Read it to me again, Daddy." It is like the moments of thanks when in the midst of crisis, a friend calls or pays you a much-needed visit. It is like the moments of thanks when you sense absolute grandeur when looking at a magnificent piece of nature. All of these great treasures are gifts from God, and giving praise and adoration in return is a giant step toward discipleship.

I believe that prayer is thanksgiving. It is important look at the distinction between praise and thanksgiving. In thanksgiving, we give glory to God for what God has done for us. In praise, we give glory to God for who God is. To me, it is evident that these two elements of prayer are molded as one, and the more we give thanks for what God has done for us the more we tend to offer praise for who God is. Giving thanks is a way of intensifying our awareness of the abundance of life we experience each day we continue to breath and view the splendor of creation. Giving thanks when we are able to make small changes in our lives and knowing it was with God's help these changes occured is a developmental piece of discipleship. Disciples are stronger when giving thanks for the smallest and grandest happenings in their lives.

I believe that prayer is a way of loving others. Disciples truly love people and desire far more for them than it is within our power to give. Look around us and we see marriages shattered. Children suffer because of lost love between parents. Look around and see the individuals who are living lives of quiet desperation. I believe we can make a difference when we learn to pray on their behalf.

Disciples are effective at confessing a lack of faith, admitting to avoiding needs of others, and of hardheartedness. And when all is said and done, disciples ask forgiveness and they worship God. To worship, disciples gather in the community of faith in praise and prayer, hear the Word, receive the bread and cup, and go out to serve others for the glory of God. In the Wesleyan tradition, reading the Bible is one of the means of grace. Reading is a passage through which God's love is found. Through the Scriptures, we encounter God's saving power and God's leadership in forming our thoughts, words, and actions. Disciples read the Bible, find the human experiences of Old and New Testament characters, and discover the divine when we read of repentance and faith, just and compassionate laws, acts of devotion and self-sacrifice, and ultimately, the unending love of the forgiving covenant God.

Disciples discover great diversity in the Bible. We find poetry, laws, historical narratives, liturgies, songs, prophetic utterances, wise sayings, short stories, parables, Gospels, letters, and sermons. Studying the Bible forms our lives as disciples. We read it for information about the people, cultures, and history of our faith. We read it for insight into our own thoughts and feelings as human beings. We read it to discover the experiences of others and their encounters with God. We read it to discern God's presence in our lives and as a compass that helps us set a course for our living. In so doing, we become servants of others through God.

The result of servanthood is often sacrificial giving. In 2 Corinthians 8:1-5, Paul shares a personal story on this idea sacrificial giving. During his third missionary journey, Paul had collected money for the impoverished believers in Jerusalem. The churches had given more than Paul expected. The point is not so much the amount given, but why it is given. God does not want gifts given grudgingly. Instead, disciples give out of a dedication to Christ, love for fellow believers, and the joy of helping people in need, as well as being aware that it is simply the good and right thing to do.

As we leave this place today, we begin a journey to discipleship that includes prayer, worship, and study. God has blessed and will continue to bless those of us who remember Paul's admonition to "Rejoice always, pray without ceasing, give thanks in all circumstances; for this is the will of God in Christ Jesus for you. Do not quench the Spirit. Do not despise the words of prophets, but test everything; hold fast to what is good; abstain from every form of evil." Growing as a disciple means being disciplined in prayer, worship, reading the scripture, and serving the needs of God's people. Today is a good day to begin. Amen. (Ted L. McIlvain)

Worship Aids

Call to Worship

Today we draw on the strength of the living God who has been our hope and our help. Today we draw strength from one another and feel comforted. Today we worship and sing praises to the Creator.

Words of Assurance

God is merciful and provides hope to we who are believers. In times of weakness and failure, God is there to stand us tall and place our feet on solid ground. In the face of temptation, God is the source that helps us turn away. In the name of Jesus Christ, we are forgiven. Amen.

Benediction

The grace and love of God be with you as you leave this place. Sow the seeds of care and comfort for those less fortunate. Be ever mindful of the perfect pattern of the Lord and Savior, Jesus Christ. Amen. (Ted L. McIlvain)

JUNE 15, 2008

❧❧❧❧

Fifth Sunday after Pentecost

Readings: Genesis 18:1-15, 21:1-7; Psalm 116:1-2, 12-19; Romans 5:1-8; Matthew 9:35–10:8

Becoming a Part of God's Covenant
Genesis 18:1-15, 21:1-7

My husband hung up the phone and in an instant we started into action. He focused on the kitchen and I focused on the living room. Company was coming and they were only a few minutes away. We had just been lounging around the house watching a video with our one-year-old. Now my husband was quickly filling the dishwasher and I was shoving a mound of toys into the cabinet beneath the television.

In this passage in Genesis, I cannot help but image that Abraham was relaxing on a hot day in his tent when, in an instant, company came. And it wasn't the same company that came to my house; my company consisted of earthly beings. Abraham's company were holy beings; three individuals delivering a message. Abraham sprang into action. He offered water, washed their feet, and gave them a place to rest. Sarah made cakes. The servants hurried to prepare the tender and good calf. Company had arrived and hospitality was everywhere.

Once the three men were well cared for, the message was delivered. The message the men delivered should have come as no surprise, for God had promised Abraham children, but what a surprise it was. Sarah will have a son. We do not know Abraham's response, but Sarah laughed, and rightly so. She was old and well past the childbearing years. These three men, who appeared out of nowhere, informed this couple that they would soon become parents.

In an instant, Sarah is made a part of the covenant. Through Sarah, God worked a miracle that began a series of miracles redeeming the generations of children that God promised Abraham and Sarah. In an instant, Sarah went from being Abraham's wife to God's vessel for building a kingdom of God's children. How could Sarah ever have known on that hot, quiet day that her life would change in an instant?

Isn't that how God works? God brings us into the covenant when we least expect it. When we are relaxed in our tent, hiding from the heat, God arrives in our life, gives us a message, and then waits for us to respond.

I called on one of our church visitors one afternoon. I wanted to take her to lunch and visit with her about joining our church family. The food was good, but the conversation was difficult. For every reason I had to join the church, she had a good reason not to join. We decided to agree to disagree, wished each other well, and went our separate ways. God had given her a message. I had simply given up. A month or so later, I received a phone call from this same guest who now invited me to lunch. I accepted, but, based on our last time together, I was not looking forward to our conversation. When we were served our food, she began to explain to me why she thought she should join the church and asked how she could begin to tithe. She gave God a response and she was brought into the covenant of the church by promising to serve the church with her prayers, presence, gifts, and service.

As people of the covenant, we have two roles. First we must respond daily to God's message to love God and love our neighbors. Secondly we must work to bring others into the covenant with God. We are called to answer God's call on our life and we are called to create opportunities for others to answer their calls as well.

Through the teachings of Jesus, many people were given the opportunity to respond to God when they heard the good news and witnessed healings. Jesus worked hard to bring people into the covenant with God, and Jesus learned that he needed others to do the same. Therefore he summoned the twelve disciples and sent them out into the world to respond to God's call on their life and to create opportunities for others to respond as well.

Disciples today do not know the time or the place where God will come into our lives and call us to be an instrument of God's work, but we do know that God will call in God's time and we will have the opportunity to respond. God has been calling some of us for many years and we have yet to respond. Others of us became part of the covenant long ago, yet we live our lives outside of its boundaries. Many of us strive to be like

Sarah. When God changes our daily plans in an instant, we respond with "laughter" as we carry through with God's desire for our life.

The guest of my church who joined God's covenant is working to grow in her faith and relationship with God. God changed her life in an instant and she will never be same again. She is now filled with a new purpose in life, one that she did not understand until she became a part of God's family. Her life before was consumed with a challenging work schedule as she climbed the career ladder. She was focused on her life and desires alone. Today, in addition to her successful career, she volunteers at a women's shelter and hospice care program. Weekly she meets with abused women and dying patients. Her presence is a ministry that God has called her to and she has received a new life through reaching out to others. She is a modern day Sarah responding to God's call to love others. May we all be willing to be a modern day Sarah by answering God's new opportunity for our life. We know that in that instant our lives will never be the same again. And we will forever be thankful! (Meredith Remington Bell)

Lectionary Commentary
Matthew 9:35–10:8

This passage in Matthew is the calling of the first disciples. How exciting it must have been to be one of the chosen. They were given specific instructions; heal the sick, minister to the lost sheep, and do not expect any payment for your actions. Spreading the good news was so important that Jesus recruited helpers to be his hands and feet even while he was present among them. Today Christ recruits all of us to be disciples. We are to search out the marginalized people and give them a voice or we are to sit beside the bed of a dying child of God and give peace. We all have God-given gifts to spread the good news and we all have been called by Christ through the power of the Holy Spirit to share this life-changing news with someone we already know.

Romans 5:1-8

Justification occurs in an instant. Once we acknowledge our sins and ask for forgiveness, the power of the Holy Spirit begins the process of sanctification—the process of becoming more like Christ little by little every day. In our sanctified life, we boast about the ways in which God works to make us stronger and more faithful. We talk about the little ways we see God at work in our life and we are eager to share our experience with anyone who has ears to hear. It is an exciting moment in the life of a Christian. And as it is written in Romans, we also boast about how God sustains us even in our weakest moments. God is revealed in difficult times and it is these times that help us grow in our faith, although they are never easy. (Meredith Remington Bell)

Worship Aids

Opening Prayer

Holy Spirit, fill us now with your presence. As we hear the message from Scripture, may our hearts be open to hearing your desire for our lives. May all that we do and all that we are honor you and glorify you. Bless our time of worship today. Amen.

Call to Worship

In our busy world today we want to hear your soft voice and feel your silent spirit.

Guide us in your ways and speak to us so that we may understand.

Benediction

May you feel the presence of God in your life as you go from this place, hearing God's call for your life and responding with energy and excitement. May your ministry to others be blessed by God. Amen. (Meredith Remington Bell)

Our Quest for Love and Belonging

First in a Series of Two on Family Life

Ruth 1:1-19a

Nearly all modern psychologies say that we humans are driven by needs. The only thing that varies is the list of needs. Reality therapy says that aside from our survival needs, we need four basic things: love and belonging, power and recognition, fun, and freedom.

Today and next Sunday we'll explore these needs in the context of family life. Few things are tied together more closely than are our needs and our families. We all meet our needs in the same way: by interacting with other people. Our family is where we learn to interact.

When we meet our needs, we're like a piece of well-oiled machinery. We're healthy and whole. But when we don't meet our needs, we manifest symptoms that reveal sickness.

All of us have a biological family, but God has provided most of us with several other families—a circle of friends, professional colleagues, civic organizations, a church, and so on. We can't simply take our families for granted. We have to feed and nurture them. Through healthy families God bestows life's greatest blessings.

Today we look at how our families help us meet our need for love and belonging, which is the first of our four basic needs. Today's scripture is one of the tenderest stories about love and belonging in all of literature. It begins with an unlikely relationship: a relationship between a mother-in-law and a daughter-in-law. These family members often don't normally get along with each other.

Naomi is a Hebrew woman who goes to live in Moab, where her husband and both of their sons die. She concludes it's best for her to go back to Israel. Ruth, one of Naomi's daughters-in-law, decides to stay with Naomi and go to Israel to live. In 1:16 Ruth expresses a beautiful sentiment: "Do not press me to leave you / or to turn back from following you! / Where you go, I will go; / Where you lodge, I will lodge; / your people shall be my people, / and your God my God." This relationship has a spiritual as well as a human dimension. It transcends geography, kinship, and ancestral ties.

Naomi plays an important nurturing role in her relationship with Ruth. She's the older woman who knows how to get things done. She quickly figures out that Ruth and Boaz need to get together. So in 3:3 she instructs Ruth, "Now wash and anoint yourself, and put on your best clothes and go down to the threshing floor. . . ." Now we see why Ruth didn't want to leave Naomi. Everyone needs a father or mother figure like Naomi—someone who's experienced and has a gentle way of sharing wisdom.

I remember the first two supervisors I had as a young pastor. They had that way of nurturing and guiding. They didn't smother me with advice, but they knew how to point the way. I'm sure there have been people like that in your life who you will never forget. Sometimes father and mother figures are within our biological family, sometimes they're outside.

It's interesting that Ruth proposes to Boaz and not the other way around. How's that for 1100 B.C.E.? Ruth and Boaz marry and have a son named Obed. Like many good Hebrew stories, this one closes with a genealogy. The genealogy tells readers that Ruth was the great-grandmother of King David. And thus, as Matthew 1:5 notes, Ruth was directly in the bloodline of Jesus of Nazareth. Therefore, this story appears in Jesus' family album.

In his book *Reality Therapy*, William Glasser says that at all times in our lives we must have at least one person who cares for us and for whom we care. If we don't have this person, we'll not be able to fulfill our basic needs. Ruth and Naomi had each other, and that was enough. Out of their relationship they drew the strength to survive at a time when it was very difficult for widows to survive.

In the 1950s Pat Sherrill grew up in Oklahoma City. He was trying to survive, too. He was a loner except for his positive relationship with his mother. When Pat's mother died, he was alone; his world grew smaller. Now he had no one with whom he could process the ups and downs of this life. He started acting out and became "crazy Pat" in the neighborhood. His supervisors at the Edmond Post Office counseled him about his job performance. Of course, his performance had slipped; everything had slipped for Pat! On August 20, 1986, he entered the post office and killed fifteen employees. This event originated the term "going postal."

In his poem "The Death of the Hired Man" Robert Frost gives one definition of a family: "Home is the place where, when you have to go there, they have to take you in." What happens when people don't have a place like that to go to?

God gave us many families or possible families. One of the most significant of these is the church. It's sad that church membership means nothing to millions of people, including many people whose names are on our church rolls. Leslie Weatherhead points to church membership as the most wonderful privilege we mortals can know. He reminds us that the church is from God. It developed from the fellowship that Jesus had on earth with his disciples. We become part of that fellowship when we enter the great family called church. This fellowship will go on long after our planet has ceased to exist. "To see such a vision," writes Weatherhead, "is to realize that being a church member is the most wonderful privilege life can offer, and one of the most powerful ways of maintaining faith during days of stress and storm" (Leslie Weatherhead, *The Christian Agnostic* [Nashville: Abingdon Press, 1965], 174).

That's belonging with a capital "B." That's the kind of belonging that's intended for all of God's children. The church could hold out no greater promise or treasure. (Sandy Wylie)

Worship Aids

Invocation

O God of all love and belonging, we bring before you our hunger for right relationships. We long for a fellowship with you and our neighbors that will sustain us all. Abide with us in this hour and help us nurture our bonds with each other. Amen.

Prayer of Cxonfession

O God of mercy, we live much of our lives apart from your will. You made us for love and belonging, but often we practice alienation and rejection. We do not love as you do. We pray your forgiveness and ask that you guide us into greater friendship with others. Amen.

Words of Assurance

In the name of Jesus Christ, you are forgiven.
In the name of Jesus Christ, you are forgiven. Amen.

Benediction

Go forth to practice friendship and hospitality. Make your homes places of belonging, and give to others those things that have been given to you. The Lord be with you. Amen. (Sandy Wylie)

JUNE 22, 2008

❧❧❧

Sixth Sunday after Pentecost

Readings: Genesis 21:8-21; Jeremiah 20:7-13; Psalm 69:7-18; Romans 6:1b-11; Matthew 10:24-39

Alive to God
Romans 6:1b-11

There were foolish folks in Paul's day who actually argued that since God's grace abounds, one might as well go right ahead and sin, knowing full well that God will continue to redeem a person over and over. While we wouldn't want to put any limits on God's grace, we wouldn't want to put God to the test, either. Paul's assumption, as expressed in the opening verses of Romans 6, was that a person who has been baptized has participated not only in the baptism of Jesus, but in the death of the Christ as well. And when we died with Christ, Paul says that we effectively died to sin. At the very least, there would be no more desire to sin, and a baptized person would make every effort not to sin. One should be able to identify baptized persons by noting that they tend, and intend, not to sin.

That is to say, you can tell a lot about a person by watching the person. Jesus was fully aware of this truth. In Matthew 11, for example, when the imprisoned John the Baptizer sent messengers to Jesus to inquire if he was the One for whom they had been waiting, Jesus answered, "Go and tell John what you hear and see: the blind receive their sight, the lame walk, the lepers are cleansed, the deaf hear, the dead are raised, and the poor have good news brought to them" (vv. 4-5). In other words, look at what Jesus was doing and you would know who Jesus was. Jesus was the Messiah; all the predicted good things were happening in his presence.

As is often the case, Paul's arguments are quite wordy and quite complex. Let's see if we can sort things out and draw a few conclusions from Paul's theological discussion contained in today's lesson.

01

First, in participating in Christ's death, we have been freed from sin. Never mind that we may still sin from time to time. It is part of the human condition. Paul warned of that tendency when he wrote of his own nature. Paul wrote, "I do not understand my own actions. For I do not do what I want, but I do the very thing I hate" (Romans 7:15). He further emphasized this point when he added, "I can will what is right, but I cannot do it. For I do not do the good I want, but the evil I do not want is what I do" (vv. 18b-19). Try as we might, we are not perfect people. Yes, we have died to sin, but sin still sometimes gets the better of us. John Wesley recognized this. Wesley would ask, "Are you going on to perfection?" He never asked if his listeners were perfect. That would have been foolishness. Still, the goal was perfection. Wesley wanted to know if we are making progress in that direction. Are we living a better life today than we were at this time last year, or last week, or yesterday?

Secondly, in baptism we died to sin, wrote Paul, but what he really seemed to mean is that we are no longer controlled by sin. Sin will not often get the better of us. And when we do slip and do what we do not want to do, God's grace will rescue us and we can begin again with a clean slate. Praise be to God! In our baptism we are given hope that the things in our lives that cause us pain, the things in our lives that are self-destructive, the quirks of our behavior that cause others grief may be left behind. They may be buried with Christ, and we may be raised with Christ into a new life in which we are better people. There is hope that things can be turned around and we can become the people that we desire to be—the people that God intends us to be and created us to be.

Thirdly, in participating in Christ's resurrection, we "will never die again; death no longer has dominion" over us. There is a certain freeing of the spirit in this. It places our focus clearly on life. But more important, in participating in Christ's death, we died to sin, and through his resurrection, we live to God. Hear that: we live to God. If God is the central focus of our living, then everything else will fall into place. Our worries about wealth or poverty take a back seat. Our worries about health or sickness take a back seat. Our worries about success or failure take a back seat. Our worries about whether we live or die become less important. All of the things that used to vie for the number one slot in our thinking and our living are no longer given the power of prominent ranking. God is first. Turn first to God. Understand that God will provide for us in at least as grand a measure as God has provided for the feeding of the sparrows and the clothing in beauty of the lilies of the field. We will be all right, all because we live to and with God.

I once heard a man say that in this life God is with him, and when he should die, he will be with God. In either case, he knew he would be well cared for. That kind of thinking brought that man a sense of peace. That kind of peace is what the Apostle Paul had in mind for us as he argued that death no longer has dominion over us, and that we could be alive to God.

As Paul wrote in the final verse of today's epistle lesson, "So you also must consider yourselves dead to sin and alive to God in Christ Jesus." It is possible to live that way, and it will bring you peace. (Douglas Mullins)

Lectionary Commentary
Genesis 21:8-21

The Genesis texts for the sixth, seventh, and eighth Sundays after Pentecost all reinforce a central tenet of the Scriptures, namely, that God will provide. I have used the stories in the texts for the sixth and eighth Sundays after Pentecost as illustrative material in the sermon for the seventh Sunday, demonstrating diverse ways God may care for his people and come to their rescue. Each of these three stories could stand alone, suggesting a three-sermon series on different expressions of the gracious ways of God.

Alternately, this text is a story illustrating two lessons. First, it is a story of the strong will of Sarah, paired with Abraham's love of Sarah shown by his willingness to do as she wished despite his own sadness. If Sarah desired Isaac, her son by husband Abraham, to be the inheritor of all that was Abraham's and of all that had been promised to Abraham, he would honor her request. Abraham would send away Ishmael, his son by Sarah's slave girl, Hagar.

Second, we see the origin of a second kingdom, parallel to the line God was establishing through Abraham and Sarah's son, Isaac. God would do this because Ishmael was also a son of Abraham. The establishment of this second kingdom would be an extension of the promise God had made to his servant Abraham that a great nation would grow from his seed and that his offspring would number more than the stars. Here is spelled out the origin of the people who historically opposed the Jews and those who supported the Jews, and who do so even into the present day. Here is a reminder that these people are God's people, too.

Jeremiah 20:7-13

Occasionally the lectionary provides alternate readings that may be used in a season. Such is the case here, where the Old Testament lessons provide a Genesis track, but also a prophetic track. It is rarely popular to be a prophet. Such is the case for Jeremiah as he sees and speaks to the deteriorating morality and increasing faithlessness of the people of Judah. In chapter 19, Jeremiah had broken a pottery jug. He threw it to the ground and it shattered into so many pieces that its repair was impossible. It was a graphic image of what was about to happen to Judah and Jerusalem. Judah would be overrun by the Babylonians, who would destroy its buildings, plunder its wealth, and take its people into captivity. So unpopular was Jeremiah's message that he was beaten and put in stocks on public display. When Jeremiah was released, he reiterated his prophecy and spoke with candor and directness about the fate of the one responsible for his harsh treatment.

What follows, in today's text, is a beautiful poem in which Jeremiah laments the sad state of affairs, including his maltreatment and public ridicule. But that is not the last word. While the poem concludes with further lamenting in the verses that follow today's designated lesson, today's lesson ends with a single verse of praise. It is the praise of a faithful servant who knows that his word is true and that God will prevail. "Sing to the LORD;" he shouts, "praise the LORD! For he has delivered the life of the needy / from the hands of the evildoers."

Matthew 10:24-39

This text would have been easier to consider if it had been spread over several Sundays. Verses 24-33 offer something worthy of a preacher's endeavor with almost every sentence. For instance, don't think you can surpass the master; it is enough that you emulate the master. Or, know that the Father keeps track of every sparrow, and you are worth more than many sparrows. Or don't ever deny knowing the Son! It will cost you eternity. Each of these themes may be preached.

One idea that jumps out, however, is the single theme expressed in verses 34-39. Peace is illusive, for we want to keep peace with our mother or our father, with our son or our daughter, but sometimes that is not possible. There is always a higher calling, and sometimes that higher calling conflicts with the needs or the desires of those closest to us. Our allegiance to the Christ is always primary. If you place any other consideration—even your family—ahead of the Christ, you are not worthy. If you place anything at all ahead of the Christ, thinking it right or reasonable or good, you will lose your life. Only in losing yourself in Christ and his calling will you find your life. (Douglas Mullins)

Worship Aids

Call to Worship

There are times we do the very things we do not want to do.
All: There are times we fail to do the good we desire to do.
The Apostle Paul said we do not have to be that way; that in our
baptism we have died to sin and are alive to God.
All: Thanks be to God!

Prayer of Confession

O Lord God, our lives seem never quite to be what we had hoped they would be or what we think God intends for them to be. We too often do the very things we know we should not do, and fail to do the good things we wish to do. We ask, O Lord, that you will forgive us our shortcomings and instill in us new life. Help us be alive to you, and to be fellow servants with Christ Jesus. It is in Jesus name that we ask these things. Amen.

Words of Assurance

In the name of Jesus Christ, you are forgiven.
In the name of Jesus Christ, you are forgiven. Amen.

Benediction

We go forth now into all the world, hoping and praying that we may be the people you intend us to be, and hoping and praying that all people with whom we come into contact will come to know you through us; in the name of the Father, and of the Son, and of the Holy Spirit. Amen. (Douglas Mullins)

God's Yes-I-Can Children

Second in a Series of Two on Family Life

Joshua 14:1, 6-14

Last Sunday we discussed how we humans are driven by our needs. Aside from our survival needs, we have four basic needs. Last week we looked at our need for love and belonging. Today we explore a second need: our need for power and recognition.

You and I meet this need as we meet all of our other needs—through interaction with others. The social unit in which we learn to interact is the family—the biological family and the other groups of which we are a part. Families are living and dynamic; we have to feed and nurture them. They don't look after themselves. We help make them stronger or weaker. Only healthy families generate power and recognition in us.

What's involved in achieving power and recognition? It's largely the development of personal competence and strength. When you become competent and strong, you can exercise power; you can do and accomplish. If you're not competent, if you're not strong, you're going nowhere. You have no power to focus. You can't do and you can't accomplish.

In order for us to acquire competence and strength, we have to be nurtured to that end. We have to give support and recognition to each other. Positive stroking and recognition have amazing power. They're the sunshine of human development. A family unit that's strong is one that has found ways to support its members and boost their self-esteem.

One year Green Bay Packers quarterback Bart Starr decided to encourage his oldest son to make good grades. For every A the boy made, Dad would give him ten cents. One Sunday the Packers and Starr had a terrible game. When Starr finally got home and entered his bedroom late at night, he saw a note from Bart Jr. It read, "Dear Dad, I thought you played a great game. Love, Bart." Taped to the note were two dimes! When is twenty cents worth a million dollars?

William Glasser, the founder of reality therapy, gives his best analysis of strength and weakness in his book, *Positive Addiction* (New York: Harper and Row, 1976). Here Glasser grapples with a major question: *Why is there so much human misery in this world?* The primary answer, he thinks, is that people are weak, and weakness hurts. Many people are too weak to meet their needs effectively. Only strength can bring happiness and fulfillment. Glasser discusses strategies for making us stronger.

Glasser lists six characteristics of strong people: (1) they don't give up; (2) they have many more options than weak people; (3) they have faith in the power of their brains; they feel strong; (4) they accept themselves and avoid unhealthy self-criticism; (5) they transmit their strength to others; (6) they're not about to settle for the passive pleasure of negative addiction. Chemical substances make us feel good only for a while.

Strong people seek the active pleasure that comes from love and worth. This pleasure generates a "natural high" that always satisfies.

One of my favorite biblical characters is Caleb, who appears in the books of Numbers and Joshua. A model of strength, he was one of the twelve spies whom Moses sent out to explore the land of Canaan.

When the mission was over, the spies came back and reported. There was a majority report and a minority report. Ten of the spies reported this way: This is a rich and fertile land, but the people who live there are powerful giants, and their cities are very large and well fortified. We're not strong enough to attack them. Why, we're only grasshoppers (Numbers 13).

Then came the minority report from Caleb and Joshua: We should attack now. We're strong enough to conquer the land. The Lord is with us.

The people believe the majority report. All night long they cry out and complain against Moses and Aaron. They want to select another leader and return to their bondage in Egypt!

God has a ready response: None of those who have rebelled will enter that land. "But my servant Caleb, because he has a different spirit and has followed me wholeheartedly, I will bring into the land into which he went, and his descendants shall possess it" (Numbers 14:24). So the children of Israel, for their timidity, wander in the wilderness for forty more years; and all of the adults of that generation except Caleb and Joshua die.

Today's scripture carries us forty-five years down the road. Caleb and some of his clan come before Joshua at Gilgal. Caleb says to Joshua, "I was forty years old when Moses the servant of the LORD sent me . . . to spy out the land. . . . Here I am today, eighty-five years old. I am still as strong today as I was on the day that Moses sent me." In the next chapter Caleb at age eighty-five goes up against the cities of Hebron and Debir and prevails in a battle that he was hindered from fighting forty-five years earlier!

What this world needs is more Calebs. People like Caleb come from only one place: they're grown in families. A rule of strength and weakness is that the strong get stronger and the weak get weaker. Strength isn't a matter of body size or physical power. It resides in the human mind. Some of the strongest people are physically handicapped.

One other thing about Caleb: he knew where his power came from. God had given it to him for a purpose. When you and I feel the power that surges up from deep within us, we can know that that power is the presence of God in our lives. If the church's Christian education program is to turn out people like Caleb, then it has to do more than give students the facts. It has to give them courage and strength and self-esteem.

Forty years . . . that's a lot of time to waste. Israel and Caleb found that out. I don't think we want our children to wait that long. (Sandy Wylie)

Worship Aids

Invocation

O God of power, we come into your presence with feelings of inadequacy. We want to be stronger; we want to live out of the boundless energy that you have put within us. Move among us in this hour, and help us gain strength for this and every day. Amen.

Prayer of Confession

O God of grace, you constantly give us gifts to make us stronger people. But we don't use your gifts, and sometimes we even reject them. Forgive us our disobedience. Help us embrace your gifts and become strengtheners of one another. We pray this in your holy name. Amen.

Words of Assurance

In the name of Jesus Christ, you are forgiven.
In the name of Jesus Christ, you are forgiven. Amen.

Benediction

Be of good courage. Hold fast to the strength that God has given you. Encourage those who are weak and lonely. And may God's blessing rest on us all. Amen! (Sandy Wylie)

JUNE 29, 2008

❧❧❧

Seventh Sunday after Pentecost

Readings: Genesis 22:1-14; Jeremiah 28:5-9; Psalm 13; Romans 6:12-23; Matthew 10:40-42

God Will Provide
Genesis 22:1-14

There are a lot of directions one can run with a Scripture passage like this, but there is one prominent biblical truth that surfaces here, and is reinforced in the Genesis readings for the Sundays on either side of this date, as well as in a multitude of other passages: God will provide. Here is a one-point sermon. We can use these and other readings to provide varied illustrations of this axiom: God will provide.

Abraham and Sarah had long wanted a child. In fact, they grew old wanting a child. At some point, they probably accepted the fact that they simply were not going to have children. They did not understand it. They did not understand how they could be so faithful to their God, and that same God would fail to bless them in this way. Never mind the way it sounds today, in order to have offspring, Sarah gave Hagar, her Egyptian slave girl, to Abraham, and she bore him a son, Ishmael, which means "May God Hear" or simply, "God Hears." Once there was a child in the home, life seemed better. However, it was still God's pleasure that Sarah should have a son by Abraham. Therefore, in their old age, Sarah was found to be with child. She bore Abraham a son, and they named him Isaac, which means "He Laughs," probably because Sarah laughed at God's messengers when, as an old woman, she was informed that she would give birth.

When Isaac was born, Sarah became very territorial and was no longer pleased to have Ishmael or his mother in her presence. She had her son, the rightful heir of all that belonged and would belong to Abraham, and so she pressured Abraham to send Ishmael and Hagar away.

With regret, but at the direction of God, Abraham did send Hagar and Ishmael away. God had told Abraham to listen to Sarah and do what she asked, for God would establish Abraham's line, a great nation, through his son Isaac. Abraham was not to despair, for God would also establish a great nation through Ishmael.

Early in the morning, Abraham took bread and a skin of water to Hagar and her young child Ishmael and sent them on their way. They wandered in the wilderness until their water supply was depleted. Then Hagar placed Ishmael under some brush and went off some distance and sat down. She could not bear to watch the death of her child. God spoke to Hagar through an angel. " 'Do not be afraid. . . . Come, lift up the boy and hold him fast with your hand, for I will make a great nation of him.' Then God opened her eyes and she saw a well of water. She went, and filled the skin with water, and gave the boy a drink" (Genesis 21:17b-19). The boy lived in the wilderness, and when he was grown, his mother got him a wife from Egypt. The moral of this lesson from the Genesis reading of the previous Sunday is that there is no cause to despair; for when you are doing what God intends you to do, God will deliver you. God will provide whatever it is that you need to see you through.

That lesson sets the stage for today's lesson. With Ishmael out of the picture, Abraham had one son, Isaac. He loved this son very much. It seemed strange then, considering how much Abraham loved this son, and how God had waited so long in Abraham's life to give him this son, and in light of the promise God had made to Abraham to establish a great nation through this son, that God would tell Abraham to go into the wilderness and sacrifice his son. Puzzled as he was, Abraham stayed the course, remained faithful to his God, and proceeded to do as God had requested. He cut the wood for a burnt offering, and set out with his son to a distant place where God was directing him. Abraham built the altar, he prepared the wood, he bound his son and placed him on the wood. He took his knife in hand and prepared to kill his son. Only then did God stop him. "And Abraham looked up and saw a ram, caught in a thicket by its horns. Abraham went and took the ram and offered it up as a burnt offering instead of his son. So Abraham called that place 'The LORD will provide'; as it is said to this day, 'On the mount of the LORD it shall be provided.' " The Lord will provide. We cannot ask for more than that.

The Genesis lesson for the following Sunday, from chapter 24, is the story of how God led a variety of people through extraordinary circumstances to bring to Isaac the absolutely right wife for him. And again, the moral of the story is that God will provide.

In these lessons, one of the major themes of the Bible is established. God can be counted on to deliver God's children from despair, God can be counted on to deliver God's people, God can be counted on to provide whatever is needful for the welfare of God's people and the building of God's kingdom. God will provide. Further biblical illustrations of this great truth abound. It might be in sending Moses to Pharaoh to seek the release from slavery of his people. It might be in sending the young lad David to bring down the giant Goliath. It might be in bringing his people out of exile to rebuild Jerusalem and reestablish the kingdom founded through the offspring of Abraham. It might be in sending God's own Son to redeem a lost generation. Time and again we see that God will provide.

I am reminded of an oft repeated refrain in the African American religious community that never fails to bring forth a rousing chorus of knowing amens. It goes like this: Jesus never comes when I call him, but he always comes in time. It is one more way of saying that God will deliver his people; that God will provide. Jesus never comes when I call him, but he always comes in time. And the people said, "Amen." (Douglas Mullins)

Lectionary Commentary
Jeremiah 28:5-9

Occasionally the lectionary provides alternate readings that may be used in a season. Such is the case here, where the Old Testament lessons provide a Genesis track, but also a prophetic track. Jeremiah's reluctant prophecy began as King Josiah undertook his reforms. Unfortunately, Josiah's successors did not follow Josiah's lead, and took the people of Judah ever more quickly down the slippery slope of apostasy. Jeremiah, under great duress and hardship, prophesied the destruction of Jerusalem at the hand of Babylon. In chapter 28 we encounter Hananiah, who claims to be a prophet, but who preaches that Babylon will not prevail and that all the misery that is presumed to be coming will be short-lived. Others, before them, had prophesied death and destruction, and here was Hananiah prophesying peace. Today's lesson concludes with Jeremiah's words, "As for the prophet who prophesies peace, when the word of that prophet comes true, then it will be known that the LORD has truly sent the prophet."

Unfortunately, if one reads further, that is not the last word. While it would seem always to be worthy to prophesy peace, it is never appropriate when that is not the Lord's word. If it is false prophecy, then the prophet is guilty of misrepresenting the Lord, and more damaging, the prophet is guilty of offering his people a false hope. Jeremiah proclaimed that Hananiah had done just that, and for his punishment, he shall die. Jeremiah 28:17 reveals that Hananiah died within the year. It is a not too subtle reminder to the preacher that he or she must not water down the hard lessons of the Bible. The truth is to be proclaimed whether it is harsh judgment or glorious redemption. And in almost all instances, that is precisely the order of things.

Matthew 10:40-42

What does it take to earn one's reward from the Master and his Father? It takes, to the very best of one's ability, a sincere effort to emulate the Master. If a person will try to think and speak and act like the Master, it not only paves the way for that person to be rewarded in heaven, but it opens that same door to everyone with whom that person comes in contact. If you behave in the same manner as the Master, and someone welcomes you, that person has, in effect, welcomed the Master himself. And if that person has welcomed the Master, the Father has likewise been received. This is the very definition of effective evangelism. It isn't that one knocks on every door, or says the right words at a given time, or sometimes does good things. It is that one lives like the Master in such a manner that others will see the Master in that person. This is an extension of Jesus' teaching from the Sermon on the Mount in Matthew 5:13-16, a lesson about letting one's light shine. Live in such a way that others will see you and the things you do and will, therefore, give glory to the Father.

Romans 6:12-23

Thanks to the grace of God, sin no longer has a foothold in us. That does not mean that we should ignore sin in the world, or that we should let down our guard when confronted by sin. In fact, we should redouble our efforts at keeping sin out of our lives. It is the height of arrogance to think that because God's grace abounds, it does not matter whether we sin. It matters! The truth is that the battle lines are always drawn. We will either be the slave of sin or the slave of obedience. The servant of the Christ will always be the slave to obedience. Grace may redeem us when we hit a pothole in the road of life, but we have no right to count on grace when we have willfully and wittingly turned our back on obedience and done that very thing that we were to avoid. Grace abounds, but it must never become our excuse for being a lesser person than we were called to be. As Paul says, "For the wages of sin is death, but the free gift of God is eternal life in Christ Jesus our Lord." (Douglas Mullins)

Worship Aids

Call to Worship

There are so many times when we think that all is lost.
All: There are so many times we have experienced despair.
And then something happens that turns the tide, and we are
delivered from our despair.
**All: That is when we are reminded once again of the
biblical promise that God will provide.**

Prayer of Confession

O Lord God, there have been too many times when we have doubted
you. We have looked at our lives and all that we are up against, and we
are sure that you have abandoned us. We are heartily sorry for our lack of
faith and insufficient trust. We should never have doubted that you will
deliver us; that you will provide for us. Forgive us and deliver us from this
present darkness that we may walk in the light of your Son, our Savior,
Jesus Christ. Amen.

Words of Assurance

In the name of Jesus Christ, you are forgiven.
In the name of Jesus Christ, you are forgiven. Amen.

Benediction

We go forth now into all the world as your people, having been
reminded of your great caring for us. We have been delivered. We have
seen the ways in which you have provided for your children. May we go
forth and live as redeemed people; in the name of the Father, and of the
Son, and of the Holy Spirit. Amen. (Douglas Mullins)

Following Jesus: Grounded Upon Authority

First in a Series of Three on Evangelism

Matthew 10:1-4; 28:16-20

The Great Commission of Jesus to the disciples is one of the foundational texts of the Christian faith. In it we find the claim to authority, the
commission to make disciples, and the call to remember the abiding presence of Jesus. It is a passage that is complex and packed with meaning, yet

it is amazingly simple. Today and for two more Sundays we will explore the Great Commission as we work together to determine its meaning for us in this time and place. During each of these three weeks, we will read the Great Commission and then another text from the Gospels that sheds more light on the subject matter in the Great Commission. Perhaps this will help us better appreciate the marvelous call that comes from Jesus to the church today!

As a teenager, I did not easily submit to authority. I disliked authority. More than being under authority, I never really wanted to be in charge of anything. I did not want to have authority myself. Even to this day, I am still not sure if I have completely resolved all of my issues with authority. As a young minister coming through the ordination process in our annual conference, we were subject to annual interviews conducted by the conference Board of Ordained Ministry. Following those interviews, many of the candidates (including me) would gather somewhere (usually a fast-food restaurant somewhere) and we would share our interview stories. Without fail, after every series of interviews, at least one of my friends would say that he or she was informed that he or she had a problem with authority. These were my friends who seemed to normally be very compliant, and I often wondered why I wasn't challenged about the same thing. Then after working through the process for a couple of years, it finally happened to me. I was being interviewed, and because of something I said or wrote, someone in the group said, "It seems that maybe you have a problem with authority."

I will never forget what happened next. At that point, another member of the group, who was a trusted and respected mentor of mine, said, "You know, we so often use that phrase when dealing with candidates. Of course, he has a problem with authority. I have a problem with authority. If the truth is known, most of us in this room have or have had or will have a problem with authority. It is not that he has a problem with authority that concerns me most. It is how he works through being under authority, being granted authority, and using that authority that concerns me."

All of my life I will never forget that challenge. It never occurred to me to question the authority of Jesus. At least, it didn't occur to me in the cognitive realm. As I have reflected upon my life, however, I am not so sure that I haven't questioned the authority of Jesus at a deeper level. In the Great Commission, Jesus says, "All authority in heaven and on earth has been given to me." Earlier in Matthew's Gospel, Jesus shares that same authority with his disciples even as he does at the Great

Commission. Here, however, the authority is not just bestowed upon random, nameless people. No, here the authority is given to specific people: "Then Jesus summoned his twelve disciples and gave them authority over unclean spirits, to cast them out, and to cure every disease and every sickness. These are the names of the twelve apostles: first, Simon, also known as Peter, and his brother Andrew; James son of Zebedee, and his brother John; Philip and Bartholomew; Thomas and Matthew the tax collector; James son of Alphaeus, and Thaddaeus; Simon the Cananaean, and Judas Iscariot, the one who betrayed him."

It is that concreteness that I have had such difficulty trusting. It is one thing to say that Jesus has shared authority with the church or with his followers. But when we start naming names—Matthew, John, Peter, Susan, Bob, Melissa, and Jeff—then we are getting serious. This is not about authority given to the followers of Jesus; rather, it is now about authority that has been given to me. And yes, I have a problem with that. It is not the same problem with authority that I had as a teenager. It is not that I have a problem being under authority, but I do have a serious problem with being entrusted with such authority. If only the people knew who I really was—if only people could see my clay feet—if only they knew that I have moments of uncertainty myself—then they might think it a mockery that I have dared to assume the authority of Jesus himself.

Yet this is the authority that Jesus has given to us. It is the authority to share in his ministry. It is the authority to defeat demons. It is the authority to bring healing. It is the authority to make disciples for Jesus. It is the authority to be the body of Christ. Such authority can be overwhelming, yet we who are in Christ are endowed with just such authority.

The question for us now is how we will use that authority. There are many who do not consider that they have a problem with authority, yet they use their authority to hurt others. Many lives have been damaged by ministerial misconduct in its various forms. No matter the nature of the offense, the common factor is that a member of the clergy who has authority and power has often overstepped a boundary and used that authority and power for personal gain or personal pleasure.

Then there are those who refuse to take up authority. I have encountered men and women who could have positively influenced their family—their church—their community—their world—had they only dared to take up the authority. Women, believing that they are subservient to men, have refused roles of spiritual leadership when God is clearly calling on them to be the spiritual leaders in their families or their churches. I know people who, in the shadow of a very strong, charismatic pastor, have declined to take authority (especially if it meant taking a stand against something espoused by the pastor).

So our challenge is to take authority. Take it appropriately, yes, but take it. Do you have a problem with authority? If you do, remember that the disciples themselves had problems with authority, but it was theirs nonetheless. (Jeffery Smith)

Worship Aids

Call to Worship

Come let us worship the author of all life!
We bring ourselves to you, O God.
Come let us worship the author of our salvation!
We offer anew to you, O Christ.
Come, O God, and empower us with your Spirit.
Renew us with the authority to be your disciples, O Holy Spirit!

Prayer of Confession

O God, we come as children who are afraid, not of failure, but of success. We are afraid, not of powerlessness, but of what to do with the power we have. You have offered us power to become children of God, yet we have failed to take up that power. We are frozen by doubt, and we are stifled by fear. Forgive us, O God, when we forget who we are. Give us power to become your children. Grant us the authority to speak your word. And may we find ourselves fitted for ministry in the body of Christ. This we ask through Jesus Christ our Lord. Amen.

Words of Assurance

In the name of Jesus Christ, you are forgiven.
In the name of Jesus Christ, you are forgiven. Amen.

Benediction

Go forth with power from on high. May God empower your life, grant you the authority to speak a holy word, and enliven your spirit to witness to the power of God in this world. In the name of the Father, and of the Son, and of the Holy Spirit. Amen. (Jeffrey Smith)

JULY 6, 2008

❧❧❧

Eighth Sunday after Pentecost

Readings: Genesis 24:34-38, 42-29, 58-67; Zechariah 9:9-12;
Psalm 145:8-14; Romans 7:15-25a; Matthew 11:16-19, 25-30

Rest for the Weary
Matthew 11:16-19, 25-30

It is amazing how a little bit of wisdom can get in the way of seeing what is truly important. That is probably why Jesus championed the little children and those who are like them in their simplicity of thought. That is also probably why Jesus gave the Pharisees such a hard time. They were wise people, they were scholarly people, and they advocated a lot of rules by which to live. Yet, for all of their wisdom, for all of their law keeping, for all of their ingenuity, they just didn't get it. When the kingdom festivities begin, the Pharisees and those like them will be on the wrong side of the door, while those who know far less—those who seem so ordinary or are the least among all people—will be with Jesus in the banquet hall.

In the midst of today's lesson from Matthew's Gospel, Jesus muttered a one-sentence prayer to his Father. "I thank you, Father, Lord of heaven and earth, because you have hidden these things from the wise and the intelligent and have revealed them to infants." Jesus, in verse 17, had just compared his generation to people who had heard the message proclaimed and ignored it, to people who heard the children playing the lute, but did not dance, or who heard the children wail, but did not mourn. Jesus was speaking of John the Baptizer with the crowd, and how so many had given no credence to anything John had told them. Oh, they had gone out into the wilderness to see John, but they did not find what they were expecting. They thought John might be a learned scholar. He was not. He was a simple man who had stepped out of the wilderness. They thought John might be wearing fine robes. He wasn't. He was dressed in whatever he could fashion from materials found in the wilderness. They thought he was a prophet. John was, and so much more, but they were offended by what he had to say.

Jesus made an observation that could get us in trouble today if we were to take it too literally, but which seemed reasonable to his listeners. Jesus seemed to believe that cities were places where knowledge and learning abounded, but were also places where Jesus was rejected. Meanwhile, Jesus suggested that the villages and the rural areas, while not viewed as centers of learning and sophistication, were the very places where Jesus was heard and welcomed. Notice that almost all of Jesus' ministry takes place in the villages and rural areas, on both sides of the sea, right up until those few tragic days following his triumphant entry into Jerusalem. The generalities may not stand up today, but the truth he was expressing contains a lesson worth hearing. Taking Jesus into your heart has little to do with the accumulation of vast amounts of knowledge, and more to do with simply opening your heart and mind, and saying yes to the one whom God sends.

Remember the arrogance of the disciples that day they were all heading for Jerusalem for the last time, when they would have driven the little children away from Jesus? They begged people not to let them bother the Master or waste his time. Remember what Jesus said? "Let the little children come to me, and do not stop them; for it is to such as these that the kingdom of heaven belongs" (Matthew 19:14). Jesus knew that it was in their innocence and simplicity of thought that they modeled what it would take for any one of us to join them in the kingdom.

Jesus was not belittling knowledge or book learning or wisdom, but he was warning of its perils. Sometimes, the smarter we get the more self-absorbed or self-important we become. The Apostle Paul understood, for he later cautioned that we ought not think too highly of ourselves (Romans 12:3). As we gather more and more knowledge, we are apt to think that we can function by ourselves and do not need anyone or anything else. It is like the people of Babel who learned how to build a tower that they thought could reach right up into the heavens (Genesis 11:1-9). Then they began to believe that they didn't need God, not even to get into heaven. God said it wasn't so.

Learning tends to make us feel that we are in control of our lives. We aren't. Jesus begs us to let go of the reins and acknowledge Jesus' lordship. There is learned truth. We can know math and science and laws and history and so much else. Then there is revealed truth. Simplicity and openness are the keys here. Open your hearts and let God come in. There is a vast difference between knowing about God, and knowing God. Books may try to teach us about God, and it may well be worth our effort to learn all we can about God. But only in our childlike innocence and simplicity will we be able to receive Jesus Christ, whom God in his wisdom and mercy has chosen to send to us.

Where is Jesus going with all of this? Finally, he came to the point of saying, "Come to me, all you that are weary and are carrying heavy burdens, and I will give you rest." Learn all you can. Read all you want to. Understand to the best of your ability your environment and the world. Still, when you want to be part of the kingdom, assume an attitude of humility and turn to Jesus. Lay down your burdens and turn to Jesus with the innocence of little children, and invite Jesus into your heart and life. Jesus will welcome you home, and will give you rest. (Douglas Mullins)

Lectionary Commentary
Genesis 24:34-38, 42-49, 58-67

The Genesis text illustrates God's apparent interest in keeping Abraham's line pure. Here is the intricate story of God's leading and nudging and ultimately providing a wife for Abraham's son Isaac from among Abraham's kinsmen. This is such a beautiful story that it simply telling it could provide the sermon. The story begins at Genesis 24:1, with an aged Abraham's insistence that his son Isaac should have a wife from among his people rather than from the Canaanites. The assignment to find such a wife for Isaac is given to a servant, who immediately understands the significance of his role. The servant bows before the Lord in prayer for guidance. There is the servant's plea that he shall meet the right woman at the well, and it comes to pass when Rebekah approaches the well. Only after the meeting does the servant discover that this woman, in fact, meets the criterion that she be from among Abraham's kinsmen. Finally, before being introduced to Isaac, whom she is to marry, she sees him from a distance and instinctively knows that he is the one. This is a story of God breaking into history to make something very good and very right happen. This is God working out God's plan according to the promise he had made to his servant Abraham.

Zechariah 9:9-12

Occasionally the lectionary provides alternate readings. Such is the case here, where the Old Testament lessons provide a Genesis track, but also a prophetic track. As Zechariah writes, some of those captive Jews who were in Babylon for seventy years return to Jerusalem. Interestingly, those who had achieved a measure of prosperity during the long years of captivity remained in Babylon. Therefore, it was mainly the poor who returned home. They were despondent, and seemed more interested in trying to eke out a living by whatever means they could than rebuilding the temple, which would have been understood to be the priority. Finally, the temple was rebuilt as a sign that the Lord God was good, a power to behold, and whose favor was to be sought. Accordingly, people from many different nations came, and a new day was beginning.

This lesson from Zechariah contains a verse that every Christian who has ever been in worship on a Palm Sunday will have heard. "Rejoice greatly, O daughter of Zion! / Shout aloud, O daughter of Jerusalem! / Lo, your king comes to you; / triumphant and victorious is he, / humble and riding on a donkey, / on a colt, the foal of a donkey." As surely as the people of Zechariah's day would come to the temple to find favor with God, Jesus would choose this dramatic symbolism as he, too, approached the temple. However, Jesus would come to the temple in an attempt to restore it to its former greatness and its true purpose. Still, it is Zechariah who proclaims that when the king shall come, he shall do so humbly, riding on a donkey. And so it came to pass. It is a reminder that humility is the appropriate stance for anyone coming to the temple or approaching God.

Romans 7:15-25a

Paul's theme of grace continues. We are complex people. As Paul discovered, there is always the propensity to do the wrong thing while failing to do the very thing we ought to do. Paul is clear that even when we know the hazards of sin, even when we know with all our hearts the things we ought not do, too often we succumb. Just as certainly, we all have a fairly clear vision about what sorts of things we should do, but too often we simply fail to do them. More often than not, we actually choose not to do them. Such behavior is a testimony to the fact that sin is real. Sin is not an abstract concept, but a very real force with which to be reckoned. Paul is candid enough in this text to admit that we will not always choose correctly, we will not always avoid the pitfalls, and we will not always stand on the side of right. The war with sin is a constant. We will not win every skirmish. But wait! Paul asks, "Who will rescue me from this body of death?" It is Jesus Christ, the Son of God. "Thanks be to God through Jesus Christ our Lord!" That is to say, there is hope and there is redemption. (Douglas Mullins)

Worship Aids

Call to Worship

We come into the house of the Lord weighed down with the burdens of life.

We come seeking rest, or at least some help with carrying our burdens.

Jesus said, "Come to me, all you that are weary and carrying heavy burdens, and I will give you rest" (Matthew 11:28).

In Jesus we will find rest for our souls.

Prayer of Confession

O Lord God, we too often get caught up in the cares of the world and in our own self-importance. We are sorry that we have so cluttered our lives. We ask that you will cleanse our souls. Give us the innocence of little children so that we may receive you and love you and live with you in our hearts. We give thanks to you for your great mercy, in the name of Jesus Christ, our Savior. Amen.

Words of Assurance

In the name of Jesus Christ, you are forgiven.

In the name of Jesus Christ, you are forgiven. Amen.

Benediction

We go forth from this house of God feeling refreshed. Our burdens have been made lighter and our souls have been cleansed. Everywhere we go, may others we encounter sense that we have been with you. May we go in peace; in the name of the Father, and of the Son, and of the Holy Spirit. (Douglas Mullins)

Following Jesus: Making Disciples

Second in a Series of Three on Evangelism

Matthew 28:16-20; John 1:35-42

Today we continue our series on the Great Commission of Jesus to the disciples. Previously, we considered the issue of authority as related to those who have been commissioned by Jesus. Next week, we will discuss the abiding presence of Jesus, and today we will consider the commission to make disciples.

The call to make disciples is considered by many to be the primary task of the Christian church. It is certainly the dominant theme in the Great Commission, and it is the basis of much programming in most of our churches today. While it does not give specific instructions (other than to baptize the disciples in the name of the Triune God), it does not let us off thinking that the message of Jesus is one that is easily kept secret. The truth is that sharing the message of Jesus is amazingly simple.

As a young minister serving a student appointment while still in seminary, I remembered thinking that evangelism was all about a complex program of advertising, outreach, and visitation. I had assumed that it needed various structures and resources to be successful. Further, I had assumed that it was a task so complex that I probably wouldn't be very good at it.

Then one day I was required to attend a training session for our district. The training had breakout groups that focused on various topics. The groups I had wanted to join were full, so I was more or less forced to attend the breakout group on evangelism. I reluctantly went into the room, but I was pleasantly surprised by what I learned that day.

The instructor (a man whose name I have long since forgotten) had several handouts that confirmed for me that an evangelism program must be multilayered and complex in order to be successful. He handed us the papers and then told us to put them away for another day because he had something important to share. He said, "Most of us think of evangelism as something that requires a lot of work. Many people are out there trying to identify evangelism and tell us what program will work most effectively in evangelism. I'm here to tell you that it is all wrong."

He paused to let the words sink in. We all looked rather quizzically at this new revelation. He continued, "I'm sure some programs may work, but my experience is that we spend all of this time trying to figure out what evangelism is and how to implement some detailed program that we forget to evangelize." That was a new concept for me. In seminary, I had learned how to think things through. I had learned how to critically evaluate things. I had thought a lot about things like evangelism; it's just that I had never really done evangelism.

Then the instructor continued and said the one thing that I will never forget. "Evangelism is as easy as one beggar telling another beggar where to find food." It hit me. Beggars are people who are desperate. They are starving. The only thing they can think about is where their next meal is coming from. When they find an abundant supply of food, they don't need a complex program to tell their friends where they got the food.

We live in a world that is starving. It is a world lost in darkness. Hate, greed, war, poverty, and neglect are among the many evils that plague us. It is a world desperately in need, and there are so many people who are themselves starving. They may not be starving for food. It may be that they are starving for hope or joy. Perhaps they are starving for love or friendship. I see a world starving for a word of peace. No matter the hunger, we know people who are starving for something.

That something is the good news. We are the people who know. We know of the joy and love that comes from following Christ. We know of hope amidst a world of despair. We know of love amidst a world of hate. We know a Savior amidst a world that is lost. It is that simple message we are called to share.

Andrew was one who had encountered the man named Jesus. He had followed him to the place where Jesus was staying, and it was there that Andrew spent the day with Jesus. In that short amount of time, Andrew had his hunger filled and his thirst quenched. This was the one who himself was the bread of life. Jesus was the cup of salvation. Andrew knew that this man was someone very special. Jesus was the anointed one. He was the Messiah!

Andrew had a brother who was likewise starving. He was looking for something. Andrew had come to the conviction that he had encountered the one who was the answer to their parched souls. He then came to his brother, Simon, and brought him to Jesus. Jesus, upon meeting Simon, told him that his name was Cephas, which translates to Peter—"the rock"! Because of Andrew, Peter's thirst was quenched, and he was empowered with a faith that became the foundation for all who followed him.

How would the story have changed had Andrew not shared the good news with Simon Peter? As important, what would our story have been had he not shared the good news? Thank God that he didn't look for a complex program with a long list of resources. All he had to do was share with one who was hungry, and a disciple was born.

Do you know someone around you who is starving for the bread of life and the cup of salvation? Give them a taste of the bread and a drink from the cup. Yes, it's just that easy. (Jeffery Smith)

Worship Aids

Call to Worship

Come, let us worship!
We worship the God of all hope.

Come, let us worship!
We worship the God of all life.
Come, let us share the good news!
**We give ourselves, O God, to sharing your gospel with our
world!**

Affirmation of Faith

Let us proclaim with our mouths what we believe with our hearts:
**We believe in God, who has created everything good
and who cast humanity in the image of God.
We believe in the goodness of creation,
in the inner goodness of the human heart,
in the goodness of life amidst a world of death.
We believe that God has called us to be the children of God,
and we believe that we are stewards of that calling.
We believe in Jesus Christ, the perfect image of God
    manifested among us.
We believe that we are the living disciples of the living Christ
who are called to proclaim the good news to the whole world.
We believe in the new life of hope and love
that Christ has set before us,
and we pray to be sustained in that new life.
We believe in the Holy Spirit as the one
who empowers our ministry,
who pushes us out the door into our world,
who gives voice and power to our feeble efforts at sharing
    the good news.
We believe that we are called to be witnesses to everything
God has done in our world,
and we believe in the power of the Holy Spirit
to move us forward as we witness to our faith.
We commit ourselves to ministry in the body of Christ,
and we offer ourselves to God as disciples of a living Lord!
    Amen.**

Benediction

Go forth in peace! Be bold in your proclamation of the gospel of Jesus
Christ! Shout from the housetops the love of a Savior. In the name of the
Father, and of the Son, and of the Holy Spirit! Amen. (Jeffrey Smith)

JULY 13, 2008

❧❧❧

Ninth Sunday after Pentecost

Readings: Isaiah 55:10-13; Psalm 119:105-112; Romans 8:1-11; Matthew 13:1-9, 18-23

God's Gracious Rain
Isaiah 55:10-13

In human experience, it is often easy to associate disappointment with failure. In God's infinite wisdom, our disappointment may be simply a misunderstanding of God's purpose and timing. One of the greatest messages we have as a Christian people is that our life is in God's hands. Isaiah tells of the rains and the nourishment that sent to Earth, and always fulfills its purpose before returning to the heavens. In much the same way, God's will may get us wet, and may even cause some unexpected damage if we are not properly prepared for the rain, but it will fulfill God's good and perfect plan for us.

In our independent, self-sufficient society, we want to be the cause and effect of all action that might touch our lives. In so doing, we miss out on the mysterious blessings of the newly fallen rain sent from God. Although we will be caught off guard by God's will, God's purpose will always be ready to nourish our life and help us grow into God's likeness, but we must let the rain fall, and we must go outside and be willing to get wet, even when we are not prepared for rain.

Too often we allow our plans and preparedness to get in the way of God's surprising mysteries. I am a planner, and I love to have everything planned out in advance, but by doing so, I miss some opportunities for growth and valuable experiences that I could have. One of the best and most fulfilling vacations that I have ever had was to the French countryside. I found very quickly that in the planning and the implementation of that trip that neither my English, nor my limited Spanish, did me much good at making arrangements. I was forced to sit back and allow others to plan and allow things to just happen along the way. I would have never given up this control freely, but I was forced into submission by my lack of knowledge, and was blessed with the most wonderful experience. I was invited to see sights I would have never visited, meet people I would have never met, and eat food that I still do not know exactly what it might have been. All of this made for one of the most relaxing and informative trips in my life, but I had to get wet by the rain of discomfort in order to experience it.

When we protect ourselves from the rain and the mystery in life, we stay a bit cleaner and more comfortable in the present, but we miss out on the future growth and blessing that awaits all of God's children. In life, we must live spiritually like we are dancing in the rain of God's mysterious will. We must listen to the word of God that Isaiah refers to as nourishment that gives us the ability to grow into new light. In our secular lives and in our spiritual lives, we have become accustomed to using umbrellas to protect us from God, or we simply stay inside so we do not have to mess with the unpredictable rain. As faithful Christians, we must embrace Isaiah's understanding of God's word as a blessing, even when it might interfere with our plans.

The second important aspect of this scripture text is the acknowledgment that God is the one who is to be glorified by the blessings we receive. There are two purposes to the life-giving rain, one to bless the land, and two is to bless the Creator of the land through the new life and beautiful growth. If our only reason for allowing the rain to fall on us is for our benefit, then we have missed the point. We are assured that we will be blessed by God's nourishing word, but the effects of that are to be glorious for God. We do not receive blessings and growth simply for ourselves. God blesses us in order that we might praise the Creator of all good things, and so we might become a blessing to others. It is only in the receiving of God's rain and the offering of growth back to God that we find the true meaning in God's purpose.

We must remember to allow the unexpected rain of God's love to pour down on us and help us grow, but we must do so in order to offer praise and glory to our God. Living lives of protection hides the goodness of God's will for us, but it also keeps us from reaching out to others. God wants us to be blessed and to grow, but one reason for that desire of God is for us to offer blessings to those around us. Hoarding the rain and nourishment we have been given, while others are experiencing painful droughts is not God's intention. When we are blessed with rain, our first response should be to praise God, and our second response should be to bless others and share God's goodness. (Chris Hayes)

Lectionary Commentary
Matthew 13:1-9, 18-23

The parable of the Sower is one of the best known of Jesus' stories. Perhaps it is so well remembered because it speaks such truth to the nature of evangelism and the human experience. All of us know that each person hears and sees life through a different set of filters, and therefore no two people ever see and hear one event in the exact same way. Perhaps a good example of this is in a traffic accident. If we ask the drivers of the two cars involved, we get two very different versions of what transpired. It becomes even more complicated when we ask witnesses about what they saw happen, because from each differing angle and each different perspective, things look a bit unique. This same concept applies to the hearing of the gospel. We never know how the words we say will be heard by those we share with, but the parable of the Sower tells us that our job is simply to sow the seeds. We are not responsible for the way the gospel message is interpreted or heard. We are responsible for sowing the seeds for people to hear. God will take care of the growth and the timing of fertile ground.

Romans 8:1-11

In this passage of Romans, justification of sin is explained through the Christ event. Jesus was sent in the likeness of sin, to put sin to death, so we might have righteousness. Paul writes that we are not capable of finding righteousness on our own as humans, because we are flawed by sin. But Jesus, who knows no sin, becomes our sin, so we might have life. Justification is not an easily conceptualized theological idea. It is difficult to wrap our minds around God cleansing our sin through Christ. Romans tells us that although we cannot obtain this justified state through our own efforts, and although we might not understand the concept in all its complexity, we can nevertheless be assured that Jesus took that task upon himself for our sake.

Even with great scholarly work, there are, and should be, mysteries to God's way. In the light of our justification by God through Jesus Christ, our response is faith and thanksgiving, with or without full understanding. (Chris Hayes)

Worship Aids

Call to Worship

We gather in God's presence for worship.
Let us lift our voices to praise God.
We gather in God's presence for worship.
Let us open our hearts to hear God's Word.
We gather in God's presence for worship.
All: Let us be transformed into God's likeness.

Prayer of Confession

Merciful God, we confess we often try to live life without your guidance. We sometimes think our knowledge is sufficient, but we know in our hearts we fall short without your help. Allow us to remember your will for our lives, and put aside our self-centeredness for your glory and reign. Amen.

Words of Assurance

In the name of Jesus Christ, you are forgiven.
In the name of Jesus Christ, you are forgiven. Amen.

Invocation

Loving God, we gather in this place as your children. We come from different places and from different points of view, knowing that you can unite us in the oneness of your Holy Spirit, that we might glorify you. Come Holy Spirit, Come! (Chris Hayes)

Following Jesus: An Abiding Presence

Third in a Series of Three on Evangelism

Matthew 28:16-20; John 14:25-27

Today we conclude our series on the Great Commission of Jesus to his disciples. Two weeks ago, we considered the issue of authority. Last week, we focused on the primary emphasis of this passage—the commission to make disciples. Today we conclude by focusing on the abiding presence of Jesus as the one thing that gives evangelism it intrinsic value.

If we take our role seriously as evangelists—namely, those who have been given authority and who are called to reach out and make disciples—then we will also understand the central message of the evangelist. It is the timeless message handed down from ancestral Judaism all the way to the modern church. It is the message of the abiding presence of God through Jesus Christ.

As I considered the text from Matthew 28 and its message concerning the abiding presence of Christ, I thought of the many funerals I have officiated over the years. Two of the primary texts from those services are Psalm 23 and the passage we read from John 14. Prior to Jesus' promise in John 14 to send the Holy Spirit (here called the Advocate), Jesus has told his disciples that he is going to prepare a place for them. Jesus has told them that God's house is a place where there is room for everyone. He has told them that he is going away, but not before he lets them in on a little secret. The Holy Spirit will come and abide with them. The primary task of this Advocate is to remind the followers of Jesus that Jesus is near. The Advocate is here to make real the presence of Jesus in and among his followers. Jesus is not the Messiah who has left us on our own; rather, Jesus is the Christ who lives in and through his disciples.

I learned early on in my ministry about the ministry of presence. I first served as a student pastor during my junior year in college. I was only twenty years old, and there in my tiny little church, I soon found just how much I didn't know. I remember my first funeral all too well. The man had suffered from Alzheimer's disease, about which I knew little. I didn't know what to say to the family as this man was dying, and I had no real understanding of pastoral care. I visited him anyway, all the while feeling woefully inadequate.

When he died, I had no idea how to conduct a funeral. I called another minister who mentored me through the planning. I met with the family three times during the two days following his death, each time not having the slightest idea what to say or do in those situations. The day of the funeral came, and I fumbled my way through the service. I don't remember much about the service.

What I do recall, however, was the response of the family. They were so grateful. They said how wonderful I had been and how comforting I was to the family. As I recounted this incident to one of my favorite college professors in the religion department, he said something I have never forgotten. He said, "In times of crisis, you don't have to know everything. You don't have to be the most skilled counselor or the best preacher. All you have to be is present." It was that knowledge that has most profoundly affected and shaped my ministry through the years.

The greatest evangelistic tool we have is the gift of presence. As a pastor who has experienced both growing and declining churches, I have learned that presence is the key. People who are present in their communities as Christians tend to draw people to Christ. This doesn't mean that we must wear our Christianity on our sleeves with acts of false piety. It does mean that, if we live our lives in the shadow of the life of Christ, we will find that people who are seeking will want what we have.

Likewise, the church must be present in the community. Churches that tend to focus on inward needs—the desires and wants of its own membership as opposed to being open to ministering to the hurt and suffering of those so often excluded by organized religion—find themselves in decline. Churches that focus on outreach and refuse to place their own needs above the needs of others are churches that are growing precisely because they are present to needs outside their own walls.

The message of presence is perhaps the greatest message of the entire Bible. God is present in creation, and in Genesis 2, we find that God is as present as our very breath. God is present to the people of Israel even in their suffering, and they are told that they will not be forgotten. God is the one who leads us as a shepherd and will lead us even "through the valley of the shadow of death" as promised in Psalm 23 (NIV). The prophets remind us that God has never deserted the people of God, even during exile and judgment. God who created us and called to be a holy people will never leave us in our hour of need.

That is the eternal promise of God, and it is here confirmed in the Great Commission. Jesus' promise to be present is not an idle promise. It is the promise that we will not be forgotten. It is a promise that we will be forever loved as the children of God.

So when you seek to share the good news of Jesus with others—when you seek to bring others into fellowship with the living Christ—it doesn't require that we have some complex skill or know everything there is to know about evangelism. It only requires that we be present as God is present. When we are present to our hurting world, we have become evangelists and Christ is made known through our presence. (Jeffery Smith)

Worship Aids

Invocation

Come, O God, and walk with us a while. Send your Holy Spirit among us. Enliven our hearts. Enrich our fellowship. Remind us of your love.

Make Jesus real to us today that we might become real in our discipleship, and bless us with grace that we might rise up above ourselves to worship you. Amen.

Call to Worship

Come and see what God has done!
God has brought us the gift of hope!
Come and taste the goodness of God's love!
God has brought us the gift of faith!
The Spirit of the Lord has come among us!
Come, O God, and abide with us!

Benediction

You have experienced the abiding presence of our living God. Go now in peace, and take this abiding Christ with you into the world that Christ may abide with the world through you, the body of Christ. Amen. (Jeffrey Smith)

JULY 20, 2008

❦❦❦

Tenth Sunday after Pentecost

Readings: Genesis 28:10-19a; Psalm 139:1-12, 23-24; Romans 8:12-25; Matthew 13:24-30, 36-43

Adopted by God
Romans 8:12-25

I do not think there is a more beautiful image of God's love for us than the image of adoption. I have a friend, Tina, who was adopted. She tells me of her experience growing up with the confusion of what it means to be adopted. One day, while at school in the second grade, Tina began to be teased about being adopted. When children do not understand something, it seems natural to make fun of it as a coping mechanism. (Perhaps children are not the only ones who react this way to misunderstandings.) Tina went home in tears not knowing how to react to the other children telling her that her parents were not her real mom and dad. With large tears flowing down her cheeks, Tina walked in the back door of her home and was greeted by a worried mother. "What is wrong?" her mother asked. Tina told the story of being teased at school about not having real parents and not being as good as the other children because of it. Tina's wise mother took Tina into her loving arms and told her that all of those other children were born into their families and their parents had absolutely no choice about the kid they got, "But we got to pick you because you were so special," her mother said.

Romans 8 reminds us that we too are special enough to God to be chosen and claimed as God's very own child. We are not born into that righteous family, but adopted into it by God's choice in Jesus Christ. The Romans text acknowledges that there will be pains and troubles, but through the spirit of adoption we are to have a hope in the inheritance of Christ. Being a part of the family of God opens up the future glory of God's kingdom to us. Therefore, when the pains of this life seem to be overwhelming, Romans tells us that we cannot even compare those pains to the future we have promised in God through Christ Jesus.

Hope can be a tricky part of life. No one likes a true pessimist who sees everything as negative all the time, but in some ways the opposite is true as well. Overly optimistic people are not the most popular to be around in our daily life. Life is too frustrating and difficult, at least at times, to always hear that everything will be fine. The difference between this overly optimistic stereotype and the hopeful nature of the Christian life is the time frame. "Humanly" optimistic people believe that everything will be taken care of soon, in this life. Hopeful Christians know that things may never seem quite right on this side of God's kingdom, but in God's timing, perfection will come. This hope does not downplay the agony and pain of life's experiences, but it offers a perspective on that pain. When we are adopted into God's family, through the actions of God through Jesus Christ, then we find ourselves hoping in God's glory, which transcends the human experience and speaks to something larger than any one person's problems.

Part of the Romans message is that trial and even suffering will be part of the Christian life. This is not said to frustrate us or make us worry about life, but rather to prepare us for the realities that come with being a faithful Christian. Even in our world today, there are times when Christian people must stand up for what is right according to God, over and against what seems right to the world. For the early Christian church, this often meant putting your life on the line; for most of us today, it means putting our reputation and the way others think about us on the line. We must find the courage, through the hope in the future glory of God, to stand up when the word of God must not be silent. When this happens, it will not always be popular, and it certainly will not always be easy, but we must be faithful and hold on to our hope in God.

Without hope in the future, there is little motivation to take action in the present. For Christian people, Romans describes a hope in the future that must be primary in our lives. This hope must come from a firm understanding of our adoption into God's family and our trust in God's eternal plan. When we have been offered such a gracious acceptance, and given such an awesome hope, we must not waste our lives living silently without joy. We must become a people who live out our hope and proclaim the adoption spirit of a loving God who wants to redeem all of God's children.

This is not a false optimism, because we balance the realities of human suffering with trust in God's ultimate plan. We must not be pessimists, and not optimists, as the world might define these two camps. Rather we are called to understand the reality and pain of human suffering, while having a greater hope than can be found by humanity alone. Romans 8 invites us to combine the realities of the human life (including the unique pressures of the Christian life) with a hope that comes from being loved and adopted into God's family. (Chris Hayes)

Lectionary Commentary
Genesis 28:10-19a

The story of Jacob's ladder and his dream about the future land promised to his people is filled with descriptive images and hope-filled theology. One of the greatest things about this story is the promise of God's presence through good and bad. Verse 15 tells Jacob that God is not only in that holy place but also God will be with him wherever he goes, and God promises to guide and direct him for the future. Both land and descendants are mentioned in this story, two of the most valued parts of life for the early Hebrew people, but the grandest promise is the promise of God's presence and guidance. No matter how blessed we are with the things of this world, no matter how much we might acquire, without the knowledge of God's presence and steady hand of direction, we will be lost.

Matthew 13:24-30, 36-43

It is difficult to understand justice from a human perspective. We want to see evil and wrong be destroyed as soon as it is identified. Our sense of justice requires immediate results, but Jesus tells a parable about a justice that supersedes our human time line. The first reaction when weeds begin to grow is to pluck them up and destroy them quickly, but in the wisdom of God, we are told that in so doing, a good crop will be destroyed as well. Part of our task as Christian people is to put aside the human understandings of timing, and focus on God's understanding of when things are best done and even left undone. Jesus' parable reminds us that we will rarely make good decisions about justice and what is right and wrong if we rely solely on a human understanding. Taking a step back and focusing on God's justice and timing is always the better course if we wish to reap a good wheat harvest. (Chris Hayes)

Worship Aids

Pastoral Prayer

God of love, we come before you as people who do not deserve your glory and your acceptance, but you take us in under your wing in spite of our own actions. You care for us as your own children and you love us even when we fall short of your hope for us. Allow us to see today your loving presence in our lives, that we might be thankful and joyful people. Amen.

Words of Assurance

Know that the Creator of all things, the Redeemer of humanity, and the Perfector of our faith offers you hope in this life and the life to come through Jesus Christ. By the power of the Holy Spirit, arise and know that the Lord your God can make all things new. (Chris Hayes)

Benediction

May the grace of God, which is bigger than any sin;
The love of God, which is deeper than any mistake;
The peace of God, which is greater than any human knowledge;
Go with you and be real to you now and forever more. Amen.

War . . . The Judgment of the Earth

First in a Series of Two on War and Peace

Isaiah 24:1-24

It is only a personal conclusion but it seems that as America endures this global war on terrorism, the church and her leaders are often strangely silent. I do not hear much, if any, significant moral discourse from our philosophers, any significant theological reflection from our apologists, or any significant pastoral sermons from our preachers on war and the church's response to it. I wonder whether we see ourselves as being part of a nation at war or whether we have relegated the business of its conduct only to our armed forces? If this is our stance, then I contend we preachers must speak a warning to the church and our nation, and declare that Scripture beckons us consider war as a foretaste of God's judgment on the earth for humanity's original sin. While this may sound passé to our contemporary minds, I believe the church must proclaim humankind's culpability in war as a harbinger of the Lord's wrath.

The prophecy of Isaiah develops the idea that our world will devolve from human conflict brought on by God's holy justice. Chapters 24–27 of the book are sometimes referred to as a "little apocalypse," and each chapter has distinct movements. Following a series of oracles against Israel's surrounding enemies (e.g. Babylon, Tyre), Isaiah launches a moving vision of the *eschaton*. Key to his apocalyptic interlude is today's text, because it details God's execution of judgment upon the world. Isaiah opens with an arresting announcement in 24:1a: "Now the LORD is about to lay waste the earth and make it desolate." This contrasts with the vision of God's glory provided in Isaiah's call experience in chapter 6:3b, when the winged seraphim affirm that "the whole earth is full of his glory." The Hebrew word *kabod* (glory) literally entails a tangible physical presence of the Lord. Thus the first assertion Isaiah makes signaling the judgment of God is a withdrawal, an emptying, of God's presence from creation. This shall impact every level of society, including daily routines of religion, home, and marketplace so that every aspect of life will be subverted.

In the ensuing description of the effects of judgment, however, are parallel accusations of humanity's guilt. I believe these crucial verses relate to considering war as an aspect of God's wrath. Note the congruency of structure, tone, and wording between these two passages:

Isaiah 24:4-5	Isaiah 24:19-20
The earth dries up and withers;	The earth is utterly broken
the world languishes and withers;	the earth is torn asunder.
the heavens languish together with the earth.	the earth is violently shaken.
The earth lies polluted	The earth staggers like a drunkard,
under its inhabitants,	it sways like a hut;
for they have transgressed laws,	its transgression lies heavy upon it,
violated the statutes,	and it falls, and will not
broken the everlasting covenant.	rise again.

Whether using the metaphor of a wilting plant or a shattering vessel, the effect of God's judgment is to cause society to fall into complete disarray. Moreover, these verses declare that this is unequivocally an outgrowth of the abrogation of God's covenant at creation with humanity. Were this vision presented as evidence within a court of law (and here the prophecy connotes such a scene), then Isaiah wants any observer to come to one conclusion: all humanity is guilty because it has foresworn God in favor of itself!

Now, why and how does this relate to war as an aspect of God's judgment? In my high school English class, we learned types of conflict in stories: self vs. self, humans vs. nature, humans vs. humans, and humans vs. God. Isaiah is setting the stage for his prophecy in terms of this last conflict. Yet the prophet wants us to see that God's judgment will be so total that society will devolve into conflict on all these levels. As humanity contends against God because of his withdrawal from creation, it will produce further conflict within us, our relationships, and our corporate life. To my thinking, the closest experiential parallel we can draw to such a cataclysm is that of war.

I fix my experience to Isaiah's vision. I have seen firsthand the effects of war on societies: its production of refugees and orphans, its destruction of friendships and families, its rending of human bodies and spirits. I have lived through its execution and carry its burdensome effects within me: my fear of loud noises and unwanted memories, my battle against corrosive grief and anger, my struggles with doubt and hopelessness. Such are the particular lot of those who live through war, and although they are a part of me I would want no one else to suffer; I would never offer them in trade to another. Writ large on society, these are terrible costs to pay and in their face, we can only sit in silent sorrow at the price we exact on ourselves and others through war. I do not question whether it is necessary, at times, to protect others from tyranny or to defend those values we consider sacred. Yet, if my witness today states anything it is this: we must candidly count this cost, for it is always far higher than first imagined, and it is a toll that both we and the nations or people we fight must pay.

Akin to my experience, Isaiah's warning to Israel is God's warning to us: "Mark carefully what price you will pay for your sinfulness, because my judgment is both sure and complete." Like war, his judgment will be total; unlike war, which carries possibility for settlement, we will never know peace without God's sovereign decision to return to creation. So war is a foretaste of the destruction humanity will bring upon itself, and thus a sober reminder of our sin. We are then brought to a final consideration: *What source of hope is there in the face of this coming judgment?* Behold, "the LORD will empty the earth and make it desolate." (Timothy S. Mallard)

Worship Aids

Call to Worship (Psalm 24:7-10 ESV)

Lift up your heads, O gates!
And be lifted up, O ancient doors,
that the king of glory may come in.
Who is this King of glory?
The LORD, strong and mighty,
the LORD, mighty in battle!
Lift up your heads, O gates!
And lift them up, O ancient doors,
that the king of glory may come in.
All: Who is this King of glory?
The LORD of hosts,
he is the king of glory!

Responsive Pastoral Prayer (Adapted from The Heidelberg Catechism, Question 28)

What advantage is it to us to know that God has created,
and by his providence does still uphold all things?
All: That we may be patient in adversity,
thankful in prosperity and that in all things ...
we place our firm trust in our faithful God and Father,
that nothing shall separate us from his love.... Amen.

A Benediction from Aaron's Blessing, Numbers 6:24-26 (ESV)

The LORD bless you and keep you; the LORD make his face to shine upon you and be gracious to you; the LORD lift up his countenance upon you and give you peace. Amen. (Timothy S. Mallard)

JULY 27, 2008

❧❧❧❧

Eleventh Sunday after Pentecost

Readings: 1 Kings 3:5-12; Psalm 105:1-11, 45b; Romans 8:26-39; Matthew 13:31-33, 44-52

The Kingdom of Heaven Is for the Birds
Matthew 13:31-33

If you and I were birds, we'd have to be pretty happy with the outcome of this parable. Let's face it, birds of the air come out pretty well here: they get the natural shelter of this big mustard shrub; they get a place to mate and nest and raise their young; a virtual playground to flit and flutter and chirp and play in. If we were birds, we'd probably be downright thrilled about the outcome of Jesus' little parable about the kingdom of heaven. But we're not birds, and, speaking for myself, I'm not sure I'm altogether happy with how this parable turns out. Here's a perfectly good story about a tiny little mustard seed being planted, then growing up to become a shrub so large it could be called a tree; a massive thing.

Now at this point, we naturally start thinking about harvest. Mustard makes medicine. It makes oil. It makes spice. And, of course, it makes the stuff we spread (some of us spread) on our sandwiches. Let's harvest this huge shrub that started from a tiny seed, get a return on our investment. Isn't that the way a good story ends?

But that's not how this story ends. In this story, the huge mustard shrub goes to the birds, and they end up getting the run of the place. That little conjunction of purpose, "so that" turns everything in their direction: "so that the birds of the air come and make nests in its branches."

Don't get me wrong; I have nothing against birds. They're beautiful creatures; colorful, graceful, musical to rival Mozart. The inspiration of a bird in song, a bird in flight, even a bird at rest, has generated countless poems, photographs, and paintings. One of the first poems I ever wrote I created for a fourth grade contest, taking my inspiration from birds:

Birds that live in treetops, birds that live on ground
It doesn't matter where they live, they make a pretty sound.

Needless to say I didn't win the contest. But let's face it; aside from all their idyllic and poetic qualities, birds have their drawbacks. How many times have you found birds trying to build a nest in a place you didn't want them to? You tear it down; they build it back. You tear it down; they build it back. Before you have a chance to tear it down again, little baby chicks appear, and then, of course, you couldn't possibly tear it down. You're left to wonder if it wasn't all planned just that way by bird brains smarter than you.

Birds will eat the corn right out of your cornfield. No shame. No embarrassment. They make messes with suspicious accuracy right on the hood of your car. They carry diseases right across borders and right into our lungs. When something's "for the birds" that means it's not worth much. Bad ideas are for the birds. Crumbs are for the birds. Dead carcasses by the road are for the birds. But the kingdom? The kingdom of heaven . . . for the birds?

There's not a word in this little parable about the one who planted this mustard shrub reaping the yield; not a breath about the owner of the field; not a single mention of people enjoying the benefits of this big shrub. Jesus' parable gives us the idea that the kingdom of heaven is completely given over to birds—no strings attached, no questions asked.

Birds didn't buy the land. They didn't till the soil. They didn't plant the seed. Birds didn't water or cultivate the shrub. They did absolutely nothing but flutter down and make nests in its branches. And it's theirs. Now who plants a mustard seed so that it can grow up and become overrun with birds? And who designs a kingdom in which not only are the gates open to freeloaders but there seems to be nobody else there? On the other hand, who would be able to afford the kingdom of heaven any other way? Could any of us buy our way in? Work our way in? Deserve our way in?

One of the most profound mysteries of our faith is that not only is the grace of God free, it's only free. No amount of money can buy it, nor can good works earn it, nor does self-sacrifice deserve it. The only way we can receive God's gracious kingdom is by grace. In other words, as a free gift. In other words, like birds.

Years ago a close friend wrote these words in a letter to me: "As I struggle with my faults (and there seem to be so many) what is it that I need more of? Do I need more resolve to live a better life? Do I need to manage my time or money better? Do I need to control my thoughts more? I don't believe any of these are at the heart of it. I believe that what I need most is probably a greater experience of God's grace."

A greater experience of God's grace. Not more achievement, more accomplishment, more conquest, more acquisition, more earnings, more merit points. More grace. Maybe what my friend was expressing is what all of us really hunger for; a greater experience of God's grace, enfolding us like the compassionate father opening wide his arms to receive his wayward son, and then again, for his older, self-righteous son; like a mother hen spreading her wings over her brood; like Jesus blessing the children within his embrace; or, like a mustard shrub, spreading its branches, as if to welcome into its wide embrace the birds of the air, every last one of them. As if to welcome into its shade the very likes of you and me. (Paul Escamilla)

Lectionary Commentary
1 Kings 3:5-12

Solomon's hallmark prayer is noteworthy in that its focus is not on himself, but other significant relationships in his life: Solomon's father, David; Yahweh; and the people of Israel. In that last regard, Solomon asks for wisdom to govern "the people whom you have chosen." Perhaps even Solomon cannot anticipate the irony in his petition—his words sound very much like the plea of an exasperated parent praying for insight in the face of the tall and tiresome challenges of parenting.

The very next episode, a quarrel between two prostitutes over maternal claim to a newborn child, will illustrate both the timeliness and precision of Solomon's appeal for wisdom with which to govern, and, relative to the Matthean parable, the messy and motley nature of leadership among God's people. To be a church leader of whatever sort is to gather many sorts of birds under wing and to know both the aggravations and rewards of bringing wisdom to bear for the common good.

Romans 8:26-39

In this well-loved text is cast what could be considered the most stalwart vision of spiritual haven in all of Scripture. Paul constructs a framework of assurance that God is about the comprehensive work of redemption for all creation. Upon this framework is tethered a sacred canopy consisting of various theological claims: the Spirit helps us in our weakness; all things work together for good; God has established our "belonging" status from before time and beyond time; and finally, whatever is against us, and would seek to separate us from God, will simply not prevail.

In the very heart of the masterwork we know as Paul's Roman epistle, the great canopy is hung, and we are persuaded by the most eloquent rhetorical means that it will endure not merely long, but forever. The parabolic branches in which the birds of the air find their nest are nothing less than the infrastructure of grace, a reality from which nothing will be able to separate us. (Paul L. Escamilla)

Worship Aids

Prayer of Confession

Merciful God, we confess that we have often considered ourselves the guardians of your kingdom, as though we, not you, decide who enters. Forgive us our presumption; grant us a vision of your new creation that stretches far and wide, and by your mercy may include even us. Through Christ our Lord. Amen.

Words of Assurance

Listen for the good news: As a great tree extends its branches for the birds of the air, so God's arms are opened wide in mercy to all who repent and seek God's refuge. In the name of Jesus Christ, you are forgiven. Amen.

Benediction

Go forth to be the church of Jesus Christ in the world—a living sanctuary to all who are in need, extending your care and compassion to the least among you, so "those for whom love is a stranger may find in you generous friends." Amen.

Peace ... The Fulfillment of God's People

Second in a Series of Two on War and Peace

Isaiah 25:1-12

In light of God's righteous judgment upon the world for humanity's sin, where does the church lead others to find hope for tomorrow? Isaiah's announcement of God's pending wrath in 24:1-24 leaves no answer for our question. Rather, its suspense invites us to continue in the so-called little apocalypse to 25:1-12. Here, a new truth emerges: peace is the special gift God gives his people despite of God's wrath, and is our fulfillment beyond the circumstances we face. This text proclaims that although God does not spare his people the experience of his wrath, God will preserve his saints through the divine's matchless mercy.

Although in the previous chapter Isaiah opened with a bold, arresting statement, he shifts in this chapter to begin with an affirmation of God's covenant relationship: "O LORD, you are my God." For Israel, since its Exodus experience, there had never been a more passionately stated intent on God's part than that he desired to be in relationship with God's people. Contrasting Isaiah's prior image of God as justifiably angry with the world for its sin, this text portrays God's desire that "I will be their God and they shall be my people" (Jeremiah 31:33b). The basis for our life together and with God must begin with this relationship. This is a quality of spiritual fulfillment that only those who share in the provision of God's love can and do know.

But how to describe this? Again, contrasting today's text with its precursor, chapter 24 contained the parallel threefold correspondence of structure, tone, and wording between verses 4-5 and verses 19-20 to impart the travail of the earth. In chapter 25, Isaiah switches to a series of metaphors connoting a sense of God's sustaining power. The mixed repetition of these metaphors reinforces the notion that God is the peace of his people even amidst his judgment. What are these images? In verses 6, 9, and 10 successively, Isaiah uses the images of the mountain, the day, and the hand of the Lord as symbols for God's divine provision. None of these is unknown in other prophetic literature, but taken together here they remind Israel that in the wake of God's judgment of the earth, God is their portion. This is key, for whereas verses 1-5 refer in the past tense to the destruction portended in the previous chapter, verses 6-12 look forward to a reimagined future in which God lavishes tender mercy on the people.

Now as with last week, I offer my own experience in war as a supporting, although less credible, witness in affirming that God alone preserves the church by divine grace. In my life, I have both observed and experienced the effects of war on a communal and a personal level. Cumulatively, these effects have combined to produce two principle reactions in me. In my counseling with soldiers and their families, I find my experience parallels theirs and these reactions are typical. How do we as people react to war? Principally, we tend to lose two things that are vital to life: perspective and hope. The first aspect of perspective is a literal loss at the moment one comes under attack: *Where am I and what's happening to me?* A soldier can and usually does quickly recover that immediate sense due to training, discipline, and love for his buddies, but that is only for that moment, that day. What happens over time with repetitive occurrences of combat is a cumulative loss of perspective in spirit, such that we begin to ask: *Where is God and does he know what's happening to me?* This is a deeper crisis of meaning in which a soldier loses touch with the innate truth that God ordains our lives and we are safely within God's moral order.

This loss of perspective is closely tied to a subsequent loss of hope, or an inability to see any type of logical, good, or beautiful future. It is this loss that leads to a more noticeable sense of meaninglessness, or, in very extreme instances of combat stress, "nihilism." However, its roots lie in a loss of hope, again, a part of our human makeup we carry, being made in the image of God. Whether we ever reach a conscious level of understanding our own sin and need for redemption or of God's love manifested for us in Jesus Christ, my experience tells me that in war, we can suffer a loss of perspective and hope that is the most lasting casualty of war.

This is a truth that I believe Isaiah understood, albeit in a deeper way, as a part of experiencing God's righteous anger. In essence, like our modern experience of war, the cataclysm of chapter 24 leads, inevitably, to a loss of perspective and hope on the part of God's people. Thus it is in chapter 25 that the prophet seeks to answer the implicit question the people of Israel must have faced: *Where may we find hope in the midst of such judgment?* By portraying the power of God as being displayed on his holy mountain, on God's righteous day, and through his outstretched hand, Isaiah provides the people with touchstones of perspective and hope to see them through their circumstances despite their fears.

As the church continues to live under the threat of terror, and as we also hear the timeless prophecy that the earth will be judged according to God's justice, we also need a fresh outpouring of perspective and hope. Moreover, America looks to the church and asks whether we have a similar affirmation for it. In tandem with the message of chapter 24, this is our twofold acclamation: although God's judgment is coming, God is our portion and will preserve us through the provision of his grace, and so we are free to live. And so with all the people of God let us proclaim as Isaiah, "O LORD, you are my God."

Worship Aids

Call to Worship (Psalm 105:1-4 ESV)

Oh give thanks to the LORD; call upon his name;
make known his deeds among the peoples!
Sing to him, sing praises to him;
tell of all his wondrous works!
Glory in his holy name;
let the hearts of those who seek
the LORD rejoice!
All: Seek the LORD and his strength;
seek his presence continually!

A Prayer of Contrition (Saint Augustine, The Confessions, book ten, chapter XXVII)

Belatedly I loved thee, O Beauty so ancient and so new, belatedly I loved thee. For see, thou wast within and I was without, and I sought thee out there. Unlovely, I rushed heedlessly among the lovely things thou hast made. Thou wast with me, but I was not with thee. These things kept me far from thee; even though they were not at all unless they were in thee. Thou didst call and cry aloud, and didst force open my deafness. Thou didst gleam and shine, and didst chase away my blindness. Thou didst breathe fragrant odors and I drew in my breath; and now I pant for thee. I tasted, and now I hunger and thirst. Thou didst touch me, and I burned for thy peace.

An Assurance of Pardon (Romans 9:14-16)

"What shall we say then? Is there injustice on God's part? By no means! For God says to Moses, 'I will have mercy on whom I have mercy, and I will have compassion on whom I have compassion.' So then it depends not on human will or exertion, but on God, who has mercy." (Timothy S. Mallard)

AUGUST 3, 2008

❧❧❧

Twelfth Sunday after Pentecost

Readings: Genesis 32:22-31; Psalm 17:1-7, 15; Romans 9:1-5; Matthew 14:13-21

Wrestling God
Genesis 32:22-31

Let's get something straight. So far as the biblical witness would suggest, angels are not dainty. In Genesis 18, three of them are eating enough for fifty people. In the New Testament, they routinely scare the living daylights out of people, including tough-as-nails Roman soldiers. And in this passage, an angel is more than a match for Jacob, a man who has proven he can hold his own in the worst of situations.

Rather than thinking of angels as perfumed, cherubic, light-on-their-feet ballerinas, we might do better to imagine them as nightclub bouncers, roughnecks, or heavy equipment operators, with names on their birth certificates like Mack, Bulldog, and Bruno.

They are God's professional movers—they never leave a scene without having changed people, moving them from here to there, from one way of looking at the world to another. "Your life was moving in this direction before; now you're going to be heading a different way." And the response they are likely to elicit in thanks for their efforts is probably not, "Oh, you're such an angel," but something more like, "You angel, you!"

This angel doesn't disappoint. Jacob is on his way to success, on the fast track of patriarchal ascendancy, and nothing is going to get in his way. Jacob's brother didn't. His father didn't. His twisted uncle Laban didn't. So far, Jacob has always grabbed or finessed his way successfully toward achieving his goals. At this point in his life, he has hit his stride, and is only going up from here. Except Jacob hasn't reckoned on angels.

Two things I've found to be true in the spiritual realm: No matter how small we are feeling, how broken, how low, how discouraged or disheartened, how much grief or illness we have suffered, there's always a force great enough to lift us to life again. And it will. It may be to the skies at the end of our days, but lift us it will.

The other truth, or so it seems to me, is that no matter how big we are feeling, how powerful, successful, brilliant, clever, how much of a shaker and mover we have become in our field, how celebrated and congratulated by others and ourselves, there is always a force great enough to bring us down to earth again. It may be six feet under at the end of our days, but bring us down it will.

In Jacob's case, the force was of the down-to-earth variety. An angel wrestles with this can-do, win-at-all-costs guy who's at the top of his game, and hobbles irreversibly his winning stride. By the end of the encounter, Jacob is mud-drenched, limping, and branded with a name that could almost qualify as playground teasing: Israel, which translates, "one who strives with God."

A star patriarch striving with God? Nonbelievers we would expect to strive with God. Pagans. The heathen. Antagonists to the faith. Francis Thompson in his early life was one of those, his epic poem describing that hound of heaven whose pursuit was relentless: "I fled him down the nights and down the days ..." Surely those who resist God's purposes strive with God. But God's chosen people?

I like the bumper sticker, "God will not let you go to hell in peace." That's fair enough. But God will not let you go to heaven in peace? Evidently not.

How was it Teresa of Avila put it? "If this is how you treat your friends, is it any wonder you have so few of them?" In some ways, to be part of the Christian community is to choose a life of extending the history of Israel, a history of struggling with God. It is to choose a life in which we raise questions, wrestle with doubts, with trust, with lifestyle, and with sacrifices called for by compassion or justice.

If there are not aspects of God that scare the living daylights out of us, then we've probably skipped some pages of the good book. To trust in a God whose blessings are such that they sometimes leave our hip out of joint is a dare all its own, because there are times when the journey of faith involves wrestling with God—unanswered questions, unresolved dilemmas, unlit valleys, irreconcilable differences. In such times, the only reason we cling to God is because the alternative is to cling to nothing. "I will not let you go," Jacob says—whether from sheer panic or steel resolve, we can't be sure—"unless you bless me."

And so the angel does. Which is, if you twist the logic just so, what we might call good news: This mysterious stranger in the night, with power to wound but also to heal, blesses Jacob, Israel, the one who strove with God.

Therein lies the promise of this story, and of the Christian faith: there will be struggle in the walk with God—dark nights, confusion, feeling forsaken—but there will also be blessing. From the struggle itself emerges a new way of defining blessing: blessing isn't always poise and polish, sweetness and light. Sometimes blessing bears the satin scars of struggle, and walks with a discernible limp. (Paul L. Escamilla)

Lectionary Commentary
Matthew 14:13-21

The encounter between Jesus and his disciples, and the claims they make upon each other, reveal similarities with Jacob's encounter with the stranger. Jacob directs the angel to "tell me your name." Similarly, the disciples direct Jesus to "send the crowds away." Both the angel and Jesus have things in mind far more expansive than what was asked by Jacob and the disciples, respectively. Instead of offering a name to Jacob, the angel blesses him; instead of sending the hungry crowds away, Jesus charges the disciples with the task of feeding them.

Here the differences begin—Jacob receives a blessing, the disciples, a gargantuan job. Upon more careful consideration, however, we realize the burden Jacob's blessing is to be, and the blessing the disciples' "burden" must be "to become." In both encounters, the divine push-and-pull results in far more than bargained for—and distinctions between burden and blessing begin to blur.

Romans 9:1-5

Paul's painfully scribed words illuminate the far more painful irony of Jacob's wrestling match with the stranger at the Jabbok. The encounter earns Jacob a new name, Israel, whose literal meaning, "one who strives with God," describes not only that tempestuous encounter, but also the relationship God is to have with God's chosen people. The patriarch's wrestling with God's angel becomes emblematic of a future history of strife between God and those represented by Jacob/Israel in that nocturnal test of wills. To be sure, "striving" is an ingredient of most any relationship—certainly a divine-human relationship. What Paul will assert (he majors in the word "strive" later in this chapter) is that there are different ways of striving with God. Careful, however: the sort of self-righteousness which suggests that "I" or "we" have chosen the proper ways of striving with the divine while others have not is a self-incriminating danger to be avoided at all costs. (Paul L. Escamilla)

Worship Aids

Prayer of Confession

Merciful God, we confess that we sometimes choose not to meet you face to face, but to deal with the outsides of holy things, afraid that to encounter you truly would frighten rather than bless us. Forgive us our unwillingness to know you on your own terms, and free us for a relationship with you that demands our all, but also promises the blessing of life. Amen.

Words of Assurance

Hear the good news: God is nearer to us now than we know, ready to meet us night or day, and enfold us in life-giving mercy. In the name of Jesus Christ, you are forgiven. Amen.

Benediction

Go forth to wrestle with God in faith—to seek, to ask, to knock—knowing that your labors are not in vain, but will yield up the blessing—life forevermore. Amen. (Paul L. Escamilla)

An Odd Couple

First in a Series of Two on Ruth

Ruth 1:15-22

"Look! Here she comes. It's about time she returned to her roots after all these years of living abroad. She doesn't even look like herself, must be the Moabite air ... it's contaminated you know. And who is that following in the distance? Why it's a young Moabite woman! I heard Naomi was returning home with serious baggage, but a Moabite! We haven't had one around here in at least a year. What an odd couple they make: a widowed Moabite clinging to her widowed Israelite mother-in-law. Well, I certainly don't like my mother-in-law enough to follow her to another country! Anyway, I wonder what her name is? You know how difficult those foreign family names are to pronounce, and she probably has at least three of them."

No doubt the people in Bethlehem were scratching their heads and engaged in similar conversations as they watched Naomi return to Bethlehem with a foreigner tagging along. I mean seriously, what business did Israelites and Moabites have being together? You remember where the Moabites originated: Lot's incestuous relationship with his daughters in Genesis. How's that for a family tree? The Israelites would run into them on the way to Canaan, when many Israelites ran after Moabite women and gods. It is no surprise then that Deuteronomy prohibits Moabites from even entering the assembly of YHWH.

As interesting as Naomi's return to Bethlehem may have been, the daughter-in-law tagging along in the distance likely consumed the rest of people's conversation. "Who is she?" "Why didn't she stay in Moab?" "One dead Israelite husband wasn't enough, now she comes here looking for number two?" "She better not try any of that funky, foreign worship in our town!" "Why would one widow follow another? Doesn't she know that one widow can barely support herself here, much less two!"

Can you picture Naomi as she walked toward Bethlehem? Was she rolling over her speech in her head? How could she tell all that had gone wrong while living abroad? She hadn't even sorted it all out yet. How would she explain the younger woman standing in her shadow? Was Naomi even thinking of Ruth by the time she reached the gates?

When she finally arrived and old friends asked if it was really her, her response was brief, painful, and piercing. "Call me pleasant Naomi no longer. Refer to me as bitter Mara from now on. God has dealt me a bitter hand indeed. I left you a complete woman with a complete family, a husband and two strong sons; now God brings me back here with no one. Can you really call me Naomi after I have been dealt with so harshly, after God has done this to me?" (1:20-21, paraphrased).

Naomi's short speech is full of polar opposites: pleasant and bitter, full and empty. In rejecting her given name in favor of a new name, Naomi (which means "pleasant") refused to understand her world in anything but theological terms. Her words are profoundly theological and surprisingly self-centered. Isn't that what crisis often produces initially: theologically driven blame? We tend to blame God and victimize ourselves. And don't miss that the author refrains from defending God or Naomi. Instead, Naomi's words hang ambiguously in the heavy air. Was YHWH responsible for Naomi's trauma? Perhaps Naomi was partly to blame for her own situation? She did cohabitate with foreigners after all! Or perhaps it was Ruth who bore the most guilt?

Speaking of Ruth ... where was she during this little exchange at the city gates? Had Naomi forgotten about her trusty—if unwanted—companion? Possibly, but how could one so quickly forget an oath like the one Ruth so eloquently took? How many times in your life has another human promised to go anywhere with you, join your country, and be buried next to you upon death. Okay, that promise might have been a little intimidating to Naomi, but who else did she have? At least Ruth could identify with her situation.

Naomi probably wanted to deny her attachment to Ruth in front of the women or even to herself, but the Moabite's presence was actually highlighted by her foreignness. Naomi failed to acknowledge her existence, yet Ruth was there. Ruth silently waited in the background because, in her mind at least, the two were, as they say, attached at the hip. Naomi's implicit rejection of her in the presence of others likely hurt Ruth deeply, yet Ruth was there. Naomi claimed to have no companion, yet Ruth was there. It's interesting that, as Naomi retreated, Ruth committed. Naomi's rejection stimulated Ruth's identification with her. Don't we all need that at some point? There are times when retreat seems like our only option, but thankfully others see it differently. Retreating was never an option for Ruth.

Questions of family, race, ethnicity, and immigration are at the heart of conflicts all over our world. Humanity seems to have progressed very little—if at all—since Naomi and Ruth set out from Moab. At times it seems that we have too many Naomis and too few Ruths. Yet something deep within us longs for a world where in-laws cling to each other, Moabites walk with Israelites, and diverse ethnic groups peacefully coexist. In that world, diverse couples walking the road of life together are not shunned; rather, they are welcomed and affirmed as visible conduits of reconciliation. We can work toward that world by clinging to each other. Chances are you know an odd couple or two. They are easy to spot: friends whose bond is stronger than their differences, or two people whose commitment swallows up their disagreements. Maybe you need a Ruth but are too afraid to acknowledge it. Or perhaps it's time to reaffirm your commitment to the Naomi in your life. In the end, regardless of where you begin, my hunch is that we're all widows who need each other. Our fragmented world could benefit from an odd couple like that. Amen. (John D. Essick)

Worship Aids

Call to Worship

Welcome to this time of worship and renewal. I invite you to this place as you are. Let go of the baggage of the past week during these moments of silence. Encounter the Lord. Encounter the Lord and make peace with yourself. Encounter the Lord and make peace with others. Encounter the Lord.

Prayer of Confession

Eternal God, instruct us in the way of discipleship. We encounter so many who are alienated by indifference, discrimination, racism, and sexism. We think of those imprisoned in small worlds of fear and ignorance, or those in worlds inflated by pride and arrogance. As we confess the prejudices, which dampen our own concern and repent of the excuses which mask our own shortcomings, lead us into the light of your truth. Although we feel pressed to turn away, strengthen us to stay. Grant us the courage to seek out the needy and the commitment to make our home with them. For the sake of your kingdom, Amen.

Words of Assurance

In the name of Jesus Christ, you are forgiven.
In the name of Jesus Christ, you are forgiven. Amen.

Benediction

May the God of Naomi and Ruth unify you in all truth and peace. Cling to what is holy and forsake all else. In the name of the Father, Son, and Holy Spirit, one God, now and forever, Amen. (John D. Essick)

AUGUST 10, 2008

Thirteenth Sunday after Pentecost

Readings: Genesis 37:1-4, 12-28; Psalm 105:1-6, 16-22, 45b; Romans 10:5-15; Matthew 14:22-33

Getting Wet
Matthew 14:22-33

There's a great deal of mystery and miracle in this story—Jesus walking on water; Peter walking on water; the sudden quieting of the storm. A great deal of mystery and miracle, but this is my question: Why did Peter do it? Why did Peter step out of the boat and go to Jesus?

Was it fear of the storm? There's no mention of the disciples being afraid of the storm—their only fear is of Jesus, who they take to be a ghost. Was it bravado? The big, tough fisherman showing off in front of his friends? I don't believe at this point Peter possesses that much courage—even of the show-off variety.

Maybe Peter's gesture was a fleece, a test of God's faithfulness, and of Jesus' authority. Do you remember Herod's challenge to Jesus in *Jesus Christ Superstar?* "Prove to me that you're no fool—walk across my swimming pool."

I wonder if there's something else that motivated Peter to do such a crazy thing. I wonder if Peter stepped out of the boat because he simply wanted to be near Jesus. It was true of the crowds just earlier; it was true of the four disciples—including Peter—when Jesus first called them. Over and over the Gospels provide examples of people who want to be near Jesus—touch the hem of his garment, have him bless their children, listen to his teachings.

I wonder if Peter wanted to walk on water not for fear of the storm, nor for show, nor to test Jesus, but simply to share in the power of Jesus' presence, to be near him, to be doing what he was doing.

Peter had taken a leap of faith some time before, throwing caution to the wind, leaving nets and boats and fishing trade and stepping out into the shallows and onto dry land—and would again before it was all over. Maybe this was simply another leap.

Would you do what Peter did? Or would you stay in the boat with the other disciples to wait and see what would happen next? Do we seek out adventure, or hide from it? Maybe, like Peter—who eventually faltered—there is in us a little of both.

Some years ago I visited Silver Dollar City, an amusement park in the Midwest with rides and attractions of all kinds. In the middle of the afternoon the park was visited briefly by thundershowers. In the sudden downpour, people were darting into retail shops right and left, where the top-selling commodity suddenly became three-dollar rain parkas. Just hours earlier, these same people had paid a handsome sum of money for admission to a park that promised to drench them on log rides, rapid river adventures, and the like. Now, it seemed, their lives depended on protection from the rain!

Which is closer to true human nature? The log ride, or the parka? It's a mixed verdict, isn't it? All I can say is, people paid a lot more for the log ride than for the parka.

Something within us wants more than safety and security—staying within the snug and predictable boundaries of the familiar. What is that something? A hankering for adventure? A thirst for meaning?

William Sheldon, a clinical psychologist, has written that the great body of research into psychological motivators indicates that humans have a motive that runs deeper than sexuality, the desire for social power, or the yearning for acceptance and approval. That motive is for orientation, meaning, and purpose. Humans want more than social status or another bite of chocolate—they want their lives to count for something worthy and true.

In other words, as attractive an option as it may be to remain safely in the boat, a deeper part of us wants to step out of it—even if it means getting wet. It is not enough that I am wealthy—I need to know how to direct my wealth in meaningful ways; not even enough that I am happy—I need to share that happiness; not enough that I know how to win friends and influence people—I need to see ways in which to direct that influence for the sake of something that matters. To be secure from life's storms is not what satisfies us; what satisfies us is to hold a hand that can lead us through life's storms.

Would you do what Peter did? I don't mean go boating in a storm and step over the edge. There's water all around us—it's calling living. And to step out of our boat into that water may be as simple as making certain decisions in certain ways. Stepping into the water is what we do when we share our faith with another person. It's what we do when we show compassion in a time and place where others scorn and scoff. Stepping into the wind-swept waters is what happens when we stand up for what is right, even in the face of inconvenience or opposition. Getting wet is what we do when we say in a way we mean more than ever before, "I am going to place myself in every moment of every day in the frightening, caressing presence of God, praying the psalmist's prayer, and meaning it: 'You, Lord, are all I have; you give me all I need; my life is in your hands.'"

There's a great deal of miracle and mystery in this story; just as there's a great deal of miracle and mystery in our own decisions to choose purpose over security, usefulness over convenience, involvement over comfort. Why did Peter step out? Why do we?

Over and over, it seems, we are willing—am I wrong about this?—to test the wellness and wetness of our baptism by reaching for a hand that's just beyond the safety of our boat. After all, if there's one thing that means more to us in life than staying dry, it's getting wet. (Paul L. Escamilla)

Lectionary Commentary
Genesis 37:1-4, 12-28

When Jacob proposes to send Joseph to check up on his brothers in a faraway pasture, Joseph responds, "Here I am," setting into motion a world of events he could never, in his most colorful dreams, have imagined. "Here I am" are words we have lofted into the realm of sacred odyssey. To say or sing them, as we often do, is to imagine ourselves following God's bright path in the fulfillment of our vocation. It was certainly the sense in which Samuel and Isaiah each spoke those words (1 Samuel 3:4; Isaiah 6:8). Their application by Joseph, however, results in a more mixed outcome—not unlike what Peter experiences as he offers his own version of "Here I am" to Jesus in the storm. Does the ragged meadow through which Joseph will pass over the years that follow qualify as "sacred odyssey?" It qualifies just as much as the drenching baptism experienced generations later by the man named Peter.

Romans 10:5-15

Concerning life in the law, "the person who does these things will live by them." Would that the life of faith were so, to borrow from logic class, "if p then q." Instead, faith involves the heart, which, the good book reminds us elsewhere, is "deceitful above all things." Hence this stretch of apologetic from verse 6 onward, in which the apostle attempts to explain the faith response, feels less like a walk across hardwood floors than a walk across a waterbed—or to borrow from Matthew 14, a stormy sea. From the swelling and receding of Paul's articulations come echoes of Peter's existential dilemma. From whence does faith emerge? Heart or voice? Formula or failure? Strength of resolve or surrender of weakness? Where was the *saving* faith for Peter—in his bold summons to Christ or in his disintegrating cry of doubt? In the very middle of the waterbed-walk, Paul finds help from the prophet to resolve the matter: "Everyone who calls on the name of the Lord shall be saved." (Paul L. Escamilla)

Worship Aids

Prayer of Confession

Merciful God, we confess that there is within us a fear not of heights but of depths. We often prefer to maintain a comfortable shallowness in our relationship with you, rather than risk moving deeper in trust. Forgive us the fear or convenience that keep us from that place of true communion, we ask in the name of Jesus, who awaits us there. Amen.

Words of Assurance

The good news of our faith is that no matter where we are in our journey, God's mercy is within reach. Accept, then, this gift of pardon and assurance: In the name of Jesus Christ, you are forgiven. Amen.

Benediction

The world waits for the people of God to claim the mark of our baptism, and step from the boat and into life. Go forth, then, to love and serve God and your neighbor beyond the safety of the sanctuary, in the sustaining presence of Jesus the Christ. Amen. (Paul L. Escamilla)

Another Odd Couple

Second in a Series of Two on Ruth

Ruth 2–3

"He's too old." "She's too young." "He's really not in shape." "I don't even work out." "He has a high-profile job, and I really don't know anything about his background." "She is a wandering widow who still lives with her mother-in-law." "He hates my kind." "She hates my kind."

You don't have to read too far into Ruth to see that Ruth and Boaz were as different as any two people in history. Then again, are any two people all that similar in the details? He was ... well, a he, which meant rights, authority, and a position at the top of the food chain. She, on the other hand, was female, foreign, and widowed—not a situation conducive to upward mobility in the ancient world. On the surface Ruth and Boaz reflect a top-down world where the needy rely on the needless. Yet below the patriarchal assumptions of this biblical story there is a subtle undercurrent. The reader is invited to envision redemption and work for it relentlessly. The author offers us a fresh pair of glasses with which we can read our world.

These new glasses don't change everything about Ruth and Boaz. In fact, they often highlight things we already know. We know, for instance, that Ruth's world followed patriarchal patterns. Moreover, as a widow— and a Moabite widow at that—Ruth dropped another rung on the Israelite social ladder. We also know that Ruth (with Naomi's help) recognized Boaz as a way out of her current situation. There was no attempt to lift herself up by her bootstraps. She may not have liked the boundaries of her world, but she worked within them.

Now hold on before running me offstage. Redemption rarely preserves the status quo or placates those in power. No, redemption doesn't occur without tough choices, without taking a stand, or without—in Ruth's case—a little cunning. These fresh glasses offered to us by the author also reveal ways in which Ruth challenged her boundaries in search of redemption. Remember that Ruth had already left her world in search of a new people and a new god. Ruth had already volunteered to glean in the fields, which was apparently dangerous for a single, unprotected woman. Ruth had already made a name for herself as a hard worker, and Boaz had noticed. So Ruth, at Naomi's bidding, took control of her own future and placed the burden of redemption squarely on the stable shoulders of Boaz. There was no question that Ruth was in need of redemption. Redemption for herself. Redemption for her dead husband. Redemption for Naomi. If Ruth had any chance at redemption, she knew it was up to her to make it happen. She would have to take risks, face rejection, put her life on the line. She would have to make her presence known in the male-dominated world of politics and tradition.

When we turn to Boaz with our new spectacles we should not be surprised to find that he was a man of his times. He was a wealthy and powerful citizen of Bethlehem. People probably looked to him for advice and counsel. Yet he had a kind way about him. He noticed you; he paid attention to everyone. You could count on Boaz to do what was right, or at least whatever Boaz did seemed to be right. Boaz would probably be your first choice in the eligible redeemer pool. He knew about the real world, he knew politics, and tradition was on his side. Boaz had already give Ruth more attention and help than she could have hoped for!

Now hold on before you crown Boaz the great redeemer of Bethlehem. Sure, he has all the makings of an ideal man, but these new glasses help us read Boaz more carefully. Upon a closer reading of this man, we notice—or don't notice—any mention of a family. And there was likely a hint of romantic interest in his conversations with Ruth. Naomi picked up on it, even if Ruth hadn't. But he wasn't about to run after a younger, Moabite woman in front of the whole town. "Sure," Boaz may have thought, "I may be an ideal redeemer for one of the Golden Girls, but Ruth, she's . . . she's young and interested in life guards and fitness instructors." Maybe that's part of the reason he was surprised to wake up to Ruth. He was quick to praise her loyalty and grant her request, but just as quick to highlight her choice of him. Boaz knew about the real world, politics, and tradition. Or, at least he thought he did. He thought she was too young. He thought he was too old. He thought he would redeem her. But redemption is funny that way. She wasn't too young. He wasn't too old. He was redeemed by her.

If we read the book of Ruth carefully we see that both Ruth and Boaz needed redemption. It is not just the poor and weak who need to be redeemed from the effects of sin; the strong and rich are held captive in our fallen world too. The author of Ruth invites us to enter into redemptive relationships that challenge our assumptions and prejudices. We have a lot to learn from this couple. Matthew thought so. Why else would he remind his readers that Jesus' genealogy includes even includes a Moabite widow named Ruth. What is odd, that Ruth challenges us to practice redemption, or that Boaz reminds us of our need for it? Whatever it is that made them odd, our fragmented world could use another odd couple like that. Amen. (John D. Essick)

Worship Aids

Call to Worship

Neither chance nor destiny has brought us here today. We are here to commune with something larger than ourselves, larger than our problems, larger than our sin. We never happen upon God. Our God encounters us and is encountered by us in serendipitous ways. Come, let us worship the One who works in mysterious ways.

Pastoral Prayer

Eternally Triune God, have mercy on us and hear our prayer. Our world groans under the weight of sin. All creation longs for redemption and reconciliation. Make us instruments of peace and healing. Open our eyes; move our feet. Lead us down the path of righteousness. Amen.

Benediction

May the God who redeems be your guide and compass this week. Go and practice redemption. Amen. (John D. Essick)

AUGUST 17, 2008

❦❦❦

Fourteenth Sunday after Pentecost

Readings: Genesis 45:1-15; Psalm 133; Romans 11:1-2a, 29-32; Matthew 15:(10-20), 21-28

A Brief Moment but a Long Look
Genesis 45:1-15

A few months ago my husband and I visited our son, Kyle, a first-year college student. We had left him months earlier as a young, first-year student excited about going to college, leaving home, happy to be living no longer under the shadow of his parents but confident in the joy that comes with finally leaving the nest. As he relished his newfound freedom, I contemplated the sadness of his departure, wondering where the time had gone. The time has passed so quickly—the baby, the toddler, the elementary school years, the middle and upper school years, and now college as a physically strong, mentally alert, vibrant young adult. I wondered if we had provided him what he would need to face his own life experiences. As I walked into his empty bedroom at home, now uncomfortably clean, I wondered, as I had right after his birth, "Will Kyle be glad that he was born?" I certainly hoped that he would.

In late fall we invited him to dinner in honor of his nineteenth birthday. We spent a fun evening laughing about times past and exciting days to come. As we parted in the parking lot, he walked to his dorm while we moved toward our car to return home. While we were getting in the car, he yelled from the dormitory steps, across the large parking lot, "Thank you, Mom!" I turned around to see this beautiful young man glowing in the street light in the yard of his dormitory, his arms lifted wide open, with one hand raised high in the air. In that second I heard a voice that projected straight to the stars and moon, as Kyle unabashedly hollered, "Mom and Dad, thank you for the dinner and thank you for my life!"

Time collapsed for me in that moment. In that split second of time, the only markers of time that I know—past, present, and future—melted into one. In that one moment, frozen in space, I remembered the little baby Kyle, for whom we had prayed for years to come into our life. I instantly saw the endless sea of diapers and corrections for the life of the young toddler learning about his world. I remembered the challenge of his teenage years, the academic hurdles, the loud rock and roll music coming from the basement, and the usual clutter of his room. I could also see in that same moment his future, the joy that he would have as he learned more life and himself, as he met the experiences of college, perhaps even found a soul mate, then move into the world with a career and family. That moment in time took on a more circular form, not contained by the strict measuring lines of yesterday and tomorrow, but fused into one dimension, where yesterday cannot be separated from tomorrow, and today is yesterday, and yesterday is today.

I stood there frozen, watching his arms wave and hearing his voice ring through the still, cold winter air. The walls between past, present, and future melted. All was one. All was good. The moment was brief, but the look was long.

Perhaps Joseph had a similar experience. The narrator suggests a similar freeze-frame moment when Joseph stood face to face with his brothers as he prepared to identify himself. The earth stopped moving. Time stood still—at least as a linear marker. Joseph was standing in front of his brothers, the ones who had despised him and placed him in a pit to die. His life had been saved by traders on their way to Egypt. Joseph had made a life for himself in a foreign land without family: first in the household of Potiphar, the captain of the Egyptian guard, then in the house of the Pharaoh, the king of Egypt. More than twenty years had passed. Famine had ravaged Canaan. Joseph, who somehow knew that famine would come, had urged the Egyptian government to stockpile food. Thanks to Joseph, Egypt had vast stores of grain. The inhabitants of Canaan, however, were starving. Jacob, Joseph's father sent the brothers to go purchase grain from Egypt so that they could live and not die from hunger. Now the tables were turned.

Now they are all there in the magnificent hall of the Egyptian Pharaoh. The brothers were hungry; Joseph had food. The brothers were begging; Joseph had power. The brothers stand before Joseph, who is called the "father of Pharaoh" (chief minister), begging for food, negotiating their little brother's life, so that they and their father might live.

They do not know that the man to whom they are speaking is their brother. Joseph looks different; he speaks differently; he has assumed the Egyptian ways (Genesis 42:8). The brothers have no clue. Joseph, however, does.

Hear the narrator describe the moment of decision: "Then Joseph could no longer control himself before all those who stood by him, and he cried out, 'Send everyone away from me.'" Joseph needs thinking space, solitude. Joseph, in this moment of time, will rehearse his past and project his future. Time—past, present, and future—will melt into one dimension.

Joseph could have chosen just to look back to the past, only seeing his youthful arrogance, his brothers' hatred, and the injustices experienced. Or he could choose to see the future, the hunger of his father, and the eventual death of his entire family. Joseph, rather, visualizes the entire drama from a richer and wider perspective. George McLeod, founder of the Iona community in Scotland, called these moments in time as "thin places." Those places in our life where the veil that separates heaven and earth are lifted. Where one can see clearly and in more careful detail all of the events surrounding our lives. The Apostle Paul described it in this manner: "For now we see in a mirror, dimly, but then we will see face to face. Now I know only in part; then I will know fully, even as I have been fully known" (1 Corinthians 13:12).

Joseph, however, did not need to wait for some great eschatological morning for full clarity as the Apostle Paul describes. Joseph saw the end from the beginning and beginning at the end. That is why he could say, even while weeping "so loudly that the Egyptians heard it," that he had no remorse, that he could forgive his brothers, that he could see the end from the beginning. Joseph finally speaks with words that are considered to be the hermeneutical key to the entire Joseph story: "And now do not be distressed, or angry with yourselves, because you sold me here; for God sent me before you to preserve life." This key point will be repeated again at the end of Joseph's life, when he says again: "Even though you intended to do harm to me, God intended it for good, in order to preserve a numerous people, as he is doing today" (Genesis 50:20).

Joseph had the long look in order to make the right decision in that eventful moment. He could see his own personal shadows as well as those of his brothers. Joseph could also see the rich path that had been his, the opportunities to live and prosper in his adopted homeland. Joseph could also see the possibility of a meaningful future, both food and forgiveness for this entire family. In that "thin place" Joseph had the clarity of vision to make the right choice—he forgave himself and his brothers. Joseph died an old man, surrounded by his family in their adopted land. (Linda McKinnish Bridges)

Lectionary Commentary
Matthew 15:(10-20), 21-28

In Matthew 15:10-20, the question appears again, *Why do the disciples break the tradition of the elders?* This time the issue is hand washing. Jesus responds by saying that "it is not what goes into the mouth that defiles a person, but it is what comes out of the mouth that defiles." In other words, greater transgressions, such as evil intentions, murder, adultery, fornication, theft, slander, false witness, can be ignored if the focus is only on the external keeping of the law. Jesus announced that change is on the way. Jesus is breaking with the legal tradition of the past, which had determined the nature and focus of Jewish piety. This move to a new paradigm is not easy to grasp for the law-abiding, faithful Pharisees. They are not comfortable with change. The external law is much easier to keep. Follow the rules and be safe. Jesus, however, wants to follow God instead, and that path is never safe! Even for Jesus.

In the next section, however, Jesus' own piety in action comes to a test. A foreigner, a Canaanite woman, comes to Jesus asking for help. Jesus shows his intensity of focus and mission, as he states, "I was sent only to the lost sheep of Israel." Jesus also shows his human side of prejudice and unwillingness to adapt to new paradigm. Change is not easy—even for Jesus. His actions do not differ from those of the Pharisees, whose strict adherence to cultural and religious matters he has been trying to change. When Jesus realizes that this woman is also a recipient of God's blessings, even though she is a foreigner not belonging to the house of Israel, then he is willing to shift the paradigm. "Even Gentiles can eat the crumbs that fall from the master's table," she says. Jesus changes his mind, amends his old way of thinking, praises her courage and faith, and heals her. Even Jesus must change his old ways of thinking. (Linda McKinnish Bridges)

Romans 11:1-2a, 29-32

Throughout this section of Romans, Paul has written of Israel's rejection of God's Messiah. However, Paul argues that Israel's rejection of the

Messiah does not lead to God's rejection of Israel. One reason is that God's promise is steadfast. Indeed, Paul's capstone argument is simply: "For God has imprisoned all in disobedience so that he may be merciful to all."

Worship Aids

Call to Worship (from Psalm 133:1-3)

How very good and pleasant it is when kindred live together in unity!
It is like the precious oil on the head,
running down upon the beard, on the beard of Aaron,
running down over the collar of his robes.
All: It is like the dew of Hermon, which falls on the mountains of Zion.
For there the Lord ordained his blessing, life forevermore.

Offertory Prayer

Gracious God, we know that as we place our gifts in the receptacles to gather the gifts of the people we only are giving back to you what you first gave to us. We pray that these gifts represent the best we have to offer you and your realm. Bless those who receive these gifts and we who give them; in Jesus' name we pray. Amen.

Benediction

"Grow in the grace and knowledge of our Lord and Savior Jesus Christ. To him be the glory both now and to the day of eternity. Amen" (2 Peter 3:18).

Singing Faith

First in a Series of Two on Music and Worship

Zephaniah 3:14-18

Isaac was a sick boy. He was often attacked and beaten up by other children. His only refuge was the church. There he enjoyed the peace that came with the great music of the church. Perhaps because of his unhappiness he became one of the first students and teachers of the new discipline called psychology. But even in that he could not find happiness.

One day he heard the great evangelist, John Wesley, preach. Isaac suddenly realized his calling to serve Christ. He would reclaim the music of the faith. Over the years church music had become music of the state reserved for royalty and the highborn. Few poor people ever heard it.

Isaac was especially concerned about the children of the poor. He wanted to give them hope. He believed that they could find hope in the story of a Savior who was himself born poor. But there was a problem. Most of the poor could not read. Many would not listen to sermons.

Isaac had a plan. He could write the kind of music that people of all classes would enjoy. Even people who could not read or listen to sermons would have a means to memorize the stories of Christ. Isaac had a kind of genius about him. He could take a beer drinking song and set powerful words of faith to the music. He could lift the melodies from the great composers, place them in simple arrangements and set them to Christian poetry.

Isaac prepared such a piece. He used music by Handel and his own words as his audition for John Wesley. We know that audition piece today as "Joy to the World." Isaac Watts became the song leader, choir director and composer of the greatest revival to ever hit Europe. He became that man because he believed singing the songs of faith could change the world.

I always liked Zephaniah. The prophet who encouraged song in the hearts of God's people is the same prophet who had once been a prophet of doom for his people. If the records are correct, Zephaniah was a Judean, born of royal blood in the latter part of the seventh century B.C.E. A descendant of King Hezekiah, he probably was a cousin of the noble King Josiah. However, Zephaniah's role in the royal courts was that of a prophet.

Zephaniah sized up the condition of his people as ripe for judgment in the light of world events. He also envisioned a day when all nations would suffer judgment from the wrath of God. Zephaniah could be specific about the enemies of Judah who would have to pay the price for their opposition to the people of God. All creatures, people and animals, in fact, everything on the whole face of the earth, would feel the full weight of this judgment. Judah would suffer, because Judah had engaged in the worship of idols. Judah had been guilty of violating the covenant relationship with the God who had created and redeemed Judah. None of these harsh judgments sounded like good reason for the people of God to join in a lusty song of praise. However, the prophet also had another word for his people, a word of promise.

Even as God calls us from sin, God opens the door for our redemption! The very nature of God is love. That love that God manifests in so many ways is also an assurance of God's faithfulness. Zephaniah could entertain notions of how utterly severe judgment would be, but he also could affirm the goodness of God. He called for his people to sing and shout aloud.

Although the group of people who consistently trusted God's promise was relatively small, they were the people who could be counted on to keep alive the promise of God for others to hear and trust. And they would keep the promise alive in song. The prophet and his people sang aloud with joyful hearts, even as their nation was invaded and destroyed. They sang about God. They sang about God's promise of a Messiah. They sang and kept the memory of the promise alive.

How important it is in difficult times to keep the stories of God's fulfilled promises alive. That is why we sing. It is worship. It is remembering. It is something we do together as the body of Christ, no matter our age or ability.

A couple, who had one beautiful little girl and then struggled through a string of miscarriages, became pregnant again. They prayed with their pastor, Mark, for God's mercy and help. But the pregnancy was very difficult. It seemed especially hard on five-year-old Julie. Would she be a big sister or not?

One afternoon a few days before Christmas pastor Mark received the call. The baby was coming much too early. Things looked very grim. At the hospital the father asked Mark to watch Julie so that he could be in the room with his wife.

"What should we do," Mark asked?

"Welcome the baby," Julie replied with the absolute faith of a five year old.

"How?" he asked.

"Let's sing the baby home." Julie said. Sing the baby home? Mark couldn't imagine where she got an idea like that. She held his finger and faced the door. Then she started to sing a favorite song, "Joy to the World . . ."

It was absurd! The tall preacher and the tiny girl facing a closed door in a busy hospital and singing a song written nearly three hundred years before that little girl was born.

But Isaac Watts taught that song to somebody. They taught it to someone else. They taught it to someone else to teach them about Jesus. Now Julie thought it was the most important thing in the world to sing that song to the baby in her mommy's tummy.

And then it started from the other side of the door. A little squeak that turned into a raging, unmistakable squall. The cry of a baby. A nurse stepped out, looked down at Julie, and said, "You have a beautiful little brother."

Singing is an act of utter faith in God! (Robert Gorrell)

Worship Aids

Invocation

Heavenly Lord, be in our songs and praise today. Pour out your Spirit here. Let our worship be an offering of gladness and joy for you. Let us celebrate your presence and join in worshiping you. Amen.

Call to Worship

Let us sing aloud!
Let us rejoice together!
God is with us. We are forgiven!
Let us rejoice with gladness and celebrate with singing!

Prayer of Confession

Oh God, we confess we have been slow to sing. We have thought of ourselves and neglected the needs of others. Fill our hearts with song and lead us out to serve in your name! Amen. (Robert Gorrell)

Words of Assurance

In the name of Jesus Christ, you are forgiven.
In the name of Jesus Christ, you are forgiven. Amen.

AUGUST 24, 2008

Fifteenth Sunday after Pentecost

Readings: Isaiah 51:1-6; Psalm 124; Romans 12:1-8;
Matthew 16:13-20

Looking to the Rocks
Isaiah 51:1-6

The Chinese wedding was about to begin in the family home. We had been invited as special guests to an intimate family gathering. We gathered with the family in the front hall, bowed low to the parents as required by traditional Chinese custom, then gave appropriate, individual, Chinese greetings to the bride and groom, wishing them peace and prosperity in their new life. We then moved to the side of the room for the special family festivities to begin. Trying not to intrude on this very intimate family moment, we observed the traditional customs that began the Chinese wedding day.

In the front room of the home was a long, oblong, black-lacquered table. On the table stood two vases of tall red gladiolas and white chrysanthemums beautifully arranged in the two corners. In the center were black, long, marble tablets with Chinese characters, written in a beautiful, flowing Chinese script. Other items, such as prayer stones and family portraits, were scattered on the lace doily that was in the middle. As the day of special celebration began, after the greeting of family and friends, the couple made their way to the table. The groom, dressed in fine attire, formal suit with white shirt and shiny black shoes, and the bride, in a white wedding gown and long veil, looking more like a model from a magazine in the USA than a traditional Chinese bride, stood reverently in front of the table. In a few moments, words were softly spoken, so soft that we could not fully hear. The ritual bowing began, bowing to the table, to the parents flanked on either side of the table, and then to one another. The central point of interest for the wedding party was not the table, the flowers, or the prayer stones, but the large, black tablets with ancient Chinese words. Later I would learn about those important tablets.

My friend, the brother of the beautiful bride, would tell me the meaning of the ritual at the end of day, when the bride and groom had left the house and we could talk in private. I learned that we had observed a very important and intimate family ritual in a traditional Chinese household. I learned that before every important family event, the ancestors are remembered. The large table, which featured the tall, black tablets, symbolized the presence of the many generations of ancestors, gone on before. Their names were carefully written on the tablets, representing more than ten preceding generations. In moments of joy or sadness, despair or celebration, members of the family would stop by the ancestor shelf and remember their dead relatives, or as our text calls them, "the rocks from which you were hewn." My friend told me that in moments of great decision making, regarding a job, a marriage, buying a house, the ancestors were always consulted. Likewise, in the times of loss, of death, of financial anxiety, the ancestors were also remembered. They were always there.

The author of Isaiah 51 knows the power of remembering the ancestors, especially in the time of trouble. Chapters 40–55 were written during the time of the Babylonian exile. Loneliness, despair, homesickness, financial destitution, loss of family and property describe the state of affairs for the Israelites. In 586 B.C.E., Babylon conquered Israel, taking all the citizens into exile, forcing them into slavery, using their skills as carpenters and artists for the strengthening of the Babylonian Empire. Jerusalem was a distant memory. The precious temple was gone. They were in a strange land. The psalmist describes this pain and longing: "By the rivers of Babylon— / there we sat down and there we wept / when we remembered Zion. / On the willows there / we hung our harps. / For there our captors / asked us for songs, / and our tormentors asked for mirth, saying, / 'Sing us one of the songs of Zion!' / How could we sing the LORD's song / in a foreign land?" (Psalm 137:1-4) What are they to do in this state of constant despair?

They listen to the words of the Isaiah: "Look to the rock from which you were hewn, / and to the quarry from which you were dug. / Look to Abraham your father / and to Sarah who bore you." These words of comfort give strength. The rationale is clear. Even while living in exile, in the Diaspora, among the many dislocated, distressed citizens of Jerusalem, one can know that the blessing is not gone, that life is not over. Even

Abraham, who was just one person, was given hope when he was called. So much more will the blessing be for an entire nation, who has been brought into the pit of despair by a dominating power of oppression. God will bring comfort and power to the weary child of Abraham and Sarah. The way to hope, however, is to remember the "rocks from which you came"—your family of generations past.

The promise is there, written in the words of the earlier prophets. The reality is even closer in the presence of the dead ancestors. We can receive strength by remembering those who have gone on before. The ancient church placed in the calendar a special day of remembrance, called All Saints or All Soul's Day. The modern church remembers those who have died by special memorial offerings, memorial plaques in stained-glass windows, special flowers at Easter and Christmas. Country church cemeteries provided a constant, weekly reminder for the family walking the familiar path to the door of the church, while glancing toward the tombstone or grave marker of a dead relative. The saints, the great cloud of witnesses, still speak to us today. From their faithfulness, the lessons in courage, examples of persistent living, we gain hope for the living of these days. (Linda McKinnish Bridges)

Lectionary Commentary
Matthew 16:13-20

Jesus queries his disciples about his own identity. Some people think that Jesus is a new John the Baptist, perhaps because of his bold, maverick style of teaching. Others think that he is Elijah, another spokesperson for God (Malachi 4:4). Peter responds by saying, "You are … the son of the living God." And Jesus is pleased. He is so pleased that he responds by saying, "Peter, you are the rock, and on this rock I will build my church" (16:18, paraphrased). The Greek name for Peter is "rock," *petra*. The metaphor abounds, but who or what is this rock?

Romans 12:1-8

Paul begins what many scholars call the "ethics section" of Romans (chapter 12) with an exhortation to "present their bodies as a living sacrifice." This kind of sacrifice, no doubt, Paul contrasts to the types of sacrifices the Hebrew ancestors previously offered to God. Now because of Christ and "the mercies of God," all sacrifices come via human agents who are living disciples of Jesus Christ. There are many gifts within the congregation and if believers offer these gifts, then Christ's ministry will flourish. (Linda McKinnish Bridges)

Worship Aids

Call to Worship (Psalm 124:1-6, 8)

If it had not been the Lord who was on our side when our enemies attacked us,
then they would have swallowed us up alive.
When their anger was kindled against us; then the flood would have swept us away
The torrent would have gone over us; then over us would have gone the raging waters.
Blessed be the Lord, who has not given us as prey to their teeth.
All: Our help is in the name of the Lord, who made heaven and earth.

Offertory Prayer

God of Grace and Mercy, hear the prayer in our gifts as we place them in the collection plates. They represent our first fruits and we pray that by accepting these gifts, the best we have to offer, you may know, O God, our absolute devotion to you. Jesus came to give us life and we give to celebrate that life and to offer life to others through our gifts. Bless these gifts and bless us that we may be your people. In Jesus' name we pray, Amen.

Benediction

May the great cloud of witnesses, *(name the deceased pillars of the church: pastors, and leaders)* who have guided and guarded the walls of this place, continue to lead and direct us as we follow the one who has gone before us all, our Lord and Jesus Christ. (Linda McKinnish Bridges)

Dancing with God

Second in a Series of Two on Music and Worship

2 Samuel 6:12-15

My first experience in orchestra was playing for a ballet performance. I had a strange experience. As I sat in the back of the orchestra pit holding one of the big bass violins, something happened. While holding the instrument and without ever touching a string I felt and heard the instrument as it began to play itself! This sympathetic vibration of strings occurs when a nearby instrument, usually a cello, strikes a perfectly in tune note. Then the big bass string will begin to vibrate as it is touched by the sound waves from the nearby instrument.

This blending of sound is a powerful experience. In the same way, worship is a blending of our spirits. It occurs when we come together in song and praise. We are affected by those around us even as we affect them. And just as the members of an orchestra must focus on the conductor to achieve beautiful music, so worshipers must focus on God. As the individual musicians must play their part (not necessarily their favorite) to complete the whole, so worshipers must provide their part (not necessarily their favorite part) in order to complete the whole of worship.

At the core of worship is a sense of real celebration. Second Samuel describes David's joyful return of the ark to Jerusalem, "David danced before the LORD with all his might; David was girded with a linen ephod. So David and all the house of Israel brought up the ark of the LORD with shouting, and with the sound of the trumpet."

David's great celebration soon consumed the whole house of Israel.

Do you like to dance? I have to admit, I am a terrible dancer. I have a rule with my wife, I only dance when I am out of town. So she has to wait until we are on vacation every year to get me to dance my one dance of the year.

Still, after all these years, I still get excited when my wife wants to dance. Recently I have had the joy of dancing with each of my grand-daughters (they stand on a chair and I do most of the dancing). To dance with someone invites a kind of intimacy. You have to give part of yourself away and blend in with their movements. You lose some control. To dance with someone, you have to think about his or her needs.

Worship is a kind of dance. We learn to move together. We find the beat together. I worship to your favorite song and you worship to mine.

Worship requires the blending of our spirits to serve God just as dance requires a blending of movement. The invitation to worship with God represents a kind of real spiritual intimacy. It is an intimacy we share with every other worshiper.

A bandleader picks the music and sets the tempo. A bandleader is in control. God has that covered. That is not your job or mine. God wants dancers. In worship we learn to allow God to control the music and tempo of life.

Worship, like dancing requires a willingness to check our ego at the door. The dance is more important than the individual dancer. Worship is more important than the individual worshiper.

My youth group had two young people with special needs. They blended in well and were generally accepted by the other kids. When our church was asked to host a district dance I wondered how these two would fit in with the event. I even went and talked to both sets of parents who assured me their kids would be fine.

Finally the night of the dance came. The church was decorated. Refreshments were set out and various youth groups arrived. The music played but no one danced. The young people were afraid of looking silly in front of their peers.

Then the young man from our group stood up and walking with his two canes he made his way across the floor. He stood in front of a young lady from our youth group. She stood with the help of her walker and they made their way to the center of the gym. They began a slight, gentle swaying to the music. Soon the entire floor was filled with dancers but none were more graceful or content than the boy with the canes dancing with the girl with the walker.

The scripture says that David danced before the Lord. Soon all of Israel joined in the dance. Every worship service begins with someone who comes prepared to celebrate God. David's people celebrated the return of the ark and God's powerful presence. Don't we also gather to celebrate God's powerful presence?

Each of us has our role to play in worship. Some are visible and some are not. But all are important.

When we finished the ballet the starring dancer stopped to talk to me. She had been the featured dancer, spending the performance centered in the spotlight. I had been one of several bassists hidden in the back of the orchestra pit. But Susan stopped, tapped me on the shoulder and said, "Thank you for being part of the dance."

In our worship God is the featured dance. But we are called to play our part as best we can ... until we hear God say, "Thank you for being part of the dance!" (Robert E. Gorrell)

Worship Aids

Invocation

Most Holy God, grant this day that we join in worship to serve you with our praise and prayer. Grant that we may worship you with joy and celebration in our hearts.

Call to Worship

As all Israel joined in celebration.
We gather in joy to celebrate your presence.
As David danced before God.
We gather before God to worship with joy in our hearts.

Words of Assurance

As God restored the ark to Israel, so God restores our hearts in worship. (Robert E. Gorrell)

AUGUST 31, 2008

❧❧❧

Sixteenth Sunday after Pentecost

Readings: Exodus 3:1-15; Psalm 105:1-6, 23-26, 45c; Romans 12:9-21; Matthew 16:21-28

That's What I Like About That
Matthew 16:21-28

Familiarity breeds contempt, the old saying goes, but to my mind the greater and more dangerous occasion of familiarity is indifference. We come to a text and we have read it so many times or heard so many sermons preached on it, that we lose not only the freshness of the text but its edge, its blessing, as well as its judgment. Part of the task of preaching or teaching is to shake the dust of familiarity off the text, to open a reader or listener's ears and let a text speak again.

A few years ago during Lent I taught a Sunday school class of young adults. We did not use a quarterly or topical study; instead, the material for each week's class was the gospel reading for the following Sunday. My intent was twofold: to let the class inform me of their curiosities regarding the Scriptures, thereby to assist my sermon preparation; and at the same time to help them engage the text a bit more deeply, so that our reading one week would help their listening the next.

In our very first class Mark's account of this same episode was up for grabs. I made copies of the parallel versions and we read them aloud. Then, knowing no better way to begin, I asked the class to consider, simply, what they liked about Jesus' predictions and pronouncements, and what they didn't like.

There was a long pause. Someone said, a bit sheepishly, that there was not much to like, frankly—all that talk of satan and suffering and crosses. "Not the aspects of discipleship we most often advertise," I said, and the class seemed to agree that it was a bit unsettling. In another minute, however, a former Marine decided that he very much liked the clarity with which Jesus issued his summons to discipleship—"If any want to become my followers, let them deny themselves and take up their cross and follow me."

"That is pretty clear," I said.

"It kind of lets you know where you stand," said he, and then, softly, after a deep pause, "and it lets me know that I am still pretty much sitting on the fence."

Someone else, who really liked the passion prediction, thought that, sad and horrible as it was, it was comforting to know that Jesus was not clueless, not like the rest of the characters in the story, not like we are. Jesus knew what was happening to him.

"Why is that a comfort?" I asked.

"If Jesus knows what is going on, he can give his disciples a way to endure and even interpret the days ahead. If Jesus knows where he is going, the rest of us, if we are listening, will know how to follow."

Another liked the promise of glory, others the promise of repayment, the certainty of God's justice being done. "Okay, so what don't you like?" I asked, and someone said, "The very same things: I don't really like the certainty of God's justice, the promise of repayment according to what we have done." And then someone said, "I don't like the conflict, and I don't mean between Jesus and the authorities, the rulers and such. I don't like the conflict between Jesus and Peter, the argument between Jesus and the disciples."

Indeed, it is most uncomfortable to read of Peter speaking harshly to Jesus, and of Jesus speaking harshly to Peter, to see them on different sides of an issue. Just moments before all their words were blessing words, each for the other: "Thou art the Christ," Peter said to Jesus; "Thou art the Rock," Jesus said in return. Now the blessing has become cursing, a mutual rebuke, Peter barking at Jesus, "You don't know what you are saying!" and Jesus barking right back, "You don't know how you are thinking!"

Jesus is often at odds with his followers, of course. That is another aspect of discipleship we don't often advertise. Sometimes, because of over-familiarity with our texts, our traditions and practices, we don't realize that we, too, have our minds set on earthly things. We don't always see how we, who are called to help convert the culture, are instead converted by the culture and so much so that we do not talk about crosses or suffering or the evil powers of this world.

In our churches we can be so seduced by the theology of glory (which is a part of the gospel to be sure, but only a part, lest it become triumphalism) or, failing that, the theology of success (one writer notes that many churches study and master their ABC's—attendance, buildings, cash—and nothing else) that we are as reluctant as Peter to embrace the cross. But when we empty the cross of its power we empty discipleship of the cross, thereby emptying our church programs of discipleship. Jesus speaks sharply to those of us who set our minds not on heavenly things.

Class was almost over when I said, "Let me tell you what I most like about this passage." I went on to say that I, too, found it very uncomfortable to see Jesus and Peter at odds, and to know that Peter represents me, all of us, in the church, but how wonderful that although Peter misunderstands, Jesus does not abandon him. Yes, they are at odds, but they are still friends. Jesus corrects Peter; he does not excommunicate him. Having loved him, having called him—having loved and called us—Jesus will keep us in the fold, keep correcting and teaching, keep showing us the way till our minds are finally, fully, always set on heavenly things. (Thomas Steagald)

Lectionary Commentary
Exodus 3:1-15

This episode in the life of Moses—and in the life of God—is among the most famous of biblical epiphanies, and one of the three or four emblematic pictures of God's self-revelation. God is indeed with us—here, with Moses, in fire and voice. This fire of God burns but does not consume; it fascinates and confuses; the entire scene is poetic, fantastic, as God's presence and voice reveals much and at the same time raises many unanswered questions.

Moses was tending the flock of his father-in-law, Jethro, "beyond the wilderness" ("backside of the desert," KJV). God will call him from beyond his fearful escape from Pharaoh, will send him back into the crucible of the past to forge a future. Both God and Moses have names that are variously and erroneously construed among those in Egypt, whether slaves or royals; the events of the Exodus and Sinai will rename and redefine both. There are a thousand good reasons for God to choose Moses for this task, and a thousand more reasons for God not to choose him at all. It is the fullness of who Moses is that gives God opportunity to fully reveal and use the divine majesty.

Romans 12:9-21

All the documents of the New Testament work from theological suppositions. In some of the documents, the Gospels especially, the author's theology must be discerned as a subtext and application made more by way of imitation—either of Jesus or the faithful—or on the specific instruction of Jesus to his disciples.

In many of the epistles, both Pauline and otherwise, the theological subtext is either implicit or occasional, and the instructions for individual or community life have the feel of common sense or general wisdom, leading to the charge then and now that many Christian teachers buttress existing social mores and opinion rather than calling for a radically reoriented lifestyle.

Whether that charge has any merit, Romans is unique in that the instructions and admonitions flow from the theological character of the book. Of all the New Testament documents, Romans is the most thoroughly and explicitly theological. Its argument leads rather naturally to what we might call, mundanely, "practical applications." (Thomas Steagald)

Worship Aids

Call to Worship (Psalm 105)

> O give thanks to the Lord, call on his name,
> **Make known [God's] deeds among the peoples.**
> Sing to him, sing praises to him;
> **Tell of all his wonderful works.**
> Seek the LORD and his strength;
> **All: Seek his presence continually.**

Collect

O God, who would call us back from beyond the wilderness of our sins and into the places of your service, grant us such a vision of your holy fire as to humble and kindle our hearts, and the authority of your name by which we might set your people free. Through Jesus Christ our Lord, who lives and reigns with you and the Holy Spirit, one God, forever. Amen.

Benediction

Now may the Lord, the Unnamed and Named, who has called us and claimed us, commissioned and gifted us, go with you into your home country, there to bring his liberating and constituting and gracious power to his suffering children. Amen. (Thomas Steagald)

The Mysterious Power of Prayer

First in a Series of Two on Prayer

James 5:13-16

"Are any among you suffering? They should pray. Are any cheerful? They should sing songs of praise. Are any among you sick? They should call for the elders of the church and have them pray over them, anointing them with oil in the name of the Lord. The prayer of faith will save the sick, and the Lord will raise them up; and anyone who has committed sins will be forgiven. Therefore confess your sins to one another, and pray for one another, so that you may be healed. The prayer of the righteous is powerful and effective."

At the tender age of fourteen, I bought my first automobile. I paid cash ... exactly fifteen dollars! The catch was that the four-cylinder engine in the old jalopy was "frozen," the pistons rusted tight to the cylinder walls. After applying penetrating oil to soak the piston rings, I prayed feverishly for days that God would "heal" my little engine. I've never prayed with more intensity and sincerity and childlike faith, and certainly never with a purer heart than I possessed at that age. I promised God that if the car could be made to run, I would use it to help people. I had done my part by applying the oil—exactly as recommended in the Epistle of James! I'll never understand why God did not grant that prayer.

You may chuckle, but the serious point is that my childish prayer is not the only one that goes unanswered. We have all had prayers not answered, at least not answered in the ways we want them answered, with the immediacy we demand. We forget that God's plan for the world is far bigger than our view of things, and we forget that for God, "a thousand years are like one day" (2 Peter 3:8). We tend to forget all the answered prayers of the past in the face of one unanswered prayer today. In all of this we can easily miss the larger point: whether God answers prayers in the way we demand should not be our first concern regarding prayer. Prayer is not about getting the things we want.

Sometimes we act as if God were just a genie in a bottle, and kneeling and praying were the equivalent of rubbing the bottle to get our three wishes. If my prayer is little more than the recitation of a "Christmas wish list" for Santa, and thus I treat God as a glorified Santa Claus, I have wandered far from the truth and richness of a scriptural understanding of prayer and I have reduced God from being the almighty sovereign of the universe to being little more than a telephone receptionist for the Sears catalog.

Understanding God and enriching our prayer life are obviously related: the bigger my view of God, the better my prayer life will be. Two things we know about God, most assuredly: God is a God of love and power. These two things come together in the phenomenon of prayer.

First, the very fact that God desires to hear our prayers is indicative of God's love. Sometimes, if I've had a hard day and my children get a bit too long-winded, I can grow impatient and weary of hearing their sweet voices, and I only have two daughters! Imagine the love of our heavenly parent, who listens patiently to the prattling on of millions of "children." God demonstrates love by listening.

Second, prayer is indeed powerful, the most potent force available to humans. Prayer connects us to the almighty, omnipotent Creator of the universe. Through prayer, we are invited to ask and seek God's awesome power. Indeed, prayer is the way we invite a nonintrusive God—and the divine power thus associated—into our lives and world.

In 2 Timothy 3:5, the Apostle Paul warned about "holding to the outward form of godliness but denying its power." The power of God comes into our lives through prayer.

Allow me to return to my illustration of that car I bought as a teenager. I was never able to get the jalopy running, but I longed to enjoy the pleasure of driving my first automobile. So a buddy and I pushed the car up a big hill, huffing and puffing, straining and sweating, just so I could have the brief thrill of steering it down the hill in a short coast. The absurdity of pushing a lifeless two-ton hunk of metal up a hill without a motor is a vivid metaphor of what religion without the power of prayer can become: a weary exercise in futility.

Granted, I do not understand why God did not grant my childish prayer for my old jalopy, nor do I understand why God has not healed a young woman in my parish, paralyzed from the neck down, despite the frequent prayers lifted up by me and by many parishioners for her. Nevertheless, she has not given up on the power of prayer. Nor will I. We understand that the mystery of prayer will not be solved in this lifetime. We also believe, by faith, that the power of prayer is real and palpable. We continue to pray. (Lance Moore)

Worship Aids

Call to Worship

O Spirit of God, descend upon us now. Guide our worship, fill our mouths with praise, and our hearts with love and gratitude in this hour, and in the week to come.

Litany (based on the Lord's Prayer)

Heavenly Father, we praise your holy name, and invite your will into our lives.
O Lord, teach us to pray.
Feed us that we might feed you.
O Lord, help us listen.
Steer us away from the cheap temptations of life and toward a deeper faith.
O Lord, create in us a longing for prayer.
Show us your power that we might be encouraged to strive to build your kingdom.
All: O Lord, teach us to pray continually and forever. Amen.

Pastoral Prayer

O Divine Source of Wisdom, one gift that sets us apart from your other creatures is our ability to learn. We thank and praise you for endowing the human race with the ability to discover, invent, and teach increasingly wonderful things with each generation. So with the start of another school year, we ask for your blessings upon all those who teach our young people, from elementary school teachers to college professors to Sunday school teachers. Be present in all the schools of our community. Bless and encourage each student. Instill in them a desire to learn, to excel, to be fruitful, and to grow in stature and wisdom. Forgive us for our ignorance and pride, and hear our sincere prayer that our children might gain greater knowledge and wisdom than we, their parents and elders, have demonstrated. In the name of Jesus, our greatest teacher. Amen. (Lance Moore)

SEPTEMBER 7, 2008

❧❧❧

Seventeenth Sunday after Pentecost

Readings: Exodus 12:1-14; Psalm 149; Romans 13:8-14;
Matthew 18:15-20

The Way to a Nation's Heart
Exodus 12:1-14

Holidays are like every other day, only more so. People travel everyday;
they just travel more for holidays. People have reunions every day, get
together with family and friends; they just plan it better, go to the extra
trouble, do it more at holidays. People buy and give presents everyday;
they just do it more expensively and with greater intensity at holidays.
People receive gifts every day; they just do it with more expectation at
holidays. People eat every day; they just do it more at holidays. People tell
stories every day; they just tell more of them at holidays.

There is something about eating together—something about the gathering and preparing, the seeing and sharing, something about the bounty
of the table that makes us pause, reflect, remember, and tell. Special occasions call for special food and special folk, friends and kin; special
occasions with special food and folk call for those special stories that
make the circle whole, even when there are holes. There is a kind of
unbroken circle in even the most broken of families—if we are able to
gather the folk, break the bread, and tell the stories.

The text before us, Exodus 12, concerns food, memory, and celebration. It reflects not a perennial human strategy so much as an annual
Jewish (and then Christian) strategy of gathering certain people, eating
certain foods, remembering certain stories. We are called to remember
not generally but particularly, in this time and in this way—and it is a
strange text, really, full of strange menus and confusing mandates. It is,
nevertheless, a text we can get our teeth into because it concerns a party,

282

a celebration supper, a special meal with special stories. That is something we understand.

The text is about Passover, what comprised it, who was to eat it, how and when, and what was to be said along the way. The Passover was, and is, the central celebration of the Hebrew faith, and it gives us the basic shape and outlines of our own central celebrations of Good Friday and Easter. In fact, some scholars believe that Jesus and his disciples shared the Passover as their final meal together (with certain various reinterpretations by Jesus). Anytime we partake of the Eucharist, we too recall Passover. Yet, this text has its own discreet history and purpose—to remind Jews of every generation, and those who are heirs by faith, of God's regard for the plight of his people and also of God's mighty work to rescue and reconstitute the people. This story is at the heart of Jewish identity: the way to that heart is through the stomach.

If the Jewish Passover recounted God's deliverance of God's enslaved children—how with a mighty hand and an outstretched arm God acted to liberate his poor, enslaved children—both Jews and Christians believe that work is not yet done. Still God works to deliver the oppressed, those suffering in exile or servitude or sin. So the Passover meal and the Passover story commemorate not just what God did, but what God is doing yet in the world, and the means by which God does it.

But why eat to mark the time? We might answer, theologically, that as a people we taste and see that God is good. Whether we are commemorating the first Passover, or the Last Supper, whether we are anticipating our family's circle being unbroken or the Great Feast the prophets saw, when all the world's families will be one around the great mountain table where God will prepare a meal for all his children, we set the table and eat. But that only begs the question.

That humans have to eat as celebration is in fact a kind of confession—a confession of need. In the strength of high celebration we are, fundamentally, confessing our weakness each to the other, and all of us to God. In the presence we are demonstrating our need of food to survive, our need of others to share, our need of stories to make meaning of the seemingly disconnected episodes of our lives. The food is impermanent, the company less so—although it is not without frailty—but the stories last, tell us who we are and where we come from, tell us what we are doing and where we are heading. Some stories have the power to move us and our meal from the plain of mere celebration to a grander height, to commemoration—which means, "remembering together." We remember together with the past, and together with the future, and together in the memory and presence of those who one way or the other are blessed and named and summoned by the stories.

For the Passover commemoration, every part of the meal is prescribed. The time is prescribed—on the anniversary, more or less, of the original event. The guests are prescribed—families, sometimes unto themselves, sometimes with neighbors. The menu is prescribed—a lamb roasted whole, and yeastless bread, lots of horseradish and sweet fruit, too, and all of it to be eaten and nothing left till morning, or if it is, then the remainder is burned.

The stories are prescribed—this is the heart of it. The faces around the table and the food on the plate all in service of the story, to help us see that God is good by tasting: the lamb, slain, so the blood could save us; the bread, flat, to remind us that salvation comes in a moment; the herbs, bitter, to bring forth our tears at the weeping of those who are oppressed; the sweet fruit, dipped in saltwater, to remind us that life's goodness is ever marinated in grief.

Eat quickly, but reflect slowly; hurry, but slow down, to recall the acts of God, the power of the Lord, the salvation that is ours by grace. This is who we are—the needy community blessed by a giving God. Eat and never forget. (Thomas Steagald)

Lectionary Commentary
Matthew 18:15-20

One of the ways to read Matthew is as a manual for church life. Whether this general designation would ultimately withstand the sometimes withering examination of critical scholarship, it is nonetheless a helpful lens for hearing and appropriating the wealth of pronouncements and didactic texts one finds in Matthew.

This selection is one of many that can be read through such a lens: instructions for disciples who live one or two generations after the life, death, and resurrection of Jesus, and still a minority in the prevailing culture. Jesus said that a house divided against itself cannot stand (Matthew 12:25), and here there is a strategy for keeping the house whole. The unity of believers guarantees the abiding presence of Jesus. It is when disciples agree that God's power is demonstrated.

While there is evidence in Matthew 13 that Jesus fully expects there to be "weeds" among the "wheat," the instruction is to make unity (if not uniformity) the goal of church life. Even the somewhat problematic passage, "let such a one be to you as a Gentile and a tax collector" might be read as saying, "with some folks you have to start over." They are expelled from the community, but perhaps for the purpose of reentering it.

Romans 13:8-14

This lection offers us no culture-friendly advice. Indeed, Paul affirms that the culture is passing away, that the world's dark night is far spent and that living according the distinctive message of the gospel will require believers to don the "armor of light." The salvation of the world will not be easy, although the outcome is assured; we are to be awake, on guard, reflecting the light that some will inevitably want to extinguish.

There is continuity between the Decalogue, here abbreviated, and the patterns of behavior that will characterize faithful Christian life in the world, which is to say that Paul wants to groom a distinct and holy people.

As is the case in Matthew, Paul is concerned to achieve and maintain the kind of unity and community that will help the minority Christians survive and flourish in their pagan world. These pieces of advice are not prerequisites to salvation, but demonstrations of the salvation that is ours in Christ. (Thomas Steagald)

Worship Aids

Greeting (Psalm 148)

Praise the Lord from the heavens, sun, moon and stars, angels and
heavenly host!
**Praise the Lord from the earth all women and men, both
aged and young!**
Let everything praise the name of the Lord, for his name alone is
exalted!
All: His glory is above earth and heaven. Praise the Lord!

Collect

O God, who has given your people both the experience and the memory of your gracious acts of salvation, and through them, hope. As we tell of your mighty hand and outstretched arm, let us await the coming feast with patience, rejoice to receive the good gifts you provide, and taste and see again and ever that you are good. Through Jesus Christ, the bread of heaven, our Savior and Lord, the King of the world. Amen.

Benediction

And now may the Lord Jesus Christ, who bore the holy cross to Calvary, give you grace and strength to shoulder your cross and with it your share of another's burdens, to bring it all to him for healing. Amen. (Thomas Steagald)

The Mysterious Power of Prayer

Second in a Series of Two on Prayer

Matthew 7:7-8, 17:20

"Ask, and it will be given you; search, and you will find; knock, and the door will be opened for you. For everyone who asks receives, and everyone who searches finds, and for everyone who knocks, the door will be opened."

Jesus said to them, "For truly I tell you, if you have faith the size of a mustard seed, you will say to this mountain, 'Move from here to there,' and it will move; and nothing will be impossible for you."

Suppose you could travel back in time a few hundred years to visit a proverbial Renaissance man. Even to such a genius as Leonardo da Vinci, could you truly explain the many miracles of modern technology? Could you convince Leonardo that a handful of plutonium could create enough power in an atom bomb to destroy an entire city? Would he believe that three tons of metal the size of a house could lift him into the air and carry him across Europe in an hour? Unbelievable powers, yet true.

I know little about the principles of aviation; I do not understand the power of a jet engine; yet I will climb aboard a 747 and fly cross-country without hesitation.

Likewise, I do not understand the power of prayer. I have spent most of my life studying religion, but I cannot fully fathom the mystery of prayer. Prayer is an incredible power, this open and direct contact with God. It is difficult to believe what Jesus said, that if we have faith the size of a mustard seed we can move mountains. That power is as hard for me to mentally grasp as it is for a monkey to decipher jet engines. But the monkey's ignorance does not bring planes crashing to the ground. Our limited understanding of prayer does not destroy prayer's efficacy. If we trust the mysterious powers of modern technology with our lives, shouldn't we trust even more in the power of prayer?

It is not necessary to understand the mystery of prayer to be able to utilize prayer's power. The power of prayer is God, and God invites us to use divine power. The first part of this two-part series on prayer gave the warning that prayer should not, first and foremost, be about getting the things we want. But let us not throw the proverbial baby out with the bath water. Jesus actually encouraged his disciples to ask God for the things they (we!) need. "Ask, and it shall be given. Seek, and you will find."

It is to be hoped that most of what we ask for in prayer will not be for ourselves, but for others. Do I need to elaborate on our dire need for prayer in the world today? Aimless teenagers; corruption in government; greed in big business; war; families in crisis; suburban malaise; epidemics and famines in the Third World. You see the news; you hear the statistics. We know the problem, and we have a solution: prayer. As R. A. Torrey said, "If we are too busy to pray, we are too busy to have power." Let's use this divine power that is so available to us—not just today, but every day.

Prayer is about paradox: we pray for God's intervention, but God prefers that we become the agents of reconciliation and care; we must pray God's will be done, yet God invites us to ask for favors; we cannot understand prayer fully, yet we should try to know more about it. There are some things we can understand, and there are some practical methods of prayer that can be beneficial. For prayer to work, it should be done in a way that is consistent with scriptural guidelines. A few:

- Pray regularly and frequently. Jesus did. Paul said, "Pray continually."
- Jesus warned not to pray to be seen by others. Though he prayed publicly at times, he seemed to prefer private prayer. In Matthew 6, Jesus instructed us to go into a room (the "closet," the King James Version calls it), and pray alone and unseen.
- Don't babble. Jesus said we will not be heard for our many words, but for our sincerity.
- Indeed, communion with God means more than verbal communication, it means connecting with God at every level: our minds, our hearts, even our physical posture.
- Humility is at the core of most of Jesus' teachings on prayer. Pray for others. Pray for God's will and kingdom to come. Pray for self last.

- Intercessory prayer tends to focus on the physically ill, and that should always be a part of our prayers, but don't just pray for the sick; remember those who do not seem like they need prayer (they probably do). Pray for everyone, even the ones who appear to be rich materially or spiritually. Ephesians 6:18 advises: "Keep on praying for all the saints" (NIV).
- Use scriptural models of prayer: the Psalms and the Lord's Prayer lead the list.
- Include silent meditation or listening prayer. Your mind will drift. Just try to keep your thoughts centered on the Divine—be still and wait on God.
- Add actions to your prayers—make prayer "real" in the physical sense by putting legs on your prayers. Become a servant so that you might be available as God's agent, to actually be, yourself, the answer to prayer! The final purpose of most of the prayers of Jesus were to make this world a better place. Be the embodiment of prayer. (Lance Moore)

Worship Aids

Call to Worship (adapted from Psalm 103)

Praise the Lord, O my soul, and forget not all God's benefits, who forgives our sins and heals our diseases.
Praise the Lord, you angels.
Praise the Lord, all heavenly hosts.
Praise the Lord, all things created in God's dominion.
Praise the Lord, O my soul.

Prayer of Confession

God of Eternity, despite the amazing advances in modern technology, we dwell in troubled times, a day and age where even those who seem to have it all can suddenly lose it all. For the rest of us, the fragments of broken promises are strewn about our marketplaces, courthouses, churches, offices, schools, and homes, the wreckage of once great hopes and ideals, the debris of shattered trust. In all creation, you alone, O Lord, are truly fail-safe. You faithfully keep your promises to us even when we carelessly disobey and break your heart, even when we crucify our Lord anew by breaking faith and abandoning responsibility. Forgive us for the times we have failed to live up to the name "Christian." Heal whatever hurt we have caused. Help us in turn forgive those who have violated the trust we once put in them. May your grace flow over us, washing away the stain of bitterness. Above all, remind us to pray, that through prayer we may remain connected to the One who is trustworthy and merciful. In the name of Jesus, who taught us to pray. Amen. (Lance Moore)

Words of Assurance

In the name of Jesus Christ, you are forgiven.
In the name of Jesus Christ, you are forgiven. Amen.

SEPTEMBER 14, 2008

✑✑✑

Eighteenth Sunday after Pentecost

Readings: Exodus 14:19-31; Psalm 114; Romans 14:1-12;
Matthew 18:21-35

How Can I Make It Up to You?
Matthew 18:21-35

"How can I make it up to you?" Isn't that what we say when we have
done wrong to someone? You know how the saying goes: To err is human;
to forgive is divine. There is another version of this saying I came across
recently that rings a bell for me. "To err is human. To forgive is darned
near impossible!"

For those of us who have been wronged, experience suggests that there
must be limits to patience with misbehavior. To those of us who have
done wrong and want to make up for it, we wonder what must people do
to make up for sin and misbehavior?

As we talk about reconciliation, the question comes to us, *What do you
do when someone has hurt you deeply? What do you do when someone continually hurts you?* Through habit or mean intention, some people create an
atmosphere of pain that makes living the Christian life almost impossible. As much as we try, forgiveness seems to slip away. Hatred and emotional distance take its place. During these times, we want to cry out,
"Lord! I have really tried, and I've had enough!"

So Peter bluntly asks Jesus that same sort of question, "At what point
is forgiveness absurd?" Peter knows human nature: some people get away
with metaphorical murder over and over and over, and at some point we
must stop it. But Jesus also knows human nature. For those of us who have
been hurt, we often allow these hurts to fester in our spirits. Jesus answers
we must forgive, not seven times (that perfect and whole number), but
seventy-seven times (for all you math majors, it's forgiveness to infinity).
Then Jesus tells the parable to illustrate.

Because restitution would be impossible for the servant, the king takes pity on him and cancels the debt and lets him go. He was fully freed. The forgiven servant, however, goes out to someone who owed him a small debt and does not show pity. The parallel nature of the stories grabs our attention. Word on the street travels fast and the king hears of the servant's ruthlessness and lack of compassion.

Our parable is really about the kind of lifestyle we will choose for ourselves. Do we know how to live the life that sets us free? Or are we bound to a world of resentment, anger, and bitterness? It appears as if this servant who had been forgiven much learned nothing about mercy, compassion, and forgiveness. So often, our selfish hearts are unaware of God's grace that surrounds us.

We live in a society in which we like to hold others responsible for things. When an accident occurs, we want to know who is to blame. Someone has to pay, we have been taught. We begin to interpret life from the point of view of debt. In a world where debt rules, nobody gets away with anything. In a world of debt, blame is the name of the game. In a world of debt, we might expect to hear Jesus cry from the cross, "Someone has to pay for this! Who is responsible for this? You'll get yours! What goes around comes around!" But instead, we hear Jesus cry, "Father, forgive them, for they know not what they do."

Jesus won't be in bondage to hatred, jealousy, frustration, and greed, but rather chooses a future that is open with us. Endless forgiveness makes no sense to our human way of thinking, but without it we can never live open-ended lives. Being a Christian involves daily choices between a way of life that ends in death or an open-ended way of life that goes on through eternity.

How can we make it up to each other? To be honest, sometimes we can't make it up—the sin has left its stain, the debt is too big to repay—but through the grace and love of Jesus Christ, we forgive, just as we have been forgiven. (Ryan Wilson)

Lectionary Commentary
Exodus 14:19-31

This lectionary text tells the story of the Israelite crossing of the Red Sea, or in some manuscripts the Sea of Reeds. One of the things that this lesson emphasizes again and again is God's providential care of God's people. God leads them as "the pillar of cloud" and protected them as God also "lit up the night." This story of the sea crossing was one of the seminal Hebrew stories about God's loving-kindness for Israel. The story had great effect on the people of Israel, for we read that, "the people feared the LORD and believed in the LORD and in his servant Moses."

Romans 14:1-12

Paul's discussion here concerns divisions or quarreling about questions of faith. Paul uses the adjective "weak" (and implies "strong") to identify Jews and Gentiles who have difficulties over the practice of faith. Paul urges concern for others and reminds the believers in Rome that unity in Christ is paramount. Paul writes, "If we live, we live to the Lord, and if we die, we die to the Lord; so then, whether we live or whether we die, we are the Lord's."

Worship Aids

Pastoral Prayer

O God, forgive us when we think of forgiveness as only a fancy word. Help us recognize that our forgiveness is modeled after your gracious and compassionate heart. Help us not just talk about forgiveness, but embody forgiveness in our daily lives. For we pray in the name of the one who said, "Father, forgive them, for they know not what they do," Jesus Christ our Lord, Amen. (Ryan Wilson)

Call to Worship

As we have wandered away from God's presence, let us ask for forgiveness and return to Christ. Jesus says, "Come to me, all of you who are weary and heavy laden and I will give you rest." (Ryan Wilson)

Litany

For our sins of commission,
We ask for forgiveness.
For our sins of omission,
We pray for pardon.
Just as you sent the Messiah, Jesus Christ, to reconcile the world
All: Grant us forgiving hearts that seek to reconcile our sisters and brothers.
(Ryan Wilson)

Healing Forgiveness

First in a Series of Two on Health and Wholeness

Mark 2:1-12

In an article that appeared in *U.S.A. Today*, December 10, 2002 titled "Psychologists Now Know What Makes You Happy," writer Marilyn Elias discovered a not-so surprising fact: "Forgiveness is the trait most strongly linked to happiness." If forgiveness is tied that strongly to happiness, perhaps some of the ideas we have grown up with need to be thrown away. We tend to associate happiness with education, success, good health, and so forth. Not that those things are unimportant, but when a psychologist notes that forgiveness is the single most important trait that leads to happiness, we of faith have good texts on which to rest.

The story from Mark 2 tells of four men who bring their paralytic friend to our Lord on a cot. But they can't get their friend to Jesus. So what do they do? They go up to the roof of the little house and tear it apart. The story tells us that Jesus looked up at the four friends and then said to the paralytic, "Son, your sins are forgiven." At that point, everybody got quiet. The religious types were there and began to debate the matter, as we who embrace theology tend to do. They grumbled, cleared their throats and said, "This is blasphemy. Who can forgive sins but God?" The answer is only God can forgive sins.

What is the relationship among sin, sickness, and forgiveness? Sin sickness can manifest itself in many ways: loss of energy or your passion for life because you said or did something that hurt another or yourself. Sin sickness afflicts us when we break God's laws for living. Sin sickness leaves us weak, lifeless, embarrassed, at times even shamed; always estranged from God and others.

We in the sophisticated twenty-first century still struggle with this issue. Sin is a politically incorrect word today. No one sins anymore. We simply have poor judgment. It is very difficult even to hear the word *sin* used in a positive, healthy way outside of the church; often not even in the church.

The ancients offer great wisdom, and we would be wise to listen. When we look at our lives and realize what sin does to us and others, forgiveness is always the needed thing. The ancients, however, took this another step. They believed that sin and sickness were hardwired to each other. In fact, many people in the ancient world believed that God visited sickness on people. Jesus debunked that. Jesus almost said, "That is not the way God works." No, when you and I sin, sin has consequences built into it. Those consequences are not the work of God, but rather the results of sin's work.

Let me hasten to say, in some cases sin does cause sickness. Let's not be naïve. There are all manner of diseases today that afflict the human species that are caused by human sin. Lifestyles and life choices can make us sick. So how do we find healing forgiveness for what we have done, for the injuries we have inflicted on others, and for those things we have left undone we should have done?

The story offers us a good counsel. First, notice, not incidental to this story, that the man is lowered into the presence of Jesus. If we are going to find healing forgiveness for our lives, we must come into the presence of Jesus. We must have a connection, an encounter with the person, the power, the presence of Jesus Christ. The healing forgiveness God brings comes in and through Jesus. This is the message of the Christian church. We must come into the presence of Jesus.

There is something else here, and we almost miss it. The story says the man was lowered into the presence of Jesus. A University of Michigan study of 1,423 people found among other things that "asking for forgiveness is one of the greatest stressors in life" (Marilyn Elias, "Psychologists Now Know What Makes You Happy"). To ask forgiveness from God or to ask forgiveness from another person is to say, "I'm sorry I hurt you." "I said the wrong thing." "I did the wrong thing." "It was not really my best self." "I apologize." The story says the man came to the place of healing when he was lowered into the presence of Jesus. There is a sense of humility that comes when we seek forgiveness that says, "I need what only God can give." It is not a sign of weakness to ask for forgiveness. It may in fact be your crowning strength.

There is one last thing here. Healing forgiveness is really a lifestyle reality. Healing forgiveness is not something we do and then we are done with it. No, healing forgiveness is a reality in which we live. We pray the Lord's Prayer, "Forgive us our trespasses as we forgive those who trespass against us," and we pray it often. Why? Because giving and receiving forgiveness makes us fully alive.

When we think about it, forgiveness is like a river that flows through our lives. It is always moving, generating and nourishing life. Forgiveness that is God's gift and God's life moves through our lives constantly. But, like many rivers in our world, we can pollute God's good gift. Things we do or we leave undone can pollute the river of forgiveness. It is only to the degree we shut off the pollutants and let the forgiving grace of God flow in life that we discover again the reality of God's forgiveness.

How simple it would be if we could simply find God's forgiveness and say, "I've done that. Check that off my list of things to do. Thank you very much. What's next?" Repeatedly, throughout our Christian experience, we discover we must confess our sins. We must receive the renewing grace of God. We must come back to the nourishing, healing gift of God's forgiveness. Why not now? Why not today? Jesus says, "Your sins are forgiven. Walk!" Amen. (Timothy Owings)

Worship Aids

Call to Worship

Come now and worship the Lord our God, the maker of heaven and earth!
Gathered and grateful, we honor the Lord.
Come now and praise the God of our salvation!
Gathered and joyful, we praise the giver of life.
Come now and celebrate new life in our Lord Jesus Christ!
Gathered and open, we worship our God.

Invocation

God of healing love, we worship you as the source of all life. Open our stubborn wills to your will, free us from the noise of hurried living, welcome us into your renewing presence that we may offer the gifts of praise and confession, and receive the gifts of forgiveness and grace. Through Jesus Christ our Lord we pray, amen.

Prayer of Confession

Loving Lord, we confess that we have made a mess of so much of our lives. We hold tightly to our hurts, we nurse old wounds, we fail to acknowledge our own brokenness. Grant us the courage to forsake every crippling emotion that keeps us from you and others, through the power of your forgiving grace, amen. (Timothy Owings)

Words of Assurance

In the name of Jesus Christ, you are forgiven.
In the name of Jesus Christ, you are forgiven. Amen.

SEPTEMBER 21, 2008

❧❧❧

Nineteenth Sunday after Pentecost

Readings: Exodus 16:2-15; Psalm 105:1-6, 37-45; Philippians 1:21-30; Matthew 20:1-16

Forgetting and Remembering
Exodus 16:2-15

"How soon we forget," Moses must have thought! Not long before, the Israelites had been slaves in Egypt. How quickly the people could forget how ruthless Pharaoh could be. But all the Israelites remembered was that at least they knew the routine. Do what Pharaoh wanted and most of the time, you'd at least get something to fill your belly. The people were looking at their hard slave life through rose-colored glasses. Although they had been mistreated, all they remembered was a comfort zone and a routine.

Their memory of God's activity in their lives had been erased. When there was a shortage of food, instead of looking to God, they only remembered Pharaoh. They were also quick to blame Moses and Aaron for leading them into the wilderness to starve. Complain, complain, complain! Accuse, accuse, accuse! Ultimately, God was to blame, and so the implication is that the people are turning from God. They were losing their faith.

But God must have heard the cry of the Israelites, and God responds to this need. The gift of food is tied to God's good intentions for God's creation. God has promised to provide for our every need, and God does not break God's promises.

God, however, wants us to be in a covenant relationship. Therefore, God gives Moses special instructions on how the Israelites are to harvest the food. There is an order to their harvesting. Normally, they are only to harvest enough food for their daily portion. However, as they prepare for the Sabbath, they are to harvest enough for two days. God provides for their daily needs, and God provides a way for them to keep the Sabbath.

There is something vital about this passage and its relationship to creation and in relationship to the Sabbath. As God was creating, God brought order out of chaos. There is something sacred about having order to our lives. There is something holy about having lives that are not out of control. The one way to help assure that we are able to have ordered lives is by keeping the Sabbath.

While many of us view the Sabbath as something that God orders us to keep for God's sake, the truth about the Sabbath is that it is for our sake. Jesus makes that very clear in his conversation with the Pharisees in Mark 2:23-28. By observing Sabbath, we take the time to rest and refocus our lives. It helps our memory be clearer and allows us to reflect on God's sustaining grace and provision for our lives. In essence, keeping the Sabbath helps us find order amidst the chaos of the world. (Ryan Wilson)

Lectionary Commentary
Philippians 1:21-30

The Apostle Paul here writes to his beloved in Philippi and shares part of his innermost thoughts. He tries to impart his confidence in his own deep faith in Christ. He also wishes for the Philippians the same kind of joy in faith that Paul himself experienced. Paul even reminds the church that suffering for Christ is a privilege. He suggests that they have much the same struggle that he had, but it is Christ who will pull them through.

Matthew 20:1-16

This lesson from *The Revised Common Lectionary* begins with Jesus telling a parable that begins: "For the kingdom of heaven is like a landowner who went out early in the morning to hire laborers for his vineyard." In modern times, this parable is a difficult one given our tendency to give people what they earn. Yet, God gives grace in the measure God deems fitting and to whom God wills. The landowner's final questions are as pertinent today as they were in Jesus' day: "Am I not allowed to do what I choose with what belongs to me? Or are you envious because I am generous?"

Worship Aids

Pastoral Prayer
Lord, our memories play funny tricks on us. When times get tough, we often want to remember life when we were self-sufficient or when

we were slaves to something else. We tend to misrepresent the way things really were. We forget that you invite us to freedom and that you desire to be our guide. Bring to our memory a clear picture of your guiding love and sustaining faithfulness. May we remember with clarity your daily provision for our lives. (Ryan Wilson)

Prayer of Confession

Gracious God, we confess that we often forget your undying commitment to us. Our memories get flooded with thoughts that are misrepresentations of reality. We confess that we cling to the things that seem to make us feel safe. But you call us out of Egypt and into the promised land. You desire for us to be free and to rely on you for all our needs. Forgive us when we fail to remember your faithfulness. Forgive us when we try to rely on the things of this world to fill our souls. Help us look to you for our sustenance. For we pray in the name of the one who is the Bread of Life, Jesus Christ, our Lord, amen. (Ryan Wilson)

Words of Assurance

In the name of Jesus Christ, you are forgiven.
In the name of Jesus Christ, you are forgiven. Amen.

Benediction

Now may the God of freedom lead you to places of promise and hope. May the God of grace provide when we are unaware. And may the God of love bring to our memory the actions of God's sustaining provision for our lives. (Ryan Wilson)

The Nourishing Secret of the Meek

Second in a Series of Two on Health and Wholeness

Matthew 5:5

I don't know what comes to your mind when you hear the word *meek*, but the words that come to my mind are not positive. The word many hear when someone is defined as "meek" is, frankly, a wimp. This definition suggests that the meek are spineless, docile, or a pushover. An old metaphor describes a meek person as "milk toasty."

The New Testament word for "meek" is *praus*. It's a noun found only three times in the Gospel of Matthew. Rather than "weak," *praus* can mean "patient," "gentle," even "strong." Let's work with those.

"Blessed are the patient for they will inherit the land." Rather than caving in to belligerence or becoming a doormat, to be meek is to be patient, knowing God is always working in the lives of those who face the horizon of grace. To be meek is to live in confident assurance that not all of God's work in any life is always an unfolding story of wonder, but to know a happiness defined by hope and not circumstances. "Happy are those who are patient."

But there is something else here. Let's now employ the word *gentle*. "Happy are the gentle for they will inherit the land." Our word *praus* is also found in Matthew 11:28 where our Lord says, "Take my yoke upon you, and learn from me; for I am gentle [*praus*] and humble in heart." "Happy are those who are gentle." To be gentle is to express the character of Jesus. The sage of Proverbs wrote, "A gentle answer turns away wrath; but a harsh word stirs up anger" (15:1). When will we learn that our laboring, heavy laden, burdened lives can only know rest when we learn from Jesus the nourishing secret of being gentle? "Happy are the gentle for they will inherit the land."

The surprising, third insight into the word *meek* is that it means "strong." Matthew quotes the prophet Zechariah (Matthew 21:5), describing our Lord's triumphal entry into Jerusalem: "Say to the Daughter of Zion, / See, your king comes to you, / gentle [*praus*] and riding on a donkey" (NIV). A better translation would be: "Your king comes to you strong." How so?

The ancient Hebrew people believed that when the Messiah came, he would not come on a war horse, but, according to the prophet, on a beast of burden. The Messiah would come in utter humility. The Greek philosophers taught that greatness of soul was far superior to physical might. The Greek word *praus* has nothing to do with weakness. Rather, see that here *meek* means overwhelming strength.

Happy are those who know that God is their strength. There is a nourishing grace that comes to all who discover this nourishing secret of the meek. Strength comes from patience and gentleness; from an awareness of living in God's presence and grace. Happy are those who are strong; who know that God is "their refuge and strength, a very present help in time of trouble." Show me a person who has strength in their life, where there is steel riveted into their soul, and I will show you a person who knows that meekness is a strength that one finds only in God.

So tell me, what is the nourishing secret of the meek? For one, blessing has more to do with being than anything else. How strange today we define happiness by what we have, who we know, where we live, and what we do. You take the survey. Ask anybody, "Are you happy? Are you blessed? What are the good realities in your life?" The answers are predictable: "I have a good job." Or, "I have a loving and faithful spouse." Or, "My children are healthy and smart." Or, "I live in a good neighborhood," "My retirement is funded," or a host of other responses all defined by external circumstances. Jesus turns our shallow definitions of happiness on their head. Jesus says that blessing has everything to do with being, not doing or having or accumulating. The meek know that life's deepest meaning comes not from the letters after your name much less on whose wall your name appears. It's who you are.

There is a second nourishing reality known only to the meek. Do you remember the Smith-Barney commercial with John Houseman? "At Smith-Barney we make money the old-fashioned way. We earn it." Not so! The old fashioned way to make money is to inherit it. Spiritually, we cannot earn our inheritance. Yet we try so hard. The only way we inherit the land God gives is to receive the gift of God, which is God's grace. The meek know that. The meek know that only God can make us new beings, the sons and daughters of our Creator.

The Bible tells us that if anyone is in Christ, he or she is a new creation—a new being. The meek—who are patient, gentle, and strong—know the land God gives away as an inheritance is rich with grace. Truth be told, the only people who are in God's estate plan are the meek. "Blessed are the patient—blessed are the gentle—blessed are the strong for they will inherit the land." The land is our birthright. It is our birthright as a gift from God. Open the arms of your heart today and confess to God, "I cannot earn what only you give." And ask God for the gift of grace in Jesus Christ. "Blessed are the meek for they will inherit the land." Such is the nourishing secret of the meek. (Timothy Owings)

Worship Aids

Invocation

Nourishing Lord, we bow our weary and grasping lives in your presence, seeking your face. Cleanse the thoughts of our hearts from every polluting intruder that we may joyfully worship you and praise your holy name. Through Jesus Christ, your son and our Savior, we pray, amen.

Litany

Blessed are the meek, for they shall inherit the land.
We would be your people of promise.
Blessed are the patient, for they shall inherit the land.
We would be your people of promise.
Blessed are the gentle, for they shall inherit the land.
We would be your people of promise.
Blessed are the strong, for they shall inherit the land.
We would be your people of promise.
Blessed are God's people of meekness, patience, gentleness, and strength.
We are your people of promise.

Benediction

Now depart in the blessing of God, knowing that it is God's good pleasure to give you the land of promise as your inheritance, the nourishing gift of meekness as your birthright, and the abiding reality of joy as your strength, through Jesus Christ, who lives and reigns in the unity of the Holy Spirit, now and evermore, amen. (Timothy Owings)

SEPTEMBER 28, 2008

֎֎ ֎֎ ֎֎

Twentieth Sunday after Pentecost

Readings: Exodus 17:1-7; Psalm 78:1-4, 12-16; Philippians 2:1-13; Matthew 21:23-32

God with Us
Exodus 17:1-7

There are many parts of the Bible that I wish I could have experienced firsthand. I would love to meet individuals like Abraham, Esther, Samuel, Rahab, David, and so many others. I would love to be in the physical presence of Jesus, and witness the great miracles found in scripture. One part of the great story, however, of which I would not have desired to be part is the Exodus. It is not only that a lifetime of wandering in the desert would have been horrific, but also mostly that I cannot tolerate whining. Perhaps it is because I am the mother of two small children. Perhaps it is because I have spent my entire life in the church. Whatever the reason, I find myself completely frustrated with the entire community of Israel throughout much of the book of Exodus. I wonder if God felt that same way.

The story of the exodus is really a story of God's mercy. Moses is clearly the first recipient of this mercy as his young life is spared through the ingenuity and wisdom of his mother and sister. As Moses' story progresses it is clear that he is part of God's greater plan of mercy for the Hebrews. God chooses Moses as the one to lead the Hebrew people out of slavery in Egypt and into the land God promised them. Their journey toward freedom is bumpy, and desperately needs God's miraculous participation. In Exodus 14, the Israelites experience their first great miracle as a community. While being closely pursued by an army, excessive in size compared to the vagabond band of slaves they were pursuing, the Israelites miraculously cross the parted Red Sea. Their pursuers are not so fortunate, and the Israelites are free to run. I believe that were it not for all of the imperfections of the human condition, the great story would have ended here. It does not, however. Instead, the story soon takes a series of turns that lead straight to the desert, and in and out of God's favor.

According to Exodus 15, it only took three days for Israel's praise to turn to complaint. After traveling three days to find water, the water they find is not drinkable. Thirsty and discouraged, they grumble. Moses cries out to God and God provides drinkable water. Now, it would seem that after experiencing such miraculous provision by God twice in just a few days that the Israelites' faith would be at a highpoint. Instead chapters 16 and 17 record the continuation of their pattern of doubt and complaint, even in the face of great divine provision. Chapter 16 takes place a couple of months into their journey. This time the Israelites are hungry. This time they do more than just grumble. They accuse Moses of bringing them into the desert to die. Forgetting apparently the hardships of slavery after just a couple of months, they remember their time in Egypt as a time when their bellies were full and they had plenty to eat. Again, God hears them, and provides for their need.

The timing of Exodus 17 is not completely clear. It is probably not long after "the manna and quail" miracle. Given their short memories, it could have been as soon as a few days later, but we do not know for sure. Again they are thirsty. Again they grumble to Moses, this time so severely that Moses believes he might be stoned. The Lord, again, hears their grumbling and provides water, this time using Moses to strike a rock with his staff. Moses named the place of the miracle Massah and Meribah because the Israelites quarreled and tested God as to whether the Lord was with them or not.

I am admittedly hard on the Israelites. They were desperate, after all, and hungry and thirsty. From their vantage point, there was much uncertainty in their future. They were putting their faith in something they could not see with their only tangible representative, Moses, being someone they were not sure they could trust. Their journey taught them that God would provide, but the hunger and thirst of their children was probably more then they could bear. They must have often felt alone and sincerely wondered if the Lord was with them or not.

There are a couple of helpful lessons I think that we can learn from the whining Israelites. First of all, it is human to feel the need to whine, grumble, and complain. Basic physical and emotional needs drive us, and we are not satisfied to not have those met. Babies, after all, instinctively cry out to have their basic needs met. Our propensity to whine, however,

303

does not eliminate or overtake God's propensity to provide. God doesn't need our grumbling to provide for our needs. All God desires is our love and trust. God does the rest.

Secondly, Jesus Christ is with us in a way that the Israelites could not fathom. Although I believe that God expected and deserved the faith and trust of Israel, it was not until the incarnation of Christ that humanity really experienced God with us. God became like us to know us better, and so that we would not doubt the presence of the Lord as the Israelites did. I still want to shake the Israelites throughout much of Exodus or at least put them in time-out. Perhaps my frustration with them is the part of myself I see in their story. May the abiding love of Jesus Christ move us from our places of selfishness and fear to a place of awareness of God's great mercy and provision. (Tracey Allred)

Lectionary Commentary
Matthew 21:23-32

Matthew 21 records the events of the first two days of the last week of Jesus' life on earth. During the first day, he entered Jerusalem and visited the temple where he angrily overturned the tables of the moneychangers. One the second day, Jesus headed back to Jerusalem, stopping long enough to encounter an unfortunate fig tree. Jesus then entered the temple for a time of teaching. It didn't take long for him to encounter the chief priests and elders who were not happy that he was there. They tried to trick Jesus into saying something to offend the crowd or break the law, but he turned the table on them by asking them a question instead. Although the question was a significant one, I'm not sure that Jesus cared as much about their answer as their process. In the end, they opted to not answer, further demonstrating the level at which they just did not understand what Jesus was about. In the end, it was not about the right answer to a tricky question anymore than it was about legalistically responding to God. Christ's authority was not given by any human, but by God.

Philippians 2:1-13

Wouldn't it be nice if churches posted Philippians 2:1-13 in the entryway? Although Paul wrote them to a group of faithful believers, it was clearly an important reminder of Christ's intended behavior in the church. The premise is clear. If we are united with Christ, as a believer, than our behavior and attitude should reflect it. We should seek to be like-minded, unselfish, humble, looking out for the interests of others, not ourselves. These concepts are relational. We are intended to serve Christ in relationship with others, and for those relationships to work, we must be Philippians 2 believers. (Tracey Allred)

Worship Aids

Pastoral Prayer

Eternal God, you are the God of our parents and our children. You are the God of our past and our future, of our beginning and our ending. Today, we gather in the present to worship you. As we gather, we bring to you our concerns and our burdens. Remind us of your faithfulness, just as you reminded the Israelites on their journey. Remind us of all of the times when you heard us and answered us. We thank you for being a God that participates in our lives, exemplified greatest in the gift of your Son, Jesus Christ. Amen.

Invocation

Oh God, we enter your presence today desiring communion with you. Enter this time of worship. Accept our gift of praise. Abide with us, and show us your way. Amen. (Tracey Allred)

Little Children, Big Lessons

First in a Series of Three on Children, Youth, and Ministry

Luke 18:15-17

As an expectant father, I have been counting the days until I get to hold my little baby. I can't wait to embrace this miracle. I can't wait to gaze into my child's eyes, hold its tiny hands, and see its first smile. I've watched other parents enjoy this moment. I've watched them lose track of time holding their precious baby. These are special moments. Holding and touching a newborn child is significant. Psychologists tell us that babies need to be touched as a crucial part of their development. Babies cannot understand words but they can recognize the cradle of love formed by their parents' arms. Throughout our lives, we will communicate love through touch. Hugs, high fives, and even pats on the back let us know that other people care about us. Touch is a small yet powerful way of expressing our love.

Through the power of touch, Jesus transformed many people who were in need of help and love. When Jesus reached out and touched a leper, or when he placed his hands on the eyes of a blind man, Jesus' love changed their lives. They were healed. They were made whole. Stories such as these circulated and drew people towards Jesus. Even parents brought their children to Jesus so that "he might touch them."

Luke doesn't tell us why parents were bringing their children to Jesus. We do know that the infant mortality rate was considerably higher than what we experience in our country today. Some estimates suggest that one in three infants died during Jesus' lifetime. Disease, famine, and war took many lives. For one reason or another parents were concerned about their children's well-being and believed that Jesus might be able to help. The Gospel of Mark provides an additional clue as to why children were being brought to Jesus. Parents wanted a blessing for their child (see Mark 10:13-16). They wanted to know that they would be rearing their child in a community of love. A blessing from Jesus would communicate just this idea. This kind of blessing would bridge the gap between the family and the community as it conveys that other people are interested in caring and loving our children.

I often receive calls during the week from people inquiring about church programs for their families. They ask if we offer child-friendly activities and nine times out of ten, they want to know if we provide childcare. People are interested in ministries for their children. Church communities should treasure children. We want children to feel loved, but not everyone understands how to meet their needs. If only babies could talk! So when we say we treasure children, we should not only welcome their cute smiles but we must also accept their crying. Some parishioners get agitated with a crying baby in worship, while others jokingly say it is God's way of telling the preacher to wrap up the sermon. Crying babies are a part of life, but for some adults, a crying baby can be a real nuisance.

When parents began bringing their children to Jesus, the disciples felt that this was a disturbance to his work and ministry. So they kept the children away. Perhaps they believed Jesus had more important matters to attend to than the disruption of crying kids. After all, the disciples were just trying to shield Jesus from the unpleasant behaviors that pop up in crowds. But the disciples missed the point. They failed to understand the nature of the kingdom of God. They failed to understand that the kingdom of God is about love and it belongs to those who are like a child.

Like the disciples, our world sometimes pushes children away by not giving them the love they need. Perhaps we just don't understand children. We hear too many stories in our own communities about children who are either neglected or abused. In our schools, teachers can quickly identify the children who haven't received the kind of love they need. These children are the ones who exhibit inappropriate or negative behaviors. They will do anything to get attention, and they inevitably fill the void in their lives with something unhealthy. Neglected and abused children need love more than ever, and it's for this reason that we should live in a way in which children receive blessings instead of mistreatment. We are called to minister to children by being their advocate. Although we have laws that attempt to look out for children, we realize our government cannot do this work alone. As the body of Christ, we are called to look out and care for "the least of these" in our world. Children surely meet this qualification.

It is ironic that the least of these not only teach us about ministry, but they show us the way to the kingdom of God. All of us are invited into this kingdom. We are invited to accept this gift as a child would, because these little ones remind us that receiving the kingdom of God isn't about what we do. It is about God. Our credentials won't get us in because it is God's gift to us. We simply need to recognize our own powerlessness and be ready to receive God's love and blessings. Jesus upholds children to us as the example to follow. Their example teaches us about warmth and freshness and excitement and enthusiasm. We might do well if we embraced any or all of these childlike traits for our lives and ministries. Today we are reminded of Jesus' word that the kingdom of God is at hand. Now let us receive the kingdom as a child would. (Mark White)

Worship Aids

Call to Worship

The kingdom of God has come near. The kingdom has come for all of us. It has come for the lost, the persecuted, and poor in spirit. Let us strive for it and receive the kingdom of God as a child. The kingdom of God is at hand!

Invocation

God of open arms, we run to you with the warmth and enthusiasm of a child. We come to worship you with enthusiasm, for we are grateful for your welcome and the invitation to follow. Now we lift up our voices with excitement and we pray that you will transform us by your word and renew us with your Spirit. Amen.

Benediction

As you depart from this place, may the love of God hold you, may the warmth of Christ guide you, and may the strength of the Spirit release you to care for the children of this world. Amen. (Mark White)

OCTOBER 5, 2008

❧❧❧

Twenty-first Sunday after Pentecost

Readings: Exodus 20:1-4, 7-9, 12-20; Psalm 19; Philippians 3:4b-14; Matthew 21:33-46

The Long Race
Philippians 3:4b-14

The history of my athletic achievement could be written in under a paragraph. Although I enjoy sports, try as I may, I'm not good at them. My one excursion into varsity sports in high school was as a member of the track team. It was the kind of team at my rural high school that any-one could join but not many did. I joined the team as perhaps a last ditch effort to prove to myself that I did have one athletic bone in my body. As it turned out, I did not. Because I could not run particularly fast, jump high or far, or heave any object more than a couple of feet, I was assigned to the long-distance events. All the other strong, fast runners were par-ticipating in other events; so we would not forfeit, I ran the one- and two-mile events each week. My only real memory from those track meets was pain in my gut, wind on my face, and the overwhelming desire to press on and finish every race no matter what. I never won, but I always finished. The Apostle Paul, no doubt, knew the pain of the race, and the over-whelming desire to finish no matter what. Paul suffered consistently for his missionary efforts. Add to his persecution a physical ailment that con-stantly plagued him, and Paul was probably a near expert on perseverance in the face of suffering.

Paul's relationship with the Philippian church began during his second missionary journey. After initially sharing the gospel with them, Paul continued to minister to them personally and through correspondence. Although Acts describes Paul's frequent contact with the Philippians as efforts to encourage them, I cannot help but think that Paul was also encouraged by the relationship. While many early believers and churches struggled morally and theologically, the Philippians were faithful—personally and corporately. They supported and partnered with Paul financially, and partnered physically with individuals from the community, joining Paul to help him.

As a person who has served churches vocationally for a third of my life, I can relate to Paul's feelings for the Philippians. There are times in ministry when the people I was called to serve and teach, served and taught me. Those brothers and sisters in Christ continue to encourage me throughout my life. Paul had that kind of relationship, I think, with the Philippian Christians. With great mutual love and respect, I can imagine that Paul wrote to them with fervency and passion to encourage them in their faith. Although scholars differ on the exact time and place, many presume that Paul was in prison as he wrote this epistle. Throughout the letter, it is obvious that Paul's situation was dismal. Paul was not sure of the outcome, that is, whether or not he would be released. Paul no doubt felt the need to encourage the Philippian Christians as he faced the real possibility that he would not see them again. He wanted their strength and faithfulness to continue regardless of his outcome. Paul also wanted to share his own faith that his death would be victory as he joined Christ.

In our lectionary text, Paul continues his spiritual pep talk to the Philippians. As he likely considers his own mortality, Paul shares with them where his own confidence lies and encourages them to consider the same. Paul shares his own impressive pedigree, one in which many have put their confidence, as one considered loss compared to his faith in Christ. (This reminder would have been good news to the mostly Gentile Philippian church.) Paul then describes his spiritual goal to know Christ better and become more like Christ even in suffering, death, and resurrection.

Verses 12-14 carry me back to the last lap of a two-mile race with the wind burning my face and piercing my lungs with every breath. I remember my cramping legs and stomach, and the backs of all my competitors barely in sight. Not that I have finished yet. Press on. Strain toward the goal. Paul must have felt that he was on the last lap of a long race that he just desperately wanted to finish. He didn't know what his earthly outcome would be or what would count as success, but Paul knew he had to press on. Even more, Paul wanted to make sure that his Philippian brothers and sisters kept their eyes on the prize of Christ Jesus and pressed on, straining toward that goal no matter what.

As twenty-first-century Christians living in the United States, we will most likely not endure the type of persecution experienced by Paul and the other first-century Christians. If we are truly serious about taking hold of that for which Christ took hold of us, however, the race is hard and long. There are few in their Christian walk who honestly sprint easily through their lives as Christians. There are even fewer who sail above the hurdles of life with the ease of a great athlete. For most of us, our lives as Christians consist of one long race. There are times when we are strong and confident and able to run ahead with ease. There are times when we get that little burst of energy we need at just the right time to overcome our opposition. There are other times, however, of pain and discouragement, and real doubt about the outcome of the journey. There are times when life makes it hard to breathe, and one more step seems unbearable. Hear the message of Paul to the Philippians. You're not there yet. Press on. Strain toward the goal. Keep your eye on the prize. As much as I am reminded of my short track career by this passage, there is one major difference. When I close my eyes and envision the race I'm running, I can see my Christ kneeling at the finish line with open arms of love and grace, even if I'm the last one there! (Tracey Allred)

Lectionary Commentary
Exodus 20:1-4, 7-9, 12-20

One of my most daunting tasks as a parent has been having the responsibility to teach my child right from wrong. I honestly did not realize how many rules and lessons there were to learn! Although the endless instruction can be tiring, I know that I must continue if I want my child to grow to be an adult who loves God and other people. I think that God felt that same responsibility with Israel. God wanted them to be people of God who were moral and honorable. The Ten Commandments were a summary of God's expectations for Israel. I love that the first words God spoke before giving the commandments were "I am the LORD your God, who brought you out of the land of Egypt." God knows that being people of God is hard. We are, after all, human. God reminds the Israelites, and us, that God was and is with them.

Matthew 21:33-46

The parable of the tenants is the second in three parables Jesus tells in the presence of the chief priests and Pharisees. Each parable shares the same basic theme. In the parable of the tenants, a landowner sends servants to collect his fruit only to have two sets of servants killed by the tenants. Finally, he sends his son who is also killed. Jesus asks the priests and Pharisees what would then happen to the tenants. Their response is that the tenants will meet a horrible fate, and new tenants will be chosen. Through our Christian lens, this parable is clear. Although it may not have been as clear to the priests and Pharisees, they obviously understood well enough to be angered and want to get Jesus for it. In our own lives, this parable is applicable as a reminder of our own tenant status in the world. As stewards of God's creation, how good is our fruit and are we returning to God what belongs to God? (Tracey Allred)

Worship Aids

Invocation

Almighty God, we humbly seek you this morning. We seek this opportunity to join our brothers and sisters in Christ and enter your presence. We desire to meet you in a way that is authentic and transforming. Enter this place and these people. Accept our gifts of praise and worship. Receive all that we do this day as an offering to you. Amen.

Confession

Oh, Lord our God, you have been faithful in our most faithless moments. As you delivered Israel from Egypt, you daily deliver us from our enemies, both internal and external. We acknowledge in this moment the many times we have failed you this week. We acknowledge the times we have ignored your commandments and will for our lives. In the words of the psalmist, "Restore us O God Almighty: make your face shine upon us, that we may be saved."

Words of Assurance

Thank you, gracious God of restoration and healing. Amen.
(Tracey Allred)

Be Transformed: Renew Your Mind

Second in a Series of Three on Children, Youth, and Ministry

Luke 2:41-52

By the time children approach adolescence, their bodies are doing all sorts of new things. Clothes and shoes don't fit for long. Voices and attitudes change. Independence and self-assurance develop. Preteens and teenagers also begin to distance themselves from their parents. It's not cool to hang out with your parents when you're twelve or sixteen. Parenting an adolescent puts into perspective all previous parenting challenges. But families still find ways to unite and appreciate each other's gifts. Occasionally they recognize that they can still learn from one another.

Growing up in an intergenerational household, I not only had my parents around but also a grandfather. Aunts, uncles, and cousins were not far away either. At least once a year we would have some kind of family reunion like a Christmas gathering or a vacation at the beach. These large family gatherings were sacred times because they provided opportunities for us to tell stories, enjoy games, and act out plays. Kids would learn from the adults, and the adults would learn from the kids. I have grown to appreciate the gifts and blessings of my intergenerational upbringing. I value what I learned.

When Jesus and his family traveled to Jerusalem for the Passover, I imagine that the group they traveled with included some close friends and extended family. I also imagine that they engaged in similar reunion activities. Enjoying one another's company would have made the journey memorable. Time together was as important for the adults as it was for the children. On my own family beach trips, date nights were created where one set of parents would have a free evening while the other adults took over the parenting responsibilities. Perhaps Mary and Joseph had other parents in their group watching Jesus, as they began their homeward journey. All the text tells us is that they assumed Jesus was in the group of travelers, but then, at some point, they realized Jesus was missing.

When Mary and Joseph find Jesus, they discover that he has been at the temple for three days listening and asking questions of the teachers. Jesus went to the temple to learn. It's not clear if Jesus was teaching the teachers, but this precocious twelve-year-old was engaged in intergenerational education. Jesus found value in learning from his elders, and vice versa. As the text states, "all who heard him were amazed at his understanding and his answers." Jesus went to the temple to train in the Torah and to fulfill God's calling on his life. He went to the temple, to his Father's house, so that he might fulfill God's work.

Jesus was an inquisitive adolescent as are many youth. He knew the temple would be an ideal place for learning and discussing the ways of God. As is the case for Jesus and for us all, the adolescent years are a time for us to raise questions and test ideas. The temple facilitated this kind of learning for Jesus. In our time, the church should be a safe place of learning where we can test ideas in order that we might grow in our faith. Community is a crucial part in this learning process because it exposes us to new ideas and helps us rethink our own positions and beliefs. It also provides us with the necessary checks and balances that are in place for our protection.

We need intergenerational communities where the young can learn from the old, and the old can learn from the young. Learning and testing ideas at any age involves risk, exploration, and freedom—including the freedom to make mistakes. Intergenerational communities that embrace learning and discovery recognize that God's presence is in each person, whatever his or her age. They validate what the Spirit of God may be saying in every person's life.

Jesus spent his first twelve years of life searching and learning; the community Jesus found at the temple was vital in this process. Jesus moved through the process of self-discovery, embracing the identity God had given. It's important that our church communities also encourage all people, but especially teenagers, to strive for understanding so that they might uncover their God-given identity. Jesus found his identity in his relationship with God. God has claimed our lives too.

We might not always understand God's claim on our lives, but all of us, young and old, can continue to learn from the example of Jesus. Mary and Joseph didn't always understand Jesus. Luke reminds us that among other things they misunderstood was his trip to the temple. They were logically upset at his disappearance, but when Mary reprimanded him saying, "Child, why have you treated us like this?" it is as if they had forgotten what God had communicated to them at the time of his birth. Had they forgotten that Jesus was the Son of God? We are not unlike Mary and Joseph. We misunderstand things and we even misinterpret Jesus' life. So we all have room to learn. The Apostle Paul most clearly stated this idea as he talked about transformation. As followers of Jesus Christ, we want to be transformed and this happens when we seek "the renewing of [our] minds" (Romans 12:2). Renew your mind and you shall be transformed. (Mark White)

Worship Aids

Invocation

Almighty God, Creator of this world, we rejoice in the beauty of this earth and the beauty within each other. We are thankful that your Spirit works in people of all ages, inspiring us to do great things. We pray that through this worship you will draw us near to you, that we might learn your ways. Amen.

Prayer of Confession

Merciful God, we have not always understood your ways. Out of our ignorance, we have sinned against you and against others. Forgive us, Lord. Help us learn. Teach us your ways and renew our minds so that we might be transformed into a new creation. Amen.

Words of Assurance

In the name of Jesus Christ, you are forgiven.
In the name of Jesus Christ, you are forgiven. Amen.

Benediction

God grant you an open mind and a loving heart. God bless you to embrace your identity. God be with you wherever you go. Now go forth to serve God as you serve others. (Mark White)

OCTOBER 12, 2008

Twenty-second Sunday after Pentecost

Readings: Exodus 32:1-14; Psalm 106:1-6, 19-23; Philippians 4:1-9;
Matthew 22:1-14

Prepare to Be Chosen
Matthew 22:1-14

There is a visual image of Jesus that I've had since I was a child.
Whether based on an actual picture I've seen or created in my own childhood imagination, it is an illustration for the phrase "gentle Savior." Jesus
is sitting on a grassy hillside, surrounded by children and lambs. It is a
warm, fuzzy image of Christ that is comforting and sweet. Although I'm
sure that reality differed significantly from my childhood image, I also
believe that there were times during Jesus' life on earth that Jesus exuded
that same sweetness and comfort. After all, people of all ages were drawn
to him. In the period between the triumphal entry to Jerusalem and the
anointing by Mary as recorded in the Gospel of Matthew, however, sweet
and comforting were not words to describe Jesus. Jesus was on a mission,
never holding back. Not that Jesus was prone to soft-peddling his ideas,
but during that last week, he shared his message loud and clear. Although
each of the Gospels includes a period of teaching by Jesus during the last
week of his life, Matthew has Jesus speaking directly to certain issues,
using object lessons, and most of all, telling parables.

The parable at the beginning of Matthew 22 follows a busy chapter. In
Matthew 21, Jesus enters Jerusalem, overturns the tables in the temple,
curses the fig tree, has an altercation with the temple officials as they
question his authority, and tells two parables to make his point loud and
clear to those who are questioning him. By verses 45 and 46, the chief
priests and Pharisees have had enough. Perhaps it is my childhood imagination again, but when I read those verses I imagine the chief priests and
Pharisees blowing their tops much like Yosemite Sam in the old cartoons

when Sam was outsmarted by Bugs Bunny. They began looking for a way to get Jesus, but they were afraid of the crowd. As a preacher I have never excited my audience to the point that they were plotting on how to get rid of me. I must admit, however, in all of my humanness, that if this did occur after my first two illustrations, I probably would not share my third one. Jesus kept on preaching. The story he shares in 22:1-14 is enough to push the Pharisees right over the edge from wishing they could get rid of him to planning their trap.

Jesus preached in a way to which everyone could relate. Even as he shared brand new ideas and theology, Jesus framed them in stories of everyday life that anyone could understand. That said, viewing these stories from outside of the culture can be a little confusing. The parable of the wedding banquet is a parable tricky to our modern world. My wedding reception was not nearly as complicated as the one in the story! Nonetheless, Jesus told the story of the wedding banquet as our image of the kingdom of God. In the parable, a king has prepared a wedding banquet for his son, and when it was prepared, he sent out his servants to alert the invited guests that the feast was ready. They paid no attention, and while a couple of them just went on with what they were doing, the majority of them seized the servants and killed them. This, of course, enraged the king who sent out his army, destroyed the murderers and burned their city.

This story suggests a lesson—if the king has invites you as his guest, come when he calls. Any other response is unacceptable. As the Pharisees and chief priests listened, I imagine their blood boiled. Aside from the apocalyptic aspect of this story, there was a clear reference to those who were chosen by God—Israel—but who refused and even mistreated their servants, the prophets, and finally Jesus. The outcome of their refusal is destruction. I wonder if the priests and Pharisees were even listening as Jesus went on, but he continued the parable perhaps more for the crowd who had gathered. After burning the city, the king sent his servants to collect whomever they could find for the banquet. They were sent to street corners to gather the good and the bad, and the wedding hall was filled with guests. One guest, however, was not wearing proper wedding attire, and he was thrown out of the banquet into the darkness.

At this point, the story gets even more complicated. Perhaps Jesus was making a side note in his sermon for the crowd. Although the original invited guests were expected to merely show up, perhaps in the second group there were higher expectations. Although whomever the servants found was welcome, the individuals were expected to be adequately prepared for the banquet. In other words, there was an expectation of change from the time the new guests were picked off the street to the time they came into the presence of the king.

Although this parable is full of gems of truth, I'd like to focus mainly on the second set of guests and the end of the parable. After all, as Gentiles, this is where we come into the story. Being an evangelical Christian, I believe that God meets us wherever we are, and desires our presence in the kingdom no matter our pedigree or background. As a matter of fact, I have heard the phrase "come as you are" throughout my life as God's invitation to all of us. Come as we are. God wants us however we are.

The king in the parable chose the new guests based on nothing more than their status as warm bodies, but he had the expectation that they would come to the wedding banquet prepared for the wedding; the king expected a change. I think that God expects a change, too. Yes, God wants us as we are, imperfect sinners in an imperfect world. When we accept the invitation, however, there are some things that we need to change to prepare ourselves for God's presence. That is not a popular concept in a world of gray morality and even grayer theology. Yet, the message of the parable is clear. Many are invited, few are chosen. May we live lives of self-examination, carefully preparing ourselves for the presence of God. Amen. (Tracey Allred)

Lectionary Commentary
Exodus 32:1-14

I believe that this passage might well be subtitled "What Was Aaron Thinking?" Although the Israelites proved to be often spiritually wishy-washy, this text is still surprising after all that they've been through with their Lord. Even as Moses and the Lord talked about the Lord's plan for the chosen people of Israel, they were smelting their jewelry and creating an idol of their own. Although I am admittedly quick to judge the Israelites, I'm not sure we are all that different. There are times in our spiritual life that it is clear that God is with us. There are other times when, for whatever reason, God seems distant. In those times, instead of seeking God fervently, many times we look for something else that seems more attainable. Temporary fixes and false gods always leave us empty and separated from God.

Philippians 4:1-9

Even as Paul wrote to the Philippians, his own physical future was uncertain. I can imagine Paul repeating these verses to himself even as he wrote. The words were important for Paul as well as for the Philippian community. No matter the circumstances, rejoice, do not be anxious, pray, and the peace of the God will guard your hearts and minds. What a beautiful promise! What a great formula for life! No matter what's going on in your life, rejoice. Praise God even when you don't feel like praising. Do not be anxious but pray about everything. In doing these things, accept the peace of God that transcends all understanding. (Tracey Allred)

Worship Aids

Prayer of Confession

O gracious Christ, we are mindful this day of the many occasions
    in our lives when we do not heed your invitation.
For the times you have called, and we have ignored you,
We confess our sin to you.
For the times, we have blatantly refused and neglected you,
We confess our sin to you.
For the times we're not prepared to be the person of God you call
    us to be,
We confess our sin to you.

Words of Assurance

From the depths of our sin and neglect, you still desire our presence and offer redemption. Thanks be to God for grace and forgiveness, invitation and acceptance. Amen.

Benediction

As we leave this place, may the words of the Apostle Paul guide our journey: "Rejoice in the Lord always. I will say it again: Rejoice! Let your gentleness be evident to all. The Lord is near. Do not be anxious about anything, but in everything, by prayer and petition, with thanksgiving, present your requests to God. And the peace of God, which transcends all understanding, will guard your hearts and your minds in Christ Jesus" (Philippians 4:4-7 NIV). Amen. (Tracey Allred)

Holding the Towel: The Value of Sharing

Third in a Series of Three on Children, Youth, and Ministry

John 13:1-20

Most children learn at an early age the virtue of sharing. It is a value parents instill in their children so they might grow up to be model citizens and respected Christians. Sharing stretches into all realms of life. As parents, we want our children to play well, and that means teaching them to share their toys. We want our children to be friendly, and that means teaching them to share their friends. We want our children to be generous, and that means teaching them to share an offering at church. Lessons like these will last longer than childhood and go beyond adolescence. Teaching a person to share lasts a lifetime.

We know it is a good thing to share but many Christians today are faced with a dilemma. We live in a consumerist society and our culture tells us that we should be looking out for number one. Our culture is about competition. It's about winning. Sharing doesn't seem to fit into the equation. We're told to protect our ideas and our interests, and that may mean keeping certain resources or information away from others, mainly our competitors. Actions like these rest on the belief that sharing doesn't help us succeed. Are we teaching our young people to resist sharing in this competitive world?

Churches are tempted to join the consumerist culture by playing the competitive game. We compare our congregation to the one down the street. We want to be like the "successful" church overflowing with members. We might even consider copying their formula for ministry so we can better compete in the religious marketplace.

Even Jesus' disciples fell victim to this kind of temptation. During a trip to Capernaum, they were arguing about who would be the greatest (see Mark 9:33-37). It was an argument about competition. The disciples didn't always understand Jesus and the nature of his work. We don't always understand either. So it's not surprising to us that when Jesus attempted to wash Peter's feet, Peter exclaimed, "You will never wash my feet." Peter did not think it was right for Jesus to serve him.

Foot washing was a standard custom known to Jesus and the disciples. The common practice was for hosts to offer guests water so they might wash their own feet. In some cases, a slave may have performed this task. Regardless of who performed the act, foot washing was a gesture of hospitality and good hygiene. A person's feet after a journey on a dusty road would be awfully dirty. Having one's feet washed not only helped a person feel clean, but also at home.

Jesus loved his disciples "to the end" and wanted to demonstrate his love for them through the act of foot washing and ultimately through the cross. Jesus broke with traditional custom by assuming the roles of both host and servant to his disciples. Holding a towel, Jesus kneels to clean their feet so that he might teach them about service and about sharing. But foot washing is about more than mere cleanliness; it is about accepting God's gift of hospitality. We embrace this gift of hospitality when we are willing to share in the ministry of Jesus Christ.

Ministry should not be territorial. Jesus knew that all things come from God and that includes the ministries of our congregations and denominations. There is little need to control "my ministry." We share in ministry together. We help each other as we share the good news of Christ with other people. There's a paradox in Christian ministry. Christian leadership is most effective when our leaders lead by serving and sharing. Just as the disciples shared in the work of Jesus, we share in the work of God when we serve together as a community of ministry rather than as lone individuals attempting to fulfill personal goals.

God shares ministry with us because we are God's hands and feet on this earth. When we share in ministry, we recognize that God is much bigger than us, but it isn't easy work. Sharing involves risk. We risk failure when we share ministry. We risk losing control and having the ministry we adore move in a different direction from our desire. Yet if we choose not to share our ministries with others, we assume a different set of risks. When we fail to share our ministries, we set a negative example about God's work for it communicates that this work is exclusive. When we choose to not share our ministries, we limit ideas. These kinds of limits convey a selfishness that isn't willing to listen to what the Spirit of God may be saying through other people and other opinions.

Churches must be willing to share ministry if they are truly interested in a healthy and bright future. Churches must share ministry with people of all ages, young and old alike. It's true that many churches minister to children and youth by loving them, teaching them, and talking to them about ministry. But churches should also go a step further and provide opportunities for young people to love others, educate others, and share in the ministries of the congregation.

The disciples had spent much of their time ministering to the needs of other people. When Jesus washed their feet, he taught them to accept the ministries others offer them. Christians of all ages should follow this example of service. We are all called to serve in some unique way and we should, likewise, be willing to accept the unique ministries of others, especially when it helps us embrace God's gift of hospitality. (Mark White)

Worship Aids

Invocation

Loving and Holy God, you welcome us with warmth and generosity. Your presence moves our hearts and touches our souls. We celebrate that you are in our midst, and we praise you for your gifts of kindness and hospitality. Through this worship, may we learn from the example of Jesus to be just as generous by sharing our whole lives with you and other people. Amen.

Prayer of Confession

Gracious God, you bestow on us blessing after blessing, but we have come up short by not following the example of Christ. We have hoarded our possessions and acted in selfish ways. We need your forgiveness. Extend your hand of mercy on our lives, Lord. May we learn that it is through serving and sharing that we are set free. Amen.

Words of Assurance

In the name of Jesus Christ, you are forgiven.
In the name of Jesus Christ, you are forgiven. Amen.

Benediction

O Lord, you have shared abundantly with us. May we also go forth with a generous spirit to share freely with others the good news we have in Jesus Christ. May we share with others in this ministry of word and deed. Amen. (Mark White)

OCTOBER 19, 2008

Twenty-third Sunday after Pentecost

Readings: Exodus 33:12-23; Psalm 99; 1 Thessalonians 1:1-10; Matthew 22:15-22

The Things That Are God's
Matthew 22:15-22

Once someone stole checks out of my mailbox, washed the checks, filled in new names and amounts, and pocketed the money. Beyond the irritation of sorting the mess out, I couldn't help wondering how successful these people might be if they put their ingenuity and energies into constructive purposes. Perhaps Jesus had the same thoughts about the Pharisees as they constantly sought to entrap him and turn the people against him. Although we are accustomed to think of the Pharisees as hypocrites, religious leaders bereft of understanding and insight into God's plan for Israel, they played an indispensable part in the life of the community. As teachers of the law, they studied Torah and helped the people understand the demands of their faith. How then could they be so blind to who Jesus was? How had they so thoroughly lost their way? How had they lost the people they were supposed to teach and shepherd?

The people loved Jesus; there was no denying that. They loved his candor, his simple approach to complex religious obligations, and his acceptance of the "less holy" members of society. They were drawn to his indefinable sense of power and authority—an authority that came, not from simply knowing Scripture, like the Pharisees and other teachers of the law, but from an inner compass, a direct connection with the divine. The Pharisees knew and understood this all too well. Some resented Jesus for it. Some even hated him for it.

But the Pharisees also knew that while the people loved Jesus, they hated their Roman occupiers even more. No one who supported the occupation of Israel could command the people's respect, much less allegiance.

Thus the Pharisees and the followers of Herod schemed to entrap Jesus: "Teacher, we know that you are sincere, and teach the way of God in accordance with truth, and show deference to no one; for you do not regard people with partiality. Tell us, then, what you think. Is it lawful to pay taxes to the emperor, or not?" With these words Jesus was trapped, and they knew it. If Jesus answered that it was okay to pay taxes to the emperor of Rome, the people would turn on him. If Jesus answered that it was not okay, he was guilty of sedition against Rome, and could be arrested for disloyalty to the empire. Either way, the cleverness of their scheme and carefully constructed question had surely finished Jesus for good.

Only an odd thing happened. Knowing the craftiness and malice in their hearts, Jesus turned the tables on his questioners, and asked them to produce the coin used to pay the tax. After producing a denarius and acknowledging that the emperor's head and title were on the coin, the Pharisees received this sage pronouncement from Jesus: "Give therefore to the emperor the things that are the emperor's, and to God the things that are God's." Stunned that their apparent victory had been dashed in so public a manner, the Pharisees went away amazed.

Although Matthew does not record where this exchange took place, Luke does, and it's important. Jesus is questioned while teaching at the temple (Luke 20:20-26). When this piece of information is taken into account, the Pharisees' defeat is much worse. While there was some disagreement among Jesus' followers about the relative evil of paying taxes to Rome, there was no disagreement whatsoever about the evils of breaking the second commandment—the commandment against graven images. According to Rome, the emperor was a god, so carrying around a denarius in one's coin purse was carrying around a graven image. To own such a coin was a necessary evil to pay one's taxes. To carry such coins into the temple was sacrilegious.

Israel had developed a system of money changers to convert Roman money into coins suitable for use in the temple. You simply could not pay tribute to God with coins bearing the emperor's head and title. As protectors of the faith, the Pharisees knew this. So did Jesus' followers. The moment the Pharisees produced the denarius in the temple, the attempt to discredit Jesus had failed, and failed spectacularly—even before Jesus' pronouncement: to give to the emperor the things are the emperor's, and to give to God the things that are God's.

As the Pharisees went away amazed, did Jesus' words continue to ring in their ears? Did they wonder if they had been outsmarted by a simple carpenter, or did they begin to see that they had been in the presence of some-one who truly understood the things that belong to God? We don't know. Matthew doesn't tell us. But one thing we do know, just as the thieves who stole checks from my mailbox were looking for an easy solution to their problems, the Pharisees had not sought to understand Jesus and learn from him; they had sought the easy solution—to discredit Jesus, rather than try to understand what he truly had to say. Perhaps as teachers of the Torah, what the Pharisees really owed God was the will to see the Torah at work in peo-ple's lives. For when they saw tax collectors repent, prostitutes turn from their ways, and the blind receive their sight, surely they could have beheld in Jesus one through whom the Torah took flesh and gave life to the people?

What does this story have to teach us? Are we like the Pharisees, want-ing to see the downfall of our adversaries? Or have we learned to thank God for those who teach us what we most need to learn? Do we know what we owe God? Since you're in church, you surely know we owe God our thankfulness and praise. Although it's hard to do, we know that we owe God an offering of our time, talent, and treasure. But more than that, we, like the Pharisees, owe God the humility to have an open mind and an open heart when we meet those who share God's words and works in ways that seem foreign. We owe God the conviction not to take the easy road, the familiar road, at the expense of journeys that lead to newness of life: for others and for ourselves. We owe God a willingness to love those who teach us lessons we do not wish to learn. (B. J. Beu)

Lectionary Commentary
Exodus 33:12-23

Having found favor in the Lord's sight, Moses pleads that God will be not just with him but with all the people. Even in the presence of God's assurances, "My presence will go with you." Moses presses the advantage on behalf of the community: "If your presence will not go, do not carry us up from here." From the moment they left Egypt, Moses consistently pleads on behalf of the people. The one thing Moses requests for himself is to behold God's glory, which God grants, but only from behind—for no one shall see God's face and live.

1 Thessalonians 1:1-10

In Paul's salutation to the church of Thessalonica, Paul gives thanks to God for the faithful and reminds them of how far they have come as believers in the gospel. Since the message of the gospel came not only in word, but also in the power of the Holy Spirit to transform their very lives, they have become an example to others who are coming to believe. In other words, others are watching; live up to your calling. (B. J. Beu)

Worship Aids

Call to Worship (Psalm 99)

The Lord is king; let the peoples tremble!
The Lord sits enthroned upon the cherubim; let the earth quake!
Extol the Lord; worship at God's footstool.
All: We will worship the Lord, for our God is holy.

Prayer (Matthew 22)

Merciful God, forgive us when we delight in our cleverness and miss the simple truths you would teach us. Help us see in others what we strive to find in ourselves. Open our hearts to the bounty you have given us that we may freely give of ourselves to others, in your holy name. Amen.

Benediction (Psalm 99)

The one who sits enthroned with the cherubim blesses us with justice.
Thanks be to God!
The one who teaches us the ways of life and death forgives all our wrongs.
Thanks be to God!
The one who gave us Jesus Christ blesses us with eternal life.
Thanks be to God!
(B. J. Beu)

What Is a Traditional Church?

First in a Series of Two on the Tradition of the Church

Matthew 16:13-20

A few years ago I received a phone call from a newspaper reporter who was writing a story on what he described as "nontraditional churches." He wanted to know what I thought about such churches. I answered by asking a series of questions, "What do you mean by 'nontraditional'? Are you talking about churches that are theologically unorthodox, churches that have a different worship style, or churches that meet in nontraditional buildings?" As you would imagine, he had no idea how to answer. What he had was a lot of questions.

Today, more than ever, Christians and non-Christians alike are asking questions about the church. Did Jesus envision an institutional church? Should the church reflect its culture or be countercultural? What is the mission of the church? In what kinds of activities ought the church to be engaged? Do we need the institutional church? Because many of these questions have gone unanswered, many folks who grew up in the church have reverted to a new mantra, "I'm spiritual, but not religious," by which they mean, "I don't belong to or attend a local church." I'm convinced that they might come back to church if Christians took their questions seriously and made a concerted effort to answer their questions.

If we are to answer these questions, it seems appropriate to study a passage of Scripture where Jesus uses the word *church*, which in Greek is *ecclesia*. Before looking at our selected text it is important to note some significant facts concerning Jesus and the church. First, Jesus went to church. Jesus was a part of an *ecclesia*, a fellowship that worshiped God. He worshiped in local synagogues and with his disciples. Second, Jesus felt free to observe and criticize the church—their hypocrisy and sincerity, their pride and humility, their selfishness and generosity. Jesus even watched when people made their contributions. Third, Jesus felt free to institute new traditions for the church such as the Model Prayer and the Lord's Supper. Fourth, Jesus emphasized discipleship and community. He stressed the need for individual commitment, but Jesus also stressed the importance of belonging to the community—the *ecclesia* that Jesus had created.

What this gospel text makes clear is that the central question for any church is: *Who is Jesus of Nazareth?* The way that we answer that question will dictate the kind of church that we want and the kind of church we will have. The reason many people are not happy in their church is that they interpret Jesus differently than the rest of their faith community. We are obligated to answer the question that Jesus asked his disciples, "Who do you say that I am?" We must answer this question individually, but local congregations must also answer it.

Peter's confession of Jesus as the Messiah was an act of faith. His confession explains the heart of the Christian faith—that Jesus is the promised Savior and the divine Son of the living God. The paradox of confession is revealed in Jesus' words to Peter. Jesus blesses Peter for his insight, but insists that this insight was a gift from God. We exercise our free will in choosing Christ, but God chooses us first.

What are we to make of Jesus' comment to Peter, "On this rock I will build my church?" At the very least it is a claim by Jesus to be the builder of the church. There are many Christians and non-Christians who doubt that Jesus intended to establish an institution. Even if you want to dismiss this passage of scripture, it is difficult to deny that Jesus did create a community of faith. It began with the twelve and extended out to other disciples who accepted Jesus' teachings and tried to follow his example. Jesus described this community as a building or temple. The image of the church as a building is used throughout the New Testament and Jesus is affirmed as its foundation and cornerstone. Believers are described as building blocks and Jesus is acknowledged as the builder. This text affirms that he is so skilled as a builder that the church will stand all assaults. Even "the gates of Hades will not prevail against it."

Is the church of the twenty-first century the *ecclesia* that Jesus envisioned? If we confess with Peter that Jesus is the Christ and the Son of the living God, then we are. The keys of the kingdom then become ours as we share with others the way into God's kingdom.

This traditional affirmation is what makes a church "traditional," because it has affirmed what has been believed at all times and in all places by orthodox Christians. Other affirmations may be important, but this affirmation is central. It is this affirmation that should unite us with other Christians whose styles of worship and way of "doing church" may be radically different from ours. The unity that results is what Jesus prayed in the seventeenth chapter of John.

Recently, our congregation had a joint Maundy Thursday worship service with a congregation of another denomination. They had preconceived notions about us and we had preconceived notions about them. Their worship was contemporary; ours was traditional. They had one label on their church sign and we had another. They drew their congregation from one socioeconomic group and we drew ours from another. We were different. The other pastor and I hoped that we could overcome our preconceptions. That didn't happen with the preaching, singing, or praying, but when we began to wash one another's feet, those preconceptions were all blown away. It was a reminder that our faith is not in some denominational label, style of worship, or social class, but in a Savior who taught us the meaning of servant leadership. (Philip D. Wise)

Worship Aids

Invocation

Lord, you have called us into this community and you have called us today into this house of worship. May we respond to your call by offering our very best in worship through Jesus Christ our Lord.

Call to Worship

The light of Christ will enlighten our worship.
The joy of Christ will echo in our praise.
The friendship of Christ will bind us together in community.
The teachings of Christ will shape our thinking.
The example of Christ will guide our actions.
**Lord, may our faithful commitment to Christ shine through
this service.**

Prayer of Confession and Intercession

Loving God, each week at this time in the service we're scheduled to confess our sins. As you well know, we don't always do that. Sometimes we're too distracted by the people around us. Sometimes we're too tired from the events of Saturday. Often, we just can't focus on confession.

It's not that we think we're too good for confession or that we have no sins to confess. No, Lord, we know that we've messed up. We know that we are not all that you want us to be. So today hear our confession of sins. (*Pause for silent confession of sins.*)

Lord, we would be awfully selfish if we prayed for ourselves and not for others. Although that's what we often do, we don't do it today. We pray for our families. We pray for our friends. We pray for our country. We pray for our world. Lord, let a fresh breath of your Holy Spirit blow over their lives, this land, and this planet where you've placed us.

Words of Assurance

In the name of Jesus Christ, you are forgiven.
In the name of Jesus Christ, you are forgiven. Amen.

Benediction

God always waits to lift our burdens, forgive our mistakes, and fill our emptiness. Go now to share this good news with all who need it, and may God's love surround you, Christ's peace dwell in you, and the Spirit's breath fill you with the freshness of new life. (Philip D. Wise)

OCTOBER 26, 2008

❧❧❧

Twenty-fourth Sunday after Pentecost/Reformation

Readings: Deuteronomy 34:1-12; Psalm 90:1-6, 13-17;
1 Thessalonians 2:1-8; Matthew 22:34-46

The Great Commandment Times Two
Matthew 22:34-46

The Pharisees were back at it again—putting Jesus to the test, trying to stump him before the crowds. This time a lawyer asked the question: "Teacher, which commandment in the law is the greatest?" As questions go, this softball toss across the home plate was probably intended to loosen Jesus up for trickier questions to follow. Jewish teaching on this subject was clear and absolute, and Jesus knew it well: "'You shall love the Lord your God with all your heart, and with all your soul, and with all your mind.' This is the greatest commandment" (see also Deuteronomy 6:5). Before the lawyer could follow up, however, Jesus continued: "And a second is like it: 'You shall love your neighbor as yourself.' On these two commandments hang all the law and the prophets."

This reply was as brilliant as it was simple. Even if the Pharisees recognized the obscure saying from Leviticus, it is doubtful that they would have elevated it to the status of a commandment, much less put it on par with the great commandment. And yet, once seen, its truth is inescapable. Jesus' genius was not that he created new doctrines that wowed the people, nor was it his ability to preach interesting sermons. Jesus' genius was his clarity of vision—his ability to distill Israel's complex cultic life to its core essence. With breathtaking clarity, Jesus is able to simplify the complex. We might say he was able to see the forest for the trees.

Nowhere is this clarity seen more clearly than in his response to the lawyer's question. Unless a reader is really paying attention, it's easy to read right over the kernel of truth Jesus quotes from Leviticus, coming as it does in the midst of a plodding, mendacious discussion of how to properly offer sacrifices, harvest a vineyard, pay servants, or choose an appropriate bed partner. The admonition even comes at the tail end of a verse, in a subordinate clause no less: "You shall not take vengeance or bear a grudge against any of your people, but you shall love your neighbor as yourself: I am the LORD" (Leviticus 19:18). Yet, Jesus saw that this insignificant-sounding pearl of wisdom supported the teachings of Torah and the prophets. It is not enough to love God. Loving God does not give us a free pass to hate our brother, sister, or neighbor—because God is in our brother, sister, and neighbor. The image of God is in each one of us. If we take the incarnation seriously, we affirm that to understand the fullness of God, we embrace and love our humanity. We cannot fully embrace and love our humanity unless we know the one who made us and who put the image of God within.

We cannot love God with our whole heart, soul, strength, and might if we do not love our neighbor. It would be like saying, "I love the poet T. S. Eliot; I just hate all his poems." If Eliot's soul is in his poetry, how much more of God's Spirit do we find in the works of God's hands? The truth of Jesus' pronouncement strikes as all true epiphanies do—how could we have failed to see it before?

The Pharisees were evidently silenced by this insight. When Jesus showed these "learned" teachers that they didn't even understand who the Messiah would be—they thought the Messiah would be David's son, as Jesus observed that David himself calls the Messiah "Lord"—Jesus silenced them completely.

When I was young, I had the great fortune of having a pastor who understood that the gospel was all about love. He would lead us in the singing of that delightful song: "Love, love, love, love, the gospel in a word is love; love your neighbor as your brother; love, love, love." As a child, to know that God is all about love was a great comfort. As I've grown older, however, Jesus' commandment to love does not bring me as much comfort. In fact, it makes me decidedly uncomfortable. It's one thing to know that God loves us unconditionally; it is quite another to realize that in the final judgment, our ability to love others is the ultimate barometer of how we love Jesus. Jesus doesn't seem to care that our theology is sufficiently up to snuff, or that we attended church regularly. No, what Jesus seems to really care about is whether we have seen the image of God in the least of our sisters and brothers, and have loved them as such. When we see the homeless sleeping on park benches and warm our grates, do we see Christ, or do we see something less? Do we become something less?

But Jesus' radical call to love does not end there. Jesus calls us to love and see the divine image even in our enemies. In terms of worldly logic, this makes no sense at all. It just seems foolish to try to love your enemies—enemies who may hate you or even want to kill you. But in terms of the soul, Jesus' call to love is the only thing that does make sense—it really is all or nothing. Paul can say that in the divine wrap up, "God will be all in all" because God is all in all. If we cannot see God in all things, we fail to perceive God. We may see beauty, power, and majesty, but it will not be God. If God is in our enemies, how can we not love them?

The Pharisees knew all the words of Scripture, but perhaps without knowing their deeper meaning. They knew that we are called to love God with all our heart, soul, and might. But they failed to recognize that one cannot love God if one does not love the neighbor. Perhaps the Pharisees can be excused. But we can't. We know we have no excuse for acting as if we don't know any better. We do. Will we act in love, or will we hold on to our fears and grievances? Ultimately, whether or not it makes sense to love our neighbors and our enemies, this I know; without this love, our lives do not make sense. They only make sense in God—the God who is love itself. (B. J. Beu)

Lectionary Commentary
Deuteronomy 34:1-12

At the end of his life, God leads Moses up Mount Nebo to view the land that had been promised to Abraham, Isaac, and Jacob—a land that Moses would not be allowed to enter. Moses stands alone as a prophet, unsurpassed in the signs and wonders he performed, unique in that God knew him face to face. And yet, God showed Moses the promised land and kept him from entering because of the people's sin. We should not expect the fulfillments of God's promises to come to us, or even in our lifetime. God's time line is rarely ours, and God's favor will not override other concerns. Yet, God's promises are sure, and while Moses died before entering the promised land, God raised up Joshua to carry on in his place.

1 Thessalonians 2:1-8

Paul proclaims that his works in the church have not been in vain. Indeed, although he had suffered and been shamefully mistreated at Philippi, this treatment had not deterred Paul from proclaiming the gospel to the church in Thessalonica—for his message had been entrusted by Christ, and it was to Christ that Paul was accountable. Paul offers himself as an example, not out of a desire for human reward or approval, but because God had given Paul the duty to do so. Even if persecuted for one's teaching, we are led to do so out of love for one another. (B. J. Beu)

Worship Aids

Call to Worship (Matthew 22)

People of God, whom do you love?
We love the Lord our God with all our heart, soul, and mind.
People of God, whom do you love?
We love our neighbors even as we love ourselves.
People of God, whom do you love?
All: We love the One who calls us and completes us in holy love.

Prayer (Matthew 22)

Eternal God, your patient love is like a mighty glacier, slowly pushing aside all that stands before it. Be patient with us as we learn to love our neighbor as we love ourselves. Nurture us in your healing love, that we may be known as a people whose love for others knows no bounds, through Jesus Christ, our Lord. Amen.

Benediction Litany (Matthew 22)

God's love has set us free.
God's love is upon us.
God love has made us whole.
God's love moves within us.
God's love has called us to witness to a world in pain.
God's love sends us forth.
Go with God's blessings. (B. J. Beu)

Is Religion a Private Matter?

Second in a Series of Two on the Tradition of the Church

Acts 2:42-47

It is a given in our world that individuals can have their own autonomous spiritual beliefs and practices. For those who believe in God, there is an almost unanimous agreement that one can have a relationship with God. There is, however, some considerable disagreement about whether this relationship should remain a private matter. The old gospel song "On the Jericho Road" expresses what many Christians believe: "On the Jericho Road, there's room for just two, / no more and no less, just Jesus and you."

For Christians, it is impossible for faith to be merely private. To begin it is impossible to become a Christian without the help of others. A person becomes a Christian through the witness of parents, friends, preachers, and so on. The Christian message would not be available to us without the continuing witness of the church through the ages, the translation and dissemination of the Bible, and the witness of Christian writers and evangelists. Even those who come to faith through a mystical experience with God do not become isolated believers.

At the end of Acts 2, Luke gives us the clearest picture we have of the life, faith, and practices of the early church. The message of Jesus, which Jesus proclaimed and was proclaimed by his disciples, was an invitation. It was an invitation to eternal life, but it was also an invitation to join a community—a family of faith.

One cannot be a Christian in isolation. You may be a believer and isolate yourself. You may not join a local congregation or attend public worship services. You may not talk to others about your faith or participate in any public religious ceremonies. Nevertheless, you are still a part of the Christian church, which is God's family and the body of Christ.

Luke says, "All who believed were together" (2:2). Wouldn't it be wonderful if that could be said about the Christian church today? Although there is a deep desire among Christians for unity among believers, it is still a distant dream. We do see some glimmers of hope as Christians cross denominational lines to help those in need. What would happen if Christians began to act in unison? Could we cooperate instead of compete? Could we compliment instead of criticize? Would we seek to serve instead of being served? How can this happen? The formula is found in this brief passage.

Unity begins in sharing. Luke writes they "had all things in common." When we consider the aspects of our faith that matter most, it's simply true that they all belong to us. The gospel story, the Holy Spirit, a place in God's family, the new life in Christ, and the great commission are not the property of some elite class of believers. Because these things belong to all of us, we can all take responsibility to protect and share them.

Sharing was encouraged among the early Christians by a devotion to the teaching of the apostles and to the fellowship of believers. They gathered around the apostles to hear the stories of Jesus' life and teachings. These earliest believers were interested in the way the Hebrew Scriptures prepared them to accept Jesus as the Messiah. They were also devoted to the community that developed around Jesus. Today some Christians are committed to the apostles' teaching and in knowledge. Other Christians are committed to their Christian community. What these early Christians knew is that both the head and the heart are important. We need a dual devotion.

The breaking of bread and the prayers were also important elements in the life of the early church. Almost certainly this was a reference to the way that they worshiped. They observed the Lord's Supper and they prayed together. Both were ways of communicating with God and experiencing Jesus. There was ritual and spontaneity in their worship practices. There was an order to their life, but it was an order imposed by the Holy Spirit.

The most surprising part of Luke's description is that they "had all things in common; they would sell their possessions and goods and distribute the proceeds to all, as any had need." In other words, they behaved like a family. This is the way we treat our family. When we share in this way we reveal the seriousness of our relationship. Sharing is an accurate barometer of spiritual life.

According to Luke, the church's faith was both public and private. These believers were seen in the temple where they engaged in public worship and talked with others about their faith. However, they did not neglect their private devotions. The result was that they were personally fulfilled and Luke describes them as having "glad and generous hearts." Also, they were esteemed by others. In our day, Christians don't often enough enjoy the goodwill of non-Christians. Perhaps the reason is that we lack the integrity of those early Christians who were the same in public as they were in private.

This authentic Christian lifestyle was attractive to the people of the first century and I'm convinced it is attractive in our day, too. Luke notes that folks were being saved "day by day." Luke gives the credit to the Lord. It was God's doing—not that of the community, but their faithful lifestyle was used by God to add new believers to the fellowship. It is important to notice that they weren't added to a list in heaven. They were "added to their number." The salvation offered in Jesus' name does save us from something—eternal separation from God, sin, but it also saves us to something—membership in the community of faith that we call the church. That salvation happens every day as we are saved from going our own way. (Philip Wise)

Worship Aids

Call to Worship

The light of Christ will enlighten our worship.
The joy of Christ will echo in our praise.
The friendship of Christ will bind us together in community.
The teaching of Christ will shape our thinking.
The example of Christ will guide our actions.
Lord, may our faithful commitment to Christ shine through our worship today.

Invocation

In the beauty and stillness of this sanctuary, O God, it is easy to feel your presence and to seek your will in our lives. What is difficult is to take what we learn and experience here into our everyday lives. Help us today to listen for your voice, and having heard it, to remember what you have said.

Pastoral Prayer

Loving God, we look to you for answers to life's most perplexing questions. We wonder why evil so often triumphs and why goodness so often goes unrewarded. We wonder why people do evil deeds and claim to do them in your name. We wonder why it is so difficult to know your will and so easy to break your commandments.

Your son, Jesus, told us that he is the way, the truth, and the life. As Jesus' disciples, we believe that. Remind us today that we can follow Jesus best by loving you and loving our neighbor. (Philip Wise)

NOVEMBER 2, 2008

❧❧❧

Twenty-fifth Sunday after Pentecost

Readings: Micah 3:5-12; Psalm 107:1-7, 33-37; 1 Thessalonians 2:9-13; Matthew 23:1-12

The Minister and Ministry
1 Thessalonians 2:9-13

During election years we hear a great deal about the President using the bully pulpit. In political jargon this means to take advantage of opportunities, wherever they come, to promote a political agenda. Sadly in these days and times many ministers of local churches use their pulpits as polished podiums for pontificating their own personal agenda.

I am convinced nothing is more important for ministers than their ministry. Primary in this responsible calling is the preaching of and living out the gospel. Some say they would rather see the gospel than hear it any day. The truth is that one without the other is meaningless and hypocritical.

In our text Paul states some priorities every minister should strive to reflect. If we do so, we make the main things the main things. We do not get sidetracked and thereby lose our effectiveness and vitality. Although these characteristics related to Paul's ministry in Thessalonica, they are relevant to our time as well.

First and foremost, our ministry must be authentic; that is, it must come from God. Paul recalls for the church that he and others worked hard to not be any burden to the people. Paul had already pointed out there was no pretext for greed, no flattering words, no seeking of personal glory, and no proud assertion of authority. No egotism or exploitation was involved. Paul and his coworkers were genuine, not hypocritical, free of deception, and with no desire to impress. The laity in our churches are quite adept at spotting phonies and know the difference between what is real and what is not. False piety and empty platitudes have no place in a valid minister's life and ministry.

This authenticity calls for "holy, righteous and blameless" living (v. 10 NIV). Granted this is asking a lot, but not too much! Our lives speak sermons before we even say a word. We will never achieve perfection, but we must continually strive toward it. Our Lord told us this and our churches expect this. Yes, a certain degree of respect comes with the office; and yes, we must work all our lives to retain it.

As a minister you may not be fantastic, super, or incredible, you may not be another Charles Wesley or Charles Allen, or you may never pastor the fastest-growing church in the country. You must, however, be authentic!

Our ministry must also be gracious, tenderhearted, and kind. Earlier in this chapter (vv. 7-8), Paul spoke of this as he does in verses 11-12. What could be more tender than a mother nursing her newborn child? This gentleness and compassion is reflective of our Lord himself and often missing in today's minister. We have far too many C.E.O.s and too few rocking-chair philosophers, too many dictatorial leaders and too few willing to lovingly guide the people like a shepherd does the sheep.

Most churches do not need the Bible shoved down their throat. Rather, the congregations need to hear the truth and be lovingly guided in the acceptance of that truth. If we love the people like a mother loves her child, if we tenderly lead the people like a mother teaches her child to walk, and if we gently correct and encourage our flock as a father would his own children, our churches would be much more apt to follow our leadership.

The ministry must meet real needs; it must be relevant. In order to do this, the message of the church must be lived out in the real world. Remember, Jesus was not crucified between two candles in a cathedral, but between two thieves in the marketplace. Often my wife, also a seminarian, reads my manuscripts. After I have polished and refined what I believe to be a great sermon, she will look up as she finishes reading and say, "So what? What does this have to do with the person in the pew who is looking for strength in a time of weakness, for courage in the time of decision, for joy in the midst of sorrow? Jesus and Paul spoke to real people about real needs!"

People have differing needs. Our message should strive to at least meet some of those varied needs. A year or so ago, I read a newspaper article concerning what to give senior citizens for Christmas. Being a senior citizen (at least by the standards of AARP) I was interested in the article. The more I read, the more I resented the article. It certainly did not meet my needs! The author suggested giving senior citizens stamps, crossword puzzles, handkerchiefs, tissues, and so on. That might be helpful to some but for those of us active and alert, this was not relevant. As an illustration, I said I wanted downloads for my iPod, more music for my MP3, and new programs for my laptop. What I am saying is—we must get relevant! Paul realized the vital importance of sharing the gospel with all its ramifications to all the people all the time. Paul refused to waste time or energy on irrelevant matters. We might want to follow Paul's example. The people who come to our churches are hungry for an authentic message from God's word, preached through an authentic minister.

Years ago I heard about an old sexton who met the pastor early on one cold but beautiful day. Snow covered the ground and the sun glistened on the day. The older preacher seemed to be relishing the work of God before him. His reverie was broken by the question of the sexton, "Any late news from God this morning?" I believe this is what the people come to church to hear—the late news from God. If we do not give this to them, who will? (Drew J. Gunnells Jr.)

Lectionary Commentary

All the texts in the lectionary for this Sunday relate to the importance of being real. They point out God will have nothing to do with hypocrisy, especially on the part of God's servants. The prophet must live the prophetic message.

Micah 3:5-12

Micah was true to his calling and a vivid contrast to the false prophets who geared their message to the favors they received. Not all who claim to have messages from God really do, a fact Jesus pointed out in the Sermon on the Mount (Matthew 7:15-20). The power in Micah's ministry was the result of the Spirit of the Lord. We cannot do the work of God in our own strength—we must rely on the power of the Holy Spirit. Micah warned the spiritual leaders of the day to speak up for what was right, not to be silent because it was expedient or personally rewarding.

Matthew 23:1-12

Jesus' warning was clear: false prophets do not practice what they preach. These prophets burden the people without any relief. They place more emphasis on human-made laws than God's laws. They know the Scriptures but refuse to live by them. They want to look holy but they did not want to be holy! They say they follow Jesus but do not live by Jesus' standards. Their love for position is more important than their loyalty to their Lord. Their leadership is self-serving. Our ministry as Christian leaders ought to focus not on ourselves but on our Christ and others. Anything less is hypocritical and unacceptable. (Drew J. Gunnells Jr.)

Worship Aids

Call to Worship

Blessed are those who seek the Word of God with their whole
heart.
O, how we love your Word, O Lord.
We meditate on it day and night.
God's holy Word is a lamp to our feet and a light to our path.
Teach us, Lord, to study to show ourselves approved to you,
people who need not be ashamed,
rightly dividing the Word of truth.
To the glory of God and Jesus Christ, the living word. Amen.

Benediction

And now Lord, send us away more conscious of our responsibility than our accomplishments, more determined to help than hinder, more aware of serving than in being served, and more committed to loving one another than in being loved.

Because in so doing we shall fulfill thy commands, emulate thy example, and be instruments of reconciliation in a troubled world. (Drew J. Gunnells Jr.)

Commodities, Stocks, Bonds, and Inheritance

First in a Series of Three on Stewardship

Luke 12:13-21

Jesus said more about money and possessions than he did about prayer, faith, or salvation. Why? Perhaps we find a clue in Jesus' words, "Where your treasure is, there will be your heart also." One man wanted legal help but Jesus gave him more than insider trading. Jesus challenged people to examine the selfish values of living. Jesus calls us to look beyond commodities, stocks, bonds, and profits to the real stuff of life.

I like the story of the church treasurer who, at his retirement celebration after thirty years of service, said "I'd say I got more out of it than I put into it, but I don't think that would be appropriate for a church treasurer."

It was not unusual for rabbis to be called on to settle disputes. But Jesus refuses to be caught up in this family squabble. I never knew what division could come to a family through an inheritance until I witnessed it myself. People become greedy, selfish, demanding their "fair share" or more. Great grief comes to people who haggle over an inheritance. The same thing has happened to the young man in the crowd. Listen to Jesus' words, "Watch and guard yourself against the spirit which is always wanting more; for if a person has an abundance real life does not come from possessions."

Plainly, the real issue was greed. To those who had an abundant supply, Jesus spoke about the farmer he calls the rich fool. Two things stand out about this man. First, he never saw beyond himself. This man's attitude is the very reverse of what Jesus taught. Instead of denying himself he aggressively affirmed himself. Instead of finding happiness in giving he sought to find it in hoarding.

Second, this man never saw beyond this world. All his plans were made on the basis of this life. I love the old story of a conversation between an ambitious young man and an older man who knew life. "I will be educated for my career." "And then?" "I will set up in business." "And then?" "I will make my fortune." And then? "I will retire and live on my fortune." "And then?" "I suppose that someday I will die." "And then?"

Jesus pointed to the problem of abundance. Jesus saw through the shallow security of affluence. Our problem is that with affluence comes a false sense of security, whether physical, emotional, or spiritual. The reality though, is that all our money cannot protect us from the ultimate experiences of life and death.

True riches are based on a real view of life. Life is uncertain and life can be fragile. We live as though the fragile nature of life happens to others, not to us. People who live calamity-free begin to be naïve about the realities of life. Then we begin to take life itself for granted. We stop thanking God for the blessedness of life. We can grow accustomed to the gift of living. One survivor of the 9/11 attack, saved from the eightieth floor of the World Trade Center said, "I will never take life for granted again."

Someone said that life is "a scandalously generous gift from a good God." What better way to live out this gift than to do what the Creator has called us to do. "Love the Lord your God." Life is a precious gift—use it. One preacher suggests putting an empty chair at your dinner table for the next few weeks as a reminder of both the ongoing presence of God in your days and the existence of others around you.

Jesus calls us to develop a life that is rich toward God. We Americans are a most privileged people. We are a fortunate people. Jesus understood how anesthetizing good times can become to the human race. The problem is that many of us begin to think that we have brought all the good times on ourselves.

What treasure are you building for the future? What will people say about you at the time of your death? What are you doing to build up a life that is rich toward God? Are you doing those things that strengthen your spiritual life? What are you doing to strengthen the lives of those around you? Are you spending most of your time looking after your own "barns and crops" rather than finding ways to release those gifts through giving?

One of the reasons Jesus gave so much attention to the stewardship of our possessions is that he understood that possessions can soon own us. Giving helps to remind us that nothing belongs to us and that we only belong to God. Still, the danger for some of us is that we believe that by giving we have met our spiritual obligation regarding our stuff. Jesus pushes us to consider that not only what we give belongs to God but also what we keep. The biggest challenge of Christian "stewardship" is answering the question, how do I handle all that God has given me?

John Wesley believed that Christians should "continue to evidence their desire of salvation, by doing good, by being in every kind merciful after their power, as they have opportunity, doing good of every possible sort, and as far as possible, to all." As a student at Oxford he learned he could live on twenty-eight pounds per year. As his income rose he still lived on only twenty-eight pounds a year so that he could give away more and more.

A friend said to me, "As I have earned more I have learned how to give away more. I believe that God has blessed me with earning potential so that I can develop more giving potential." Now, that's getting the point.

Remember the old short story of Charles Dickens, *A Christmas Carol*? Ebenezer Scrooge had an opportunity to use what he had to make life rich or to keep what he had for himself. The Apostle Paul had it right when he said, "[Remember] the words of the Lord Jesus, for he himself said, 'It is more blessed to give than to receive' " (Acts 20:35). (Guy Ames)

Worship Aids

Call to Worship

Jesus said, "Do not worry, saying, 'What will we eat?' or 'What will we drink?' or 'What will we wear?' For it is the Gentiles who strive for all these things; and indeed your heavenly Father knows that you need all these things. But strive first for the kingdom of God and his righteousness, and all these things will be given to you as well" (Matthew 6:31-33). Let's join our hearts in worship as we make an offering of our lives to the one who gives us all things well.

Offertory

(As the ushers come forward let us offer God's tithes, our offerings, and the extra dollar.)

"Do not store up for yourselves treasures on earth, where moth and rust consume and where thieves break in and steal; but store up for yourselves treasures in heaven, where neither moth nor rust consumes and where thieves do not break in and steal. For where your treasure is, there your heart will be also" (Matthew 6:19-21).

Offertory Prayer

O God, you are more concerned about what we do with all that we have than merely with what we have given to you. As we make these offerings we pray that we may bring to you all that we have, so that our treasure will be in you. In Christ's name, amen.

Benediction

It is true that it's more blessed to give than to receive. As God has made you a channel of his gifts, so go to show the world how good our God's gifts are. In the name of the Father and of the Son and of the Holy Spirit. Amen. (Guy Ames)

NOVEMBER 9, 2008

❧❧❧

Twenty-sixth Sunday after Pentecost

Readings: Amos 5:18-24; Psalm 78:1-7; 1 Thessalonians 4:13-18;
Matthew 25:1-13

What Does God Want?
Amos 5:18-24

From the barren and desolate region of Tekoa he came and Amos was
anything but your run-of-the-mill prophet. Amos heard the voice of God
in the fierce crooning of the desert wind and his communion with
God. This setting prepared Amos for ministry. God often prepares
prophets like this. Think of John the Baptist in the same wilderness and
Paul in the desert of Arabia. Many of Amos's sermons are laced with figures of speech peculiar to the desert. Because Amos was not a polished
scholar like Isaiah and was lacking in cultural refinements, Amos was
offensive to the court life in Bethel.

Amos was a careful student of human nature and his messages stirred
the people. Although it is not easy to find one brief passage in his book
to summarize Amos's message, perhaps these verses in our text come as
close as any. The lesson is simple and pointed—religious practices,
divorced from life and devoid of righteous living, are an abomination to
God. Amos cut to the heart of the problem religion has faced in every
generation—profession devoid of practice. Like many modern Americans
the people of Israel had misunderstood what God wanted from them.

These people claimed to want the "day of the Lord." This common
expression referred to the Lord's manifestation of himself in righteousness, which includes judgment for evildoers and deliverance for believers.
We talk too glibly of this event. For those who are nominally religious,
whose religion is devoid of righteousness, this will be anything but a new
day. It will be a day of eternal darkness.

Amos draws on his desert experience to point out the consequences of people who see only the evil of others. They may call on God for deliverance but fail to realize their own evil lives will bring forth judgment. They will be like a man who flees a lion only to meet a bear or who runs into the house for protection only to be bitten by a snake.

God wants worship that is vital and relevant. In Amos's day the noble ideas of sacrificial worship, which reflected the inner attitude and commitment of the offerer, had degenerated into a selfish attempt to manipulate God. In verses 21-23 the essential elements of Israel's worship are pointed out one-by-one: festivals, sacrifice, and praise. Unmistakably clear is the total rejection of Israel's worship. God delighted in the character of his people, not the aroma of their sacrifices. God not only rejected their offerings but also God would not lend his ears to their music.

God had enough of heartless and meaningless ritual; God wanted to see the basic virtues of a godly life. God wanted justice that ensured the protection and rights of all people. God wanted righteousness that had both a vertical and horizontal relationship. That is, one must be right with God as well as right with his fellow person. These two virtues were to be practiced in all legal, business, and personal relationships. The call was not to do away with ceremonial worship, but to vitalize it with righteous and holy living.

One of my seminary professors had a saying that comes to mind: "It does not matter how high you jump in a worship service; rather, it is how straight you walk when you leave." We cannot substitute things more to our liking for God's requirements. What God wants is a life-authenticating commitment to social justice and right living. The people of Israel convinced themselves that if they just built and sustained their commitment to the religious institution with attendance and support, God would be satisfied. They sought to pull what a Texan would call a "switcheroo." They substituted institutionalism for obedience, religious jargon for justice, and religious ritual for righteousness. All in all Israel replaced God-directed faith with human-made religion.

Our prosperous nation, which boasts of a church on almost every street corner, is very similar to Israel in the eighth century B.C.E. Any society that cares more for gain than honor, more about their standard of living than God's standard is sick. Any church that accepts lavish support as a substitute for righteous behavior is a sham. Any church that thinks God will accept a correct creed and perennial activity as substitutes for plain obedience to God's divine will is wrong. In the eyes of God there can be no dichotomy between faith and ethics.

If we are not careful we can also let our worship become superficial and shallow. Emotion and enthusiasm can take the place of righteousness lived out in the community. Ritual can become a substitute for reality. We might profess loudly what we believe, but unless we practice what we profess, God will reject it. Just as in the time of Amos—what God really wants still rings true today: "But let judgment run down as waters, / and righteousness as a mighty stream" (Amos 5:24 KJV). The New Living Bible paraphrases this: "I want to see a mighty flood of justice, an endless river of righteous living." (Drew J. Gunnells Jr.)

Lectionary Commentary

The texts for this Sunday all deal with living out our religion in the marketplace. Holy words without holy ways are contradictory. Worship on Sunday that does not work on Monday is false.

Matthew 25:1-13

Jesus is telling his followers how to live until he returns. In this story we are told that every person is responsible for his or her spiritual condition. This parable about a wedding tells about ten virgins waiting to join the wedding procession. However, when the time comes, five of them have no oil in their lamps. By the time other oil is purchased, it is too late to join the feast. Spiritual preparation cannot be bought or borrowed at the last minute. Our relationship with God is personal and must be real.

1 Thessalonians 4:13-18

In these verses is a teaching concerning how we are to live to please the Lord, especially in the light of Christ's imminent return. The Thessalonians were wondering about those of their number who had died and what would happen when Christ returned. Paul wanted all to know that death was not the end, and if it was, it was the front end! When the Lord returns, all believers, the living and the dead, will be reunited. Nothing is said about the time of the Lord's return and this is not as important as being ready for Christ's return. For those who are ready, God will turn tragedy to triumph, pain to glory, defeat to victory. This should bring great hope and comfort—real encouragement to every believer. (Drew J. Gunnells Jr.)

Worship Aids

Call to Worship (Psalm 42:2, 5-6a, 8, 11)

My soul thirsts for God, for the living God.
When shall I come and behold the face of God?
Why are you cast down, O my soul,
and why are you disquieted within me?
Hope in God; for I shall again praise him,
my help and my God.
By day the Lord commands his steadfast love,
and at night his song is with me, a prayer to the God of my life.
Why are you cast down, O my soul,
and why are you disquieted within me?
All: Hope in God; for I shall again praise him,
my help and my God.

Prayer of Confession

God of infinite mercy and righteous judgment, we pray that we might see your coming day; nonetheless we live as if your day will never arrive. We spend our lives as if we have an eternity on earth and that day of your final verdict, whether in grace or in judgment, will never arrive. The psalmist has sung, "So teach us to count our days that we may gain a wise heart" (Psalm 90:12), yet we confess that we have neither numbered our days nor have we gained wise hearts. Forgive us, O God, for our lack of discernment.

O Gracious One, rekindle in us once again the vision of what our lives can be when we live in conformance to you and your holy word—to us and for us. Remind us that we have life plainly because of your generous choice. Now give us the wisdom to choose you once again. In this and in all things, we praise you holy name. Amen.

Words of Assurance

In the name of Jesus Christ, you are forgiven.
In the name of Jesus Christ, you are forgiven. Amen.

Benediction

Heavenly Provider, make us mindful not only of our blessings but also of our responsibilities. Teach us anew and afresh that the authenticity of our worship is demonstrated by the way we treat our fellows, that what we do Monday through Saturday is just as important as what we do on Sunday. May we never be so naïve or immature as to believe that any type of worship not accompanied by righteous living is acceptable in thy sight. Remind us of your own admonition about judgment, namely, that our treatment of the hungry, the thirsty, the stranger, the person without adequate clothing, the sick, and the prisoner is a reflection of our treatment of you (Matthew 25:31-45). O Lord, we know that authentic living depicts authentic worship. May it be so in our lives. Amen. (Drew J. Gunnells Jr.)

The Power of Compounding

Second in a Series of Three on Stewardship

2 Corinthians 9:6-15

Jesus said, "Give and it shall be given unto you." Does that mean that Christian giving is like a sure bet at the racetrack? No, but the Bible does tell us there is much to be gained by giving. What is it?

Two business partners were on an overnight trip to Philadelphia at the height of a multimillion-dollar lottery fever. They stopped at a convenience store to try their luck but found that the ticket line wrapped around the side of the building. One partner spotted a much smaller line inside the store where people were calling out, "$5 on No.3" and "$10 on No. 2." He quickly advanced to the front of that line and asked how the game was played. "It's simple, son," the clerk said, pointing outside. "First you pump your gas, and then you come tell me how much you got."

The power of compound interest has helped many people to make a lot of money. Some time ago I heard about a man who earned no more than $30,000 annually but was buying a $250,000 house. In 1989 he had received a $30,000 inheritance, which he invested in Wal-Mart stock. Later during the tech-stock growth of the mid-1990s he transferred that Wal-Mart stock to Cisco stock. He sold out his stock before the stock market slide of 2001. The result was a $2.5 million profit out of that original $30,000 investment.

We know the stories about the power of compounding—most of us have not experienced the power as much as others have. The Bible teaches that spiritual compounding results in a great return on your financial investments when given the right way.

Paul teaches about the possibilities of investments. I love God's simple principle stated in verse 6. "The point is this: the one who sows sparingly will also reap sparingly, and the one who sows bountifully will also reap bountifully."

Scripture is filled with this analogy and the comparison between planting crops and giving to God's work. The more we invest, the better our return. Withhold your money from savings, stocks, mutual funds, or business and you will have a smaller return. There are always risks in investing. In the same way, Paul is reminding us that the person who gives sparingly will receive a cheap blessing. The simple question Paul asks us is *How cheap are your investments with God?*

Paul's letter to this church is an attempt to collect an offering for the people of the mother church in Jerusalem. Disaster had struck Palestine and the church in Jerusalem was in great need. The daughter churches of Asia Minor had the rich opportunity to give to those who had real need. I admire the way Paul goaded the rich Corinthian church by telling them how generous the poor Macedonians had already been.

Paul writes a letter to this same group in Macedonia when he is in prison. These Christians go to great lengths to send tokens of care to Paul in prison. Paul's letter to the Philippians is a thank-you note for the care package that they sent. The church at Corinth had plenty but they constantly complained. They argued about preachers, they argued about church discipline, they argued about sharing their fellowship dinners with one another. Their lives were a constant whine and a grumble. While the poor Christians of Macedonia gave more than they could afford.

"Each of you must give as you have made up your mind, not reluctantly or under compulsion, for God loves a cheerful giver." A better rendering of the word *cheerful* is "hilarious." God loves hilarious givers. This is the very nature of God—God's giving to us is scandalously generous. God wants us to learn to give with joy.

Remember who the real giver is. Paul is clear—we are not the original givers, as a matter of fact, what we give is merely what we have received. God provides for us so that we may give.

When I was a young preacher I visited regularly Josie, aged and crippled with arthritis. She prayed for me every day, and checked on me to know if I was really teaching the Bible. One day as I visited in her modest home she handed me a check for the church. She was no longer able to attend, and the $25.00 check was so very large on her $250.00 a month

Social Security income. "Jo," I scolded, "you can't afford to do this. The church will be alright, but you need this money."

Jo looked back at me with fire in her eyes and said in a stern voice, "Preacher, don't you ever try to steal my blessing from me. The joy is in giving to God and no one, not you or anyone else, can take that away from me."

Appropriately admonished I simply said, "Jo, I will put your check in the offering on Sunday."

Addition is good, but multiplication is better. In finance those who do well understand this simple principle. I remember overhearing some older women (widows and single) discussing their investment strategy. One finally commented, "You'll never have enough money if you don't save."

Preaching to a congregation in Maua, Kenya, I referenced the text of Jesus having the disciples cast their nets on the other side of the boat to make a greater catch. I casually asked the congregation if they had ever fished, assuming that there are fishermen in almost every part of the world except the desert. No hands were raised. Later I discovered that they couldn't relate to fishing at all.

Then I shared a story from Southwest Oklahoma depression dust-bowl days of a mother who would regularly take the only eggs of the morning to poor neighbors who had no food. I told this congregation that the daughter of this mother later told me that the chickens always laid a second time that day. An audible gasp rose from the large congregation. They all know the biology of chickens. In the natural sunlight without the added science of chicken farms, God has created chickens to lay only once a day. Somehow in the generosity of this mother, God gave through those hens again.

Isn't that just like God? (Guy Ames)

Worship Aids

Call to Worship

For God so loved the world that he gave.
Give and it shall be given unto you, pressed down,
shaken together and running over.
It's more blessed to give than to receive.
Today we give ourselves a living offering to God,
which is our spiritual worship.
All: Praise God from whom all blessings come!

The Offering

Let the ushers come forward as we receive God's tithes and our offerings. The Apostle Paul writes, "The point is this: the one who sows sparingly will also reap sparingly, and the one who sows bountifully will also reap bountifully. Each of you must give as you have made up your mind, not reluctantly or under compulsion, for God loves a cheerful giver. And God is able to provide you with every blessing in abundance, so that by always having enough of everything, you may share abundantly in every good work. As it is written, "He scatters abroad, he gives to the poor; / his righteousness endures forever." He who supplies seed to the sower and bread for food will supply and multiply your seed for sowing and increase the harvest of your righteousness. You will be enriched in every way for your great generosity, which will produce thanksgiving to God through us; for the rendering of this ministry not only supplies the needs of the saints but also overflows with many thanksgivings to God" (2 Corinthians 9:6-12).

Thank you God, for the freedom and ability to be givers. Let our hearts be consumed with generosity for your kingdom. Amen.

Prayer of Confession

God, so often we want a great harvest with only a little investment. It's so easy for us to complain when we don't receive what we believe we deserve and then to hoard the things that we do receive. We want you to be a great giver so that we might have all that we want. Forgive our lack of faith.

God, we confess to you that we don't handle well what you have given to us. We find it difficult to affirm the Apostle Paul's words of being content in every state whether we have plenty or are in want. When we have plenty, we want more and when we are in want we are never content. Draw our minds to the Giver of every good gift, that we can begin to learn to trust that you will supply everything that we need in Jesus Christ.

We confess that we have set our vision so very small. We have failed to believe that you are able to supply more abundantly than we can ask or imagine. Give us eyes to see the vision you have for us and the kingdom. Let us not be afraid to grasp the vision you have given to the church, and make us as generous as you in claiming that kingdom vision for the sake of Jesus Christ our Lord and the world. Amen. (Guy Ames)

Words of Assurance

In the name of Jesus Christ, you are forgiven.
In the name of Jesus Christ, you are forgiven. Amen.

NOVEMBER 16, 2008

❧❧❧

Twenty-seventh Sunday after Pentecost

Readings: Zephaniah 1:7, 12-18; Psalm 123; 1 Thessalonians 5:1-11; Matthew 25:14-30

Use It or Lose It!
Matthew 25:14-30

In every motivational book I've read or every inspirational speech I've heard, a real emphasis is placed on taking risks in order to be successful. Quotes like "Nothing ventured, nothing gained" surface, as does the statement "If you prefer security to opportunity, you're doomed from the start." Both of these have a significant relationship to Jesus' parable of the Talents.

The parable itself is part of the farewell discourse on the Mount of Olives during which Jesus predicts the fall of Jerusalem. Jesus also reveals signs that will precede his personal return. After telling the parable of the Fig Tree, Jesus gives four other parables: the Thief in the Night, the Faithful and Wicked Servants, the Ten Virgins, and the parable of the Talents—our text.

In this parable a master travels to another country, leaving his capital in the hands of three servants. Today we use the word *talent* to refer to some special ability or aptitude one might have, as for example, a talent in music or art. However, in Jesus' time *talent* referred to wealth and was not a coin but a measure of weight. A silver talent for example, was worth about $1,000. (Some translations indicate the servant hid his master's silver.) Suffice to say, a talent amounted to a considerable amount of money.

The servant who received five talents and the one who received two talents traded them, each doubling his capital. The servant with only one talent did not attempt to invest but dug a hole and hid it in the ground. When the master returned there was a day of reckoning. With joy the servants who had invested their capital made their reports. To each of them the master said, "Well done, good and faithful servant! You have been faithful with a few things; I will put you in charge of many things. Come and share your master's happiness!"(v. 21 NIV)

The man who received the single talent also reported. The reprimand of this servant was as severe as the master's commendation for the other two servants was glorious. This servant was called wicked and lazy, the opposite of good and faithful.

The master took away the one talent this servant had, gave it to the one who now had ten talents, and expelled the unfaithful servant from his presence. This is figuratively expressed as being thrown into the darkness.

Jesus adds no explanation of the parable, yet the emphasis is on service. Blessings bring responsibility and accountability. God's gifts are tools to be used in the divine kingdom and not prizes to enjoy along the way. In a very real sense we use these gifts or we lose them. This may be disturbing or sound harsh, but it is true.

What of our talents? Talents come in all sizes and shapes. God blesses everyone with some talent—the just as well as the unjust. Lest we become proud of our particular talent, the Bible notes that we are given talents "according to our ... ability." All people are created equal only in the sense that all have equal chance to prove themselves. Somewhere along the line we all realize we are unequal in looks, in opportunity, in advantages, even in mental capacity. When you get right down to it, all talents are undeserved.

One thing, however, is supremely clear. God expects each of us to perform up to our own capability. The five-talent individual is expected to produce five additional talents and the two-talent individual is not condemned if he only produces two additional talents. The one-talent person was not required to produce five talents! You might say all talents are like coins: on one side is written "endowment" and on the other, "accountability."

Never forget that the reward for faithfulness is greater opportunity and greater responsibility. Both the five-talent and the two-talent person were given additional talents, which meant more responsibility. Polio vaccine inventor Dr. Jonas Salk said it well: "The greatest reward for doing is the opportunity to do more." If you think because of your faithfulness you will be relieved of further responsibility, think again!

The "villain" in this parable is the one-talent individual. In calling this person "wicked," Jesus used the same term he used six times in reference to satan, seven times in a general sense, and only two times related to a character outside satan. "Wicked" is a strong, strong word in the Bible. Far too many church members are doing exactly what this one-talent person did. Afraid of any risk, they bury their talent and refuse to get involved in meaningful Christian service of any kind. These people minimize the talent they have.

How many church members do you know who "used to" sing, "used to" teach, "used to" visit, "used to" help around the church? Look at them now and realize this parable is so true to life—you really do lose what you refuse to use! Obviously, God expects from each of us faithfulness, dependability, tenacity, diligence, and discipline. Anything else merits no commendation from God, only condemnation. We bring it on ourselves.

George Buttrick, in his fine book, *The Parables of Jesus*, tells of visiting an ancient abbey in France named "Our Lady of the Risk." Upon investigation he found this was a reference to none other than Mary, the mother of Jesus, who risked everything to have the Christ child.

What was the master looking for from his servants when he returned from his journey? Not fame, but faithfulness. Not genius, but goodness. Not degrees, but dependability. Those God commends are those willing to work while others play, to study while others sleep, to risk all for God's sake rather than play it safe for their own sake.

The practical appeal of the parable is clear. This parable is a stimulus to faithfulness in service, knowing of a sure and glorious reward. At the same time, it is a warning against sloth or laziness, knowing the sure and certain loss. (Drew J. Gunnells Jr.)

Lectionary Commentary

All the texts listed for this Sunday deal with God's judgment. In both Zephaniah and in 1 Thessalonians, it is seen as the Day of the Lord.

Zephaniah 1:7, 12-18

Verse 7—The prophet announces that judgment is coming. The Day of Yahweh is seen in this light. A day of sacrifice was a holy occasion; therefore, when the sacrifice was placed upon the altar, the people waited in hushed silence anticipating the presence of God among them. The idea here is that the people of Israel would cease every manner of opposition to God and bow down in obedience and loving service to their Covenant God.

Verses 12-18—These verses teach that God will "search out" Jerusalem with no possibility of hiding from his wrath. The idea of "left on lees" is a reference to wine processing. If the wine remained too long on its lees, it became a bitter, unpalatable liquid. Judah had settled down on its dregs and impurities, until the good wine of obedience and service had degenerated into little more than hypocritical lip service to her God. Obviously what took place in the marketplace was consequential. Injustice to others inevitably leads to the building of houses that will not stand and vineyards that will not produce. Destruction and devastation always follow degeneracy. God will judge immoral behavior!

1 Thessalonians 5:1-11

Once again the Day of the Lord is a period of God's judgment, entailing horrible, inescapable affliction. Paul reminds the people this event concerns unbelievers, not believers. This day will come suddenly and silently. This will be especially painful to unbelievers. "But you, beloved, are not in darkness" is a welcome relief. Christians know judgment is coming and the way of escape is the cross and the empty tomb. Paul urges us to be vigilant and keep our "sentry armor" on. Here is a very practical point—we are to build up and strengthen one another as this day approaches. We are not to be indifferent because tomorrow is secure for us, neither are we to be fooled by the calm events of today. When those of us who live on the Gulf Coast hear a hurricane is coming, we know to get prepared. (Drew J. Gunnells Jr.)

Worship Aids

A Responsive Reading

We have given you during these past few weeks an opportunity to
  share your intent to participate in our programs of ministry.
Today we make these pledges reality.
We gladly give you back, O God, what you have given us because all that we have is a trust from you.
Because you have chosen us, O God, and thereby enriched our lives,
we offer ourselves, our talents, and our substance to you.
To the sharing of the gospel both here and abroad,
we offer ourselves, our talents, and our substance to you.

To the Christian education of our children,
    to the guidance of our youth,
   and to the spiritual growth of our adults,
we offer ourselves, our talents, and our substance to you.
Looking forward to that day when the kingdoms of our world
    become the kingdom of our Christ,
we offer ourselves, our talents, and our substance to you.
Let us pray. Almighty and everlasting God,
    you have given us life abundant.
Accept these gifts as our recognition of this truth.
Bless us, therefore, with additional opportunity to serve in any way
    possible.
In Jesus's name, amen. (Drew J. Gunnells Jr.)

Thanksgiving and Generous Living

Third in a Series of Three on Stewardship

Proverbs 3:9-10; Psalm 116:12-14, 17-19

Times of crises lead naturally to times of prayer. Following the attacks of 9/11, people tended to show kindness toward strangers, spend more time with family, and even pray with people of other faiths. People showed gratitude for simple joys.

In a similar way, thanksgiving becomes a focus of celebration for cultures under stress. Our contemporary thanksgiving is taken from the Hebrew feast of booths or Pentecost. It is a time to thank God for all the blessings that have come to us. I'm amazed at how people become more conscious of the small things during times of loss: ironically, more conscious than in times of abundance.

I appreciate the story told about one wealthy grandmother. She never forgot to send Christmas gifts to her grandchildren, who never remembered to write a thank you. One year she bragged to her hairdresser that after Christmas every one of her grandchildren had come to visit her. Knowing that these grandchildren had disappointed her over the years the hairdresser was surprised. "That's wonderful. It's so good to know they finally are showing their appreciation and love."

"Oh it wasn't appreciation that brought them to my house. You see, this year for Christmas I sent them all a handsome check . . . but failed to sign it."

Our national holiday of Thanksgiving comes from the feast celebrated by the early Puritans at Plymouth Rock and a group of Native Americans who offered these Europeans true hospitality. Both groups were in need, but out of their need they shared with one another. The Bible has much to say about living lives of thanksgiving. For example, "Honor the LORD with your substance / and with the first fruits of all your produce; / then your barns will be filled with plenty, / and your vats will be bursting with wine" (Proverbs 3:9-10).

How do you teach children the value of generosity? We tell them, "Say, thank you " or "Remember the magic words." One of the things that we hope children do is to watch how we give to others. I remember hearing about a family who came home from church complaining about the day. The seats were too hard, the sermon too long, the music too dull. Finally, the smallest child said with wisdom, "Well, what can you expect for a dollar?" A second thing we do is practice sharing. By exchanging gifts, teaching a child to share toys, learning how to give to others we help children begin to think of others.

Finally, we set standards. Children tend to model what they know to be the standard. How many times did you hear someone in a home say, "This is the way we do it"? Growing up, we tried to help our children learn the habits of being generous with God, with each other, with people outside our home. In my childhood home my father taught the importance of giving by setting out each Sunday morning a quarter, dime, nickel, and penny for the four children of our family to take to church. The oldest got the quarter, the youngest the penny, and so forth.

In a similar way, first fruits are God's standard for our generosity. First fruits illustrate the biblical principle of bringing the best of your crop. By faith we offer what comes in first in hopes and expectation that other produce will follow. There is always the possibility that there may only be a small crop, herd, or flock. This is an extreme act of faith.

Following the first fruits, the Hebrew Bible has established the law of gleaning. The first fruits go to God. The gleanings are the last fruits, the leftovers—those go to the poor. The standard that God's word sets is one of being generous with God's gifts back to the Creator and then to the needy. This is God's plan to build a community of generosity.

Generosity flows from thanksgiving. I helped to support myself in college by waiting tables in a local Mexican buffet. Our employer gave us the privilege to work for tips and no wages, so every customer was vitally important to us. One of the lessons I quickly learned was that the most demanding customers were generally the poorest tippers. Time and time again I was surprised to find a big tip from people who had expected and demanded little.

Here are a few lessons I learned from waiting tables. Generous people tend not to be demanding. Generous people tend to look for the positive. Generous people tend to overlook the insignificant. Generous people tend to be appreciative. Generous people are thoughtful. Generous people are thankful.

Generosity of giving comes from those who recognize their blessings. Generosity flows from lives of people who understand thanksgiving.

Contentment is the fruit of thankful living. Paul's Letter to the Philippians is really a thank-you note for their generosity while he is in prison. Paul makes note of some important principles of learning how to live thankfully and generously.

I love the way Paul instructs them. After acknowledging the gift, Paul writes, "For I have learned to be content with whatever I have. I know what it is to have little, and I know what it is to have plenty. In any and all circumstances I have learned the secret of being well-fed and of going hungry, of having plenty and of being in need. I can do all things through him who strengthens me" (Philippians 4:11-13).

Thanksgiving allows us to learn the lessons of "just enough." The amazing picture of the "first" American Thanksgiving is of a group of broken and grieving Puritans whose hopes have been dashed by a harsh winter and the loss of half of the hundred that came on the Mayflower. There was not a home that had not experienced a funeral, not a child who had not lost at least one parent. The new compound was not yet complete. The summer and fall harvest was not bountiful. Then there were the Native Americans who stumbled on this site where an earlier disease had brought death to tribal and family members. Together, in their poverty, these two peoples celebrated God's goodness, their hope for the future, with a generous spirit. Taking out of the small rations they set aside a feast. What an act of faith! In the midst of adversity and loss they were able to say with Paul, "And my God will fully satisfy every need of yours according to his riches in glory in Christ Jesus. To our God and Father be glory forever and ever. Amen" (Philippians 4:19-20). (Guy Ames)

Worship Aids

Call to Worship (from Psalm 100)

Make a joyful noise to the Lord, all the earth.
Worship the Lord with gladness; come into his presence with singing.

Know that the Lord is God.
It is he that made us, and we are his;
we are his people, and the sheep of his pasture.
Enter his gates with thanksgiving, and his courts with praise.
Give thanks to him, bless his name.
For the Lord is good; his steadfast love endures forever,
and his faithfulness to all generations.

Offertory Prayer

Let the ushers come forward as we worship with God's tithes and our offerings. The Apostle Paul wrote this thank-you note to the Philippian church from prison:

> I rejoice in the Lord greatly that now at last you have revived your concern for me; indeed, you were concerned for me, but had no opportunity to show it. Not that I am referring to being in need; for I have learned to be content with whatever I have. I know what it is to have little, and I know what it is to have plenty. In any and all circumstances I have learned the secret of being well-fed and of going hungry, of having plenty and of being in need. I can do all things through him who strengthens me. In any case, it was kind of you to share my distress.
>
> You Philippians indeed know that in the early days of the gospel, when I left Macedonia, no church shared with me in the matter of giving and receiving, except you alone. For even when I was in Thessalonica, you sent me help for my needs more than once. Not that I seek the gift, but I seek the profit that accumulates to your account. I have been paid in full and have more than enough; I am fully satisfied, now that I have received from Epaphroditus the gifts you sent, a fragrant offering, a sacrifice acceptable and pleasing to God. And my God will fully satisfy every need of yours according to his riches in glory in Christ Jesus. (Philippians 4:10-19)

Benediction

John Wesley reminded Christians to "continue to evidence their desire of salvation, by doing good, by being in every kind merciful after their power, as they have opportunity, doing good of every possible sort, and as far as possible, to all." Go in the name of Jesus Christ who is God's best gift—who has called you to be generous as you live out the image of the one who has called you to follow Jesus. Amen. (Guy Ames)

NOVEMBER 23, 2008

❧❧❧

Reign of Christ/Christ the King Sunday

Readings: Ezekiel 34:11-16, 20-24; Psalm 100; Ephesians 1:15-23; Matthew 25:31-46

The Shepherd King
Ezekiel 34:11-16, 20-24; Matthew 25:31-46

Whenever a new monarch has come to power throughout history, people have asked, *What kind of king (or queen) will this be?* Today we celebrate a king; for today is the day in the church year when we celebrate the reign of Christ. It seems appropriate for us to ask, *What kind of king is Jesus?* Scripture shows us that Jesus is an unusual kind of king—a shepherd king, much like his ancestor David.

What does that mean? It means that Jesus, in all his glory, lays aside a crown and picks up a shepherd's crook. In our Old Testament text, Ezekiel reports that God himself will search for his sheep and seek them out. It is interesting that God must seek out his sheep because they have been scattered "on a day of clouds and thick darkness." Sheep, at the best of times, have very poor eyesight. On a foggy day, they have little chance of finding their way without some guidance. Are we so different from these sheep? We, too, have a tendency to be very shortsighted when it comes to staying on the path we should follow. Sometimes, even with our good intentions, the storms of life scatter us. The good news is that Jesus is still a shepherd king today. Jesus still seeks us out, wherever we may have wandered, to bring us back to the meadow where we can be safe under Jesus' watch.

As the shepherd finds the sheep, he guides them to green meadows where food and water are plentiful. The shepherd provides for them all that they need. In Ezekiel 34:15-16, God describes this in detail: "I myself will be the shepherd of my sheep, and I will make them lie down, says the Lord GOD. I will seek the lost, and I will bring back the strayed, and I will bind up the injured, and I will strengthen the weak." A shepherd does so much more for his sheep than simply turning them loose in a hayfield. The shepherd makes sure that they have plenty of rest and goes after the lost sheep, collecting those who have strayed. The shepherd heals those who are hurting and builds up those who are frail. What a promise! Whatever our needs, our shepherd king is already working to meet them.

God's provision is not always what we are looking for, or even what we think we need. The verse we read just a moment ago does not actually end there. It goes on to say, "But the fat and the strong I will destroy. I will feed them with justice." Sometimes, the shepherd must act as judge, separating the flock. This seems harsh, but it is the shepherd's love that causes action. "Because you pushed with flank and shoulder, and butted at all the weak animals with your horns until you scattered them far and wide, I will save my flock, and they shall no longer be ravaged." There are times when the shepherd must guide and lead the sheep along a path they do not wish to follow, in order to make things right for the rest of the flock.

Ezekiel's words foreshadow today's New Testament passage in which Jesus tells of his return. Here, the king is in full regalia, shining in glory, sitting on a throne surrounded by all his angels. While Matthew's image of the king differs from the shepherd of Ezekiel, the king's actions are the same. The king sorts out the nations of the world, putting some to the right, and others to the left. The criteria for the sorting is also the same. Those who have butted their way through life without regard to the people being pushed away by their actions are chastised. The sheep, those loyal followers of the king, have followed the king's lead without even realizing that is what they were doing. Their love for the one who cares for them has led them to imitation. Thus, they ask, "Lord, when did we feed you or give you something to drink? When did we ever visit you in the hospital or in jail? When did we provide a home or clothes for you?" The king answers, "Just as you did it to one of the least of these who are members of my family, you did it to me." The shepherd king leads by example. Just as Jesus spent his time on earth with those society looked down upon, with those who most needed him, Jesus expects his sheep to do the same. Jesus walks along that path and waits for them to follow. This shepherd is not content for his sheep to simply be like other sheep. They have more potential, and so part of his feeding them involves lead-ing them to a truer understanding of who they are and to whom they belong. Only those sheep who truly know their shepherd's nature are rewarded; only those citizens who honor the king by loving other people will inherit the kingdom God has prepared for them.

And so, we come back to our question: *What kind of king is Jesus?* Jesus is a king who will seek us out where we are, a king who provides for our every need, a king who corrects us and guides us along the path we must follow. Jesus is a shepherd king who seeks us, feeds us, and leads us so that we can prosper. It is up to us to decide what kind of sheep—what kind of citizens of God's kingdom—we will be. (Melissa Scott)

Lectionary Commentary
Ephesians 1:15-23

In this passage, Paul encourages the Ephesians to continue in the path they have begun. Paul commends the trust they have placed in Jesus, and the way that this trust is evidenced through the love they show toward their Christian brothers and sisters. Along with this thanksgiving, Paul writes them of his prayer for them: that they will come to know God through wisdom and through revelation. God can be known in many ways, and Paul is encouraging the Ephesians to use both their own intelligence (in the study of Scripture and the knowledge of Jesus they have been given) and discernment (new revelation of God's glory that comes through prayer and observation). The purpose of all this is that they may more clearly know the hope that comes from being part of God's family. (Melissa Scott)

Worship Aids

Call to Worship (from Psalm 100)
Make a joyful noise to the Lord.
We will worship the Lord with gladness!
Know that the Lord is God. It is he that made us, and we are his.
The Lord is good, his love lasts forever!

Prayer of Confession
God, our shepherd and our king, we confess that we have not always followed your example. We have pushed through life, not taking notice of the needs of others. For these sins, forgive us. Teach us to recognize you in those around us and to treat others as you have treated us.

°Assurance

In the name of Jesus Christ, you are forgiven.
In the name of Jesus Christ, you are forgiven. Amen.

Offertory Prayer (from Psalm 95)

Creator God, you are the maker and sustainer of all things. In your hands you hold all the earth—the oceans, the mountains, and all in between. We know that all that we have is yours. We worship you now by returning these gifts you have granted us to be used to your glory. (Melissa Scott)

A "This End Up" Thanksgiving

First in a Series of Three on Christian Thanksgiving

Psalm 95:1-10

When buying a new appliance for our kitchen, I happened to notice that many, if not all, of the containers in the warehouse were labeled with the words "this end up." Obviously, to set the container in any other position would mean certain damage to the contents.

Psalm 95 could be labeled similarly. A Christian Thanksgiving focuses life in the context of praising God so that before we wrestle with life's demands and unfairness, even its joys, we offer praise to God first, rather than rant and rave. To focus life in terms of its hardships and struggles can harden our hearts to life and even toward God. Thus life is turned upside down. With praise and gratitude to God, we keep our lives in perspective and we do not run the risk of damaging our relationship with God and others. Jesus came that we might learn how to keep life in a "this end up" perspective. This Thanksgiving season is a wonderful time for such a focus.

This Sunday, November 23, 2008, can be an extraordinary step in the right direction. As we approach Thanksgiving, worship is a significant place for making extravagant and extraordinary sounds or what the psalmist calls a "joyful noise." The Hebrew word means "joyful voice." One of the most important aspects of worship is its music and singing features. While litanies, prayers, readings, responses, and other segments of worship are important, it is the hymnody and music that underscore worship's rhythm, making the heart soar. Coming to worship as a community of faith and singing the great hymns and listening to great anthems can help make a sore heart soar. A joyful sound lifts the spirit of the worshiper. Not only does it lift the spirit; it lifts the vision of the worshiper in order to view life as God views it. The great texts of hymns not only lift our vision of God and life but also they can lift our vision of self and other people. This community act, once a week, is an extraordinarily important event that helps us proclaim that with the Creator God, all of life is set in the right position, the right focus, for God's people.

Early in my ministry, I found that placement of the anthem in worship just prior to the sermon was the most meaningful placement for me, personally. While many traditions favor placing it after the sermon or homily, I found placing the anthem just before the sermon prepared me to preach more effectively. Hearing the choir giving witness to faith through the anthem prepared me to deliver God's good news in a more faithful manner. In fact, I would be so bold as to say my better sermons have always been those that followed the choir or the congregation making a "joyful noise to God with songs of praise." This is another way worship can help us prepare for a "this end up" Thanksgiving.

There is another way the psalmist believes worship prepares Christians for Thanksgiving. Namely, we are to raise our vision to the level of seeing the world as through God's eyes. As those who follow Jesus' teachings, we need to keep in mind that Jesus himself said, "I can do nothing on my own . . . because I seek to do not my own will but the will of him who sent me" (John 5:30). Thus, Thanksgiving for the Christian faith is to praise God for God's will to be done. Or, as Jesus' prayer suggests, "Thy will be done on earth, as it is in heaven" (Matthew 6:10).

We live in such a rat-race world. We run here and there at breakneck speed. I recall a story regarding our fast-paced world. A traveler's plane had arrived at his appointed destination. After some time waiting for the passengers to exit the aircraft, the traveler left the plane at a frantic pace, all the time fearing he would miss an awaiting taxi. To his surprise, a taxi driver was standing at the curb, door open, and smiling while greeting the man as if he were a good friend. The man, breathless, shouted, "Hurry, or I will be late for my meeting!" The cab driver immediately jumped in the front seat and off they zoomed to the man's appointment. With breakneck speed the cabby swerved in and out of traffic, all the time keeping eye on the traffic all around him. The man kept yelling, "Hurry, hurry, or I'll be late!" Finally, the driver yelled back, "But, sir, you didn't tell me where you wanted to go!"

Such a story epitomizes a culture bent on hurrying to a known destination without acknowledging God's help in getting there. Surprisingly, the church behaves similarly. Today, in our worship, the scripture text calls to us once again to put what could be called our own "Meribah moments" along life's journey in perspective. It was at Massah that the people of the exodus complained incessantly to Moses for having brought them out to the desert to die of thirst. Moses named the fountain they found *Meribah*, which means "strife." Instead of striving to trust God and Moses, they bitterly denied God's promises, even to the point of threatening to harm Moses.

However, before we condemn the Israelites for their "upside down" attitude, may we reflect this Thanksgiving season on our own Meribah moments. These are the times and events when we, too, lose our perspective and find ourselves wandering and wondering if our journey is some sort of divine comedy. In anger and frustration, we strike out at God and those who would encourage us that God has not forgotten us. The psalmist reminds his own people, his own generation, that when such moments occur, it is time to refrain from wringing the hands or facing life with the clenched fist. Instead, it is time to look around and marvel at God's wondrous world, a world given as a gift, a gift to be shared. Thanksgiving is a time not to close our hands, but to open them to God and to others.

And how might this be demonstrated in the lives of Christian folks at Thanksgiving?

The next time we find ourselves languishing in complaining and planting the seeds of strife in our life's wilderness, it is time to make one of two choices—praise God and turn our wilderness into a garden of gratitude, or rant and rave and plant the seeds of bitterness and strife.

By engaging the former we find godly rest for our souls and life can be a "this end up" thanksgiving. Then, we may arrive Thursday, November 27, taking our place at the table with the words in our hearts and on our lips, "Oh come, let us sing to the LORD; / let us make a joyful noise to the rock of our salvation!" (Mike Childress)

Worship Aids

Call to Worship

From many places we have traveled to worship God in this place.
We have come to give God thanks and praise!

O, people of God, sing with your hearts and not just your lips.
Give God your heartfelt gratitude.
It is good to give God thanks and praise!
O, people of God's own image,
let us worship God with our hands and hearts open that,
once again, we might know we are in the presence of our Creator.
All: Amen!

Prayer of Confession (Unison)

O God, we come before you today acknowledging that our ways do not always reflect your ways. Many times we are reminded by the lives of others that your creation is to be shared with all people, yet we take more than we give. In your mercy, forgive us and grant us courage to live with grateful hearts like your Son, our Savior and Redeemer. Amen.

Words of Assurance

Rejoice! God's mercy endures forever. In God's love you are
forgiven.
Now live out God's forgiveness in peace and justice with joyful
and grateful hearts.
All: Amen.
(Mike Childress)

NOVEMBER 27, 2008

❧❧❧

Thanksgiving Day

Readings: Deuteronomy 8:7-18; Psalm 65; 2 Corinthians 9:6-15; Luke 17:11-19

The Way to a Thankful Heart
Luke 17:11-19; 2 Corinthians 9:6-15

The characters were not lifelong friends; they were simply thrown together by their circumstances—and horrible circumstances, at that! Each of them had been struck with that horrible disease, leprosy. Their sickness ate away at their bodies, but even more, it ate away at their souls. They were no longer allowed to be around their families—or anyone else. Everywhere they went, their disease forced them to keep their distance, crying "Unclean! Unclean!" to prevent accidental encounters with the healthy multitude. These lepers were no longer able to approach God in the temple. They wondered what terrible thing they had done to cause this punishment from God. It was this emptiness that drew them together. After all, suffering with others is better than suffering alone.

Then, one day, everything changed. The lepers heard that a healer, Jesus of Nazareth, would be coming their way. So they quickly moved to the outskirts of the village so they could meet Jesus. As always, they kept their distance, but instead of calling out their usual "Unclean!" they raised a new cry, "Jesus, Master, have mercy on us!" Suddenly, an amazing thing happened. The healer looked—actually looked!—at them. Jesus did not simply glance and quickly turn away, as others usually did. Instead, Jesus really saw them. Hope blossomed; perhaps the stories they had heard about Jesus' compassion were really true. Then Jesus spoke: "Go and show yourselves to the priests." They looked at each other in confusion. Surely Jesus knew they could not enter the place of worship. *But,* they decided, *what do we have to lose? This healer speaks with authority. We will see what the priests have to say.*

As they made their way to the priests, one of them stumbled. As he put his hand down to catch himself, he saw clean, unblemished skin. He quickly pushed back his sleeves and lifted his robes, and everywhere he saw no disease. His companions looked back to see what was keeping him and stared at him in awe. As they looked at each other, they realized—it was true. They were healed!

In their joy and confusion, one of the men slipped away. He headed back down the road they had just traveled, shouting praises at the top of his lungs, and found Jesus. He threw himself at Jesus' feet and repeated his words of thanks over and over again. Jesus looked at him with great joy, and then looked beyond him. "Were not ten made clean? But the other nine, where are they?"

Where were the rest of the healed lepers? What kept them from returning to Jesus? Scripture never answers that question, leaving it to our imaginations to figure out why. The reasons may have been as varied as the lepers themselves. Perhaps they were just following instructions; Jesus had told them to go see the priest, and that was what they were doing. They knew that their healing was not official until the priest declared them clean. Maybe they were frightened. After all, a strange thing had just happened, one they could not understand. Perhaps they were full of gratitude, but weren't sure how to express it, so they just headed on with their lives. We cannot know the answer to this mystery; we are simply left to wonder.

It is easy for us to condemn these lepers, to point out their ingratitude. I wonder, though, if our lives are really so different. Do we always remember to offer thanks for the miracles—small and large—of our own lives? What is it that prevents us from running to Jesus, shouting our gratitude? It may be some of the same reasons that held back the lepers—fear, anger, joy—that overtakes all else, or a myriad of other things.

How then, do we become like the one who returned? What is the way to a thankful heart? Paul wrote to the Corinthians about this very thing in his second letter to them. Paul encouraged them to give generously to an offering for fellow believers who were in great need. It was not only for the sake of those who were receiving the offering that Paul encouraged extravagant gifts. The benefit of such generosity is that it leads to abundant thanksgiving as well. Thanksgiving is not always only on the part of the recipients. This offering was a test of the faith of the Corinthians. The offering showed their great gratitude for all that God had given them. A thankful heart shares the blessings given. As we do this, God softens our hearts, and we begin to understand what God has done and is doing in our lives.

This is a strange paradox: the less we have (because we are intent on sharing what we have with others), the more we will be grateful. A few years ago, I sat in a small church in a Kenyan village. As the time for the offering was announced, people moved forward with fruit, vegetables, and even live chickens, and an auction began. The members of the congregation with money purchased the offerings of food that others brought forward so that everyone could have money to give toward God's work. I was moved by this act of generosity, that all would give what they could. But there was more to come! Those who had purchased the fruit (but thankfully not the chickens!) quietly brought it to my friends and me. They were honoring us as guests, giving us food that they could little afford to spare. My new friends, who lived in small homes with dirt floors and often wondered what they would eat each day, understood Paul's words: "This most generous God who gives seed to the farmer that becomes bread for your meals is more than extravagant with you. He gives you something you can then give away, which grows into full-formed lives, robust in God, wealthy in every way, so that you can be generous in every way, producing with us great praise to God" (vv. 10-11, *The Message*).

What is the way to a thankful heart? The way is understanding that all we have is a gift from God. Share those blessing with others. Open your heart to the gratefulness that flows from these things, and you too will be like the leper who returned, bubbling over with gratitude for all that Jesus has done for you. (Melissa Scott)

Lectionary Commentary
Deuteronomy 8:7-18

Human nature has not changed much over the years. Moses' words to the Israelites in this passage indicate that then, as now, people tend to overlook God's work in their lives. It is one thing to see that God is with us when we are struggling; then, every good thing seems to be a miracle provided by God. When all is going well, we have a tendency to believe we have achieved this all on our own.

How do we avoid this predicament? The passage offers a threefold answer: after a good meal, give thanks to God for the food that God provided. Secondly, remember to keep God's commandments; an awareness of who you are and whose rule you live under will keep you mindful of God's loving nature. Finally, take time to remember past blessings. Celebrate the ways God has provided for you and nurtured you in the past. (Melissa Scott)

Worship Aids

Prayer of Confession

Giver of all good things, we do not always remember to say thank you. Forgive us for the times when our fear, our selfishness, our busyness cause us to have ungrateful hearts. Show us the way to gratitude, that we might appreciate and share the blessings you give us each day.

Words of Assurance

Know that our God is a gracious God, who says, "You are welcome," even when we forget to say "Thank you." Your sins are forgiven, and your life is made whole, simply through God's grace and love. Rejoice!

Benediction

Go out with hearts overflowing with gratitude. As you go, remember that God gives you all that you have. Honor God by sharing those blessings with others. Amen. (Melissa Scott)

Thank God! We Are All Keepers

Second in a Series of Three on Christian Thanksgiving

Psalm 121

One has to wonder what the world would be like if we all looked at each other as equal and valuable to God. How might the world be different? How might countries relate to one another in this post-9/11 world? How would spouses or partners respect one another? Would siblings behave any differently? How might the church behave differently if it looked at all other faiths as equal before God? What would America look like, if today, Thanksgiving Day, when we raised our heads from the table blessing, we looked at each and every person as a child of God as well as our brother and sister? It might just change every facet of human living. In fact, I am convinced that it can. And, it needs to start with me.

As a young boy, I loved going fishing with anyone who would take me. No matter if it was on Virginia's James River, Roanoke's Smith Mountain Lake, or off the New Jersey coast fishing for fluke with my uncle and cousins, I just loved to fish. Perhaps my love was directly connected to the moment when some unsuspecting and hungry fish, thinking a free meal awaited, would take the bait, and then the fun would begin. Reeling in the catch and finding a fish on the other end, regardless of the size, was one of my childhood's crowning moments.

My grandfather was not always so agreeable. With his help, I would pull in the fish, look at it dangling on the end of the line, and if it met with his expectations, he would announce, "It's a keeper!"

With God, everyone is a keeper.

No exceptions.

Everyone is a keeper because God is "a keeper." God keeps everything of value and God's most valuable creation is humanity—all of humanity. When people really need help, they look up those they know can help, unconditionally.

The psalmist looks up and sees an enormous mountain range. Mountains played an extremely important role in Hebrew religious practices. Whether it was Mount Sinai, Mount Nebo, or the Mount of Olives, it was on such turf that Yahweh could be found. Moses continually sought counsel from God by taking to the mountains. Just prior to his death, Moses was taken up on a high place by God and shown the promised territory, a land he would not get to visit personally. Just prior to Jesus' crucifixion, Jesus sought the privacy of the Mount of Olives to speak with God as he struggled with his own death.

These are examples of how God was sought out in the high places and mountains. These were important locations for spiritual encounters with Israel's God.

So, the psalmist does what was natural in time of need. The psalmist looked to the mountains, the high places, and was reminded once more that God was near: "I lift up my eyes to the hills— / from where will my help come?" It is not the mountains that give help or refuge to the psalmist. It is from God and God alone that help is bestowed.

And why? Because the writer realizes that he or she is a keeper with God. Many hundreds of years later Jesus arrives on the human scene and reveals God's good news. Israel's a keeper, and all people are keepers as far as God is concerned.

For the Christian, when listening to the psalmist's words, Thanksgiving can be a time we hear God calling us to higher ground. We get the larger view of God, a God who loves all people, a God who watches over those who are prone to stumble and fall. Psalm 121 mirrors our loving, rescuing, helping God who "will not slumber ... will neither slumber nor sleep ... will keep you from all evil; / he will keep your life. / The LORD is your keeper... The LORD will keep your going out and your coming in / from this time on and forevermore." Think of all the keepers in the Bible.

We are tempted to think that God only keeps those who are good, those who do God's will and never stumble or fall, or those who meet certain criteria we set. This myth has for too long shackled folks. The church has been complicit in saying and behaving in ways that underscore such an erroneous claim. I think of people like Rahab, a prostitute (Joshua 2:1). Rahab provided lodging for the two spies Joshua sent to the land of Jericho. God kept them safe through Rahab's hospitality. Rahab was a keeper. Then there was David, the king of Israel; even after causing Bathsheba to commit adultery and subsequently having her husband, Uriah, killed in battle, David was a keeper. And Matthew, a tax collector, whose detested vocation Jesus looked beyond and saw someone who would learn to fish for human beings. Matthew was a keeper. Later on, a man named Zaccheus, a chief publican residing at Jericho, would meet God when Jesus had supper at his house, a supper that changed his life. If we could ask Zaccheus what it was that changed his life, his answer could categorically describe anyone's encounter with God by saying, "When I looked into Jesus' eyes, I saw the person I could become. It was then I realized that, in God's eyes, I was a keeper."

What does all this have to do with Thanksgiving 2008?

We answer this way: namely, if we can be thankful that God sees us as keepers, then we cannot help but look at all others as keepers, as well.

So, when I sit down at the table this Thanksgiving Day, November 27, I could thank God for all the blessings in my life—my family, my friends, my fellow church members, my job, my health, and a host of other blessings. And they are blessings. They are the gifts that keep me in God's care. But I want this Thanksgiving Day to be a day like no other. I want to bow my head and include my Muslim brothers and sisters in my list of blessings. I want to learn to be grateful for those who disagree with me in life because they help me learn how to respect others' views. I want to thank God for those whom I perceive to be my enemies because they stretch me and deepen my sensibilities about what it means to love and care for those who would seek to harm me.

When I stand up to leave the Thanksgiving table, I will be able to thank God that we are all keepers and I will begin to contribute to life in ways that demonstrate the truth that God keeps us all! Amen. (Mike Childress)

Worship Aids

Call to Worship

All the earth gives praise and glory to God, its Creator.
We, too, lift our eyes and are awed
by the wonder of God's creation.
All flesh will know God's rescuing love.
God is our refuge and strength, ever present, ever caring.
In our worship we give God thanks,
who sustains us and redeems us
in the journey of life both now and forevermore. Amen.

Litany for Thanksgiving

The bounty of God's creation is set before us.
Unending are God's gifts that sustain life
and give strength to those who seek God.
With the grace of Christ, we accept God's invitation to feast at
    God's table,
A table rich in grace, love, mercy, and kindness.
A table provided by the love of God in Jesus Christ. Come! All
    are welcome!
(Note: This litany is well suited for a service of Holy Communion.)

Benediction

We have come and worshiped at God's table. We have been given generous portions of God's love. With our hearts nourished and our spirits renewed, let us enter back into the communities from which we came, empowered to serve all people through Christ's peace and justice. Amen. (Mike Childress)

NOVEMBER 30, 2008

❧❧❧

First Sunday of Advent

Readings: Isaiah 64:1-9; Psalm 80:1-7, 17-19; 1 Corinthians 1:3-9;
Mark 13:24-37

Waiting with God
1 Corinthians 1:3-9

I have never been good at waiting, but I have gotten less patient as I
have gotten older. Perhaps this is because I now have a greater sense of
how quickly time moves. Whatever the reason, I now find myself looking
anxiously at my watch and tapping my fingers anytime I am forced to
wait. Waiting for an appointment, waiting at a stoplight, even waiting for
water to boil—all of these raise my blood pressure. Even in the midst of
fun, I am impatient: a long line at an amusement park ride, and I am not
sure that it is worth the wait; a rain delay at a baseball game, and I am
ready to move on to the next thing.

Why is waiting so difficult? Sometimes it is the uncertainty; we want
to know what is coming, and the longer we are in the dark, the higher our
anxiety level becomes. But this is not always the answer, because we are
often even more impatient when we know what is coming.

Today, the first Sunday of Advent, we begin our journey toward
Christmas. All around us, the world is gearing up for a celebration of glut-
tony. It is hard to resist taking part in that frenzy, especially with our
impatient natures. And yet, the season calls us to a different kind of waiting—not a crazed rush toward an end, but an eager looking forward.

I remember as a child waking up early on Christmas morning, knowing
that I would have to wait until the rest of the family was awake before I
could rush to the tree to see what had been left there. I would wiggle
around and make as much noise as possible, hoping that I would "acci-
dentally" awaken my parents. I still wake up early almost every
Christmas, but something has changed. I now love that time just before

everyone else is up, when I plug in the lights on the tree, turn on the nativity light, and sit. It may be the one time of year when I enjoy waiting! It is not only the anticipation of the fun that will soon come; it is also the great love that fills the room, the memories of Christmases past and the expectation of future joys together that make my Christmas morning waiting such a wonderful time.

If only I could hold on to that contentment the rest of the Christmas and Advent seasons—or the rest of the year, for that matter! Instead, I am constantly in motion, headed toward the next event, working on the next responsibility, trying to find the right answer to the next question. It must have been something like that for the early Christians as well, because Paul's first words to the church at Corinth are about waiting. Paul reminds them that the day of Jesus is coming, and that they should stop worrying because they have everything they need to make it to that time. "You are not lacking in any spiritual gift as you wait for the revealing of our Lord Jesus Christ. He will also strengthen you to the end, so that you may be blameless on the day of our Lord Jesus Christ."

The Corinthians were eagerly looking forward to the event we are now awaiting—the coming of Christ. As we celebrate God's coming in the person of Jesus, we, with the Corinthians, also look for God's second arrival—for "the day of our Lord Jesus Christ." The good news that Paul shared with them is just as true for us today: we are not only waiting for God, we are also waiting with God.

Have you noticed that when someone else is waiting with you, it makes the delay a little less tedious? Having a friend to talk with as you wait for your name to be called in the doctor's office eases the tension, and sharing your hopes with a coworker about a plan at work can add joy to your excitement. Waiting, like many other things in life, is something that is often best endured in the company of others. That is what is so reassuring about these verses.

We are not waiting hopelessly in this world for the coming of Christ. Instead, we have been given all the supplies we need for the journey. All God's gifts are right in front of us as we wait. More important, our faithful God is with us in the wait. God will "strengthen you to the end." God offers us the company that makes waiting easier because God has called us "into the fellowship of his Son, Jesus Christ our Lord." That, after all, is the promise of Advent. Christ is coming—Emmanuel, "God with us." We must grab hold of that promise.

In my church, when we are traveling to mission sites or taking other trips, we have a set answer to the question, "How much longer?" We always laughingly reply, "Five more minutes." What began as a joke to prevent constant questioning has become much more. We all know that "five more minutes" is not an accurate answer to the question. Instead, it has become shorthand for "I know waiting is hard, but hang in there. We will be there soon. We are all in this together." This Advent, as we think about the coming of Christ in our lives, let us remember that phrase, "five more minutes," not as a prediction of the time of Christ's return, but as a reminder that it is coming, that we are waiting together, and that God is waiting with us. (Melissa Scott)

Lectionary Commentary
Isaiah 64:1-9

The prophet Isaiah expresses the people's great longing for God. It is a moment of tremendous agony; a desire for a God who seems to have turned his back, coupled with the knowledge that if we have been deserted, it is for a very good reason. In the midst of such pain, it is comforting to remember the type of God we have; our God who does awesome deeds, who meets gladly those who do right. An understanding of the power and righteousness of God leads naturally into an acknowledgment of our own weakness and sinfulness. And yet, it is that same understanding that brings hope. With a confession of our unworthiness, and a deep desire for God's presence, perhaps, after all, this God of great mercy will come to us again.

Mark 13:24-37

In the season of Advent, this passage reminds us that, while we celebrate the coming of Christ as the infant Jesus, we cannot contain God in that manger. Jesus comes in mysterious ways, in ways that we do not expect, and often do not recognize. What then, can we do? We can, as instructed in verses 28-29, take notice of the signs: not necessarily the apocalyptic signs so many have looked for, but the signs of God's continuing presence with us: acts of justice and kindness, moments of redemption. Also, we can do what Mark's Gospel instructs: be prepared. Never forget that God is indeed coming again. We must do our best to always be about the work God has given us. Christ is coming. What then, shall we do? Keep watching, and keep working. (Melissa Scott)

Worship Aids

Invocation (Psalm 80)

God of hosts, look down from heaven and see us now. We call on your name. Let your face shine upon us as we worship.

Pastoral Prayer

God, it is not easy for us to wait. And yet, that is what this season calls us to do. Help us wait patiently for you. Be especially with those in need of your healing and your comfort. Let them feel that you are waiting with them, strengthening them. Come now, Lord. We wait for—and with—you.

Benediction

May all the gifts that come from God our Father and our Lord, Jesus Christ, be yours. As you look eagerly for Christ's coming, know that God is Emmanuel, strengthening you and waiting with you. (Melissa Scott)

Thanksgiving Leftovers

Third in a Series of Three on Christian Thanksgiving

Psalm 8:1, 3-9

Thanksgiving Day at my childhood home was an extremely festive occasion. In fact, it received as much attention as Christmas and Easter. No fewer than two weeks of activities encompassed this holiday.

In most homes, Thanksgiving's featured centerpiece is the table. Over the years, it has been the quintessential symbol of blessing. A virtual cornucopia of recipes usually adorns it, ranging from traditional family fare to the most recent delectable culinary discoveries. Turkey, salads, chutney, candied yams, creamed spinach, macaroni and cheese, homemade breads, applesauce cake, and pumpkin pie are just some of the varied selections that adorned my family's table. Yes, arguably, the table remains the traditional American Thanksgiving icon.

In our home it was also a time for family to visit and reminisce about the past. Family picture albums, home movies, and the always-embellished stories about family events seasoned the festive mood that permeated the gathering. Interspersed through the day was the usual ritual of watching football or heading outdoors to enact our own reasonable facsimile of the sport. Admittedly, our home was patriarchal regarding Thanksgiving. The divisions of labor and play were, by today's twenty-first-century standards, embarrassingly gender-specific. Today, however, Thanksgiving in our home reflects a more modern, progressive model. Role reversal is unapologetically embraced (men cook while women play!), travel is limited to only very close friends because too many miles separate family members, and sports have been replaced with hot tub conversations. However, with such transformation, the table remains the predominant gathering place (some things never change!).

There was also an extraordinary phenomenon that accompanied every Thanksgiving holiday—leftovers. For some reason, enjoying leftovers was just as popular as the Thanksgiving Day meal itself. Perhaps it was the marinating effects that enhanced the flavors; but whatever it was, we always looked forward to sneaking into the refrigerator later that day or days afterward for leftover treats. However, there was another fact about leftovers at our home, there were times they were treated like second-class meals. As such, they would be discarded.

The psalmist says, "O LORD ... when I look at your heavens, / the work of your fingers / ... what are human beings that you are mindful of them, / mortals that you care for them?" In a colloquial sort of way, this verse could read, "O Lord ... when I look at nature, the menu of your creation, the work of your hands ... what are human beings that you are mindful of them, leftovers, that you care for them?"

We humans are not God's leftovers in the creation's scheme of things.

While the psalmist concludes that our mortality is "a little lower than divine beings" (v. 5a; Hebrew *elohim* means "God" or "divine beings"), we are "crowned ... with glory and honor. These two attributes are directly linked to our divinely appointed purpose; namely, God has given us "dominion over the works of [God's] hands." In other words, we all have been divinely appointed as God's stewards.

Therefore, I would like to propose a new paradigm for Thanksgiving, namely, that as Christians, we celebrate thanksgiving to God, not one day or even a couple of weeks but three hundred sixty-five days a year. This would be the most noble and Christian way we could arise from the Thanksgiving table—being God's stewards of all that God has created here on planet earth. Another way of putting it, instead of treating such an important holiday as strictly an American observance and then going on about our business as usual, what if we treated God's earth with the respect and love that it deserves? As Christians we are called by God to think and live theologically as we manage God's ecology.

Think of how many times we have sat at a table selfishly enjoying the bounty of God's earth and rarely, if ever, think of how and by whom such foods got to our tables. In the days that follow until we find ourselves at the Thanksgiving table again, could we take time to think of people like the Immokalee workers in Florida who work as migrant workers under such harsh conditions and receive only a pittance of what the majority of Americans earn? They are our equals. They are our brothers and sisters. They are our costewards of God's earth. How can we take our place at table this year enjoying the fruits of their labors and not be moved to advocate for better working conditions and a fairer wage?

Then there are the giant oil and fishing companies that scourge earth's majestic oceans and seas for its crude oil and fish. We are beginning to discover that such entities are taking more from the earth than they are giving back, all the time literally raping the earth of its vast reserves of oil and fish. Such activity has endangered some species of fish and all but destroyed the plankton necessary for stabilizing and promoting ocean and sea life. Yet we go to market and without any hesitancy purchase gasoline and fish at exorbitant prices and never question the injustice that serves up such commodities. As God's stewards, our thanks to God for giving all humanity such a provider, Earth, has to include calling oil refineries and fishing magnates to accountability. And, this has to be done, not in adversarial ways, but through cooperative and peaceful actions.

Then there are other food industries we can call on to promote better ways of providing food for our tables without demeaning and harming the animal kingdom. We only have to watch some of the news programs or cable channels such as the Discovery Channel to learn the horrific ways animals are treated so that the world's market demands are met with cruel efficiency. Hormones have been developed in order to speed up the growth of beef and milk cattle, chickens, turkeys, pigs, and all other species that serve the world's hunger for meat and milk. We're only beginning to learn how humanity's supply and demand for food products may be causing harm to us humans and our environment.

On and on we could go, listing the seemingly endless injustices to our world and its environment. Yet, the world and the church pull up to the table every day and may only give lip service to one of the world's most growing problems—the grievous lack of caring for our world, a world gifted to us by God.

Do not hear me offering only a diatribe against those who seek to provide us the necessities of life. There are innumerable companies and organizations dedicated to serving humankind and doing so with integrity. We must be grateful for them and even support them with our patronage. However, this is not a perfect world. And God is calling each of us to step up and claim our rightful place in the world as God's stewards.

How might we do this as Christians?

The psalmist calls us to accountability.

From now on, let us always look at the Earth as God's table. This is a table having room for all God's people, people having God's image of glory and the honor of being God's stewards!

If we can view our role as stewards who give more than we take, who call ourselves and others to accountability as partners in caring for God's global garden, then we can take our place at God's table, not just once a year, but each and every day with the blessing: "O LORD, our Sovereign, / how majestic is your name in all the earth!"

This way, there will always be plenty left over so that all God's children may come to God's glorious and bountiful table to say and experience God's grace. (Mike Childress)

Worship Aids

Pastoral Prayer

O God, our Creator, what a wonderful and glorious world you have created. Empower us with your Holy Spirit that we may live as a thankful people. Help us develop the attitude of gratitude in all we do and say so that your love and grace flourish and be reflected in our stewardship. In Christ we pray. Amen.

Invocation

Let us rise and meet our Creator. Let us raise our hands and voices in acknowledgment that God's Holy Spirit moves among us, calling us to new life in Christ. Let us raise our eyes, knowing that this new life of stewardship for all God's creation is seen in the life of Jesus the Christ, our Lord and Savior. Amen.

Benediction

Sisters and brothers, caregivers and caretakers of all God's
   bountiful blessings,
let us leave this place in the sure knowledge
that our lives are to be God's gifts to the world.
Let us live generously and unconditionally in Christ's love and
   peace.
All: Amen!
(Mike Childress)

DECEMBER 7, 2008

❧❧❧

Second Sunday of Advent

Readings: Isaiah 40:1-11; Psalm 85:1-2, 8-13; 2 Peter 3:8-15a; Mark 1:1-8

Hope-filled Waiting!
Isaiah 40:1-11

The passage for consideration is a favorite for this season of the Christian year. Isaiah 40 is a powerful passage, marking the beginning authorship of Second Isaiah. Authored during the exilic period of Hebrew history, Isaiah prophesies the imminent return of God's people to the promised land. The Hebrews have been exiled in Babylon for almost fifty years. Isaiah speaks confidently about God leading the people back to their homeland. Using poetic images Isaiah depicts God turning a merciful eye towards the Jewish people. God restores blessing and promise.

Advent begins the Christian year with a message of hopeful waiting. Isaiah sets the tone for Advent as it identifies the theme of expectant hope rooted and grounded God's love for God's people. The bold prophet of God's redemption reads as if the events have already occurred. After the exile God's people are ready for new hope from God. As God's people today we struggle to sense God's presence of our own exile. Living each day in the shadow of terrorism, staggering violence, possible threats all around us, our uneasiness with poverty, racism, materialism, we too seem to be faking our faithful response to God's mystery.

In such circumstances the last word we want to hear about is waiting. Like the exiled Jews, we want a definitive word from God. The prophet sensed such uneasiness. Isaiah begins his message with the words of comfort and reassurance. Feeling lost and cutoff the Jews hear God's words of promised comfort. Isaiah proclaims the people's waiting in a foreign land is over. Isaiah declares that God builds a highway across the wilderness. God's breath is breathing new life over the decaying grass and withering flowers. God is at work regardless of how things may appear to them. These lucid images stir God's people to a reborn hope.

This prophetic message is one we need to hear. We are so easily enticed to believe in the latest trend—the freshest story. We are inundated each moment with more news than we can ever hope to assimilate. Choices overwhelm us each day as to what we will do, where we will go, what we will buy, and what we are to believe. Although the Hebrews' exile was more related to place than ours, we too find ourselves in exile. We too need to hear a new song in this foreign land of too much stuff, too much information, and too many choices. In the midst of such despair Isaiah proclaims not only that God is present, but that God is preparing to restore God's people. God has forgiven our sin and will abide with us. God helps us find our way. We wait in expectation that God will be faithful to these promises.

When my son was born my wife and I waited for sixteen hours as she labored to deliver. It was not, however, a dull kind of waiting. Following the instructions of those who lead us, we prepared for what was to come. We acted before the event came—faithful that it would happen in its time. It was an expectant, intense, deliberate waiting. Such is the waiting Isaiah calls God's people to do. The result of such waiting is the fulfillment of the promise. For us it was the birth of our son; for the Hebrews it was going home.

Wherever people are in Advent, they long for a God who can lead them. Isaiah reminds the Hebrews and us that such a place exists. The prophet dares to offer us a vision of what God will do in a place called Bethlehem. Isaiah dangles before us God's promise of love. Today we proclaim a word of hope to a people who so desperately need it. We too begin our journey home to the place God has for each of us. (Travis Franklin)

Lectionary Commentary
Mark 1:1-8

Mark roots his gospel in a Hebrew understanding of who Jesus is as the Messiah. Quoting Isaiah, Mark wants all to know who John is as John prepares the way for Jesus, the Messiah. The structure of Mark's beginning sets the context for all that follows. There is expectancy through prophecy, a call to repentance on behalf of God's people, and the promise of what God will do through Jesus and the Holy Spirit. God confirms Jesus' identity as Messiah.

In preaching this text one might answer the central question of this Gospel: *Who is Jesus?* Mark makes it clear that there will be a part to play for not only God and Jesus, but for humankind as well.

2 Peter 3:8-15a

Second Peter prepares disciples to conduct themselves in persecution and hardship. This author seems unsure whether or not he will see those to whom he writes again. The text has a finality to it. It describes the end time and its judgment upon people. This author would find himself at home in our world with its preoccupation with the end of the world. Second Peter's description of that end becomes for him a useful tool in helping restore and strengthen the waning faith of the struggling.

Second Peter demands nothing but faithfulness in the end. Christian proclamation during persecution offers a message that believer's faithfulness God will reward. Those found to have no faith will receive what is coming to them. Second Peter lifts up a perspective of hope and faith. Whatever it is they have to endure is worth it. Second Peter brings perspective to suffering for the sake of the gospel. (Travis Franklin)

Worship Aids

Call to Worship

We gather here today to listen to what God has to say.
Give us ears to hear your word, O God.
We gather here today expecting God to move and work among us.
**Give us expectant hearts that anticipate the movement of
your spirit, O God.**
We gather here today, seeking to see with the eyes of faith
and hope for what your love has done, is doing, and will do in the
world.
**Give us ears to hear, hearts that sense,
and eyes to see your glory as it is revealed to us this day
and always. Amen.**

Invocation

Lord, we come before your throne of grace not trusting in ourselves but in your marvelous and gracious love as it seeks expression among us. May we listen for your still, small voice as it speaks to us today and as it boldly proclaims the undeniable reality of your love that will not let us go. Instill in our humble hearts, through your grace, the hope of Christmas that transforms the ordinariness of life into the extraordinary sacredness of that which has been made holy by the presence of your most Holy Spirit. Stir our hearts and our imaginations that we may see beyond the appearances of what is to the bold reality of all that can possibly become. In the name and spirit of the Holy child, Jesus our Lord, we pray. Amen.

Pastoral Prayer

O God, we come into your holy presence today anticipating the power of your love as it seeks expression among us. Help us slow our lives down, pause in order to wonder, be reclaimed by a sense of awe at whom you are and what you are seeking to do in our broken world. Stir our imagination with images of your grace and fill our hearts with the reality of your incarnation. May this incarnation explode on the scene of our predictable lives. Forgive us for insensitivity to who you are and how you are working in our lives and in our world. Pardon us for being so selfish that enough is never enough to quench our thirst and hunger for more. Direct our attention to the places that we are afraid to look in our own lives and in the life of the communities where we live. Make us realize the importance of this moment and all the moments that follow. Give to us today, in this season of giving and sharing, hearts that are humble and willing to give. Thank you for the birth of Jesus; to restore and redeem us all by your all-powerful love. Give us joy that we might come to know and claim the reality of Bethlehem. May we too be brought to our knees as we worship the Christ child who even now seeks nothing less than our hearts and souls. In the name and spirit of the babe named Jesus, we pray. Amen. (Travis Franklin)

Where Do Gifts Come From?

First in a Series of Two on Gifts

Deuteronomy 26:1-19

One Christmas, shortly after my mother-in-law had passed away, a new dish appeared on our dining room table. Our children were old enough at that time to know that it had not been among those dishes we used at special occasions. This dish, featuring a Christmas tree and ornaments, was an obvious choice for Christmas celebrations.

"Where did that come from?" was the unanimous question that sprang from their lips as the dish was placed on the table. What followed was a story of how their grandmother had acquired the dish and how it had been something she treasured and had been passed on to us and would be passed on to them. In a strange and mysterious way, an informal litany began to take shape over the years in which the story was repeated each Christmas. Each year the story of grandma's dish was one of the rituals in which we celebrated her love for us and the pleasure we shared in being together at Christmas.

In the season of Advent we prepare to celebrate the supreme gift of God's love that is ours in the birth of Jesus. At the heart of our thanks-giving and joy in receiving such a gift, at the heart of preparing to receive it anew, is the importance of remembering the source of such a gift. This ritual of remembering is important not only for a celebration of Christmas but also empowers us to experience the giftedness that sustains daily life. The rituals of remembering have power because over and over again we have the opportunity to recall the first question that springs to mind from a surprised and grateful heart. *Where did this come from?*

The question keeps us connected to the source of life's gifts. Within the litany of remembrance we recall the identity of the giver. The passage in Deuteronomy prescribes a litany of remembrance that comes at the time of harvest. It serves as an act of worship in which the participant has the opportunity to look back into history and to recognize the hand of God acting in history. In that sense it is Israel's confession of faith.

"We are the descendants of a wandering Aramean," the worshiper states. "We belong to a people who were mistreated by the Egyptians and suffered. God heard our cries and saw we were being oppressed. God brought us to this place of milk and honey."

God's actions in the past are directly related to the event of handing over the first fruits of the harvest to the priest. In that moment God's intentions toward the worshiper become clear. God's intent is to love, provide, and lead. God's power is directed toward the daily events in the life of God's children. The natural world with its capacity to provide, and the worshiper's own hands and energy become the sign of God's loving provision. Acts of worship remind the people that they have experienced God's presence in God being the source of life and life's sustenance.

The season of Advent is a part of that worship tradition. The practice of reading the prophecies helps us recall God's identity and ours as God's people. We hear our story. We are like sheep that have gone astray. Our lives are like the city of Zion, laid to waste by our selfishness and our indifference to others. God is acting in Jesus to lead us out of our slavery. We are invited to sing a new song.

Our worship provides the process in which we can connect with our experiences of God's history-making involvement in our lives. Paul tells the early church that we were once at odds with God and one another. Now we belong to God and one another through the reconciliation made real in Christ. Our worship is the declaration of our faith in who God has been and will be. We have clarity about our belonging to God. We have clarity about our belonging to one another. The God who led a people out of Egypt is still leading people out from the land of fear and death. We are those people.

There was one other lesson concerning grandmother's dish. In the discussion about where the dish came from, there was also discussion about how and when it would be used. Since it was clearly very beautiful, the children anticipated that it would go into a china cabinet and not be used. We did discuss the fact that the dish needed to be carefully used and at the appropriate times. We also discussed their grandmother's enjoyment of her family and friends and her desire that we all could enjoy using the dish.

The ritual in Deuteronomy continues as the worshiper is instructed in the purpose of the litany of remembrance just concluded. The gift is a tenth of the harvest and is used in sharing with others. The sharing is an act of obedience based on the experience of love recalled in the story of God's actions in behalf of God's people. The sharing is the expression of harmony with God and with neighbor. The act of praise is followed by acts of mercy and compassion. Once again the basic elements of life are seen in a new way. The gifts of God are fully realized in both the harvest of the earth, the work of a person's hands and the obedience of the heart. They all are extensions of God's power and love in daily life.

Our worship and our grace-filled obedience in Advent link us to our faith family in every time and place. Our gifts of heart and hands and labors are the fruits of knowing where these gifts came from. (Bob Holloway)

Worship Aids

Call to Worship

We are the beloved of God, inheritors of God's promised redemption.

As the people of God we offer our songs of praise, our gifts of love, and our lives to be shaped the Holy Spirit.

Pastoral Prayer

Holy God, we gather to once again enter the story of your saving goodness. We come to proclaim your promises and their fulfillment in Jesus Christ. Renew the image we received in our baptism. Renew in us such a sense of thanksgiving that we may praise you with joy and serve you with faith and hope.

We pray for those across your world who praise you with lives of charity, justice, and peace. Through Christ you seek to transform all creation. Anoint us with the spirit of expectation that we may be alive and awake to your presence. Through Christ we pray. Amen.

Benediction

We are the beloved of God, we live in peace, and we serve with joy. Amen. (Bob Holloway)

DECEMBER 14, 2008

❧❧❧

Third Sunday of Advent

Readings: Isaiah 61:1-4, 8-11; Psalm 126; 1 Thessalonians 5:16-24; John 1:6-8, 19-28

Will Anybody Know?
Isaiah 61:1-4, 8-11

This incredible passage of scripture from Isaiah is a third part of the prophecy within Isaiah. A disciple of Deutero-Isaiah possibly wrote this third portion. Certainly the theme is the same. Jesus used part of this passage to identify what he seeks to do in his ministry. It is an appropriate text for the Advent season as it seeks to define the place and role of this restored community of Jews in Jerusalem to the world. As we move to the birth of God's son into our own world, isn't it appropriate to ask ourselves what role will this event have in our life?

A reference in this text reflects that the prophet is anointing by God to carry out his calling from God. Elsewhere in the Old Testament, this kind of anointing is usually reserved for kings. By using powerful imagery this prophet takes on God's authority. The author obviously wants readers to understand where his message has its source. This passage shifts the role and responsibility of God's people. Written in a postexilic time frame, the Jews have now been granted their return to the promised land. They have been restored as God's chosen people. This restoration will take on a new and different role. The salvation they have experienced firsthand is to be now a salvation that they share with all people, everywhere. The restoration of Jerusalem has a purpose. The reason behind this restoration lies in the hope that all nations will come to acknowledge that God has blessed Jerusalem. God seeks to pledge God's blessing not only on the city but also on all who dwell within it. We discover the power of this passage as God seeks not only to restore and rebuild, but also to illustrate what such blessing is to the entire world.

As the church moves toward Bethlehem, it is no surprise that God seeks to use us in this redemptive event. We describe what blessing and restoration does in the lives of people. Paul is right in Romans 8 when he writes about God working for good in the world with those who love God and with those who are called according to God's purpose. Advent is filled with this sense that God is behind, in, through, over, above, under, all over this great drama unfolding before us. God is intentional as this is the focus of Advent 3. Isaiah has been anointed by none other than the Lord.

As the Hebrews needed to be reminded of their response to restoration so, too, we followers of Christ need reminding. Responsibility goes with salvation. Our experience cannot simply be reduced to a day and place. Such an experience demands a continual response. We seek to be faithful to what restoration means and how it defines us each moment we live. We too are called to become a living illustration of what it means to be blessed and restored by God. Perhaps then all may see and come to such blessing and restoration.

When the tragic events of 9/11 happened we could not believe it was happening on our soil. After that dark and yet heroic day, we began to rally as a nation to one another. We realized how much we needed one another as a nation and as a community. Such events, even tragic ones, shape us and define us individually and collectively. Such was the case of the restoration of the Jews to Jerusalem. God through the prophet wants the people to understand that this is a defining moment in their lives both individually and collectively. The events of restoration are a turning point for them as God seeks to use God's work in history. God molds who people are and who people become.

In preparation and waiting may we come to realize and to answer for ourselves how this birth at Bethlehem might shape and mold us. May its power claim us and transform us. Maybe this Christmas we will be open to what it is God is seeking to do in us. Could it be that this Christmas God wants to know what difference this birth make to us? Will God be able to tell the difference? As important, will anybody else? (Travis Franklin)

Lectionary Commentary
John 1:6-8, 19-28

John's Gospel begins by identifying John the Baptist's role, as Jesus' precursor to all that Jesus is to become. Images of light, life, and witness are all important to John. John's unique style of storytelling certainly makes this different from the other Gospels. The dramatic style makes the story come alive. However, the primary message is one we recognize from the Synoptic Gospels. The inclusion of reasons for the actions of John the Baptist sets his role in the unfolding drama. Everything in this Gospel leads to the point of this introduction—announcing the coming of the Messiah. This season of the church year God points us toward the coming birth of Jesus.

Expectancy, repentance, and promise are three key words to understanding the focus of this text. Anticipating who God is and how God works in the world is the disciple's role. In response to God there is always opportunity for God's people to turn from sin and toward God. God's confirmation of Jesus as God's Son sets in motion just how such fulfillment of promise is being established.

1 Thessalonians 5:16-24

This passage from 1 Thessalonians has been the subject of much debate in the church. It is characterized by a series of brief imperative phrases. Some believe this call for order may be an early form of church order. It is similar to some other late first-century writings that instruct the early church, including instructions for worship governance. Some scholars believe that Paul challenges the proper use of prophecy at Thessalonica. Everything that precedes these verses attempts to order the life of the Christian community at Thessalonica. Order was significant to the life of the early church. Paul believes it must be done in accordance with sound practice.

Paul wants to make sure that prophecy is truly a gift of God's spirit. The gift of prophecy as it takes form must be examined according to order and form. Prophecy has a proper place within the practicing community of faith. The early church as it began to spread throughout the ancient world endured growing pains. Sound doctrine and practice was important to Paul. These didactic verses seek to help the church at Thessalonica order itself in worship and practice according to sound doctrine. (Travis Franklin)

Worship Aids

Call to Worship

Today we come to give God praise for God's mighty works
  among us.
The Lord has done great things for us, and we are glad.

We remember God's great love today as we move towards the b
    of a baby in Bethlehem.
The Lord has done great things for us, and we are glad.
Instill in our heart today a sense of great joy and thanksgiving
    for all you have done, are doing, and will do, O God.
The Lord has done great things for us, and we are glad.

Invocation

Lord, into your most holy presence we now come. Calm our anxious
spirits. Remove the distractions that would keep us from you here today.
Break down the walls of separation that we have built to keep you from
our hardened hearts. Lead us in joy and celebration of the only reality
worth knowing, that you love us as we are. Free us for joyful obedience to
your claim and call on our lives this day and every day. Amen.

Pastoral Prayer

O Lord, how can we call you "friend" and yet not know you? Our busyness with the idols of our time has kept us from you again this week. In our
hurry to do all that we can get done and to do it all efficiently, we have forgotten once again who is most important. Forgive us we pray and pardon us
for our selfishness. Help us come to realize what it means to be in relationship with you and with others. Lead us into an understanding of your time
and the power of what it means just to be without so much doing. We
thank you this day and always for your Son, Jesus, and for all he has given
for us. In our journey to the manger may we come sense once again the awe
and power of all that you are doing through this child. May we allow this
child to have our hearts. May we surrender completely to him and all that
he would have us do in this season of giving and sharing. Bless our hurting
world and bring your peace to us as only you can. Heal us in our brokenness and may we come to care for those who need us most. In the name and
spirit of your most precious Son, Jesus, we pray. Amen. (Travis Franklin)

Gift Cycle

Second in a Series of Two on Gifts

Deuteronomy 26:1-19

It is not uncommon for the book of Deuteronomy to be seen as strictly
a book of law. The instructions for worship in Deuteronomy that have

been our focus for these two weeks could be read in such a way that the hearer feels the burden of being careful to do the right thing at the right time. After all, there are sections of the book that are filled with curses as well as blessings.

The second instruction for the required litanies of faith begins in verse 12. It reads as a rather stiff declaration of what the worshiper needs to be able to say after making the offer of gifts for the work of the temple and for the needy. The worshiper states that the portion required has been given without any of it being eaten while mourning. It is presented while the worshiper is ritually clean. All the commands and ordinances have been kept. "Now God, look down on me and bless me as you swore to my ancestors that you would bless."

We find the words *commands* and *ordinances* to be heavy words. How can Deuteronomy be read in the season of Advent in which we place so much hope in the grace born into the world in Jesus?

Perhaps our reaction is not so much a reflection on our spiritual ancestors as it is a reflection that we have made a false assumption about the connection between law and grace. We assume the words *law* and *grace* cannot be in harmony with each other. The truth is exactly the opposite.

The opening litany of remembrance centers on God's gracious acts of liberation and provision. Through the natural world and the skills and work of human beings, God provides. In the time of slavery, God leads people into freedom. These are acts of God's self giving to God's children. The response of obedience is not then an act of obtaining God's goodness but a response to that goodness. The law gives direction for the desire of the worshiper to rightly use the gifts God has so freely bestowed. The worshiper articulates the bond of covenant with God in which daily life becomes the place where God's promises are fulfilled. Daily life provides the opportunity for gratitude to be lived out in covenant faithfulness.

As a text for Advent this one joins prophecies concerning the Messiah as an historical witness to God's saving and sustaining power. The life of discipleship is the response for all those who seek to live with faith in the constancy of God's grace—not in a linear way, but in a cycle of God's action. God graciously takes initiative on behalf of humankind, the gifts returned to God through worship and compassion for others are returned to God's children as a part of God's gracious intentions.

One Christmas, our son, at the midpoint of his Peace Corps service, returned for the holidays. He had served on the island of Maewo, a part of the nation of Vanuatu in the South Pacific. He had been there fourteen months and had lived with a family on the island as he taught school. We were, of course, so grateful for their acceptance of him, their shepherding him through the waters of being far from family and in a different culture.

A few days before he arrived, we received boxes shipped with the bold writing stating we were not to open them until Christmas. We were not surprised, thinking they were souvenirs he had picked up in his travels.

On Christmas morning, he passed around the boxes and told us these were gifts from his family in Vanuatu. Amazement began to dawn as we realized these were not souvenirs he had bought but were handmade items created for us by his adopted family. There were simple dresses for my wife and daughter, carved wood for my son and me, and woven ceremonial mats handpainted with our names. Tears welled up in our eyes at the beauty and the love behind the gesture. It was that family extending their family to include us. Our first thought was what can we share? It was not thinking about reciprocating, you bought me something now I have to buy something for you. We felt connected to their family. They had shared a gift from their own culture, their own talents, and identity as a family. We wanted to do the same. We made a tape of our family singing songs and hymns that were important to us, songs we had sung in worship together. The tape we made was taken to Maewo and shared as a part of their worship.

Teresa of Avila said, "Accustom yourself continually to make many acts of love, for they enkindle the soul." The birth of Jesus is the fulfillment of law and grace found in Deuteronomy and continues to be fulfilled in us as we offer our gifts of love. Our faithfulness to our covenant with God is the means through which God kindles and rekindles our souls and the soul of the world. (Bob Holloway)

Worship Aids

Call to Worship

We are here at God's inviting.
We are invited to receive God's gifts of love.
Let our praise of God reflect our joy in God's goodness.

Pastoral Prayer

In this season, O God, our minds are on gifts and gift-giving. What we look for is something to give. Awaken us to the gifts that really matter.

Center our minds on someone we are called to serve, someone we are called to love. Center our hearts on someone we can encourage, thank, hug, forgive, or from whom we can ask forgiveness. We give you thanks for this season and for the supreme gift of the one you sent into our world. Grant us grace to receive Jesus gladly.

Benediction

Pour out your Holy Spirit on us, God, that we may joyfully receive and faithfully share the gifts of faith, hope, and love that are ours through Jesus Christ. Amen. (Bob Holloway)

DECEMBER 21, 2008

❧❧❧

Fourth Sunday of Advent

Readings: 2 Samuel 7:1-11, 16; Psalm 89:1-4, 19-26; Romans 16:25-27; Luke 1:26-38

Let It Be!
Luke 1:26-38

Luke identifies for us a common Advent story—the familiar work of God through the announcement of the angel and the somewhat surprised and confused response of Mary. The story depicts God as taking the initiative in the human drama only to be misunderstood by the human that God seeks. Such seems to be a common theme among the gospel stories as God's presence, work, or activity is met with fear, misunderstanding, a sense of mystery, awe, power, and certainly high drama. This story is yet one more example of such an encounter between God's angel, Gabriel, and Mary, the soon-to-be mother of Jesus.

Advent offers an introduction to a great drama about Gabriel's announcement and Mary's response. The story has all the characteristics that make God's work in the world such a good read. Luke portrays part of how God seeks expression among God's people by using Gabriel. Angels are messengers and mediators of God's word and will. Luke uses them regularly in his gospel story as messengers. The message Gabriel delivers to Mary is fourfold. Mary will have a son named Jesus, the child will be the Son of God, the child will sit on the throne of David, and the birth of the child will come to pass via the work of the Holy Spirit of God. It is the same form of the message the angel earlier had for Zechariah. Luke also affirms that nothing with God is impossible.

God initiates contact with people through an angelic announcement. Mary responds by listening, puzzlement, misunderstanding, questions, and eventually faith. Luke's story we have heard before many times throughout biblical history. Luke retells the ongoing unfolding of God's salvation history with the world. Yet, Luke tells it with high drama and with simplicity. In a nutshell, God acts in life. Humans are encouraged to listen, question, seek understanding, and dialogue, but ultimately respond with trust and faith to what it is God is seeking to do.

As the church makes its dramatic journey to the manger, this story invites us to respond to God's initiative once again. As Gabriel appeared to Mary we realize how God comes to us. Such intrusions into our ordered and ordinary life catch us off guard. Still such intrusions into life always demand a response from us. This process offers the opportunity to invite the congregation to examine what it means to be disciples.

When was the last time you were surprised? I remember the day my parents called a family meeting to tell us we were moving. We had lived in our community for six years and were settled. Such news came out of nowhere and caught my sister, my brother, and me completely by surprise. Our lives would never be the same. Such is the stuff of life. Such is the drama of Mary's new life, altered forever in a moment. Isn't that the way life is? Isn't that the way God works?

The real power of this story, however, we find in Mary's response to what God seeks to do in her life. Despite the surprise, Mary finally comes to that powerful place of acceptance as she responds saying, "Let it be." In light of all that has transpired, her response is incredible. She provides us an example of how we too might respond to God's surprises in our own life. The issue for us always, however, is can we just let it be? Often, we need to know and be in control. Can we simply just let it be? Such a faithful response provides us with a living illustration of who we need to be as we too ponder the Bethlehem stable. Without seeking to control or glamorize or add or overanalyze, can we just let the story be what it is this Christmas? Can we allow God to say what needs to be said through this simple birth? Can we step back in awe and wonder of a child and just ponder these things in our hearts and allow God to do what God needs to do with us, in us, and through us? Can we just let it be? (Travis Franklin)

Lectionary Commentary
2 Samuel 7:1-11, 16

The seventh chapter of 2 Samuel is the heart the Samuel narrative. It is the story of God's favor of King David. God blesses not only David but also David's line and lineage. Most of the dialogue in these verses is between God and the prophet Nathan. David proposes through Nathan to build a house for God. God, however, refuses David's offer. God rather reminds David of God's own need to be able to move among his people. The implication is that no one can contain God in a single place.

God predicts for David a son and how God's favor will be with David's line forever. God also gives the responsibility for building the temple to the next king of Israel, David's son. God reverses David's original request to build God a house. It will be God who builds David a house and a lineage forever. The power of this story inheres in how God redirects what David seeks to do. God rewards David by establishing David's house and lineage forever.

Romans 16:25-27

This text pronounces the final benediction on what is a profoundly rich theology of Christian faith. It contains nothing less than the concluding proclamation of God's final victory over the world in grace. It seeks to state once and for all that God's gracious lordship will prevail. It boldly announces God's fulfilled promise of the complete restoration of creation to a right relationship of love and devotion to its Creator. Paul seeks to affirm all that he has previously written.

These closing words to Romans remind the Christian that not only can there be joy in the first Advent of Christ but also that same joy may be celebrated in Christ's second Advent, when God's powerful plan for God's creation will become a visible reality. This is the message of Romans to the church today. This text expresses what it means to wait with anticipation and joy. The message resonates with passion and power that God is and will always be faithful to what God says God will do! (Travis Franklin)

Worship Aids

Call to Worship

Let us sing of the mercies of the Lord today and always!
With our mouths we will make known God's faithfulness to all
   generations.
Your mercy, O God, will build up forever and your faithfulness
   shall be established in the heavens.

For the heavens declare your glory and the heavens sing
    continually of your praise now and forevermore. Amen.

Invocation

Move among us once again here today in this sacred place and time, O
Lord, our God. Open us to the work of your Spirit that we might come to
realize the power of your love as it seeks to embrace once again. Empower
us as your people that we may worship you in spirit and in truth and that
your grace may soothe our hurting souls and heal our wounds. In the
name of Jesus the Christ, we pray. Amen.

Pastoral Prayer

O God, here we are together in this sacred place of worship. May we be
attentive to where you would work among us here today. May we come to
experience the stirring and leading of your Spirit as it speaks, as it leads, at
it forgives, as it heals, and as it convicts. Declare to us today through word
and table the way in which you would have us live. Give to us the courage
to make the hard choices in life, the will to live according to your prompting, and the love to shatter our pretentious illusions. Make us mindful of
the needs of others and to stop expecting someone else to take care of the
needy, or feed the hungry, or welcome the stranger, or visit the prisoner
when we certainly have the time and the means to do it ourselves. In this
season of love, help us love. In this season of giving, help us give. In
this season of hope, help us be hopeful. In this season of grace, lead us to
graciousness. Forgive us when we settle for so much less than what you
offer. May we come to see as you see, love as you love, work as you work,
share as you share, and live as you would have us live. Bless our hurting,
broken, divided world and remove whatever stands in the way of us all
finally realizing that we are and will forever be your children. In the name
of the Baby Jesus, we pray. Amen. (Travis Franklin)

Giving to Honor

First in a Series of Three on Holidays and Emotional Health

Luke 2:8-18

Only four shopping days left 'til Christmas! Those words bring panic to
some of us. How will everything get done? How does everyone else get
everything done?

During the holidays, it is especially easy to get caught up in other's expectations—especially in the gift-giving department. We are inundated with suggestions for what we should buy, how our homes should look, what we should cook, and how we should dress. I remind you of that first Christmas—when the shepherds and the wise men showed up.

Scripture says the shepherds came in from their fields. Being good shepherds, they didn't just leave their flocks, they brought them with them. They came and they offered their praise. They gave what they had. They gave a part of themselves, spontaneously, with no thought of the cost.

In the Native American community, gift-giving is done for only one reason: to show honor. Honor is acting on a decision we make to place high value, worth, and importance on another person by recognizing that person as a unique creation and granting him or her a position in our lives worthy of great respect. In many of the sovereign nations of North America, the giveaway is a crucial part of many of our rituals. In most of the nations, when someone dies, that person's possessions are shared with friends and family. In the dominant society, at funerals, the women of the church plan and serve a meal to the deceased's family. In the native culture, the deceased's family cooks the meals for the friends and family, sometimes every meal for six days!

For many of the ceremonies on the Navajo reservation, the family works for months to gather the gifts traditionally given—material for the women, gift cards for the men, and blankets for the guests of honor. At powwows, the drums, the arena director, head dancers, and the emcees are honored. To avoid shame, gifts are given to honor the elders and as treats for the children. The giveaway is a way to share what the family has and to honor those who care enough to participate in our ceremony.

We live in a society, which, for the most part, follows Hollywood and the commercials. We buy into the idea that one of the best suggestions for buying a gift is to get the other person something we would like to have. But I suggest if one does that, one is declaring the wishes and needs of that other person to be second to one's own desires and needs. In a manner, we have succeeded in doing exactly the opposite of what we wanted to do.

I am making the assumption that, if one is willing to spend the time and money to get a person a gift, it is to honor them. So what do we do when we don't honor the person for whom we still *must* present a gift? I have worked in the secular world. I have drawn a name of an office worker to get a gift for and a dollar limit is set so no one will be unable to participate. Nor can I forget the gift exchange where you grab a gift and the next person to get a gift can choose a new one or pick yours! Are you giving gifts out of your desire to share, or a sense of duty or others' expectations? The idea of gift giving originated, so the story goes, when Saint Nicholas wanted to help children in need, so he gave them gifts anonymously.

Now, it is not only how much a gift is worth, the number of gifts is important. What happened to the times when one gift, no matter what it was, was received graciously and happily? I remember watching a movie during which a boy opened his gift early because he had to go out in the snow. His present, wrapped in newspaper, was mittens that his mother had knit. That and an apple were the only presents under the tree. He needed those mittens, and valued them.

We have lost our way. Have the number of presents and their value become more important than the person receiving the gift?

Let's go back to that first Christmas—the angels brought their heavenly voices to sing heavenly songs. The shepherds offered their story and their praise. The Magi offered frankincense, gold, and myrrh. Each wanted to give a gift and each gave what they had. The Magi had the resources to offer material gifts, but every gift was important.

As you contemplate the gifts still left on your list, I encourage you to think how your gift will honor the receiver. Perhaps we have gotten caught up in the competition and the standards that the world has. Bigger, better, more expensive gifts—even for people we don't love, maybe don't even like! So who are we trying to impress?

Four more shopping days before Christmas. If you go to the mall, I invite you to look at the faces of those shoppers. What will we see if we look at your face? Yes, there are only four more days, but prayerfully examine your shopping list. These are the people in your life whom you choose to honor. These are the people who share your life to some degree. What you give does not have to be bigger or more expensive than last year. What you give need only please two people—the receiver and yourself, the giver, not your sister-in-law or your rich cousin, not your mother! Does the gift reflect the honor you want to give that person? Think of those first people who gave gifts to the King. They gave what they had and those gifts were a part of their own resources; they didn't borrow! The shepherds and the angels gave of themselves. In a society where time is money and so valuable, might you consider how you can give that to some on your list? A promise to spend time will also give those procrastinators a whole year to fulfill their intentions! Whatever your choice, I ask that you give as Yahweh has given, abundantly and graciously. (Raquel Mull)

Worship Aids

Call to Worship

Creator, we have left our warm beds and traveled to be in this place.
We have come to hear the words you have for our life.
We have gathered in your name to praise and worship you.
Give us your sense of peace and joy in this time and in this season.
Amen.

Offertory

Creator, we are surrounded by your creation and totally dependent upon it. We are grateful, especially during this time of anticipation of the celebration of the birth of your Son, for your gift of him to us. In return, we bring our tithes, gifts, and offerings. May our giving reflect our acceptance of your love. Amen.

Prayer of Confession

Creator, your promises are clear. Your desires have been set forth in your word. Your Son has shown us the path to walk. Yet we have failed. In word, in deed, and in thought, we have shown that we still have much to learn and practice as your children. Hear our prayers. For those words we wish we could take back, give us the courage to apologize. For those deeds, done and undone, help us return to your ways and begin again. For those thoughts that foment discontent and blame, we rest upon your promise that your Spirit can remind us to think of good things. Hear our prayers and grant that we, trusting in your grace and forgiveness, are restored to you. We are thankful, especially during this time of anticipation of the celebration of the birth of your Son, for your gift to us. Help us bring you honor and glory in all we say, do, and think. Amen.

Words of Assurance

In the name of Jesus Christ, you are forgiven.
In the name of Jesus Christ, you are forgiven. Amen.

Benediction

We, as believers, have been given the gifts of forgiveness, righteous-ness, and love. As you leave this place, may you share those gifts with others, in the name of the Father and the Son and the Holy Spirit. Amen. (Raquel Mull)

DECEMBER 25, 2008

❧❧❧

Christmas Day (or Christmas Eve)

Readings: Isaiah 9:2-7; Psalm 96; Titus 2:11-14; Luke 2:1-20

Life Interrupted . . . Or?
Luke 2:1-20

When were you last interrupted? Perhaps your sleep was interrupted this morning when ecstatic children bounced on your bed exclaiming, "It's Christmas, get up, get up!" Sleep interrupted. Or perhaps you were at your desk last week, trying to get those last few items finished up before the holiday, when the phone rang. You almost didn't answer it, but you were afraid it might be that prospective client. But then you picked it up and it was a telemarketer, soliciting a donation. Work interrupted. Maybe you were running late on your way to the airport to catch your flight home for Christmas when you got stuck in mall traffic, almost missing your flight. Travel interrupted.

In the book, *Reaching Out*, Henri Nouwen acknowledges the frustration and even anger that accompany these constant interruptions. But, he says, what if our interruptions are in fact our opportunities? What if all the unexpected interruptions are in fact the invitations to give up old-fashioned and outmoded styles of living and are opening up new unexplored areas of experience? (Henri Nouwen, *Reaching Out: The Three Movements of the Spiritual Life*, [New York: Doubleday, 1975], 52). Instead of viewing these interruptions as things that keep us from our work or ministry, how would we be different if we viewed interruptions as opportunities for ministry?

Most of the time, interruptions are just minor annoyances that temporarily distract us from what we are trying to do. And in these cases, Nouwen's thoughts help me manage the small interruptions. But what about those more serious interruptions, the ones that rock our worlds?

There you are at your desk, trying hard to get that report finished when the boss pops in. Perhaps he regretfully informs you that due to downsizing your job is being outsourced overseas. Or perhaps it's been a good year and you're being promoted to headquarters, which is half a continent away. Major life interruption or an opportunity for personal growth and ministry? Maybe you have worked hard and saved for years to buy or pay off your home. Then one late summer day the weatherman warns of a Category 5 hurricane headed your way. Two days later everything you own is gone. Major life interruption or an opportunity for personal growth and ministry?

Imagine that you are one of the main characters in our gospel text this morning. Imagine yourself as Mary or Joseph—your wedding plans are put on hold and your standing in the community is threatened when Mary becomes pregnant before you are married. Imagine the response from friends and family when you claim from the beginning that the child was the future Messiah fathered by the Holy Spirit! If that weren't enough, the government requires you to travel to Bethlehem for a census count late in Mary's pregnancy. The city is overcrowded with weary and short-tempered travelers, all of the inns post no-vacancy signs, and labor begins. Without proper medical help or the support of family and friends, you deliver your son in an unheated, unsanitary barn. Life interrupted or opportunity for personal growth and ministry?

And what about the shepherds? Picture this scene with me—twilight is long gone and there is no moon this night. The darkness, inky black and all-encompassing, settles over the field. Sleepy shepherds take up strategic positions among their slumbering flocks, trying to remain alert to any sign of danger. All of a sudden, the night sky explodes with light and an angel of the Lord appears before them, announcing the birth of the Messiah, the Savior, and telling them to go and find him! Sleep, work, and life interrupted, or a once-in-a-lifetime chance to worship the newborn king?

As an adult, Jesus had a habit of breaking into lives unexpectedly. Jesus called fishermen from their nets and a tax collector from his office. Work interrupted or an opportunity to embark on a whole new path? Jesus spoke to the woman at the well and dealt with the local religious leaders who were about to stone the woman caught in adultery. Life interrupted, or an opportunity for two marginalized women to receive grace and a second chance to live their lives with wholeness and dignity? Jesus interrupted the status quo and the security of centuries of established religious practices when he ushered in the kingdom of God among us. Jesus interrupted those who tried to silence him by executing him, and he interrupted the power of evil by overcoming death and rising again from the dead.

Jesus is still about the business of breaking into lives today. For some of us, we hear the call like the shepherd, "I am bringing you news of great joy for all people: to you is born this day . . . a Savior, who is the Messiah, the Lord!" We arrive at the manger in amazement, to worship our King and then we return to the work that God has already called us to do, but our hearts are changed forever.

God may be calling some of us from our offices or fishing nets, whatever they may be, to follow Jesus on a whole new vocational path. God may be calling others of us to speak up on behalf of those who for whatever reason cannot speak up or defend themselves. Still others of us may be called on to stand against the status quo, against those who can no longer see interruptions as possibilities for growth and ministry.

When was the last time you were interrupted? (Tracy Hartman)

Lectionary Commentary
Isaiah 9:2-7

Most scholars now believe that this poem originated with Isaiah in the eighth century B.C.E. It may have been part of the coronation ritual for King Hezekiah in 727 B.C.E or for another crown prince sometime after 732. Verses 2-6 speak clearly of past events. Only verse 7 looks ahead to the future reign of the one who has been born. Further, there is no indication that the prophet is portraying words of Yahweh; rather this poem is addressed to God. While primarily a birth announcement, this text also contains elements of hymns of thanksgiving and coronation. Although these words were originally written to hail the arrival of a specific king of Judah, they have been applied to other later kings, and ultimately to the arrival of Christ the King. Here, as in Luke, we are reminded that God's reign of peace and justice will come by way of a humble child.

Titus 2:11-14

This passage is commonly known as a "faithful saying" or "summary of the gospel." These few verses link Christ's original appearance with the hope of what is to come, and they challenge Christians to live holy and godly lives in the interim period. In verse 13, Jesus is called, "our great

God and Savior." This is one of the few places in Scripture where Jesus is called God (see also John 1:1, 18; 20:28 and Hebrews 1:8 for the others). (Tracy Hartman)

Worship Aids

Call to Worship (Psalm 96)

O sing to the Lord a new song all the earth!
Declare his glory among all the nations,
For great is the Lord and greatly to be praised!
All: Say among the nations, "The Lord is King!" Let us worship God.

Offertory Prayer

God, on this day when we joyfully and expectantly give and receive gifts, help us understand what it truly means to receive the gift of your only begotten Son. In turn, may we willing give our gifts to you—our time, our talents, and indeed our very selves. Amen.

Benediction

Joy to the world, the Lord has come! We have celebrated this wonderful gift of God this day. As we go, may we share the good news with all we meet! Go in peace to love and serve the Lord. Amen. (Tracy Hartman)

Time to Ponder

Second in a Series of Three on Holidays and Emotional Health

Luke 2:8-20

Christmas morning. After all the planning and shopping and cooking and decorating, the time is now. Probably most of the presents have been opened and there is almost a sense of letdown. The anticipation of Christmas morning is half the fun. Peggy Lee wrote and sang a song, "Is that all there is?"

Is that all there is? Is that all there is?
If that's all there is, my friends, then let's keep dancing.

My daughter was born on Christmas morning, thirty-five years ago, today. It was a Monday and I certainly had not planned on spending Christmas Day in the hospital. I was in strange surroundings, in a strange city with no one except my husband. I do not mean to discount my husband, but I wanted another female to reassure me. There were no presents, no decorations, and no fancy meal. All those years ago, the infant was kept in a nursery and only brought in for a feeding. I had time to think about my new role of mother during her absences. I was nervous and insecure but I thought of Mary, a teenager, alone in a strange place, a strange city with lots of strangers hanging around. Angels came, but after they sang their praises and glorified God, they left. Then the shepherds came, telling the story of how the angels had told them about this baby, and then they left. Maybe she was still a bit frightened, and amazed, and felt isolated, "but Mary treasured all these words and pondered them in her heart."

In the midst of the wrappings and the tasks to still be finished, I invite you to ponder on the things that have happened so far. Psalm 46:10 orders us to "be still, and know that I am God." If one knows how to worry, one knows how to meditate. I would imagine that we have all worried about today in some form or fashion. *Will they like their gift? Did I spend too much? If the children are disappointed, what can I do to help them through this?* Or perhaps in the rush to get here, words were spoken in anger and impatience. Or maybe you had to use a lot of energy to convince your family that this worship service is important.

Yes, I believe this service is important because it is at this time, with this community of faith, we echo the words and emotions the angels and the shepherds offered so many years ago. "Glory to God in the highest heaven, / and on earth peace among those whom he favors." We, as believers, purposefully separate ourselves from the demands and expectations of the world to remember what we are celebrating: to remember the innocence and purity of a newborn child, to celebrate the gift given by Yahweh to Yahweh's creation.

When we leave this place, I pray that any peace you find in this time together will go and stay with you for the rest of the day. Don't squander that peace on circumstances or people you can't control. How often, in times of stress, like trying to get a meal on the table for a holiday gathering, do we let the clock become the controlling factor? Or, worry that our kitchen won't be clean enough when our mother-in-law arrives? Practice, to allow yourself some time to smile, to laugh, and to be part of the party.

Remember that the photos in the magazines of the perfect Christmas are but single moments caught on film. No telling what else is going on behind the cameras! The shepherds arrived to see the marvelous gift; they dropped what they were doing and came as they were. They were not motivated by guilt. They came without critical eyes. They came as a group for a purpose.

What will your purpose be as you gather with friends and family? To compare or to share? To listen with compassion or to complain? To enjoy each other's company or to control?

Too often with family, especially, we think we know each other so well. And we anticipate reactions or assume the outcome of various situations. Or maybe we even plan to head off any uncomfortable situations. It is much easier to have peace without people around us but to be a whole person requires us to learn to respect and accept people as they were created.

Today is a birthday celebration and we are thankful. So, your plans for a good Christmas may include the traditional meal with loved ones and those we don't love as much. Another round of gift-giving and receiving may be on the agenda. For your own emotional well-being, take the time to ponder as Mary did.

Peggy Lee asked if there is more. Oh, yes there is more than just the presents and the decorations, more than the demands and responsibilities, more than the bustle and the anticipation, more than the dancing. We can have the peace if we want it.

So I invite you to sit back. Close your eyes. Take a deep breath. Listen to the breaths of others around you. Feel the air go through your nostrils. This is life. Think about your joy in getting your gifts, the anticipation. Acknowledge any disappointment and bless the giver. Picture a reaction to a gift you were so excited to give. Remember your favorite Christmas. Be still and think about the wee baby born in a stable, born for you and me, born to give us peace and joy. Savor it! (Raquel Mull)

Worship Aids

Call to Worship

I bring you good news of great joy.
Please tell us.
A Savior has been born to you; he is the Messiah, the Lord.
All: Glory to God in the highest and on earth, peace and goodwill among all.

Invocation

Dear God, we turn our faces to the east and, with the rising sun, we are reminded that we have been given a new day. We live with the consequences of our choices, yet we have a new opportunity in which to make amends, change our ways, and bless others. We still have plans and hopes for this day, so in this time when we gather as your family, give us peace. Still our minds from tasks still undone, meals still to be fixed, and presents needing to be wrapped. As we come together to celebrate the gift of your Son, prepare our hearts for your presence and your words. Amen.

Benediction

Go in peace, knowing that the One who has the power to heal and restore is in our midst. Grace to all who love not only the baby Jesus but also the man, Messiah. Amen. (Raquel Mull)

DECEMBER 28, 2008

❧❧❧

First Sunday after Christmas

Readings: Isaiah 61:10–62:3; Psalm 148; Galatians 4:4-7;
Luke 2:22-40

Redeeming Rituals
Luke 2:22-40

What rituals have you practiced lately? Is it a ritual for your family to decorate the Christmas tree together? If you have children, did you set out milk and cookies for Santa on Christmas Eve? What rituals or traditions do you follow for other holidays, for weddings, or to celebrate the birth of a child? What meanings do these rituals hold for you—what do they represent?

Now, change gears just a bit. What religious rituals do you practice? What rituals help you express your faith and give your worship (either public or private) meaning? My guess is that it was easier for you to come up with the first list of rituals than it was for you to think about religious rituals you may practice. In fact, many seeker or contemporary churches have intentionally set aside nearly all of the rituals that we associate with traditional worship. They claim, and occasionally they are right, that the rituals have lost their meaning and become rote, irrelevant, repetitious, or downright boring. Despite these thoughts, all churches, traditional and contemporary, practice the rituals of baptism and communion in one way or another. In some traditional or orthodox settings, worshipers have ritualistic ways of reading Scripture and progressing through the liturgy or order of worship. Others use candles and incense to enhance worship. In every place, all of these rituals can be powerful symbols of faith that help worshipers connect with God.

In today's gospel text, Mary and Joseph perform two religious rituals required by law in their faith tradition: the circumcision and presentation of Jesus, and the purification of Mary. However, they would not have seen these ceremonies as rote, boring, meaningless, or an unwanted interruption in their lives. For in the Jewish tradition, God was to be honored and praised in all of life's circumstances. Mary and Joseph would have seen these rituals as an opportunity to express praise and gratitude to God for God's presence and blessing in their lives.

Imagine the scene with me. According to Jewish custom, every first-born male was designated as holy to the Lord. First, Jesus would be presented to the Lord, and then they would offer a sacrifice. Mary and Joseph would like to offer a lamb, but the trip to Bethlehem has consumed much of their meager savings. Two turtledoves, an acceptable offering for those who could not afford a lamb, would have to do instead. Purchase made, they prepare to enter the temple, Joseph carrying the doves and Mary swaddling Jesus cozily in her arms. Suddenly, an old man appears before them and reaches for the child. Mary tightens her arms protectively around Jesus and steps back to shield him from the stranger, but something in his eyes stops her.

"I have been waiting for many years to see this child," he tells them softly. "The Spirit promised me I would not see death until I had seen the Messiah. And now, at long last, he has come."

Mary looks at Joseph and he nods, quietly. Gently, so as not to disturb the sleeping child, she lays Jesus in the outstretched arms of Simeon.

With great reverence, he stares at the baby. Then he begins to praise God saying, "Master, now you are releasing your servant in peace, / according to your word; / for my eyes have seen your salvation, / which you have prepared in the presence of all peoples, / a light for revelation to the Gentles / and for glory to our people Israel."

Mary and Joseph stand in amazement as Simeon hands them back their son, but they soon learn that Simeon isn't done. He has words of blessing for them too. And then, words of prophecy for Mary. The phrases swirl in her head: Jesus will be opposed, a sword will pierce her soul. What did it all mean? She glances at the baby and back up at Simeon to ask him to explain, but he is gone.

In Simeon's place is another person of great age and wisdom, a woman and prophet named Anna. She never leaves the temple, they discover, and she too has been awaiting the arrival of the Messiah. Instantly, she begins to praise God and to speak about Jesus to everyone who has been looking for the redemption of Jerusalem.

Later that day, as Mary and Joseph begin the long trip back to Galilee, they talk quietly about the day's events. Although they do not understand everything that the two messengers have told them, it is clear that God has spoken through them both that day. Although they do not understand everything, they are content to ponder for a while the mysteries of a God who has met them as they celebrated the centuries-old rituals.

Simeon and Anna lived lives of devotion that enabled them to be sensitive to the movement of God in their day. Like Mary and Joseph, they marked both daily and special events with rituals that served to recognize the sacredness of life and the presence of God in the everyday. In our hectic and harried lives, we have lost much of the practice and significance of ritual. What have we lost along with it?

"But God doesn't need ritual to work," you may be saying. "God can work in any way that God chooses!" Of course that is true. But perhaps by cultivating the disciplines that ritual practice can develop, we will become more sensitive to the ways that the God of mystery is already at work all around us. What rituals have you practiced lately? (Tracy Hartman)

Lectionary Commentary
Isaiah 61:10–62:3

These verses of praise and rejoicing are set in the middle of some of the darkest passages in Isaiah. Chapters 56 and 57 have oracles against corrupt leaders and idolatry. Chapter 59 contains a call to national repentance. Then chapter 60 begins poems on the glory of Jerusalem and God's people. In 61:10-11, the writer switches back to the first-person praise. Here, God is clothing the servant in righteousness. In 62:1-3, the writer speaks of a restored Zion that will be recognized by all nations. In chapter 63, the dark tone returns with a poem on divine vengeance and a psalm of intercession. In 64, the author makes a final plea to God who in turn pronounces judgment in chapter 65.

Galatians 4:4-7

In the gospel passage for today, Luke makes it clear that Mary and Joseph presented Jesus in the temple and performed Mary's purification ritual in accordance with Jewish law. In Galatians, Paul states that those who were under the law needed someone born of a woman and under the law to redeem them. Now, Paul proclaims, all may be adopted as children and become heirs of God. Scholars point out that only Jesus is God's own son; everyone else has been adopted into the family. (Tracy Hartman)

Worship Aids

Call to Worship (Psalm 148)

Praise the Lord!
Youth: Young men and women alike,
Adults and Children: Old and young together!
All: Let us praise the name of the Lord, for his name alone
is exalted!

Prayer of Confession

In the busyness of our daily lives and the holiday season, it is hard to discipline ourselves to recognize the sacredness of life and to find your presence in the everyday. Forgive us God, and help us, like Anna and Simeon, be attuned to your work in the world. Amen.

Words of Assurance

In the name of Jesus Christ, you are forgiven.
In the name of Jesus Christ, you are forgiven. Amen.

Benediction

As you leave this place today, may you look for ways to regularly find and celebrate God in the midst of the ordinary. Go in peace, knowing that you do not go alone. (Tracy Hartman)

Just Say No

Third in a Series of Three on Holidays and Emotional Health

Matthew 5:37a

A new year is upon us, and as we prepare to make those New Year's resolutions, take a minute to think about how you can prevent some stress. I am sure you have heard this before, but I will offer you proof that if you learn to do this, you are following the example Yeshua set for us. Learn to say no!

How many times have you wondered, as you are running to and fro, struggling to meet deadlines, juggling duties as mother or father, employee, chauffer, and church member, *How did I get myself into this situation?* Or, do you find yourself scheduled to be in two places at the same time? Multitasking is a learned behavior. Many mothers can pick up their children at school, listen to their stories, respond compassionately, decide what is in the freezer so they can fix dinner, and remember to pick up the dry cleaning. I erroneously believed that men's brain hemispheres were more finely separated and therefore could only perform one task at a time. Then, I watched my husband back up a truck with a trailer—he was able to gauge distances, work the gear shift, clutch, brake, and gas, think in reverse as he used only the mirrors to back the trailer and turned the steering wheel in the opposite direction that I would have—without becoming frustrated!

We, as ordinary people, want to please people, want to achieve, and want to be given credit for what we do. The pattern for success in the secular world, which now influences the church and other arenas, is to move up the ladder in position, responsibility, and authority. Of course, in the secular world advancement is compensated by a larger salary, more influence, more benefits, and even some envy. Leadership, in all areas, requires more of our time and energy, many times to the detriment to our families, our marriages, and our spiritual life. Yeshua was a leader and yet he managed his calendar of healing, teaching, preaching, mentoring and incurring the wrath of the Pharisees. He could say no—no to his family, to Satan, to the church, and to his disciples.

To his brothers, Yeshua said no. Yeshua had been walking in Galilee, teaching and healing. His brothers wanted him to expand his territory, "Leave this place. Show your disciples in Judea and all over the world what you can do" (John 7:1-4, paraphrased). Yeshua said no. He knew the world would hate him because he could only tell the truth and he knew the world was evil and he "remained in Galilee" (John 7:9). He explained his time had not fully come. This was exactly the same reason he said no to his mother when he met up with her at a wedding in Cana. The wine ran out, which would have brought shame and embarrassment. Mary came to Yeshua and told him, expecting him to fix the situation. He told her she was sticking her nose in another person's business, he did not plan to, and his hour had not yet come (John 2:3).

Satan tempted Yeshua three times while he was in the wilderness. He was offered bread because he was hungry. Then Satan took him to a pinnacle of the holy city to tempt him to prove that angels protected him. Finally, Satan promised everything if Yeshua would only bow down and worship him. The offers of power, authority and material things were refused (Matthew 4:1-11). Satan was told no. This is a valuable lesson—learning to say no to temptation.

During this time, the Pharisees were the religious authority in the church. Yeshua told them no on more than one occasion. He told them he would not perform signs to prove who he was (Mark 8:11). The Gospel of Matthew tells when Yeshua returned to the temple after driving out the money changers and the merchants. The chief priests and the elders of the people came and wanted to know by whose authority he was teaching and healing. He responded by saying that if they answered his question, he would answer theirs. After some discussion in which the religious leaders determined that they could not answer his question without compromising their positions, they answered that they did not know. So, Yeshua told them no—"Neither will I tell you by what authority I am doing these things (Matthew 21:27).

Yeshua was not even hesitant to tell his disciples no. In Mark's Gospel, Yeshua and his disciples are getting ready to take a little time off. They even get as far as boarding the boat and setting across the lake. There, instead of peace and quiet they find more people who need teaching. As the day progresses, the disciples, who have not eaten, come and offer a plan. They tell Yeshua, send the people away so they can go and find food. Yeshua told them no; "You give them something to eat" (Mark 6:37). Five thousand were fed with five loaves of bread and two fishes.

We each have the ability and the responsibility to make decisions regarding time, money and our thoughts. In fact, how we spend our money, time, and energy are indicative of what is most important in our lives. We know that the church is important, yet there are times when we can be overstretched, even in the church. One sure way to prevent burnout and stress is to know your limits, and with prayer, maintain them. It would be interesting to see when Yeshua spent time in prayer in relation to the times he said no.

I invite you to value yourself this year. Avoid overextending yourself. Learn to say no. Yeshua still ministered, still made disciples, and made sure he took care of himself. He said no so he could fulfill his purpose with clear conscience and intention. May your new year and its resolutions include some noes and some Sabbath time for yourself. (Raquel Mull)

Worship Aids

Invocation

Creator; we have said no to lounging around, to ignoring you this morning so that we may gather as your family to praise and worship you.

In the midst of responsibilities and desires, come into our presence and create in us a holy place. Amen.

Pastoral Prayer

We have gathered this winter day, grateful for what we have received from you, from family, and from friends. With the Christmas cards and communications, we have learned of needs and joys. We know of families who are separated by conflict and miles. We remember those who were grieving at Christmas and those who are traveling. Help us remember our blessings at all times and give us peace. In your son's name. Amen. (Raquel Mull)

III. APPENDIX

CONTRIBUTORS

Tracey Allred
2729 Mountain Woods Drive
Birmingham, AL 35216

Guy Ames
Chapel Hill United Methodist
  Church
2717 West Hefner Road
P.O. Box 4787
Oklahoma City, OK 73120

Meredith Remington Bell
First United Methodist Church
313 North Center Street at Division
Arlington, TX 76011

B. J. Beu
3810 67th Avenue Court Northwest
Gig Harbor, WA 98335

Linda McKinnish Bridges
Wake Forest University
P.O. Box 7225
Winston-Salem, NC 27109-7225

Tim Bruster
First United Methodist Church
800 West 5th Street
Fort Worth, TX 76102

Thomas Lane Butts
First United Methodist Church
324 Pineville Road
Monroeville, AL 36460

Kenneth H. Carter Jr.
Providence United Methodist
  Church
2810 Providence Road
Charlotte, NC 28211

Carol Cavin-Dillon
Christ United Methodist Church
508 Franklin Road
Franklin, TN 37069

Mike Childress
121 Laurie Vallee Road
Louisville, KY 40223

Will Cotton
St. Luke's United Methodist
  Church
3708 45th Street
Lubbock, TX 79413

Paul L. Escamilla
Walnut Hill United Methodist
  Church
10066 Marsh Lane
Dallas, TX 75229

John Essick
P.O. Box 8613
Waco, TX 76714

Dan L. Flanagan
Saint Paul's United Methodist
   Church
324 South Jackson Street
Papillion, NE 68046

Travis Franklin
1111 Herring Avenue
Waco, TX 76708

Roberto L. Gómez
El Mesias United Methodist
   Church
P.O. Box 4787
Mission, TX 78573-4787

Robert Gorrell
Church of the Servant United
   Methodist Church
14343 North MacArthur Boulevard
Oklahoma City, OK 73142-9725

Drew J. Gunnells Jr.
1205 Dominion Drive East
Mobile, AL 36695

Tracy Hartman
3400 Brook Road
Richmond, VA 23227

Chris Hayes
First United Methodist Church
313 North Center Street at Division
Arlington, TX 76011

Bob Holloway
First United Methodist Church
P.O. Box 88
Graham, TX 76450

Cameron Jorgenson
2617 Cole Avenue, #8
Waco, TX 76707

Wendy Joyner
Fellowship Baptist Church
P.O. Box 1122
Americus, GA 31709

Gary G. Kindley
First United Methodist Church
5601 Pleasant Run Road
Colleyville, TX 76034

Mike Lowry
Southwest Texas Conference
   United Methodist Church
16400 Huebner Road
San Antonio, TX 78248

Timothy S. Mallard
Combat Maneuver Training Center
CMR 414, Box 2018
APO AE 09173

John Mathis
Woodland Baptist Church
P.O. Box 206
Woodland, NC 27897

Ted McIlvain
TCU Adjunct Faculty
P.O. Box 298045
Fort Worth, TX 76129

Lance Moore
First United Methodist Church
915 Pine Street
Foley, AL 36535-2150

David N. Mosser
First United Methodist Church
313 North Center Street at Division
Arlington, TX 76011

Raquel Mull
Saint Paul's United Methodist
Church
Socorro, NM 87801

Douglas Mullins
1545 Cohasset Drive
Cincinnati, OH 45255

Timothy Owings
402 Congressional Court
Augusta, GA 30907

Cindy Guthrie Ryan
2134 Wedgewood Drive
Grapevine, TX 76051

Carl L. Schenck
Manchester United Methodist
Church
129 Woods Mill Road
Manchester, MO 63011-4339

Mary J. Scifres
3810 67th Avenue Court Northwest
Gig Harbor, WA 98335

Melissa Scott
Colonial Avenue Baptist Church
4165 Colonial Avenue Southwest
Roanoke, VA 24018

Jeffrey Smith
Woodway First United Methodist
Church
P.O. Box 20548
Waco, TX 76702-0548

Thomas R. Steagald
First United Methodist Church
217 North Main Street
Stanley, NC 28164

Mark White
Baptist Theological Seminary
3400 Brook Road
Richmond, VA 23227

Victoria Atkinson White
Baptist Theological Seminary
3400 Brook Road
Richmond, VA 23227

Jennifer H. Williams
Christ United Methodist Church
6570 Mifflin Avenue
Harrisburg, PA 17111

Rod Wilmoth
10050 N. Colony Drive
Tucson, AZ 85737

Ryan Wilson
Trinity Baptist Church
210 West South Sixth Street
Seneca, SC 29678

Philip D. Wise
Second Baptist Church
6109 Chicago Avenue
Lubbock, TX 79424

Sandy Wylie
P.O. Box 986
McAlester, OK 74502

Brett Younger
Broadway Baptist Church
305 West Broadway Avenue
Fort Worth, TX 76104

SCRIPTURE INDEX

Old Testament

Genesis

1:1–2:4a 164
2:15-17 . . . . 46, 48
3:1-7 . . . . 46, 48
12:1-4a 53, 55
18:1-15 194
21:8-21 . . . . 201, 203
22:1-14 209–10
24:34-38, 42-49, 58-67 . . . . 217, 219
28:10-19a 232, 234
32:22-31 246
37:1-4, 12-28 . . . . 253, 255
45:1-15 260–63

Exodus

3:1-15 . . . . 275, 277
12:1-14 . . . . 89, 91–92, 282
14:19-31 . . . . 290, 291–92
16:2-15 296–97
17:1-7 . . . . 60, 62, 302–4
20:1-4, 7-9, 12-20 . . . . 309, 311
32:1-14 . . . . 316, 318
33:12-23 . . . . 323, 325

Numbers

9:1-14 49–51
11:10-23 56–59
14:1-10 63–65

Deuteronomy

8:7-18 . . . . 368, 370–71
11:18-21, 26-28 179–81
26:1-19 . . . . 386–88, 393–95

Joshua

14:1, 6-14 205–8

Ruth

1:1-19a 197–200
1:15-22 249–52
2–3 256–58

1 Samuel

16:1-13 . . . . 67, 69

2 Samuel

6:12-15 271–73
7:1-11, 16 . . . . 397, 398–99

1 Kings

3:5-12 . . . . 239, 241

Psalms

8 164–67
8:1, 3-9 378–81
13 209
15 32
16 112
17:1-7, 15 246
19 309
22 97
23 . . . . 67, 125
27:1, 4-9 26

(Psalms—cont.)

29 11
31:1-5, 15-16 132
31:1-5, 19-24 .... 179, 181
31:9-16 81
32 46
33:1-12 187
40:1-11 19
51:1-17 39
65 368
66:8-20 141
68:1-10, 32-35 148
69:7-18 201
72:1-7, 10-14 3
78:1-4, 12-16 302
78:1-7 345
80:1-7, 17-19 375
85:1-2, 8-13 383
89:1-4, 19-26 397
90:1-6, 13-17 331
95 60
95:1-10 364
96 405
99 323
100 359–60
104:24-34, 35b 156
105:1-6, 16-22, 45b 253
105:1-6, 23-26, 45c 257
105:1-6, 37-45 296
105:1-11, 45b 239
106:1-6, 19-23 316
107:1-7, 33-37 338
114 290
116:1-2, 12-19..... .... 89, 194
116:1-4, 12-19 118
116:12-14, 17-19 357–59
118:1-2, 14-24 105
118:1-2, 19-29 81
119:105-112 225
121 .... 53, 371–74
123 353
124 268
126 390
130 74
131 172
133 260
139:1-12, 23-24 232

145:8-14 217
148 .... 285, 412
149 282

Proverbs

3:9-10 357–59

Isaiah

9:1-4 .... 26, 28
9:2-7 .... 405, 407
24:1-24 235–37
25:1-12 242–45
40:1-11 383–84
42:1-9 .... 11, 13
49:1-7 19–21
49:8-16a 172, 174
50:4-9a 81, 83–84
51:1-6 268–70
52:13—53:12 .... 97, 99–100
55:10-13 225–27
58:1-12 .... 39, 41
60:1-6 .... 3, 5–6
61:1-4, 8-11 390–91
61:10—62:3 .... 412, 414
64:1-9 .... 375, 377

Jeremiah

20:7-13 .... 201, 203–4
28:5-9 .... 209, 211–12

Ezekiel

34:11-16, 20-24 361
37:1-14 74–76

Hosea

5:15—6:6 187–89

Amos

5:18-24 345–47

Micah

3:5-12 .... 338, 340

6:1-8 32–34
6:8 161–63

Zephaniah
1:7, 12-18 . . . . 353, 355–56

3:14-18 264–67

Zechariah
9:9-12 . . . . 217, 219–20

New Testament

Matthew
2:1-12 3–5
3:13-17 11–13
4:1-11 . . . . 46–48, 416
4:12-23 26
5:1-12 . . . . 32, 34–35
5:5 298–300
5:37a 415–17
6:1-6, 16-21 . . . . 39, 42
6:16-18 78–80
6:24-34 . . . . 172, 174–75
7:7-8 286–88
7:21-29 . . . . 179, 181–82
9:9-13, 18-26 . . . . 187, 189–90
9:35–10:8 . . . . 194, 196
10:1-4 213–16
10:24-39 . . . . 201, 204
10:40-42 . . . . 209, 212
11:16-19, 25-30 . . . . 217–19, 221
13:1-9, 18-23 . . . . 225, 227
13:24-30, 36-43 . . . . 232, 234
13:31-33, 44-52 239–41
14:13-21 . . . . 246, 248–49
14:22-33 253–55
15:10-20, 21-28 . . . . 260, 263
16:13-20 . . . . 268, 270, 326–29
16:21-28 275–77
17:20 286–88
18:15-20 . . . . 282, 284–85
18:21-35 290–92
20:1-16 296
21:1-11 . . . . 81, 83
21:23-32 . . . . 302, 304
21:33-46 . . . . 309, 311–12
22:1-14 316–18
22:15-22 323–25
22:34-46 331–33
23:1-12 . . . . 338, 340–41

25:1-13 . . . . 345, 347
25:14-30 353–55
25:31-46 361–63
26:14–27:66 81
26:20-30 94–96
27:24-26, 45-54 102–3
28:16-20 . . . . . . 164–67, 221–23, 228–30

Mark
1:1-8 . . . . 383, 384–85
2:1-12 293–95
12:28-34 22–24
13:24-37 . . . . 375, 377
16:1-8 . . . . 98, 151–54

Luke
1:26-38 397–98
2:1-20 405–7
2:8-18 400–3
2:8-20 408–10
2:22-40 412–14
2:41-52 312–14
4:1-15 71–73
10:25-28 161–63
12:13-21 341–44
16:10-13 169–71
17:11-19 368–70
18:15-17 305–7
24:13-35 . . . . 118–20, 144–46

John
1:6-8, 19-28 . . . . 390, 391–92
1:29-36 43–45
1:29-42 . . . . 19, 21
1:35-42 221–23
3:1-17 53–55

(John—cont.)

4:5-42	60–62
6:51-58	15–17
9:1-41	67–69
10:1-10	125–27
11:1-45	74, 76
13:1-17, 31b-35	89–91
13:1-20	320–22
14:1-14	132, 134–35
14:15-21	141, 143
14:25-27	228–30
16:4b-11	85–87
17:1-11	148, 150
18:1–19:42	97–99
20:1-18	105–7
20:19-23	156, 159–60
20:19-31	112–13

Acts of the Apostles

1:6-14	148–50
2:1-21	156–59
2:14a, 22-32	112, 114
2:14a, 36-41	118, 120
2:42-47	125, 127, 334–37
2:43-47	176–78
3:1-16	115–17
7:55-60	132, 134
10:34-43	11, 13–14, 105, 107–8
17:22-31	141–43

Romans

1:16-17	179, 182
3:22b-31	179, 182
4:1-5, 13-17	53, 55–56
4:13-25	187, 190
5:1-8	194, 196–97
5:1-11	60, 62
5:12-19	46, 49
6:1b-11	201–3
6:12-23	209, 212
7:14-25	29–31
7:15-25a	217, 220
8:1-11	225, 227
8:6-11	74, 76–77
8:12-25	232–34

8:26-39	239, 241–44
9:1-5	246, 248
9:14-16	245
10:5-15	253, 255–56
11:1-2a, 29-32	260, 263–64
12:1-8	268, 270
12:9-21	275, 278
13:8-14	282, 285
14:1-12	290, 292
16:25-27	397, 399

1 Corinthians

1:1-9	19, 21
1:3-9	375–77
1:10-18	26–28
1:18-31	32, 35
4:1-5	172, 175
11:23-26	89, 92–93
12:3b-13	156, 159
15:50-58	136–38

2 Corinthians

5:20b–6:10	39, 42
9:6-15	349–51, 368–71
13:11-13	164–67

Galatians

3:23-29	7–9
4:4-7	412, 414
5:19-26	128–30
5:22-26	122–23

Ephesians

1:15-23	361, 363
3:1-12	3, 6
5:8-14	67, 70

Philippians

1:21-30	296
2:1-13	302, 304–5
2:5-11	81–83
3:4b-14	309–11
4:1-9	316, 319

Colossians

1:18-20 109–11
3:1-4 . . . . 105, 108

1 Thessalonians

1:1-10 . . . . 323, 325–26
2:1-8 . . . . 331, 333–34
2:9-13 338–40
4:13-18 . . . . 345, 347
5:1-11 . . . . 353, 356
5:16-22 191–93
5:16-24 . . . . 390, 392

Titus

2:11-14 . . . . 405, 407–8

Hebrews

4:14-16 . . . . 97, 100–1
10:16-25 . . . . 97, 100–1

James

5:13-16 279–81

1 Peter

1:3-9 . . . . 112, 114
1:17-23 . . . . 118, 120–21
2:2-10 132–34
2:18-25 183–85
2:19-25 . . . . 125, 127–28
3:13-22 . . . . 141, 143–44
4:12-14 . . . . 148, 150–51
5:6-11 . . . . 148, 150–51

2 Peter

3:8-15a 383, 385
3:18 264

CONTEMPORARY AND TRADITIONAL RESOURCES
FOR WORSHIP LEADERS

The
ABINGDON
WORSHIP
Annual
2008

EDITED BY MARY J. SCIFRES & B. J. BEU

The *Abingdon Worship Annual 2008* offers fresh worship-planning resources for pastors and worship leaders. The 2008 edition moves in a new direction from previous volumes. Using a Theme Idea based on the lectionary readings, each week's offering of prayers and litanies follows the basic pattern of Christian worship: Gathering and Praise, Proclamation and Response, Thanksgiving and Communion, and Sending Forth. Alternative ideas for Praise Sentences and Contemporary Gathering Words are offered for those who serve in contemporary worship settings. And, in response to requests from many of our readers, we have included a number of Communion liturgies as well. *The Abingdon Worship Annual 2008* is a must-have sourcebook, offering countless opportunities for planning meaningful and insightful worship.

"Commendations to Abingdon Press for offering two fresh ecumenical resources for pastors."

For *The Abingdon Preaching Annual*—"Anyone who dares proclaim a holy word week in and week out soon realizes that creative inspiration for toe-shaking sermons quickly wanes. Multitasking pastors who are wise seek out resources that multiply their own inductive initiatives."

For *The Abingdon Worship Annual*—"Not only the sermon but also the whole service dares to be toe-shaking ... and the *Worship Annual* is a reservoir of resources in that direction."

—The Reverend Willard E. Roth, Academy of Parish Clergy
    President, *Sharing the Practice: The Journal of the Academy of Parish Clergy*

Abingdon Press